ADVANCES IN ORIENTAL DOCUMENT ANALYSIS AND RECOGNITION TECHNIQUES

SERIES IN MACHINE PERCEPTION AND ARTIFICIAL INTELLIGENCE*

Vol. 19: Parallel Image Analysis: Theory and Applications
(Eds. *L. S. Davis, K. Inoue, M. Nivat, A. Rosenfeld and P. S. P. Wang*)

Vol. 20: Picture Interpretation: A Symbolic Approach
(Eds. *S. Dance, T. Caelli and Z.-Q. Lin*)

Vol. 21: Modelling and Planning for Sensor Based Intelligent Robot Systems
(Eds. *H. Bunke, T. Kanade and H. Noltemeier*)

Vol. 22: Machine Vision for Advanced Production
(Eds. *M. Pietikainen and L. F. Pau*)

Vol. 23: Machine Learning and Perception
(Eds. *G. Tasini, F. Esposito, V. Roberto and P. Zingaretti*)

Vol. 24: Spatial Computing: Issues in Vision, Multimedia and Visualization Technologies
(Eds. *T. Caelli, Peng Lam and H. Bunke*)

Vol. 25: Studies in Pattern Recognition Memorial Volume in Honor of K S Fu
(Eds. *H. Freeman*)

Vol. 26: Neural Network Training Using Genetic Algorithms
(Eds. *L. C. Jain, R. P. Johnson and A. F. J. van Rooij*)

Vol. 27: Intelligent Robots — Sensing, Modeling & Planning
(Eds. *B. Bolles, H. Bunke and H. Noltemeier*)

Vol. 28: Automatic Bankcheck Processing
(Eds. *S. Impedovo, P. S. P. Wang and H. Bunke*)

Vol. 29: Document Analysis II
(Eds. *J. J. Hull and S. Taylor*)

Vol. 30: Compensatory Genetic Fuzzy Neural Networks and Their Applications
(*Y.-Q. Zhang and A. Kandel*)

Vol. 31: Parallel Image Analysis: Tools and Models
(Eds. *S. Miguet, A. Montanvert & P. S. P. Wang*).

Forthcoming

Introduction to Pattern Recognition — Statistical, Structural, Neural and Fuzzy Logic Approaches
(*A. Kandel and M. Friedman*)

*For the complete list of titles in this series, please write to the Publisher.

Series in Machine Perception and Artificial Intelligence – Vol. 33

ADVANCES IN ORIENTAL DOCUMENT ANALYSIS AND RECOGNITION TECHNIQUES

Editors

S.-W. Lee
Korea University
South Korea

Y. Y. Tang
Hong Kong Baptist University
Hong Kong

P. S. P. Wang
Northeastern University
U.S.A.

World Scientific
Singapore • New Jersey • London • Hong Kong

Published by

World Scientific Publishing Co. Pte. Ltd.

P O Box 128, Farrer Road, Singapore 912805

USA office: Suite 1B, 1060 Main Street, River Edge, NJ 07661

UK office: 57 Shelton Street, Covent Garden, London WC2H 9HE

British Library Cataloguing-in-Publication Data
A catalogue record for this book is available from the British Library.

ADVANCES IN ORIENTAL DOCUMENT ANALYSIS AND RECOGNITION TECHNIQUES

ISBN 981-02-3744-8

Printed in Singapore by Uto-Print

CONTENTS

PREFACE

SEONG-WHAN LEE
Center for Artificial Vision Research, Korea University
Anam-dong, Seongbuk-ku, Seoul 136-701, Korea

YUAN Y. TANG
Department of Computing Studies, Hong Kong Baptist University
Kowloon-Tong, Hong Kong

PATRICK S. P. WANG
College of Computer Science, Northeastern University
Boston, MA 02115, USA

The contributions of this book were first presented at the 17th International Conference on Computer Processing of Oriental Languages (ICCPOL'97), held at the Hong Kong Baptist University, April 2-4, 1997. They were reviewed by three referees, and in many cases revised; from the 148 papers that were presented at the ICCPOL97, 15 on advances in Oriental document analysis and recognition were selected by prominent professionals and experts mainly from Canada, China, Hong Kong, Japan, Korea, Singapore, Taiwan, and USA. Most of them have been expanded or extensively reworked for publication here.

In recent years, rapid progress has been made on computer processing of Oriental languages and the research development in this area has resulted in tremendous changes in the recognition of document images, retrieval of information, input methodologies for texture and interaction of natural languages. The progress of the computer processing of Oriental languages can also be found in multimedia computing and the World Wide Web. Many results in those domains were presented in this conference.

The papers can roughly be classified into four groups:

General Description of Oriental Languages

The paper, "Intriguing Aspects of Oriental Languages" by Suen, Mori, Rim and Wang includes a description of three affiliated Oriental languages: Chinese, Japanese, and Korean. A description of the origins of these three languages and the inter-relationship among them are presented. Drawn from the viewpoints of several experienced researchers in the field of OCR and computational linguistics, it attempts to bring out the intriguing aspects of these three ideographic languages. Numerous references are given and comments on future trends are also presented.

The paper, "Differentiating Between Oriental and European Scripts by Statistical Features" by Lam, Ding and Suen uses a combined analysis of the several discriminating statistical features to identify the documents printed in different languages.

International Journal of Pattern Recognition and Artificial Intelligence Vol. 12 No. 1 (1998) 1–4

Handwriting Processing

In the paper, "The Generation of Oriental Characters: New Perspectives for Automatic Handwriting Processing", Plamondon, Guerfali and Li summarize the key concepts behind the so-called vectorial delta-lognormal model. The results from this theory and how this model could be used for Chinese character analysis and processing are presented.

The paper, "A New Synthesizing Method for Handwriting Korean Scripts" by Lee and Cho chooses 11 characteristic parameters which determine the shape of handwriting scripts to generate Korean handwriting scripts. It proposes Beta-velocity model to simulate the cursive stroke movement by manipulating curvilinear and cursive connection for consecutive strokes within a letter or a word.

In the paper, "Gray-Scale Nonlinear Shape Normalization Method for Handwritten Oriental Character Recognition" by Kim and Lee, the nonlinear shape normalization method for handwritten Oriental characters is proposed to minimize the loss of information caused by binarization and to compensate for the shape distortions of characters. The two-dimensional linear interpolation technique is extended to nonlinear space and the extended interpolation is adopted to enhance the quality of the normalized images.

Xiao and Dai in the paper, "On-Line Handwritten Chinese Character Recognition Directed by Components with Dynamic Templates" use 45 basic components for 3,755 categories of daily-used Chinese characters to direct the stroke segment matching of the whole character set. It can reduce the computational complexity of the structural matching and improve the performance. In this research, the reference templates of these components are extracted dynamically from the corresponding segment string of characters when a special matching is carried out. This strategy avoids building multiple templates for the components of the same kind but at different places of the characters.

The paper, "Comparison of Feature Performance and its Application to Feature Combination in Off-Line Handwritten Korean Alphabet Recognition" by Chung, Seo, Kim and Yoon classifies the features into three: geometrical/topological, statistical and global features. For each class, it selects four or five features and performs recognition with PE92 database using neural network. This paper compares the recognition performances and selects the top four among those thirteen features and combines some or all of the features.

In the paper, "Segmentation and Recognition of Continuous Handwriting Chinese Text", Chen, Loudon, Wu and Zitserman propose a new segmentation method for both on-line and off-line systems to recognize free-format handwritten Chinese character sentences. This method performs basic and fine operations of the segmentation based on the varying spacing thresholds and the minimum variance criteria. A lattice is created from all the segments and the Viterbi algorithm is applied to find the most likely character sequence.

In the paper, "Network-Based Approach to Handwriting Analysis" by Sin and Kim, the starting point of the research is a network of HMMs corresponding to the whole set of characters. Then it is followed by the assertion that the HMM for on-line script is applied to not only on-line but also other tasks of handwriting synthesis and pen-trajectory recovery in off-line character images. The single network of HMMs and the single principle of DP-based state-observation algorithm are used in this paper.

Document Processing and Input Methodologies

The paper, "Distributed Autonomous Agents for Chinese Document Image Segmentation" by Liu and Tang presents a novel computational paradigm for extracting text/graphic blocks for the Chinese document images, which is based on a notion of distributed autonomous agents. The paper describes the formalisms as well as the behavioral characteristics of the agents followed by a demonstration of the agents in detecting document blocks from some real-life Chinese document images.

The paper, "Ink Matching of Cursive Chinese Handwritten Annotations" by Lopresti, Ma, Wang and Crisman illustrates a pen-based electronic document annotating and browsing system and methods for searching hand-drawn personal notes employing the described matching schemes. It proposes an ink matching network that applies semantics of Chinese language early in the process of ink matching.

Printed Oriental Character Processing

Yuen, Feng and Tang in the paper, "Printed Chinese Character Similarity Measurement using Ring Projection and Distance Transform" present a new similarity measurement method. The representation of the character in ring projection space has been proven to be orientation and scale invariant. However, it will be distorted nonlinearly in the presence of noise. To contest such a deficiency, the distance transform is proposed as a nonlinear metric. The similarity measurement is performed using the distance transformed image in ring projection space.

The paper, "A Self-Organizing Hierarchical Classifier for Multi-Lingual Large-Set Oriental Character Recognition" by Park, Song and Lee proposes a practical scheme for multi-lingual, multi-font and multi-size large-set Oriental character recognition. The variations of the character shapes in multi-font and multi-size are absorbed by a modified nonlinear shape normalization method based on the dot density. A hierarchical feature extraction method is adopted to represent the different topological structures of multi-lingual Oriental characters. For classification, the SOFM/LVQ, and LVQ4 techniques have been used.

In order to increase the recognition accuracy, the paper, "Typeface Identification for Printed Chinese Characters" by Tseng, Kuo and Lee, identifies character typefaces before the recognition. Probability distributions for the six typefaces are measured, and the three features and a contextual heuristic are used to classify the typefaces of the characters. Trapezoid-shaped membership functions are constructed to represent the fuzzy numbers for the distribution of each feature. In order to obtain the higher identification rate, a two-level decision tree is utilized.

The paper, "A Reliability Design Methodology for Chinese Character Recognition Systems" by Huang, Liu, Suen and Tang establishes a novel method enabling the Chinese character recognition systems to have higher reliability. Two thresholds, class region threshold and disambiguity threshold are used in each character, and an algorithm to derive appropriate thresholds is developed. In addition, an iterative learning is applied.

We wish to thank the valuable efforts of all the authors and the referees who have made this book possible, also published as a special issue of the *International Journal of Pattern Recognition and Artificial Intelligence.* We also want to express our appreciation to Ms. Lakshmi Narayan, Editor, for her patience and help in guiding us through this task. We hope that this book will be a valuable addition to the expanding field of Oriental Document Analysis and Recognition Techniques and you will find useful the articles featured in the book.

INTRIGUING ASPECTS OF ORIENTAL LANGUAGES

CHING Y. SUEN

Centre for Pattern Recognition & Machine Intelligence (CENPARMI)
Concordia University, Suite GM-606
1455 de Maisonneuve Boulevard West
Montreal, Quebec H3G 1M8, Canada
E-mail: suen@cenparmi.concordia.ca

SHUNJI MORI

Image Processing Laboratory, The University of Aizu
Tsuruga, Ikki-machi, Aizu-Wakamatsu-City, Fukushima 965, Japan
E-mail: s-mori@u-aizu.ac.jp

HAE-CHANG RIM

Department of Computer Science, Korea University
1, 5-ka, Anam-dong, Seoul 136-701, Korea
E-mail: rim@nlp.korea.ac.kr

PATRICK S. P. WANG

College of Computer Science, Northeastern University
360 Huntington Avenue, Boston, Massachusetts 02115, USA
E-mail: pwang@ccs.neu.edu

This paper includes a description of 3 affiliated oriental languages: Chinese, Japanese, and Korean. It includes a description of the origins of these 3 languages and the inter-relationship among them. Drawn from the viewpoints of several experienced researchers in the field of OCR (Optical Character Recognition) and computational linguistics, it attempts to bring out the intriguing aspects of these 3 ideographic languages, including the formation and composition of pictograms, special features, learning, understanding, contextual information, and recognition of characters and words, and their relations to poetic expressions and pattern recognition techniques. Numerous references are given and comments on future trends are also presented.

Keywords: Oriental languages, Chinese language, Japanese language, Korean language, Hangul, Chinese characters, Kanji, OCR (optical character recognition), language processing.

1. INTRODUCTION

Language is one of the most important means of human communication. Current languages in the world are usually the products of hundreds and thousands of years of evolution. They can be grouped into several families. Among these families, oriental languages are probably the mostly spoken in the world. Of these and of special interest to the co-authors of this paper are Chinese, Japanese and Korean, which are quite unique. These 3 oriental languages have a common structure of pictogram elements. They are inter-related either through usage of a common set of characters, or through usage of loaned words or meanings. Due to the diverse backgrounds of the 4 co-authors, different aspects of the above will be presented and they may not be entirely coherent in structure and content, but all of them have

Advances in Oriental Document Analysis and Recognition Techniques (1998) 5–29

the intention of providing the readers a lead to the right materials and places for further reading and research. As well the space limitation of this paper has forced us to consider only the written forms of these languages.

We start with a description of the Chinese language, of which some characters form a large portion of Japanese texts, and some words form the vocabulary of an equally large proportion of Korean expressions. Then we introduce the origins of Japanese and Korean, their interesting properties, and methodologies of recognizing them by a computer.

2. THE CHINESE LANGUAGE

Chinese is a hieroglyphic language which has a history of more than 4,500 years. It is being used in many places especially in the Far East, e.g. China, Hong Kong, Macau, Taiwan, Singapore, and Malaysia. Its writing system is unique in the world because Chinese characters give people the impression of a picture. The characters are built from a combination or permutation of about 220 basic patterns, known as radicals. Both Japanese and Korean have adapted many of the Chinese characters or expressions. While Japanese still uses about 4,000 Chinese characters (called Kanji in Japanese), Korean script has evolved into pure syllabaries though the structure of its characters (called Hangul in Korean) is similar to that of Chinese characters. A few examples of these characters are presented in Fig. 1. As shown in this figure, the characters of these 3 languages are rather complex in structure, hence it is of no surprise to see that automatic recognition of these languages has always been a great challenge to scientists working in this field.

2.1. Chinese Word Recognition

In this section, we shall discuss some aspects of the advantages of Chinese characters and words, and how "learning by pattern and knowledge" can make it more interesting and easier to learn, understand, memorize and recognize Chinese characters and words. Unlike alphabetic and one-dimensional western languages such as English, Chinese characters are well known to be two-dimensional and non-alphabetic. Each Chinese character is confined in a rectangle or square area known as the "square word" (方塊字). There is essentially no unique linear way of representing a Chinese character and some characters are so complicated that they have more than 30 strokes.[43] Mainly because of this nature, it was widely believed for quite some time that Chinese characters are rather backward, too difficult to learn, understand, recognize and memorize. Further, many consider Chinese characters are non-scientific and inappropriate for modern use by mechanical means such as computers. It was even once suggested that Chinese characters should be "alphabetized" (or romanized, latinized). Such an idea, if forcefully put into practice, would have essentially killed Chinese characters (and subsequently, its culture).

Fortunately, however, after years of research and experiments many effective methods have been developed for Chinese input keyboard design, internal/

English	Chinese	Japanese	Korean
Famous spots	名胜	名所	명소
Museum	博物馆	博物館	박물관
Souvenir shop	土产店	みやげ品店	선물가게
Tax-free shop	免税商店	免税店	면세점
Theatre	剧场	劇場	극장
Concert	音乐会	音楽会	음악회
Night club	夜总会	ナイトクラブ	나이트클럽
Casino	赌场	カジノ	카지노
Coffee shop	咖啡店	コーヒー ショップ	커피숍
Emergency exit	太平门	非常口	비상구
Expressway	高速公路	高速道路	고속도로
Toll road	收费的公路	有料道路	유료도로
International call	国际电话	国際通話	국제통화
Public telephone	公用电话	公衆電話	공중전화

Fig. 1. Examples of Chinese, Japanese, and Korean characters.

external codes, and output printout/display techniques, and automatic recognition by machines. Hundreds of technical papers and reports can be found in the literature, and dozens of different kinds of Chinese computers, typewriters and word processors are available in the markets.[43] It turns out that not only Chinese characters avoid the fate of being eliminated but also people have begun to realize that, after all, maybe Chinese characters are not that intimidating.

Actually, Chinese characters, indeed are not only "not intimidating" but very useful from "intelligence", "knowledge" and "pattern recognition" points of view.[43] Using "learning by pattern and knowledge" method will make recognition easier and more interesting, in contrast to the conventional "learning by rote" techniques.[1,28] Note that Chinese characters and words are not just "pictorial" (象形), they are also "indicative symbols" (指事), "logical aggregates" (會意), "phonetic complexes" (形聲), "derivative" (轉注) and "borrow" (假借), and according to Ref. 44, they have strong properties in

(i) syntax-semantics correlation,
(ii) logical relations between characters,
(iii) multi-character words hierarchical structures,
(iv) induced knowledge,
(v) culture continuity,
(vi) artistic balance and beauty, and
(vii) avoiding ambiguity.

These properties are illustrated in the following figures.

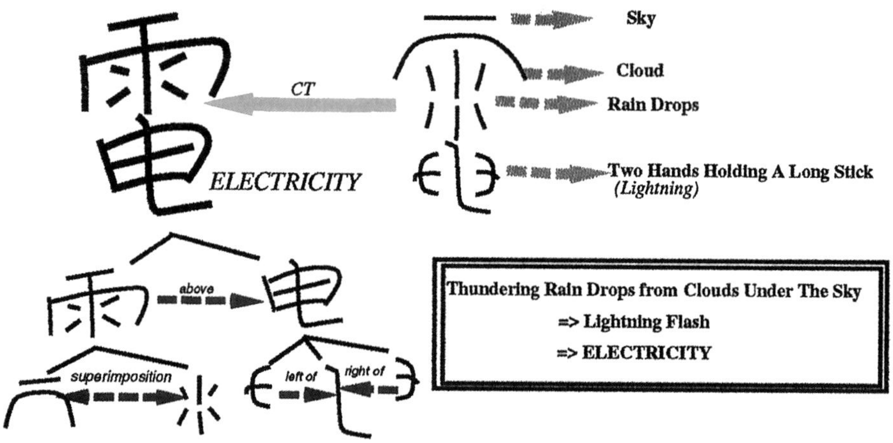

Fig. 2. Hierarchical structure and semantic network of "electricity".

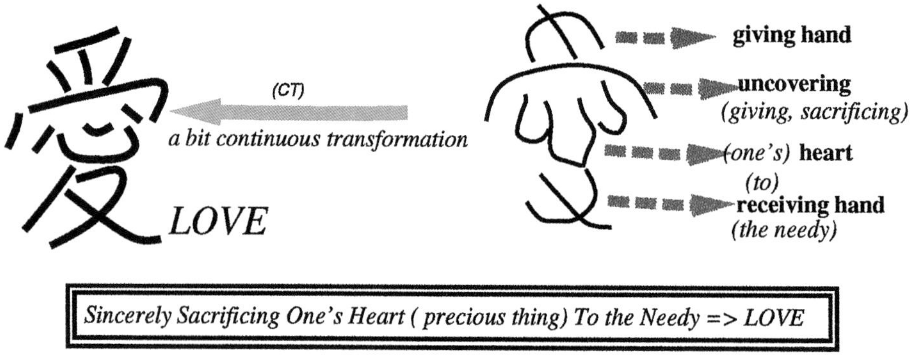

Fig. 3. Pictorial and indicative symbol of "love".

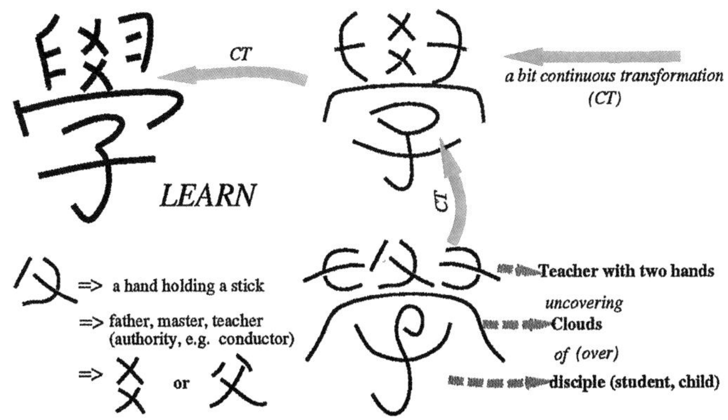

Fig. 4. Pictorial and indicative symbol of "learn".

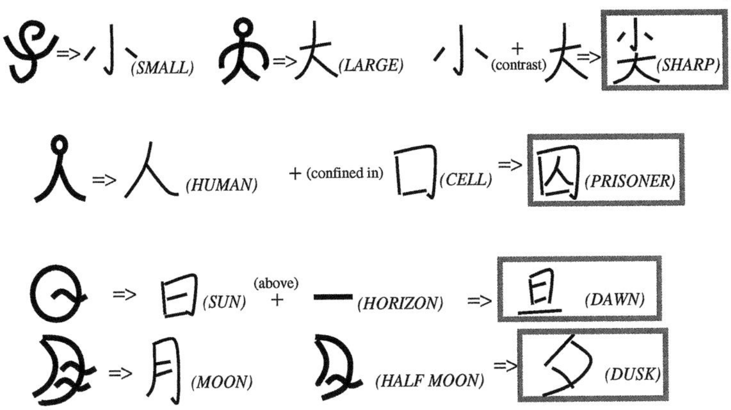

Fig. 5. Examples of logical aggregates/common properties between characters.

One of the advantages of such properties is *reinforcement learning*:

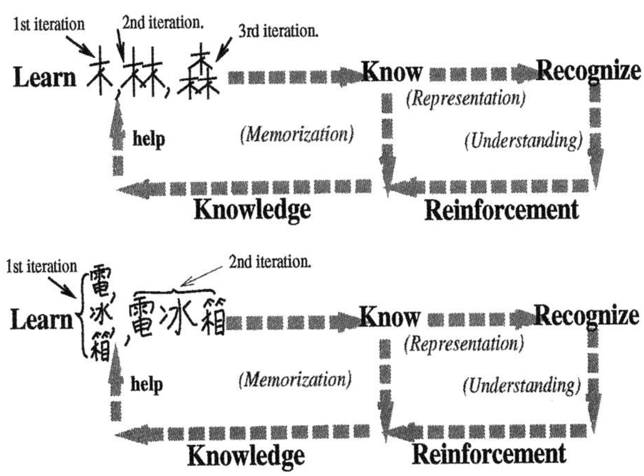

Fig. 6. Reinforcement learning, understanding and recognition of Chinese words.

For instance, knowing the words "electricity", "ice" and "box", can help one learn, understand and recognize a new word "refrigerator" very easily. In addition, all words related to "tree" share the common pattern "tree". Such property can help learning, understanding and recognition as shown in Fig. 6. According to the analysis in Ref. 44, among 7,000 commonly used Chinese characters, the largest such radical (family) is "water" (with more than 400 characters), followed by "grass" (350), "hand" (330), "tree" (319) and "heart" (260). Such strong characteristics are also reflected in multi-character words, such as *cow, ox, buffalo, bull, calif, veal, milk, beef, butter, steak, cowhide* and *horn*, etc. all of which bear the character "牛" in it. Such advantages are rather unique and can rarely be found in other languages such as English.

Further, it can also be extended to many other aspects of Chinese sentence and language levels as well, mainly because of its hierarchical and natural structures. For instance, parsing, searching and pattern matching are very efficient in address recognition on postal envelopes, name roster list handling and calendar time schedule processing, in comparison with other western languages such as English. Such a comparison is shown in Fig. 7.

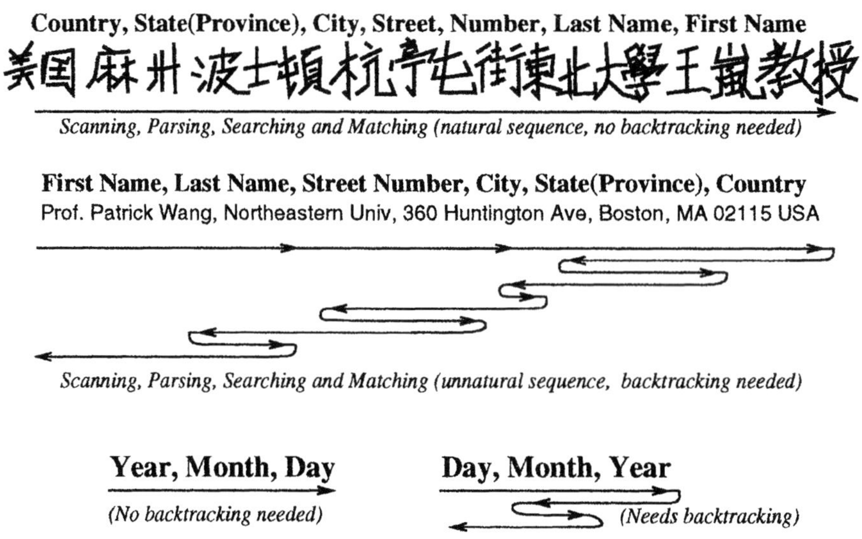

Fig. 7. Advantages of Chinese languages in comparison with Western languages.

It is well known that deterministic parsing without backtracking is more efficient compared with non-deterministic parsing with backtracking. Suppose every envelope can save one second in OCR scanning and recognition, 60 envelopes can save one minute, 3,600 envelopes can save one hour. A small scale post office which on the average handles about 360,000 letters daily can save 100 hours everyday! What a significant amount of saving time, energy and cost!

Next, we shall illustrate some poems to show the advantages of Chinese words and language. It is well known that *poem* is a form of language that is "refined", "elite", "compact", "elegant", and "powerful". It is also efficient in terms of saving memory — using as few words as possible to disseminate a certain idea or context, like the *macro* structure in programming. In a way, it is also similar to "image compression" and "decompression". Interestingly enough, the advantages of Chinese words can also be vividly seen in Chinese *poems.* Here are some illustrations.

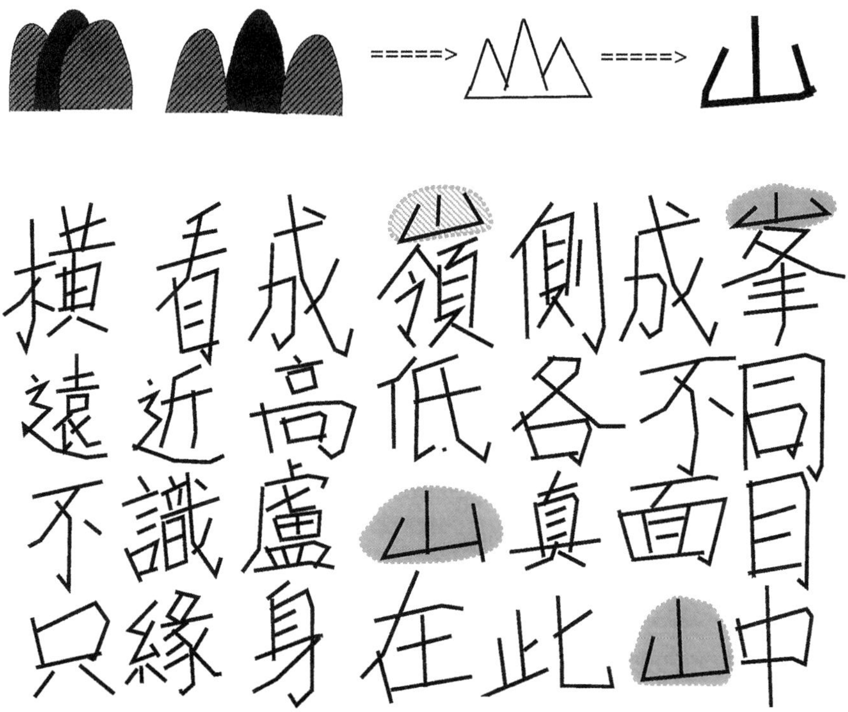

Looking from one side, mountains, from the other side, ranges
Far, near, high, low, all different
I can hardly recognize the true face of the Lu Shan mountain
Simply because I am in the middle of it

Written by Su Dong–po, 11th Century, Translated by P. Wang, 1997

Fig. 8. Some well known Chinese poem by Su Dong-po (蘇東坡).

Interestingly enough, this famous poem written by a famous Chinese poet Su Dong-po (蘇東坡) about 1,000 years ago somehow pointed out that one of the most difficult tasks of three-dimensional (3D) object recognition is due to too many "*variations*" and it is extremely hard, if not impossible, to find the object's *invariance.* This happens to coincide with the modern theory of 3D vision and object recognition by computers.

The following are some more illustrations of appreciating poems from *pattern recognition* and *knowledge/semantics* points of view.

Tu Fu: (詩聖 杜甫)

別淚遙添錦水波 (full of water, liquid characterized by patterns 水,氵)
My farewell tears added to the ripples of Jing River afar

感時花濺淚 恨別鳥驚心 (full of tears and hearts, characterized by 心,忄)
Thinking of the situation, My tears shed on flowers
Hate to depart, even birds scared me

Li Po: (詩仙 李白)

直掛雲帆濟滄海 (full of water, liquid)
Sailing boat to cross the ocean

淚下漢江流 (full of tears, water)
My tears pour unto the flowing Han River

Anonymous: 水汪汪的大眼睛 (full of water and eyes by 水 ,氵, 目)
Big, watery eyes

芬芳美麗滿枝椏 (full of grass, plants by ++ , 木)
Fragrant and beautiful buds all over the branches

3. CONTEMPORARY JAPANESE AND KANA SYSTEMS

Though Japanese is written with Chinese characters, linguists have no conclusive evidence of the linguistic kinship of Japanese because it is unlike Chinese both in structure and in vocabulary. Actually contemporary Japanese is a mixture of Kanji (Chinese characters, most nouns, verbs, and adjectives), Hiragana and Katakana which are phonetic symbols invented by the Japanese to represent particles and other grammatical devices which have no exact equivalents in Chinese. More descriptions about Hiragana and Katakana will be presented below. In technical and scientific documents, the Latin alphabet is also used. However, it is somewhat controversial to include the Latin alphabet while OCR needs to recognize them in real-life situations in Japanese language processing. Although basically each Hiragana character has a corresponding Katakana, each character plays its own role. Therefore Hiragana and Katakana must be treated as different systems.

3.1. Basic Usage of Katakana

Katakana is primarily used for words borrowed from foreign languages, e.g.

computer — コンピュータ

3.2. Differences between Hiragana and Katakana

Notice that Hiragana and Katakana do not have exactly one to one correspondence. Contemporary Hiragana uses 46 characters, i.e.

あいうえお　かきくけこ　さしすせそ　たちつてと
なにぬねの　はひふへほ　まみむめも　や ゆ よ
らりるれろ　わ　を　ん

In addition to these as voiced syllables and semi-voiced syllables, the following 25 characters are used:

がぎぐげご　ざじずぜぞ　だぢづでど　ばびぶべぼ
ぱぴぷぺぽ

As small characters, the following 4 characters are used:

ゃ ゅ ょ っ

Accordingly, a total of 75 characters are used in Hiragana.
On the other hand, Katakana has the following character set:

アイウエオ　カキクケコ　サシスセソ　タチツテト
ナニヌネノ　ハヒフヘホ　マミムメモ　ヤ ユ ヨ
ラリルレロ　ワ　ン　—

As voiced syllables and semi-voiced syllables the following 24 characters are used:

ガギグゲゴ　ザジズゼゾ　ダ　デド
バビブベボ　パピプペポ　ヴ

That is, "を" has no counterpart in Katakana. In voiced syllables "づ" and "ぢ" have no counterparts in Katakana. On the contrary, " — " is only used in Katakana. As voiced syllables, "ヴ" is used in Katakana. This is because Katakana is for phonetic expression of foreign languages. Specifically "ヴ" corresponds to "v" in English.

As small character set, Katakana uses

ャ ュ ョ ッ

as counterparts of the Hiragana. In addition, the following small characters are also used:

ア イ ウ オ

However, old Katakana characters are allowed in people's names, and so in the broadest sense, the following kana characters are also used:

Hiragana — ゐ, ゑ
Katakana — ヰ, ヱ, ヲ, ヂ, ヅ.

3.3. Combinations of Small Kana Characters

In contemporary expressions, the small kana is used as double consonants, etc. The following combinations are used in Hiragana:

きゃ きゅ きょ しゃ しゅ しょ ちゃ ちゅ ちょ
にゃ にゅ にょ ひゃ ひゅ ひょ みゃ みゅ みょ
りゃ りゅ りょ
ぎゃ ぎゅ ぎょ じゃ じゅ じょ ぢゃ ぢゅ ぢょ
びゃ びゅ びょ ぴゃ ぴゅ ぴょ

Thus, 36 combinations are used.

In Katakana, among the above combinations, "ヂャ", "ヂュ", "ヂョ" are not used and so 33 combinations are allowed. However, in the case of Katakana, since another set of small characters are used as mentioned before, an additional 21 characters are used. Furthermore, "ヂュ" is allowed as an exceptional case. This is because of the phonetic expression of:

producer ⟶ プロデューサー.

3.4. Kanji Sets

Chinese characters (also known as Kanji characters in Japanese) consist of 50,000 characters. However, in Japan, at most 4,000 are used daily. According to the older statistics taken in 1935 sampled from 60 days of 5 representative newspapers, out of 447,575 Kanji characters, 3,542 different Kanji characters were found. The first Kanji character was "一". This was used 6,500 times which accounts for 1.5% of all Kanji characters used. The most frequently used 10 Kanji characters are

"一", "日", "十", "二", "会", 大", "國", "政", and "時".

with a total frequency of 9.4%. The frequency of the highest 100 Kanji characters is 38.7%. The frequency of the top 1,000 characters is 91.7% and that of the top 1,800 is 98.0%. This statistics supported the movement to limit Kanji. After the second world war, a new preliminary common-use Kanji table was produced, which consisted of only 1,295 different characters. This was influenced by the report of the American Education Mission which predicted that Kanji would not be used in daily writing and Latin characters would be preferred.

A new committee was established for this issue including journalists. Eventually the committee proposed a new Kanji table, called Touyou-Kanji table which included 1,850 characters after adding 564 Kanji and eliminated 9 from the previous Kanji Table. This was established formally in 1936. The meaning of "*Touyou*" is "tentative", implying that new tables may be developed later. One of the scheduled tables was Education Kanji Table consisting of 881 Kanji's designed for elementary school education.

On the other hand and contrary to the American Education Mission's prediction and that of Kana-promotion association in Japan, more and more Kanji characters are being used. This is the direct result of natural culture and people's legacy, while at the same time, widely-used word processors have also facilitated the usage of more Kanji's. In this respect, there is a need to establish a standard of Kanji code system for computerization. As a result, 2 tables were established: (1) first level Kanji Table, and (2) second level Kanji Table, with 2,965 and 3,388 Kanji's respectively, totaling 6,353 different Kanji's which are enough in Japan.

3.5. Origin of Hiragana and Katakana

Japan imported Chinese characters from China more than a thousand years ago. Since then, Chinese characters, called Kanji's, were used as a standard in Japan. On the other hand, the Japanese language called Yamato, existed earlier. Hence there is a need for this language to be represented by Kanji's. The Japanese devised 2 ways of expressing Japanese by Kanji's[42]:

(1) Use Kanji's which have the same meaning, e.g.

"ame tsuchi" — 天 地,

where 'ame' and 'tsuchi' mean 'heaven' and 'earth' which correspond to 天 and 地 respectively. The corresponding Kanji's were pronounced according to the existing Japanese pronunciation. This way of pronunciation is called 'reading by *jikun*'.

(2) Use Kanji's according to their pronunciation regardless of their meanings, e.g.

"a-me-tsu-chi" — 阿米都知,

This is the phonetic way to use Kanji's, which is also called 'reading by *jion*'. This was known as Manyo-kana or True-kana. There were several kinds of Manyo-kana, however, the simple one which uses "one character one syllable" was developed into Hiragana and Katakana.

Table 1. Katakana characters and their correspoinding Manyo-kana.

ア	阿	ナ	奈	ル	流
イ	伊	ニ	二	レ	礼
ウ	宇	ヌ	奴	ロ	呂
エ	江	ネ	禰	ワ	和
オ	於	ノ	乃	ヰ	井
カ	加	ハ	八	ヱ	慧
キ	幾	ヒ	比	ヲ	乎
ク	久	フ	不	ン	
ケ	介	ヘ	部		
コ	己	ホ	保		
サ	散	マ	末		
シ	之	ミ	三		
ス	須	ム	牟		
セ	世	メ	女		
ソ	曾	モ	毛		
タ	多	ヤ	也		
チ	千	ユ	由		
ツ	川	ヨ	輿		
テ	天	ラ	良		
ト	止	リ	利		

Table 2. Hiragana characters and their corresponding Manyo-kana.

あ	安	な	奈	る	留
い	以	に	仁	れ	禮
う	宇	ぬ	奴	ろ	呂
え	衣	ね	禰	わ	和
お	於	の	乃	ゐ	為
か	加	は	波	ゑ	恵
き	幾	ひ	比	を	遠
く	久	ふ	不	ん	无
け	計	へ	部		
こ	己	ほ	保		
さ	左	ま	末		
し	之	み	美		
す	寸	む	武		
せ	世	め	女		
そ	曾	も	毛		
た	太	や	也		
ち	知	ゆ	由		
つ	川	よ	与		
て	天	ら	良		
と	止	り	利		

During the long history of Manyo-kana, it changed gradually into a new style of characters, which was divided into 2 streams, i.e. *Ryakutai-kana* (simplified-kana), and *Sou-kana* (cursive-kana). Ryakutai-kana was developed in the field of Kanji reading. In Japan, a Chinese sentence is read in Japanese pronunciation using some auxiliary markers to adapt to Japanese grammar. Therefore, the markers were introduced to write in a narrow space and deformed the original Manyo-kana, but the line-likeness of Kanji was preserved. Table 1 shows the correspondence between Katakana and its original Kanji.

On the other hand, Sou-kana was developed in the field of old Japanese sentence expression, which is called *Wa-bun* (和文). In this case, the function of Sou-kana is to express sentences, and long strings of characters. Therefore, more cursive deformation was possible in terms of convenience and speed to write with a brush. The stories and poems in the era of Heian (794-1192) were written using considerably deformed Sou-kana. For example, the world-wide famous novel "Genji-monogatari" contains 93.7% Hiragana and only 5.1% Kanji, which was written by a woman named Murasakishikibu.[29] The deformation went on further from the writing art. Sou-kana was used mainly by women and so very gentle and smooth cursive shapes were devised, which is the origin of Hiragana. Table 2 shows the correspondence between Hiragana and its original Kanji.

3.6. OCR's in Japan

A large number of electronic companies in Japan have been engaged in the research and development of Optical Character Recognition (OCR) readers. As a result, many OCR products are available in the market. Our study indicates that there were about 80 such products in February 1996,[10] for the following:

(a) Formatted documents (hardware)
(b) Office automation
(c) OCR software (document OCR)
(d) OCR software (formatted documents)

Supported by alternating demands, sale of OCR hardware continues. OCR software has been developed in recent years changing the interface and adding word processing capability for the natural way of post processing. Word processors which have OCR functions capture an overwhelming share in OCR in U.S.A. According to the catalogue, the speed is twice higher than the current OCR's, as OCR specific for Western languages was sold by Xerox. These 2 cases are typical examples of the collaboration between American and Japanese companies. An OCR which specifically uses facsimile as scanner was sold. Facsimiles which read phone numbers of a receiver and send document automatically were sold. The implementation of character recognition to the basic OS (operating system) was realized in Windows 95 in its upper-grade version.

3.7. Perspective

Both PC and business users are now familiar with character recognition because of the widespread usage of OCR software, its low cost, and the high performance of new PC's. However, it needs some skill to use OCR software in practice, and while being sold at a high volume, cases of their effective use seem to be few. In this sense, it is very important for OCR technology including on-line character recognition to establish the base for using them effectively. In order to achieve the objective, the following points should be taken into consideration:

1. Interface with neighboring application fields
2. Modularization of character recognition
3. Development of structural analysis of the document in specific areas
4. Development of segmentation of individual characters and character strings
5. Further improvement of the performance of individual OCR's

3.8. Improvements by Using Linguistic Knowledge

It is true that linguistic information can enhance OCR performance. However, it is difficult to assess the improvement quantitatively because it depends on so many factors. Here, we only describe some instances which have been reported in the literature. Actually Itoh and Maruyama described this point very clearly.[8] Their basic idea of postprocessing is to use morphological analysis with cost evaluation in the path of the lattice. They used 3 kinds of documents: (a) papers published in IEICE Transactions, 9,455 characters, (b) education document for clients for computers, 4,129 characters, (c) patent documents for electricity, 2,393 characters. Types (a) and (b) represent usual document quality, while type (c) was selected to represent low quality documents. The results are shown in Table 3.

In this table, undetection rate means the ratio of the undetected character errors to the total number of characters, and over detection rate means the ratio of the warned correct characters to the total number of characters. So they concluded that if 95% or more recognition rate is achieved without postprocessing, the recognition rate can be lifted to the 99% level and the overlooked character errors can be suppressed to $<0.2\%$. This is very good performance considering that the first class certification of word processor examination is 98.9%.

On the other hand, Mori *et al.*[30] recently reported the effectiveness of postprocessing in their method which is based on n-gram model estimated from the small size training samples using so-called smoothing technique. They used 3 kinds of testing data: (a) editorials, 80,098 characters, (b) essays, 23,315 characters, and (c) technical reports, 34,219 characters. The editorials and essays come from daily newspapers, and the technical reports are related to information science. They used the editorials of 5.8 million characters as the training data. The correct recognition rates before postprocessing are 93.63%, 91.34%, and 92.15%, respectively. Using trigrams, the recognition rates for top N_{cn} choices are 99.71%, 98.80%, and 99.07% respectively, which are the upper bounds of the recognition rates after postprocessing, where N_{cn} is the parameter, i.e. the number of candidates.

Table 3. Performance of postprocessing for each document.

Document	Recognition rate (%) Before post-processing	Recognition rate (%) After post-processing	Undetection rate (%)	Over detection in rate (%)	Total detection rate (%)
A	96.50	99.26	0.18	1.81	5.35
B	94.74	99.03	0.17	1.50	6.64
C	87.46	94.61	1.09	4.80	16.38

4. KOREAN LANGUAGE

Some linguists support the view that the Korean language belongs to the Ural-Altaic language group of central Asia which includes Turkish, Mongolian, Hungarian and Finnish. Due to proximity to China, the Korean language is strongly influenced by Chinese,[4] and more than half of its vocabulary comes from the Chinese culture, especially its Confucian classics, though it has been assimilated phonetically into Korean.

4.1. Origin

Up to the 15th century, there was no distinct Korean alphabet, and Koreans used Chinese ideographs to express their language in writing, sometimes to represent the ideographs' original meaning and sometimes to simply express sounds. However, the sounds of the Korean language differ from those of Chinese, and learning to write complex Chinese characters was a difficulty for the common people. In view of these problems, King Sejong the Great (4th monarch of the Yi Dynasty of the Choson Kingdom) commissioned a team of scholars to devise a new simple method of writing down spoken Korean so that even the common people would be able to express their thoughts in writing. As a result, Hangul (originally called Hun-Min Chong-Um, literally 'proper sounds to instruct the people') was invented in 1443, the 28th year of the reign of King Sejong. It is a remarkable syllabic system which consists of 11 vowels and 17 consonants, giving a total of 28 phonetic signs. Based on East Asian philosophy (I Ching, or the Book of Changes), each Hangul consists of initial, medial and final sounds to reflect their belief in the combination of the powers of Heaven, Earth, and Man to create the universe. This new phonetic script is now used throughout Korea though Chinese characters are still taught at schools and used to represent original Chinese loan words.

4.2. Korean Symbols and Phonetic System

Hangul uses a phonetic alphabet which is supposed to be based on the patterns seen in a window frame with two vertical bars and two horizontal ones. The letters are combined into syllables that resemble Chinese characters to the undiscerning eye. A syllable that begins with a vowel is preceded by a circle, a character that also represents the nasal sound -ng. In the latter case, the circle is written below the syllable it terminates. The frequent occurrence of the circle is distinctive of Korean and makes it easy to identify.

Korean letters can be divided into 2 categories: element signs (phonemes) and combined scripts (syllabics). One Korean syllabic consists of a consonant element, a vowel element, and sometimes one or more final consonant elements.

Consonant elements The basic signs are: ㄱ(g,k) ㄴ(n) ㄷ(d,t) ㄹ(r,l) ㅁ(m) ㅂ(b,p) ㅅ(s,sh) ㅇ(ng) ㅈ(j,ch) ㅊ(chh) ㅋ(kh) ㅌ(th) ㅍ(ph) ㅎ(h).

ㄱ(g), ㄷ(d), ㅂ(b), and ㅈ(j) at the beginning of a word are, respectively, heard as k, t, p and ch by non-Korean speakers. ㅇ at the top of a syllabic is a base for vowels; thus, 아 is not nga but a.

Double-element signs: ㄲ('k) ㄸ('t) ㅃ('p) ㅆ('s) ㅉ('ch).

Vowel elements The basic signs are: ㅏ(a) ㅑ(ya) ㅓ(o) ㅕ(yo) ㅗ(o) ㅛ(yo) ㅜ(u) ㅠ(yu) ㅡ(u) ㅣ(i).

Combined vowel signs are: ㅐ(e), ㅒ(ye), ㅔ(e), ㅖ(ye), ㅚ(o), ㅟ(i), ㅢ(wi), ㅘ(wa), ㅝ(wo), ㅙ(we), ㅞ(we).

Combination of elements Each letter of Hangul consists of two or more elements. The way of combining two elements(a consonant and a vowel) is determined by the form of each vowel element. This is shown here for the consonant ㄱ(k): 가(ka) 갸(kya) 거(ko) 겨(kyo) 고(ko) 교(kyo) 구(ku) 규(kyu) 그(ku) 기(ki) 개(ke) 걔(kye) 게(ke) 계(kye) 괴(ko) 귀(ki) 긔(kwi) 과(kwa) 궈(kwo) 괘(kwe) 궤(kwe).

Independent vowels are expressed by the sign ㅇ(silent) and a vowel element: 아(a), 에(e), 이(i), 오(o), 우(u). Examples of syllabics containing the vowel ㅗ(o) are: 고(ko) 노(no) 도(to) 로(ro) 모(mo) 보(po) 소(so) 오(o) 조(cho) 초(chho) 코(kho) 토(tho) 포(pho) 호(ho) 꼬('ko) 뽀('po) 쏘('so) 쪼('cho).

By adding a final consonant, which consists of one or two elements, to the combined letters, other syllabics can be made as follows: 각(kak) 간(kan) 갇(kat) 갈(kal) 감(kam) 갑(kap) 갓(kat) 강(kang) 갖(kat) 갗(kat) 같(kat) 갚(kap) 갛(ka') 갉(kak) 값(kap) 갔(kat). The number of possible combinations of two or more elements is enormous, but about 2,300 movable types suffice for Korean printing because some combinations are not actually used.

4.3. Korean Character Recognition

Korean characters are structured in a scientific way, i.e. each Korean character is composed of 2 or 3 Korean symbols in 2 dimensions. Moreover, the number of possible Korean characters generated this way is very large (with more than 11,000 possibilities) and there are many character shapes which look alike. These characteristics make Korean OCR very difficult.

Generally, in terms of recognition, we can classify the methodology of Korean OCR into the alphabet-unit and the character-unit. Between these 2 methods, the alphabet-unit recognition is preferred because it can utilize the formation principle of the Korean character. If we can correctly segment a character into symbols, the symbol-unit recognition method becomes much easier in recognizing a character. In recognizing Korean by the character unit, the complexity of recognition is increased because of the large number of characters to be recognized. Thus, most researchers try to reduce the complexity by limiting the number of characters to be recognized. For example, some research groups took only the most frequently used 2,350 characters as the target vocabulary to be recognized.

Many attempts have been made to develop printed and handwritten Korean character recognizers for the past 20 years. Recent development of printed Korean character recognition technology has resulted in some commercial products reporting more than 95% recognition rate although they are limited in font types and sizes. However, the performance of handwritten Korean character recognition is not so good as that of the printed Korean character recognizers. This is because it involves more problems such as the variations of a writing style.

Below we will describe some methods of recognizing printed and handwritten Korean characters, pre-processing, and post-processing. Finally, we will discuss some future trends.

4.4. Printed Korean Character Recognition

In the early period of research, some Korean researchers devised structural methods.[23] The structural methods first extract features by tracing end-points, branching points, and crossing-points from an input character, and then recognize the input character by the process of stroke matching. The extraction of Korean structural features is relatively easy. However, structural methods are very sensitive to noise and they require a lot of processing time. To alleviate these problems, many researchers tried to contrive the thinning algorithms which are tolerable to noise, and they facilitate the extraction of features directly from binary images.

The disadvantages of structural approaches have resulted in the advance of neural network approaches for printed Korean character recognition.[13,14] Among them, the hierarchical structural neural network is most popular. The hierarchical structural neural network consists of the type classification network and character recognition networks as shown in Fig. 9. The type classification network is first used for classifying the given Korean character into 1 of 6 types. Then, the corresponding character recognition network tries to recognize the given Korean character.

Another neural network approach was proposed in Ref. 18, which tried to recognize Korean documents printed with multi-fonts using the back-propagation algorithm. In this method, the pattern classifier using structure-adaptive self-organizing neural network was employed to recognize multi-font and multi-size characters.[22,25]

Many statistical methods have also been proposed for printed Korean character recognition. Most statistical approaches are based on Hidden Markov Models (HMM).[32] Statistical methods have the advantage that they can consider the variations of Korean character shapes. However, they cannot easily use the structural features of Hanguls because so many of them have similar shapes.

So far, most attempts made to recognize printed Korean characters have focused on fixed-sized and single font, especially on the Myeong-Jo font or the Gothic font. As a result, some commercial products recognizing documents printed in this font with a fixed character size are available. Nowadays, many Korean researchers are trying to develop a system which can recognize the large-set documents including multi-size, multi-font, and multi-lingual characters.

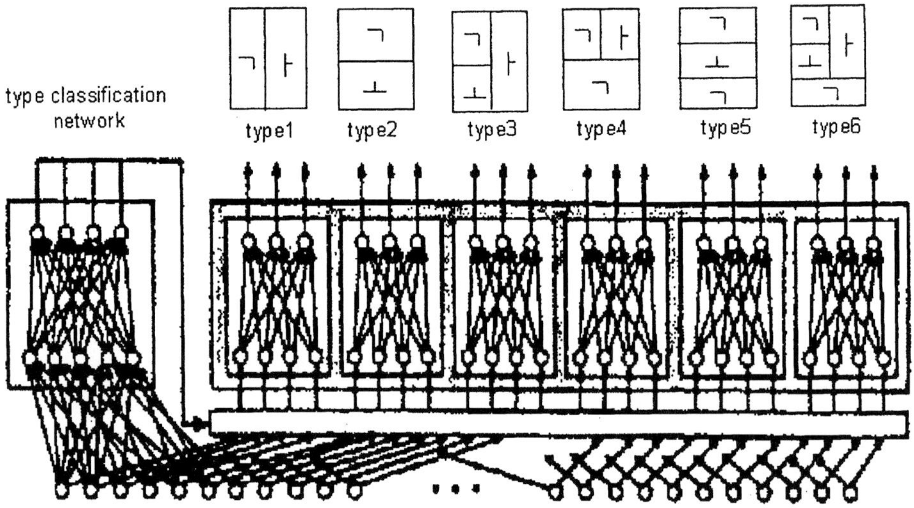

Fig. 9. Classification of Korean characters and hierarchical neural network.

4.5. Handwritten Korean Character Recognition

Interests in handwritten Korean character recognition increased in the middle of 1980's when the pen-interface technology became popular. For both on-line and off-line handwritten Korean character recognition, the main difficulty is to identify the variations of characters resulted from the symbol position, touching of symbols, and the different styles of writing. For example, 2 characters in Fig. 10 look the same although they represent different characters with variations. Actually, the character on the left-hand side is 뇌 (/Noe/, brain) and the character on the right-hand side is 내 (/Nae/, inside). Because of these variations, the recognizer is often confused and makes some mistakes. Therefore, it is very important to observe the variations of hand-written Korean characters.

Fig. 10. Example of handwritten characters with similar shapes.

For the observation of variations, the most frequently used method to resolve the problem is DP matching which can be classified into 2 approaches, viz. character-unit DP matching[17] and symbol unit DP matching.[36] The symbol-unit DP matching is preferred to the character-unit DP matching these days. An example of symbol-unit DP matching is shown in Fig. 11.

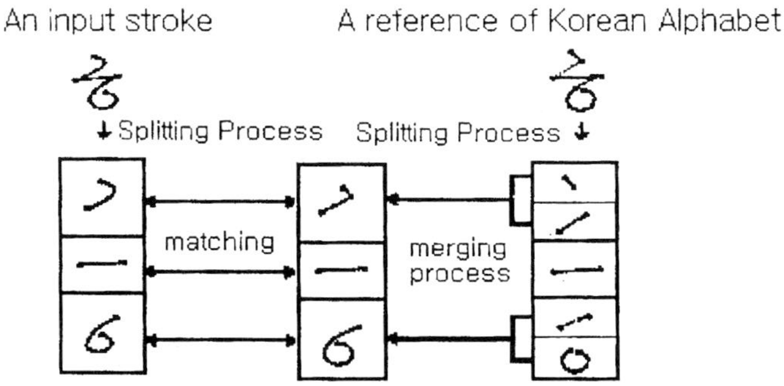

Fig. 11. Example of DP matching.

Statistical models can also handle different variations of patterns well by using statistical information. This advantage has led many Korean researchers to apply statistical models to recognize handwritten Korean characters. HMM is the most frequently used statistical model.[33,37] Representative research efforts are described in Ref. 12 which is a historical review of research at CAIR/KAIST. They tried to develop an unconstrained cursive script recognizer based on HMM and tried to extend the recognition model. They also attempted to improve the performance of recognition by integrating various types of knowledge into the HMM framework such as statistical, structural, and syntactic.

Neural network approaches are commonly employed for handwritten Korean character recognition, because they are less sensitive to partial deformations and noises of the input pattern.[35,39] Multi-perceptron and pattern classifier were mainly used in those groups. However, neural networks require a lot of training time and they are not effective when there are too many candidates to be recognized. Nevertheless, we expect that neural networks can solve many difficult problems that other methods cannot.

Recently, Korean researchers tried to solve the variation problem by integrating the segmentation and the recognition methods.[27] Such an integration turned out to be very effective for recognizing handwritten Korean characters especially when the degree of variation was high. The integration method using the recurrent neural network was also presented.

Another group of researchers tried to combine the statistical and structural methods.[11,38] By integrating 2 methods, it can reflect the local features of the given character, and also it can learn the variations of writings.

4.6. Pre-Processing

In order to improve the accuracy of Korean character recognition, pre-processing is required, e.g. the analysis of noise, the segmentation of character, and the restoration of deformed shape. Lee *et al.*[26] investigated the distribution of quantity and entropy of character images and proposed a method of correcting the skew of the input character.

There have been 2 well-known methods for segmenting Korean characters: (1) the direct segmenting method, and (2) the segmentation and recognition integrating method. The former method segments the Korean characters into symbol-unit fragments before the recognition process, but this method can hardly observe the variations of Korean characters.[5,19,24] The segmentation and recognition integrating method performs both the segmentation task and the recognition task simultaneously,[9,16] but this method has the drawback of being too much dependent on the recognition module. Because of these limitations, many Korean researchers try to develop a method of optimizing the segmentation and the recognition of the characters.

With respect to the other step of pre-processing, normalization techniques for shape variations play an important role in the performance of Korean OCR. Lee and his colleagues[26,34] studied many different normalization techniques and made quantitative evaluations.

4.7. Post-Processing

Due to errors introduced by pre-processing or recognition, post-processing of Korean character recognition is also required. So far, most research in this aspect has been done for the printed Korean character recognition. Previous works for the post-processing of Korean character recognition can be classified into the following 2 methods: (a) the isolated word error detection and correction method, and (b) the context dependent word error detection and correction method. The isolated word error detection and correction method uses dictionary information and morpho-syntactic information of a word,[6,21] and the context dependent word error detection and correction method uses contextual information of adjacent words.[7,46] The isolated word error detection and correction approaches try to detect the position where the error occurs through morphological analysis and correct the error by using the N-gram dictionary. However, those methods are too much dependent on the dictionary information, and they cannot correct the error if there are more than 2 in a word. On the other hand, the context dependent word error detection and correction methods utilize the co-occurrence or mutual information of a word, and the part-of-speech as contextual information.[46]

4.8. Future Works

So, we have described the current status of OCR for both printed and handwritten Korean characters. Many attempts have been made to develop printed and handwritten Korean character recognizers. Some commercial products which can recognize single font and fixed-type font Korean characters at a high recognition rate are available. However, there are still problems in recognizing documents with multi-font and multi-size printed Korean characters. As well, the performance of recognizing handwritten Korean characters has to catch up with the printed Korean character recognition.

5. CONCLUDING REMARKS

We have described 3 major oriental languages with 3 different views and perspectives. It is hoped that the readers will understand more about the intriguing aspects of these fascinating languages, and be able to find useful pointers to conduct further research in character recognition and language analysis. Due to the complex structures of the characters and symbols used in these languages, it is the common view of all the co-authors that automatic recognition of these languages in documents with high performance will remain a great challenge for the next few years.

To achieve the ultimate goal of recognizing the document with multi-font, multi-size, multi-lingual characters, the following problems must be solved in the near future. Because the input document is usually represented in various structures, the structure of the document must be accurately analyzed while being processed. Furthermore, a more precise method of separating the given character string is required. Effective methods of combining the separation and the recognition methods must also be developed. Moreover, the post-processing method using linguistic information is also required in order to attain a higher accuracy. It seems that the collaboration of people in different disciplines such as computer scientists, engineers, mathematicians, psychologists, and linguists, is particularly desirable.

REFERENCES

1. D. P. Ausubel, J. D. Novak and H. Hanesian, *Educational Psychology: A Cognitive View*, Second Edition, HRW Co., New York, 1978.
2. S. B. Cho and J. H. Kim, "Integrating hidden Markov model and neural network classifier for on-line handwritten character recognition", *J. Korea Information Science Society* **20**, 3 (1993) 328–337.
3. K. Chu, *Cognitive Aspects in Chinese Character Processing*, IEEE Workshop on Automaton Language, Spain, 1985, pp. 141–163.
4. D. Crystal, *An Encyclopedic Dictionary of Language and Languages*, Penguin Books, London, England, 1994.
5. J. I. Doh, "A study on the letter segmentation of Hangul characters for printed Hangul character recognition", *Proc. Conf. Korea Information Science Society* **17**, 2 (1990) 175–178.
6. N. H. Hong, W. I. Lee, J. H. Lee and G. B. Lee, "A study on the correction method of misrecognized characters using string and Eojeol information in character recognition system", *Proc. 1st Korean Character Recognition Workshop*, 1993, pp. 109–113.
7. Y. Y. Hur, M. J. Kim and H. C. Kwon, "Linguistic and heuristic constraints on the post-processing for Korean OCR", *J. Korea Information Science Society* **24**, 1 (1997) 25–31.
8. N. Itoh and H. Maruyama, "A method of detecting and correcting errors in the results of Japanese OCR", *Trans. Information Processing Society of Japan* **33**, 5 (1996) 664–670.
9. M. W. Jang, D. N. Chun and H. S. Yang, "Segmentation and recognition of document information based on the connected component", *J. Korea Information Science Society* **20**, 12 (1993) 1741–1751.
10. JEIDA, "Report of a study on the standardization of human-media information processing", Japan Electric Industry Development Association, 1997.

11. H. J. Kim and P. K. Kum, "Recognition of off-line handwritten Korean characters", *Patt. Recogn.* **29**, 2 (1996) 245–254.
12. J. H. Kim and J. O. Kwon, "A historical perspective of handwriting recognition research at CAIR/KAIST", *Proc. 1994 Korean–French Character Recognition Workshop*, Sept. 1994, pp. 1–12.
13. W. S. Kim and S. Y. Bang, "A study on Korean and Chinese character document reader using neural network", *J. Korean Institute of Telematics and Electronics* **29-B**, 2 (1992) 50–59.
14. J. W. Kwon, S. B. Cho and J. H. Kim, "Multi-size/multi-font Hangul document recognition with hierarchical neural networks", *J. Korea Information Science Society* **19**, 1 (1991) 69–79.
15. D. H. Lee, W. G. Cho, H. S. Yang and J. H. Kim, "Hangul character type classification with neural network", *Proc. Conf. Korea Information Science Society* **16**, 1 (1989) 215–218.
16. D. J. Lee and S. W. Lee, "Character segmentation and recognition in Hangul document mixed with alphanumeric characters", *Proc. Conf. Korea Information Science Society* **21**, 2 (1994) 403–406.
17. H. D. Lee, T. Aagui and M. Nakajima, "On-line recognition of cursive Korean characters by descriptions of basic character patterns and their connected patterns", *Proc. SPIE Conf. Visual Communications and Image Processing*, 1988, pp. 1001–1111.
18. H. K. Lee and S. Y. Bang, "Recognition of handwritten Hangul characters using backpropagation neural networks", *Proc. Conf. Korea Information Science Society* **19**, 1 (1992) 681–684.
19. J. G. Lee, J. H. Lee and H. J. Kim, "A study on the extraction and segmentation of the picture and characters in Korean document", *Proc. Conf. Korea Information Science Society* **17**, 2 (1990) 167–170.
20. J. S. Lee, O. J. Kwon and S. Y. Bang, "An improved 2-stage classifier method for printed Korean characters by expanding the input subimages for grapheme identification", *Proc. 3rd Int. Conf Document Analysis and Recognition*, Aug. 1995, pp. 548–551.
21. J. Y. Lee and S. H. Oh, "A correction algorithm for misrecognized words using N-gram Hangul dictionary", *Proc. 5th Conf. Hangul and Korean Information Processing*, 1993, pp. 271–283.
22. K. M. Lee, S. B. Cho and Y. B. Lee, "Structure-adaptive self-organizing neural network: Application to Hangul character recognition", *Proc. 7th Conf. Hangul and Korean Information Processing*, Oct. 1995, pp. 137–142.
23. S. H. Lee and J. H. Kim, "A study on stroke extraction for structural recognition of Korean characters", *Proc. Conf. Korea Information Science Society* **14**, 2 (1987) 151–154.
24. S. H. Lee, J. I. Cheon, Y. J. Cho and J. C. Namkung, "A study on the classification of character for newspaper automatic recognition system", *Proc. Conf. Hangul and Korean Information Processing*, Oct. 1989, pp. 209–215.
25. S. W. Lee and J. S. Kim, "Multi-lingual large-set oriental character recognition using hierarchical neural network classifier", *Proc. 3rd Int. Conf. Document Analysis and Recognition*, Aug. 1995, pp. 177–180.
26. S. W. Lee and J. S. Park, "Quantitative evaluation of normalization methods for large-set handwritten character recognition", *Patt. Recogn.* **27**, 7 (1994) 895–902.
27. S. W. Lee and E. J. Lee, "Integrated segmentation and recognition of connected handwritten characters with recurrent neural network", *Proc. 3rd Int. Conf. Document Analysis and Recognition*, August 1995, pp. 413–416.

28. R. B. Millward, "Models of concept formation", in *Aptitude, Learning, and Instruction*, (eds.), R. E. Snow *et al.*, L. Erlbaum Assoc., Hillsdale, N.J. Also *A Survey, Proc. Int. Conf. Pattern Recognition*, Rome, 1988, pp. 1123–1132.
29. T. Miyazima, *Tables of Vocabularies Used in Classical Novels*, Tsukuma, 1989, in Japanese.
30. H. Mori, H. Aso and S. Makino, "Robust n-gram model of Japanese characters and its application to document recognition", *IEICE Trans. INF&SYST.* **E79-D**, 5 (1996) 471–476.
31. A. Nakanishi, *Writing Systems of the World*, Charles E. Tuttle Co. Inc., Tokyo, Japan, 1980.
32. H. S. Park and S. W. Lee, "Off-line recognition of large set handwritten Hangul hidden Markov models", *Proc. 3rd Int. Workshop on Frontiers in Handwriting Recognition*, May 1993, pp. 51–61.
33. H. S. Park and S. W. Lee, "Hidden Markov mesh random field: Theory and its application to handwritten character recognition", *Proc. 3rd Int. Conf. Document Analysis and Recognition*, Aug. 1995, pp. 409–412.
34. J. S. Park and S. W. Lee, "An adaptive nonlinear pattern matching method for off-line recognition of handwritten characters", *J. Korea Information Science Society* **22**, 2 (1995) 292–303.
35. T. J. Seong and S. Y. Bang, "On-line handwritten Hangul recognition by learning character composition rules", *J. Korea Information Science Society* **20**, 3 (1993) 305–316.
36. D. G. Sim, Y. K. Ham and R. H. Park, "On-line recognition of cursive Korean characters using matching and fuzzy concept", *Patt. Recogn.* **27**, 12 (1994) 1065–1620.
37. B. K. Sin and J. H. Kim, "A statistical approach with HMMs for on-line cursive Hangul (Korean Script) recognition", *Proc. 2nd Int. Conf. Document Analysis and Recognition*, Oct. 1993, pp. 147–150.
38. B. K. Sin and J. H. Kim, "Network-based approach to handwriting approach", *Proc. 17th Int. Conf. Computer Processing of Oriental Languages*, 1997, pp. 101–106.
39. H. H. Song and S. W. Lee, "A self-organizing neural tree for large-set pattern classification", *Proc. 3rd Int. Conf. Document Analysis and Recognition*, Aug. 1995, pp. 1111–1114.
40. C. Y. Suen, *Computational Analysis of Mandarin*, Birkhäuser Verlag, Berne, Switzerland, 1979.
41. C. Y. Suen, *Computational Studies of the Most Frequent Chinese Words and Sounds*, World Scientific Publishing Co. Ltd., Singapore, 1986.
42. Y. Takabe, *The Expression of Japanese Language*, Kadokawa, 1988.
43. P. Wang (ed.), *Intelligent Chinese Language, Pattern, and Speech Processing*, World Scientific Publishing Co., Singapore, 1988.
44. P. Wang, "Learning, representation, understanding and recognition of words — an intelligent approach", in *Fundamentals in Handwriting Recognition*, ed. S. Impedovo, Springer-Verlag, Heidelberg, Germany, 1994, pp. 81–112.
45. P. H. Winston, *Artificial Intelligence*, Addison-Wesley, Reading, Massachusetts, 1994.
46. J. H. Yoo, J. H. Lee and G. B. Lee, "Post-processing for character recognition using morphological analysis and linguistic evaluation", *J. Korea Information Science Society* **22**, 6 (1995) 880–890.

Ching Y. Suen received an M. Sc. (Eng.) degree from the University of Hong Kong and a Ph.D. degree from the University of British Columbia, Canada.

In 1972, he joined the Department of Computer Science of Concordia University, Montreal, Canada, where he became Professor in 1979 and served as Chairman from 1980 to 1984. Presently he is the Director of CENPARMI, the Centre for Pattern Recognition and Machine Intelligence of Concordia, and the Associate Dean — Research of the Faculty of Engineering and Computer Science.

Prof. Suen is the author/editor of 11 books and more than 250 papers and his current interests include pattern recognition and machine intelligence, character recognition and expert systems, document processing and computational linguistics.

Dr. Suen is an Associate Editor of several journals related to Pattern Recognition and Artificial Intelligence. He founded Computer Processing of Chinese and Oriental Languages, an international journal of the Chinese Language Computer Society in 1983 and served as its Editor-in-Chief for 10 years.

A fellow of the IEEE, IAPR, and the Royal Society of Canada, Prof. Suen is the recipient of several awards, including the 1992 ITAC/NSERC award for outstanding contributions to pattern recognition, expert systems, and computational linguistics.

Shunji Mori received the B.E. degree in 1956 and Dr. engineering degree in 1978 from Hokkaido University. From 1957 to 1983 he was with the Electrotechnical Laboratory of the Ministry of International Trade and Industry of Japan.

There he served as head of the Pattern Processing section from 1969 to 1981 and as supervisor of the Pattern Information Processing System (PIPS) from 1971 to 1973. In 1975 he was a visiting researcher at the Computer Vision Laboratory, University of Maryland, for half a year and from 1981 to 1982 he was a visiting professor in the Department of Computer Science, Concordia University, Montreal. From 1983 to 1987 he worked for Nippon Schlumberger as head of the Modeling Department of System Engineering. From 1988 to 1992 he worked for Ricoh Company, Ltd. as head of the Artificial Intelligence Research Center of the Research and Development Central Research Center. Currently he is a Professor of Computer Science at the University of Aizu, Aizu Wakamatsu, Fukushima, Japan. He serves as Chairperson of Software Department.

His research interests include pattern recognition, image processing, and knowledge engineering. Dr. Mori is a member of AAAI, IEEE, the Information Processing Society of Japan.

Hae-Chang Rim received the Ph.D. degree in computer science in 1990, from the University of Texas at Austin where he was a member of Artificial Intelligence Laboratory during 1986–1990 (Natural Language Processing division).

He is currently associate professor of computer science in Korea University (Seoul, Korea). His research interests are natural language processing, information retrieval, and artificial intelligence.

Patrick S. P. Wang is an IAPR Fellow and has been tenured full professor of computer science at Northeastern University since 1983, a research consultant at MIT Sloan School since 1989, and adjunct faculty master of computer science at Harvard University Extension School since 1985. He received his Ph.D. in computer science from Oregon State University, his M.S. in I.C.S. from Georgia Institute of Technology, his M.S.E.E. from National Taiwan University and his B.S.E.E. from National Chiao Tung University. He was on the faculties of the University of Oregon and Boston University, and senior researcher at Southern Bell, GTE Labs, and Wang Labs prior to his present position. In addition to his research experience at MIT AI Lab, Prof. Wang has been visiting professor and has been invited to give lectures, do research and present papers in more than a dozen countries in Europe and Asia and many universities and industries in the U.S.A. and Canada. He has published over 120 technical papers and 16 books in pattern recognition, AI and imaging technologies and has three OCR patents by US and Europe Patent Bureaus. As IEEE senior member he has organized numerous international conferences and workshops and served as reviewer for many journals and NSF grant proposals. Prof. Wang is currently founding Editor-in-Charge of the *International Journal of Pattern Recognition and Artificial Intelligence*, Editor-in-Chief of the series on *Machine Perception and Artificial Intelligence* by World Scientific Publishing Co., and elected chair of IAPR-SSPR (International Association of Pattern Recognition). In addition to his technical interests, he has also written several articles on the operas of Verdi, Puccini, and Wagner, and the symphonies of Mozart, Beethoven, and Tchaikovsky.

THE GENERATION OF ORIENTAL CHARACTERS: NEW PERSPECTIVES FOR AUTOMATIC HANDWRITING PROCESSING

RÉJEAN PLAMONDON*, WACEF GUERFALI and XIAOLIN LI

Laboratoire SCRIBENS, École Polytechnique de Montréal
Département de génie électrique et de génie informatique
C.P. 6079, Succursale Centre-Ville, Montréal QC, Canada H3C 3A7

We recently developed a general theory of rapid human movements and applied it to the generation of western handwriting. The goal of this paper is to summarize the key concepts behind the so-called vectorial delta-lognormal model that results from this theory and to show how this model could be used for Chinese character analysis and processing.

Keywords: Human movement modeling, delta-lognormal model, handwriting generation, oriental character analysis.

1. INTRODUCTION

Over the past thirty years, a tremendous effort has been made to understand handwriting generation and control using different types of models.[1,6,10,17,18,21,22] None of these models is alphabet-specific, although most applications and examples provided by the authors deal with the handprinted or cursive Latin alphabet.

We recently developed a general theory of rapid human movements[8,9,11,12] and applied it to the generation of handwriting.[10,16,17,19] This model is general enough to encompass numerous basic psychophysical phenomena concerning simple movements[13,15] and it leads to a realistic and robust definition of a stroke.

The goal of this paper is to summarize the key concepts behind the vectorial delta-lognormal model[10,16,17] and to show how this model could be used for Chinese character processing. We first conduct a short survey of the principal characteristics of the major oriental alphabets. Second, we describe the handwriting generation model and then we present an algorithm for the analysis-by-synthesis of Chinese characters, to highlight some of the specificities of the oriental alphabets in terms of kinematics. We finally conclude the paper by conducting a short survey of some potential applications of this methodology to the problem of handwriting recognition.

2. ORIENTAL CHARACTERS: A SUMMARY

Oriental characters are the written symbols that represent spoken language in oriental countries and areas. They can be broadly classified into three main categories: Chinese, Japanese and Korean (Hangul) characters. There are also many countries where people use other alphabets of their own devising.

*Corresponding author. E-mail: rejean@scribens.polymtl.ca

Advances in Oriental Document Analysis and Recognition Techniques (1998) 31–44

2.1. Chinese Characters

Chinese characters are ideographical characters which have evolved from picture-like symbols over thousands of years. As a result, the Chinese alphabet is very large: There are more than 50,000 characters in total, of which about 3,000 to 5,000 characters are in daily use.[24] In many cases, a single Chinese character represents a word, but very often words are formed by combining different characters.

Chinese characters have a complex structure. Most Chinese characters consist of sub-patterns called radicals. In Chinese dictionaries, there are more than 200 different radicals, and a radical can itself be a character.

The complexity of Chinese characters varies dramatically: The simplest character has only 1 component,[a] while the most complicated has more than 30 components. On average, a Chinese character has 8 to 10 components. There are basically two styles of Chinese handwriting: block style and cursive style. Block style is usually taught at elementary schools and secondary schools. In block style, a character is written component by component, radical by radical, all within a character box (real or imaginary). By contrast, when a character is written in the cursive style, there is no constraint on the number of components and several block style components may be connected to form a single component.[25]

Another important feature of Chinese handwriting is that all handwritten Chinese characters are usually separated spatially, so there is no need for segmentation between characters. An exception is artistic writing, in which a whole line of characters can be written using just one component.

While Chinese characters in Taiwan and Hong Kong remain almost as they were 50 years ago, many Chinese characters have been simplified in the mainland of China since the 1950s. This further complicates the character alphabet.

Entering Chinese characters into a computer is a difficult problem due to the size of the alphabet and the complex structure of the characters. Recently, some keyboard input methods have been developed (such as Wang's keyboard coding method in mainland China), but all of them are cumbersome, even for professional users. In this respect, on-line Chinese handwriting recognition will provide an easy way of entering these characters into computers through an electronic pen-pad.

2.2. Japanese Characters

The Japanese alphabet is considered the most complicated alphabet in the world and contains the following character sets: (1) Hiragana, (2) Katakana, (3) Kanji, and (4) English.[24,26] Hiragana and Katakana (called Kana) are phonetic alphabets and each of those has 46 characters. Kanji characters are Chinese characters which were introduced into Japan in the old days. Consequently, Kanji characters and Chinese characters have essentially the same meaning and the same structure. There are about 2,000 Kanji characters in daily use in Japan, and a subset of 6,349 Kanji characters forms the Japanese Industry Standard JIS6226-1978. In addition to the

[a]We define a component here as a pentip trace from pen-down to pen-up[1,4,7] to avoid confusion with what we will define as a formal stroke in the subsequent sections.

above, the English alphabet is also used in Japan, which adds 26 upper-case letters and 26 lower-case letters to the alphabet.

The Japanese developed many kinds of pen-pads and a large number of on-line handwriting recognition systems since the 1960's,[24,26] as there was a definite need to find efficient ways of entering the Japanese characters into computers. Their systems are usually based on syntactic and structural approaches by means of some exhaustive strategy.

2.3. Korean Characters

A Korean (Hangul) character represents a syllable, which is composed of 2 or 3 simple letters in the CV or CVZ format, where C is an alphabet of 19 initial consonants, V is an alphabet of 21 vowels, and Z is an alphabet of 26 suffix consonants.[20] A Hangul character is usually written in a square box. In cursive writing, its components may be connected to one another. Apart from Hangul characters, the Korean alphabet also contains some others, such as Chinese characters.

Although the above character alphabets are different from each other, there are a few factors that are common to them all:

1. Most oriental characters are written in square boxes and are spatially separated from each other.
2. All these characters have a complex structure, but can be decomposed into subpatterns.
3. It is difficult to enter these characters into a computer through a keyboard.
4. When written in cursive style, components in a character are usually connected to one another, this superimposition phenomenon resulting in curvature peaks.

In view of the above, computer processing of oriental characters with applications in handwriting segmentation, signature verification and on-line recognition is most interesting to researchers. In this aspect, the generation of oriental characters may present new perspectives for automatic handwriting processing. In the following sections, we will apply the kinematic theory of human movement to the generation of Chinese characters as an example to illustrate the basic concepts and involved possible applications.

3. CHINESE CHARACTER GENERATION

Figure 1 illustrates the general model used in this paper. It is based on the kinematic theory of human movements.[10,12] According to this theory, a character is represented at a high level in terms of an allograph that is an ideal model described by a sequence of virtual targets connected by circular strokes. To generate a character, this map is converted into an action plan that results in a temporal sequence of synchronous commands (D_1, D_2) that are fed into an agonist and an antagonist neuromuscular system from a synergy whose output is the velocity of the pentip.[19] Some of the strokes are produced pen-up and do not leave any handwritten trace. These strokes are, in fact, 3D trajectories that can be analyzed with the same approach after proper generalization. Since we do not have access to precise XY data while the pentip is not in contact with the digitizer, we limit our study to 2D movements and we will refer to the term component to describe any complex trajectory followed during a pen-down trace.

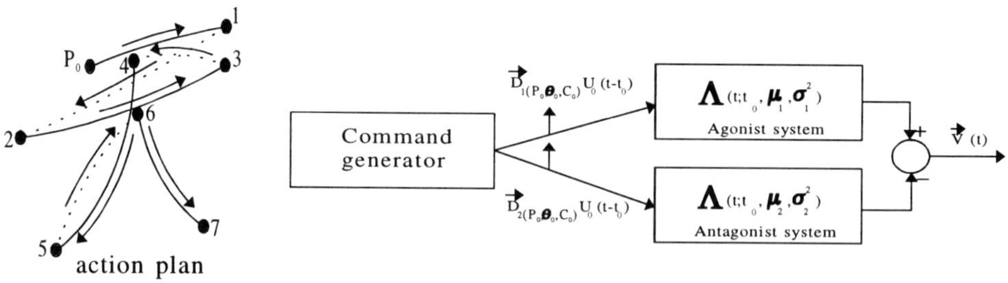

Fig. 1. Basic concepts underlined by the delta-lognormal model.

The representation used in Fig. 1 leads to a simple and robust definition of a formal stroke: a circular path of curvature C_0 and initial orientation θ_0 with respect to an arbitrary reference, executed with a velocity whose magnitude versus time obeys a delta-lognormal law[9,11]:

$$|\vec{v}(t)| = D_1 \Lambda(t; t_0, \mu_1, \sigma_1^2) - D_2 \Lambda(t; t_0, \mu_2, \sigma_2^2) \tag{1}$$

where

$$\Lambda(t; t_0, \mu_i, \sigma_i^2) = \frac{1}{\sigma_i \sqrt{2\pi}(t - t_0)} \exp - \left\{ \frac{[\ln(t - t_0) - \mu_i]^2}{2\sigma_i^2} \right\} \tag{2}$$

D_i = amplitude of the agonist ($i = 1$) and antagonist ($i = 2$) commands.
t_0 = time occurrence of the synchronous input commands.
μ_i = logtime delay of the agonist ($i = 1$) and antagonist ($i = 2$) systems.
σ_i = logresponse time of the agonist ($i = 1$) and antagonist ($i = 2$) systems.

The angular direction $\theta(t)$ of the velocity vector is described as a time function:

$$\theta(t) = \theta_0 + C_0 \int_{t_0}^{t} |\vec{v}(\tau)| d\tau \tag{3}$$

One of the very basic properties of such a formal stroke is that its length (D) as well as its duration (MT) can be predicted from the values of the two inputs commands[8,12]:

$$D = D_1 - D_2 \tag{4}$$

$$MT = K \left(\frac{D_1}{D_2} \right)^{\alpha} \tag{5}$$

where K and α are constants[b] depending on μ_i and σ_i.

[b] In a more general case, a quadratic law links $\ln(MT)$ with $\ln(D_1/D_2)$.

A human subject can thus voluntarily control the length and duration of each stroke using a strategy based on the control of D_1 and D_2 for each stroke.

Consequently, it is easy to understand that a human subject can anticipate what will happen once a pair of commands has been fed into his neuromuscular system. He can therefore start a new stroke at the proper time, before the previous stroke has been completed.

The generation of a complex trajectory pattern is thus the result of a vectorial addition of stroke velocity vectors.[10,16,17]

$$\vec{\nu}(t) = \sum_{i=1}^{n} \vec{\nu}_i(t - t_{0i}) . \tag{6}$$

Figures 2 and 3 summarize the key concepts of the model with a Chinese character generated in block style and in cursive style, respectively.

Each trajectory of the character was computed and generated from the shape and the kinematics of the allograph previously depicted in Fig. 1. Figures 2(a) and 3(a) show typical executions of this allograph using the block style and the cursive style, with their respective curvilinear (Figs. 2(b) and 3(b)) and angular (Figs. 2(c) and 3(c)) velocities.

As one can see, each pen-down stroke in the block style almost corresponds to a component and there is no superimposition effect observed in the velocity profiles. In view of the curvilinear velocity (Fig. 2(b)), where dotted lines correspond to pen-up strokes, one can distinguish components (or strokes in this particular case) by their transition from a high to a low or null amplitude. On the other hand, to write cursively, strokes have to be superimposed and components therefore become more complex. This can be easily observed from the curvilinear velocity in Fig. 3(b) where all the strokes of Fig. 2(b) have been merged into a single component. With respect to the angular velocity, component frontiers correspond, in general, to angular discontinuities where the amplitude of the signal varies dramatically. One can also see that there is a time correspondence between the valleys of the curvilinear velocity and the crisps of the angular velocity (comparing Figs. 2(b) with 2(c), and Figs. 3(b) with 3(c)), as predicted by the vectorial delta-lognormal model.[10,17]

Comparing Fig. 2 with Fig. 3, it is easy to understand why the cursive style is more rapid, and that this rapidity is obtained, at the expense of some loss of legibility, by time-superimposing the individual strokes. This results in a more fluent trajectory, without pen-up or discontinuity.

4. ANALYSIS-BY-SYNTHESIS

Analysis of oriental handwriting with the vectorial delta-lognormal model can be completed in a few steps. The data captured for our study comes from a Wacom SD-510C electronic digitizing tablet. The raw data $x(t)$ and $y(t)$ collected from the digitizer was sampled at 100 Hz. These signals were filtered with a Chebychev second-order low-pass filter with a cut-off frequency of about 12 Hz. The curvilinear

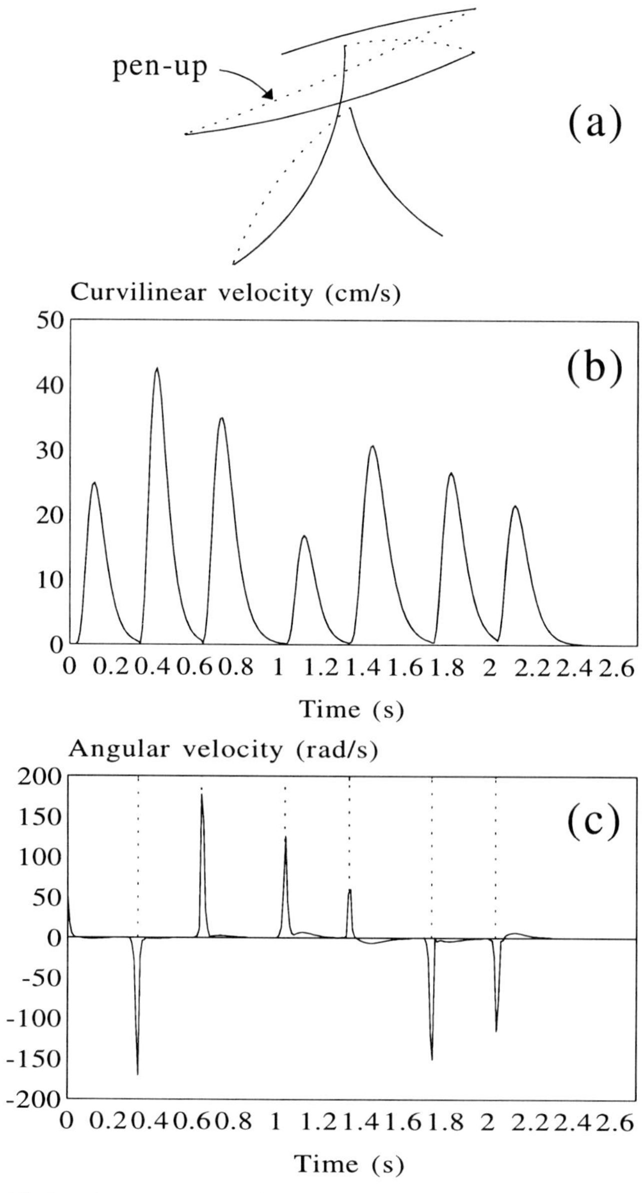

Fig. 2. Chinese block-style handwriting (a) typical execution (b) curvilinear velocity (c) angular velocity.

velocity $V(t)$ and the angular velocity $V_\theta(t)$ (see Eqs. (7) and (8)) are then computed using a second-order derivative filter with finite impulse response (FIR).[23] Figure 4 shows a handwritten Chinese character ("want") and its corresponding curvilinear and angular velocities.

$$|\vec{v}(t)| = V(t) = \sqrt{\left(\frac{dx(t)}{dt}\right)^2 + \left(\frac{dy(t)}{dt}\right)^2} \tag{7}$$

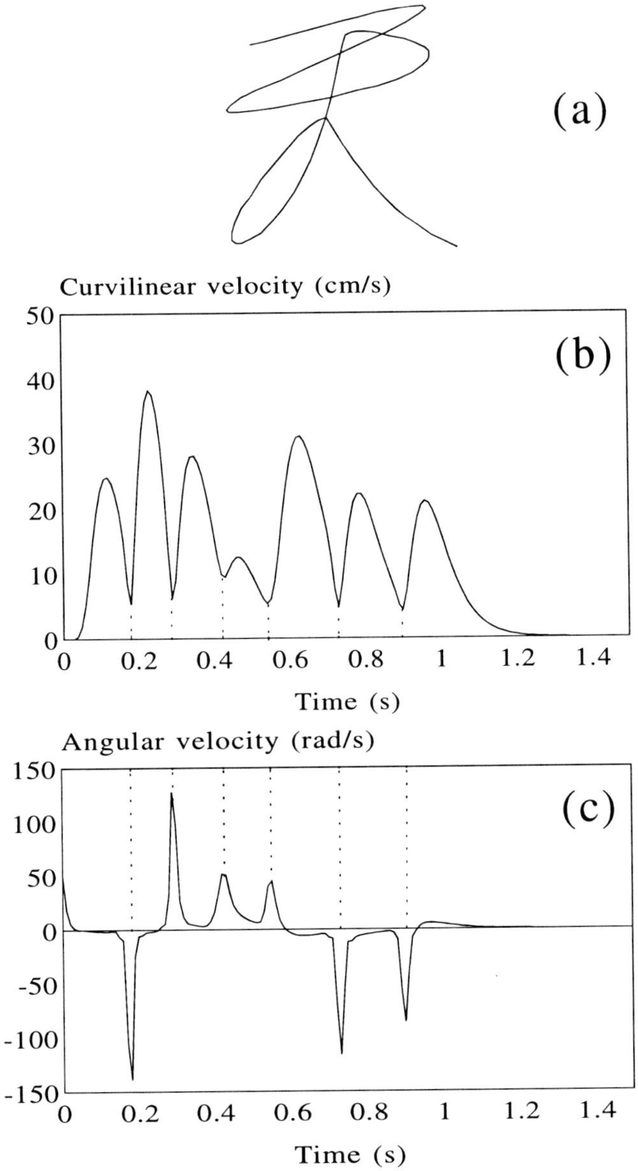

Fig. 3. Chinese cursive-style handwriting (a) typical execution (b) curvilinear velocity (c) angular velocity.

$$\frac{d\theta(t)}{dt} = V_\theta(t) = \frac{\frac{d^2y(t)}{dt^2} * \frac{dx(t)}{dt} - \frac{d^2x(t)}{dt^2} * \frac{dy(t)}{dt}}{V(t)^2} \tag{8}$$

Handwritten words (or characters) are then segmented into components. (For example, there are five components in Fig. 4(a).) Each component is made up of one or more strokes, and is the result of a vectorial superimposition of time-overlapped

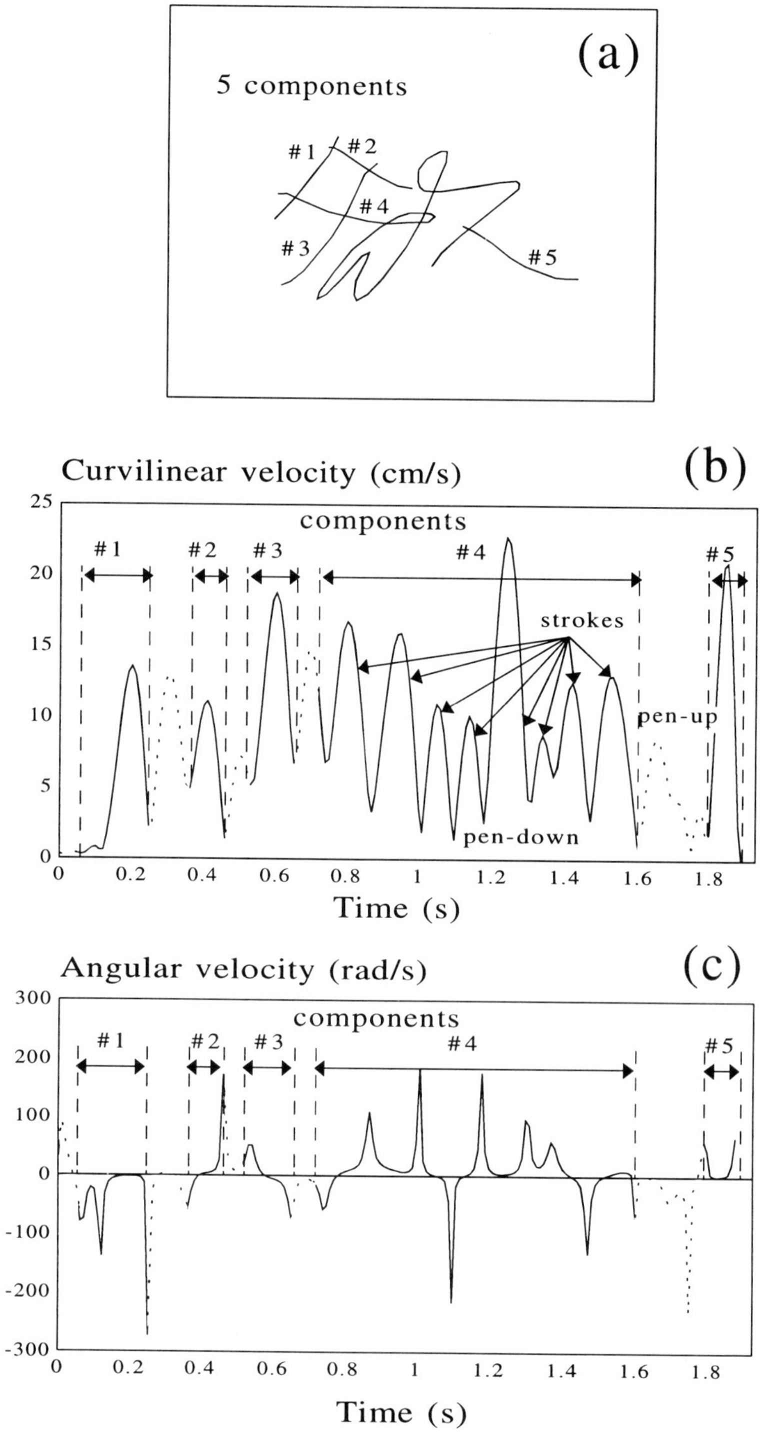

Fig. 4. Example of handwriting signals (a) original handwriting (Chinese word "want") (b) curvilinear velocity (c) angular velocity.

velocity profiles. The curvilinear velocity of each individual stroke obeys the delta-lognormal law. However, the difficulty of analyzing natural handwriting comes mainly from retrieving the strokes and is due to two phenomena: First, there exists a multitude of combinations of strokes that can be employed to generate a single complex movement, and second, in fluent handwriting, the majority of strokes are partially hidden in the measured signal, as a consequence of the time-overlapping process.

To extract the set of parameters that best fits the handwriting velocity signals, we need follow several steps according to the vectorial delta-lognormal model. First, we have to estimate the number of strokes for each component. An analysis of the extrema and inflexion points of the curvilinear velocity signal is applied to estimate the number of strokes and their approximate location. Second, we combine a heuristic method[2,17] and a graphical approach[17,27] to locally estimate the 9 parameters of each stroke. Third, once the initial local estimation has been done, a simultaneous global optimization of all parameters of each component (9 parameters per stroke) is carried out, taking the time-overlapping effect into account. The Leevenberg-Marquardt nonlinear regression technique is used for the optimization process.[2,5] Figure 5 shows an example of the Chinese word "want" as written by a human subject and as generated by the vectorial delta-lognormal model using the parameters extracted with our analysis-by-synthesis method.

The algorithm described above for the analysis-by-synthesis of a given handwritten trace can be summarized as follows[2,16]:

BEGIN
    Compute the module and the direction of the curvilinear velocity from the pentip coordinate $x(t), y(t)$.
    Make a first-level segmentation of the word into components, using the pen-paper contact information.
    FOR** Each component **DO
        Determine the number of hidden strokes.
        FOR** Each stroke **DO
            Compute an initial estimate of the 9 parameters.
        ***END** (for)*
        Extract the optimal group of parameters of the partially hidden strokes by optimizing the matching of the resulting curvilinear velocity vector (Eqs. (4) and (5)).
        Save the group of parameters that best fits each component.
    ***END** (for)*
END.

Although we have shown just a few typical examples in this paper, there is no reason to believe that the vectorial delta-lognormal model is not language and culture independent. After all, the model is based on neuromuscular attributes that belong to all human beings.

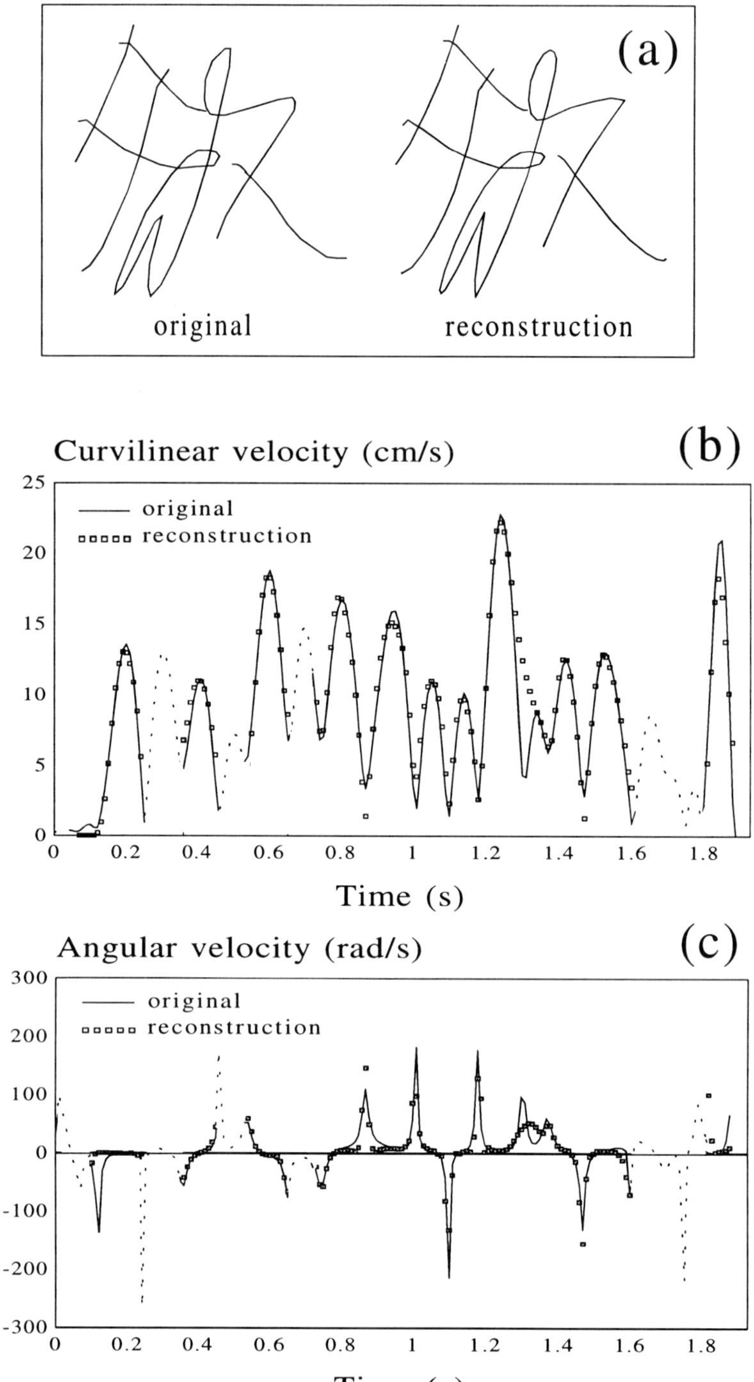

Fig. 5. Model-based reconstruction of the Chinese word "want". (a) Handwritten samples, original and reconstructed (b) curvilinear velocity (c) angular velocity (continuous lines: original data; block squares: reconstructed signals).

5. FORTHCOMING APPLICATIONS

We have shown that the flexibility and the reproduction capacity of the vectorial delta-lognormal model goes far beyond the analysis of simple strokes. The representation supported by the model of complex movements intrinsically proposes an original solution for the problem of segmenting cursive handwriting components into basic handwriting units (or strokes). Using this model, each individual stroke can be analyzed and studied on the basis of the set of parameters associated with it. This opens the way to two types of analysis: the study of writer-specific parameters and the study of message-specific parameters. Work on writer identification by analyzing the properties of their signatures is an example of the first type of application. High-level handwriting representation and recognition based on a small set of parameters constitutes an example of the second type of application. In both cases, models of parameter variability can be used to theoretically generate a very large number of variations of a single allograph.[3,14,17] This might be a possible solution for the case where large databases are used and characterized for algorithm validation as well as for neural network training. Immediate applications for high-rate data compression of handwriting signals are also possible using the model. Apart from neuropsychological and remedial applications,[13,15] these are some research avenues to explore with the vectorial delta-lognormal model in the context of handwriting analysis and recognition.

ACKNOWLEDGMENTS

This work was supported by grant OGP00915 from NSERC, a grant from project IC4/IRIS, National Center of Excellence, grant ER-1220 from FCAR and strategic grant STR0192785 from NSERC.

REFERENCES

1. D. Bullock, S. Grossberg and C. Mannes, "A neural network model for cursive script recognition", *Biol. Cybern.* **70** (1993) 15–28.
2. W. Guerfali, "Modéle delta-lognormal vectoriel pour l'analyse du mouvement et la génération de l'écriture manuscrite", Ph.D. Dissertation, École Polytechnique de Montréal, 1996.
3. W. Guerfali and R. Plamondon, "Effect of variability on letter generation with the vectorial delta-lognormal model", in Advances in Document Image Analysis, invited talk, *Proc. First Bresilian Symposium on Document Image Analysis*, eds. Curitiba, N. A. Murshed and F. Bortolozzi, Lecture Notes in Computer Science **1339**, Springer, 1997, pp. 74–83.
4. G. Lorette, "Méthode de traitement automatique d'images de points et de lignes en reconnaissance de formes", Thèse de doctorat d'états. Université Paris-Val-de-Marne, 1984.
5. D. W. Marquardt, "An algorithm for least-squares estimation of nonlinear parameters", *J. Soc. Industrial and Applied Mathematics* **11** (1963) 431–441.
6. P. Morasso, V. Sanguineti and T. Tsuji , "A model for the generation of virtual targets in trajectory formation", *Advances in Handwriting and Drawing: A Multidisciplinary Approach*, eds. C. Faure, P. Keuss, G. Lorette and A. Vinter, 1994, pp. 333–348.

7. R. Plamondon, "A model-based segmentation framework for computer processing of handwriting", *Proc. 11th Int. Conf. Pattern Recognition*, 1992, pp. 303–306.
8. R. Plamondon, "The Generation of Rapid Human Movements. Part II: Quadratic and Power Laws", Technical report EPM/RT-93/5, École Polytechnique de Montréal, 1993.
9. R. Plamondon, "The generation of Rapid Human Movements. Part I: A Delta-Lognormal Law", Technical report EPM/RT-93/4, École Polytechnique de Montréal, 1993.
10. R. Plamondon, "A delta-lognormal model for handwriting generation", *Proc. 7th Biennial Conf. Int. Graphonomics Society*, 1995, pp. 126–127.
11. R. Plamondon, "A kinematic theory of rapid human movements. Part I: Movement representation and generation", *Biol. Cybern.* **72** (1995) 297–307.
12. R. Plamondon, "A kinematic theory of rapid human movements. Part II: Movement time and control", *Biol. Cybern.* **72** (1995) 309–320.
13. R. Plamondon, "The Kinematic Theory: A New Window to Study and Analyze Simple and Complex Human Movements", *Behavioral and Brain Sciences*, vol. 20, 1997, pp. 45–75.
14. R. Plamondon, "A kinematic theory of rapid human movements. Part III: Kinetic outcomes", *Biol. Cybern.*, 1998, to appear.
15. R. Plamondon and A. Alimi, "Speed/accuracy tradeoffs in target directed movements", *Behavioral and Brain Sciences* **20** (1997) 1–31.
16. R. Plamondon and W. Guerfali, "Why handwriting segmentation can be so misleading", *Proc. 13th Int. Conf. Pattern Recognition*, 1996, pp. 396–400.
17. R. Plamondon and W. Guerfali, "The generation of handwriting with delta-lognormal synergies", *Biol. Cybern.*, 1998.
18. R. Plamondon and F. J. Maarse, "An evaluation of motor models of handwriting", *IEEE Trans. Syst. Man Cybern.* **19**, 5 (1989) 1060–1072.
19. R. Plamondon and C. M. Privitera, "A neural model for generating and learning a rapid movement sequence", *Biol. Cybern.* **74**, 2 (1995) 117–130.
20. B. K. Sin and J. H. Kim, "A statistical approach with HMMs for on-line cursive Hangul (Korean script) recognition", *Proc. ICDAR*, 1993, pp. 147–150.
21. Y. Singer and N. Tishby, "Dynamical encoding of cursive handwriting", *Biol. Cybern.* **71** (1994) 227–237.
22. O. Stettiner and D. Chazan, "A statistical parametric model for recognition and synthesis of handwriting", *Proc. 12th Int. Conf. Pattern Recognition*, vol. II, 1994, pp. 34–38.
23. S. St-Laurent, "Réalisation et comparaison de divers filtres numériques", Mémoire de projet de fin d'études, École Polytechnique de Montréal, 1995.
24. C. C. Tappert, C. Y. Suen and T. Wakahara, "The state of the art in on-line handwriting recognition", *IEEE Trans. Patt. Anal. Mach. Intell.* **12**, 8 (1990) 787–808.
25. Y. T. Tsay and W. H. Tsay, "Attributed string matching by split-and-merge for on-line Chinese character recognition", *IEEE Trans. Patt. Anal. Mach. Intell.* **15**, 2 (1993) 180–185.
26. T. Wakahara, H. Murase and K. Odaka, "On-line handwriting recognition", *Proc. IEEE* **80**, 2 (1992) 1181–1194.
27. M. E. Wise, "The geometry of log-normal and related distributions and an application to tracer-dilution curves", *Statistica Neerlandica* **20**, 1 (1966).

Réjean Plamondon received a B.Sc. degree in physics, M.Sc.A. and Ph.D. degrees in electrical engineering from Université Laval, Québec. P.Q., Canada in 1973, 1975 and 1978 respectively. In 1978, he joined the staff of the École Polytechnique, Université de Montréal, Montréal, P.Q., Canada, where he is currently a Full Professor and Head of the Department of Electrical and Computer Engineering.

An active member of several professional societies, a senior member of IEEE (85'), Dr. Plamondon is the President of the International Graphonomics Society, and Canadian representative on the board of Governors of IAPR (International Association for Pattern Recognition). He has coedited four books and also published a children book, a novel and and a collection of poems.

His research interests deal with the automatic processing of handwriting: neuromotor models of movement generation and image perception, script recognition, signature verification, signal analysis and processing, electronic pen-pad, man-computer interfaces via handwriting, forensic sciences, education and artificial intelligence. He is the founder and director of Laboratoire Scribens, a research group dedicated exclusively to the study of these topics.

Wacef Guerfali received a B.Eng, M.Sc.A and Ph.D. from Ecole Polytechnique de Montreal in electrical engineering in 1988, 1990 and 1995 respectively. He joined the staff of the Scribens Laboratory at Ecole Polytechnique in 1995 as a research associate.

His research interests are in handwriting modelling, generation and recognition.

Xiaolin Li received a B.Sc. degree in electrical engineering from Guangxi University, China, a M.Sc. degree in electrical engineering from East China Institute of Technology, and a Ph.D. degree in computer science from University of Birmingham, England in 1978, 1987, and 1994, respectively. In the 1980s he was an assistant lecturer (instructor) at Guangxi University, and then a lecturer (assistant professor) at Guilin Institute of Electronics. From 1995 to 1996 he worked at Hong Kong University of Science and Technology and then at Laval University. At present, he is a research associate in Laboratoire Scribens, Ecole Polytechnique de Montreal. His research interests are in pattern recognition and signal processing. He is a member of IEEE Computer Society.

A NEW SYNTHESIZING METHOD FOR HANDWRITING KOREAN SCRIPTS

DO-HOON LEE*

Department of Computer Engineering, Miryang National University
Miryang Kyungnam 627-130, Korea

HWAN-GUE CHO

Department of Computer Science, Pusan National University
Pusan 609-735, Korea
E-mail: {dhlee, hgcho}@pearl.cs.pusan.ac.kr

So far there have been models for generating handwriting scripts of western languages. Since the basic structure of oriental languages such as Chinese, Japanese and Korean, is quite different from that of alphabet-based western languages, western handwriting models cannot be applied directly to oriental languages except for a few models. In this paper, we propose a new generation model for generating Korean handwriting scripts. For this we choose 11 characteristic parameters which determine the shape of handwriting scripts. These parameters were selected experimentally by investigating ample Korean scripts. Furthermore we propose the Beta-velocity model to simulate the cursive stroke movement by manipulating curvilinear and cursive connection for consecutive strokes within a letter or a word. In order to generate these oriental cursive strokes, we adopted Beta distribution curve basis which enables one to make easy asymmetric velocity profile. By combining all these features, we synthesize various handwriting Korean scripts by controlling 11 characteristic parameters. In the final section of this paper, we give experimental results. These easy-to-synthesize Korean scripts can be used in evaluating off-line character recognition system and a word processor by supporting handwriting-style fonts.

Keywords: Handwriting model, Korean letter, motor theory.

1. INTRODUCTION

Understanding human handwriting is one of the most interesting topics in current neurophysics, neurology, computer science and cognitives science. The study of handwriting is now being used to diagnose the state of patients by psychologists and neurologists.[2] Several research groups, working from different perspectives, have proposed handwriting models aimed either at generating movement or at explaining certain psychophysical phenomena.

Currently there are two major trends in studying human writing. One trend is to study how to recognize given handwriting scripts, another is how to synthesize scripts similar to the script written by humans. For the first subject, there have been numerous methodologies developed in both on-line and off-line modes. The main difficulty in these works lies in that we do not fully understand the general theory of human writing, since each one has one's own writing habit and style. Currently only narrow domain character sets, e.g. numerals and English text, are recognized successfully.[14,16]

*Corresponding author.

Advances in Oriental Document Analysis and Recognition Techniques (1998) 45–61

So far, several handwriting models have been proposed, mainly aiming at digital or analog regeneration of existing samples of handwriting. There are several different approaches to the description of handwriting in general.[12] One is the so-called ballistic model based on human motor system,[2] and the other is the mathematical model based on the algebraic curve that is presented with parameters of time and directions.[3] Kondo proposed a model using the vector-matrix of successive strokes.[5] Another computational model for the production of handwriting was proposed by Schomaker *et al.*[13] It started with allograph codes as inputs and gave a target pen-tip trajectory as outputs.

In the view of character synthesizing, a signature generation model has been proposed by Plamondon.[8] In his paper, the signature generation process was structured in terms of curvilinear and angular velocity generators that control the magnitude and orientation of the pen-tip velocity vector, each of these generators being characterized by an appropriate impulse response. Recently Plamondon proposed a general theory of rapid human writing movements, the Delta LogNormal model based on a kinematic theory. This model proved to be of interest, since it has demonstrated its consistence with major psychophysical phenomena while at the same time enabling a very realistic representation and generation of the dynamics and shape of handwritten characters.[4,9,10]

Until now there have been only a few concrete models to synthesize various oriental language scripts including Chinese, Japanese and Korean, since they have different structures and writing styles. Recently one synthesizing method for handwritten Korean scripts was proposed using the Hidden Markov Model (HMM) which is a typical methodology to recognize the handwriting scripts.[15] Some synthesized Chinese scripts were shown by Plamondon using the Delta LogNormal model.[11] Though the model based on HMM is the first theoretical model for the generation of Korean, the final output seems to be poor and quite different from any human handwriting.

1.1. Motivation

The purpose of character synthesizing is threefold. First, it uncovers important characteristics hidden in human writing. For example, the sign verification is one application in characterizing distinguishing features of human scripts.[8] However, in practice, human experts have been responsible for the identification of the writer of a script because there are many characteristic features which cannot be easily measured quantitatively by a computer.

Second, synthesizing human script can be used to develop natural and graceful fonts to be used in word processor or document processing system. We can see that the development of computerized fonts has been focused on the aesthetic aspects of script.

Third, we give here a new purpose of this work. Our Korean script synthesizing system enables us to build a large set of testing characters.[1] Suppose that we are asked to evaluate two character recognition systems. According to the current testing procedure, we should prepare some benchmark character set obtained by tester. Applying these data sets, we can estimate the recognition rate of the system. However, there is no standard on how to measure the "roughness" of a handwriting letter in character recognition. It is a matter of course that rough data (such as a bad style script or fast handwriting) gives a low recognition rate, while easy data (such as typewriter script) gives a higher recognition rate.

Let us assume that a recognition system S_M can recognize perfectly (e.g. 95%) for the well and clearly written letter (Data A), but S_M does not work for the fast-written scripts (Data B) less than 50% success rate. Assume as well that another recognition system, S_B, works with a 75% recognition rate for both Data A and B. In this case it is very difficult to decide which one S_A, S_B is a "better" system, since there is no metric function to estimate how input scripts are easy to recognize. Therefore it is very important how to prepare testing data set for evaluating a recognition system fairly. If we synthesize scripts with a given degree of "difficulty" at will, we can use these scripts to evaluate any recognition system more accurately and fairly.

Additionally there are various writing styles in oriental language script since most oriental characters are composed of many disconnected line segments, while all Roman letters are connected in a cursive form. Thus the previous generating procedure designed only for western letters cannot be directly used for oriental languages, especially for Korean.

In this paper we propose a new synthesizing method for Korean handwriting script with given parameters, which determines the shape of scripts by controlling the degree of noise added, the speed of writing, connection style of cursive segment, line and unit syllable spacing, etc. Therefore we can generate most kinds of letters from a clearly readable one to a very poor script (hard to read) by adjusting parameters.

2. CHARACTERISTICS OF KOREAN HANDWRITINGS

The Korean letter is a phonetic letter like Roman. The shape of the letters originated from the old Chinese ideograph letter set. However, the structure of Korean characters is rather simpler than that of Chinese characters.

Each Korean syllable consists of two or three basic components that are consonants and vowels in the square form. The unit of Korean letter is called / *Um-jeul*/ (in Korean) that is one syllable. It is divided into three parts, the *first-*, *second-*, and *third-syllable*. The first and third-syllable should be consonants and the second-syllable should be a vowel in all Korean letters. Note that the third-syllable may be null in some cases. Figure 1 illustrates the general structure of Korean letters, where consonants or vowels should be put into each small box. Each Korean letter is classified into one of six different structural types depending on the existence of the third-syllable and the position of consonant and vowel in a square.

Table 1. Structure of Korean letters.

Type	(a)	(b)	(c)	(d)	(e)	(f)
Character	구	곤	가	감	귀	권
Pronunciation	/ku/	/kon/	/ka/	/ka:m/	/kui:/	/kwon/
First-syllable	'ㄱ'	'ㄱ'	'ㄱ'	'ㄱ'	'ㄱ'	'ㄱ'
Second-syllable	'ㅜ'	'ㅗ'	'ㅏ'	'ㅏ'	'ㅟ'	'ㅝ'
Third-syllable		'ㄴ'		'ㅁ'		'ㄴ'

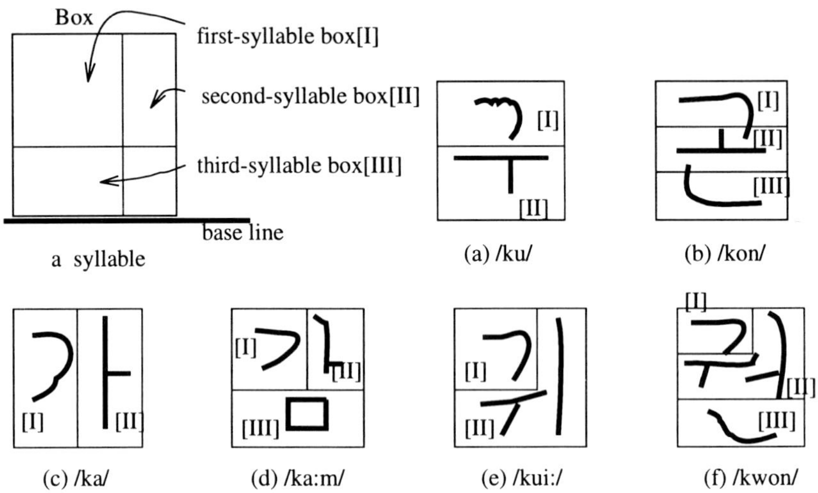

Fig. 1. Six different structures of Korean letters.

As far as we know, there had been few studies on the characteristic measure for handwriting Korean scripts. The final shapes of handwritten Korean letters are determined by the various characteristic parameters. Since all Korean characters consist of many disconnected strokes, a human writer must lift up his arm or move it in various directions.

We investigated more than 2000 handwriting samples obtained from Korean adults. By examining these samples, we selected the following 11 characteristic parameters. Table 2 explains these parameters and the corresponding character scripts.

2.1. Control Parameters for Korean Handwriting

(1) The connection unit in a letter. Almost all Korean handwritings have inter-syllable connection depending on the writing velocity or the writer's habit. In faster writing, each stroke tends to be connected to the next stroke in a letter or to the first-syllable of the following letter in a word. These connecting phenomena are classified into five types. In Type (a), the basic type, we draw each stroke as a straight line. Therefore Type (a) is the same as the skeleton font of our synthesizing system. In Type (b) all connected strokes within a syllable are connected in a curve preserving C^1 continuity. In Type (c), all segments, not necessarily connected, in each syllable are connected in a cursive form. In Type (d), the first- and the second-syllable are connected. Type (e) shows that all segments in a letter are connected along one connected curve.

(2) Speed. In order to write fast, the total length of the trajectory of a pen is shorter than that of letters written at normal speed. Each basic consonant or vowel in a letter tends to be connected in one curve so as to decrease the length of pen movement, which increases the writing speed. This parameter is important, since it determines the curvature of consecutive strokes and it distinguishes mainly the writer of a script. In our model, the speed is controlled by the degree of overlapping the velocity vectors of two consecutive strokes in a syllable. The wider two velocity vectors overlap, the faster a pen moves from a starting point to ending point.

(3) Shearing. A shearing is a transformation shortening or extending one side of the bounding box of each letter. It is natural that handwritings should be declined in the right side rather than stand upright to make an arm move easily.

(4) Scaling. In writing someone likes to subscribe the first-syllable in the larger shape comparing with the second- or third-syllable. By examining lots of sample handwriting scripts, we have noticed that the scaling factor for each syllable is nearly constant in a human writing. Table 2(4)-(b) and (c) show the x-scale up and y-scale up letter, respectively.

(5) Script Noise. Every line stroke in handwriting is perturbed due to the slight tremble of a human arm/elbow/hand. Also the straightness of the line stroke depends on the quality of the pen-tip and the quality of the paper. We call all these factors the script noise. We have noticed that children's writing samples or slow handwriting samples include more noise than those from fast or adult's handwriting. Table 2(5)-(b) is a handwriting with noise. We made the script noise by perturbing the control points of the skeleton fonts randomly within a small circle.

(6) Dragging. Within the Korean handwriting letter, the leading stroke effects the position of the following stroke, since the preceding stroke tends to be linked to the following one. Table 2(6)-(b) shows that the first "ㄱ" syllable moves left slightly and the third "ㄱ" moves right. Dragging is one of the distinct characteristics in the Korean handwriting. This effect cannot be found in any other oriental languages, such as Japanese or Chinese. Without considering this dragging effect, no Korean handwriting could be natural and real.

(7) Segment moving. The stroke for the first-syllable pulls the third-syllable of the preceding character due to the fast pen movement. Thus the overall position of the last syllable in a preceding letter moves right in proportion to the writing velocity. In Table 2(7), "ㄴ" of letter (a) moves to the right side, and has appeared in (b).

Table 2. Characteristic parameters.

Parameter Name	Script Example
(1) Syllable connection type (P_1={1,2,3,4,5})	 (a) (b) (c) (d) (e)
(2) Speed ($0.0 \leq P_2 \leq 1.0$)	 (a) (b)
(3) Shearing ($-1.0 \leq (P_3^x, P_3^y) \leq 1.0$)	 (a) (b) (c)
(4) Scaling ($0.0 \leq (P_4^x, P_4^y) \leq 2.0$)	 (a) (b) (c)
(5) Script noise ($0.0 \leq P_5 \leq 10.0$)	 (a) (b)
(6) Dragging (P_6={0,1})	 (a) (b)
(7) Segment moving (P_7={0,1})	 (a) (b)
(8) Size of each syllable ($1.0 \leq P_8 \leq 2.0$)	 (a) (b)
(9) Box-Transformation ($1.0 \leq P_9 \leq 2.0$)	 (a) (b)
(10) Vectorized connection (P_{10}={0,1})	 (a) (b)
(11) Line alignment and spacing ($0.0 \leq P_{11} \leq 1.0$)	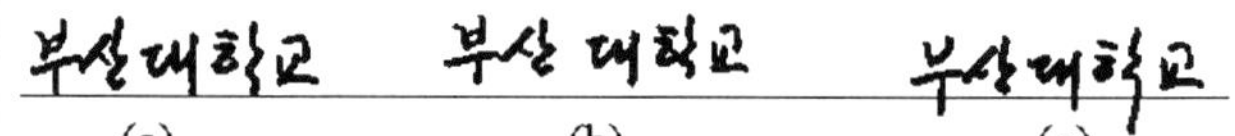 (a) (b) (c)

(8) Size of each syllable. Within a letter, each size of syllable is not fixed. The size of the script character and the relative size of the three components in a letter depend on one's writing style. Usually Korean women prefer to make the first-syllable bigger, compared with those of a man's writing. In Table 2(8), (b) shows a bigger first-syllable than that of character (a).

(9) Box-Transformation. In elementary school, students learn they ought to write each letter in the square box fully. But in handwriting mode this rule is not maintained, so each letter is placed in the box of the arbitrary shape such as Table 2(9). The shape of this bounding box is distinct to each writer's style.

(10) Vectorized connection. In fast handwriting, we have found one different connecting effect, namely vectorized connection, which seems to be similar to the dragging effect. We can observe that some segments in a certain letter are not connected even in a fast movement, since the pen should be lifted to change its direction to the opposite side. This phenomenon depends on the writer's habit, not on the velocity of the pen-tip, which is one of the unique features of Korean letters on comparing with western languages. When the adjacent strokes are similar or of the same direction, these strokes tend to be connected in a cursive form. If this parameter is set, then two consecutive strokes with the nearly same moving direction are connected in a cursive form. (See Table 2(10).)

(11) Line alignment and Spacing. This last parameter controls the inter-character distance and the distance between the character and the baseline, and the regularity of line spacing alignment.

3. BETA-VELOCITY MODEL FOR HANDWRITTEN KOREAN SCRIPT

The Delta-LogNormal model was already proposed by adopting a curvilinear stroke generator composed of two parallel neuromuscular networks which control, respectively, the agonist velocity $V_{\sigma 1}(t)$ and the antagonist velocity $V_{\sigma 2}(t)$ associated with a specific movement. The resultant velocity $V_\sigma(t)$ is obtained by subtracting effects as follows:

$$V_\sigma(t) = V_{\sigma 1}(t) - V_{\sigma 2}(t)$$

and

$$V_{\sigma i}(t) = \frac{D_i}{\sqrt{2\pi}\sigma_i(t-t_0)} e^{\frac{1}{2\sigma_i^2}(\log(t-t_0)-\mu_i)^2},$$

where D_1 and D_2 reflect the respective amplitude of the agonist and antagonist input commands; and μ_1, σ_1 and μ_2, σ_2 reflect the time delay and impulse response times of a LogNormal curve on a logarithmic scale. t_0 represents the starting time of the input. These four parameters, $\mu_1, \mu_2, \sigma_1, \sigma_2$ control the timing of the neuromuscular network of the human arm.[4,9,10]

Plamondon showed the usefulness of this model to generate the handwritten alphabets as well as the Chinese characters.[11] For the Delta-LogNormal model the writing velocity, angular velocity and other parameters are extracted from the handwritten letters that come from a tablet, and these are regenerated using this model. Thus this model is effective to regenerate the given input character.

However our purpose is to generate a large handwritten data set and various fonts that can be used on word-processors. So we propose a new method whose idea is based on the Delta LogNormal model, which uses the skeleton font and some parameters. The proposed model is simple to generate the handwritten scripts although it cannot describe delicately the pen movement in the aspects of kinematics and psychologics.

In addition to velocity control capability, our model considers the antagonist and agonist effects in pen-lifting, since the final shape of the Korean letters are greatly subjected to the pen-lifting strategy. Therefore, our Beta-Velocity model describes the overall pen movements with two main aspects, pen velocity function and pen lifting vector function shown in Fig. 2.

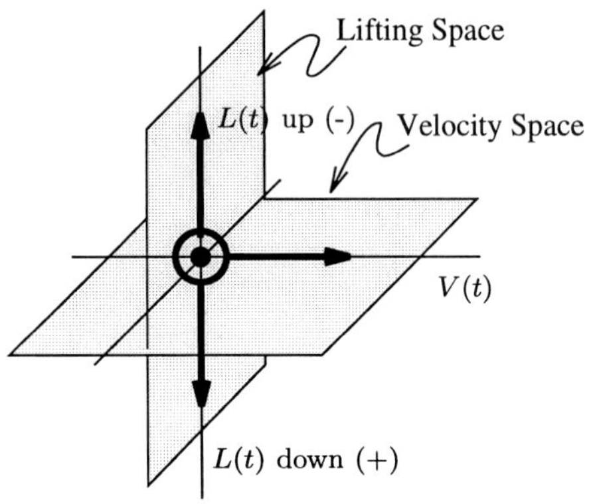

Fig. 2. Working space of pen movement.

Figure 3 shows how to generate the character segment into two-dimensional (2-D) space from given set strokes. Even though the results of pen tip movement is generated into 2-D space, the trajectory of pen tip is depicted into three-dimensional (3-D) space.

A Korean character C (e.g. "란") is composed of a set of successive strokes $\{s_i\}$, so we denote $C = \{s_i\}$. The velocity vector V^{s_i} for a given stroke s_i is denoted in the following.

$$V^{s_i}_{\alpha,\beta}(t) = d \cdot \frac{|s_i|}{D} \cdot V_{\alpha,\beta}(t), \tag{1}$$

where $|s_i|$ is the length of a stroke s_i, and $D{=}\sum_i |s_i|$, d is a constant. The function $V_{\alpha,\beta}(t)$ is defined as

$$V_{\alpha,\beta}(t) = \frac{\Gamma(\alpha+\beta)}{\Gamma(\alpha)\Gamma(\beta)} t^{\alpha-1}(1-t)^{\beta-1}, \qquad 0 \le t \le 1, \Gamma(n) = \int_0^\infty t^{n-1}e^{-t}dt\,. \tag{2}$$

If n is a positive integer, then it is easy to see that $\Gamma(n) = (n-1)!$ α and β are parameters controlling the shape of the velocity profile for a stroke segment. Figure 4 shows various shapes of beta curve with different α and β values.

The velocity vector of two consecutive strokes overlaps due to rapid pen movement. For example, Fig. 5(a) shows that the stroke velocities of s_1 and s_2 overlap, and describes the velocity at time t_c, which is the vector sum of s_1 and s_2.

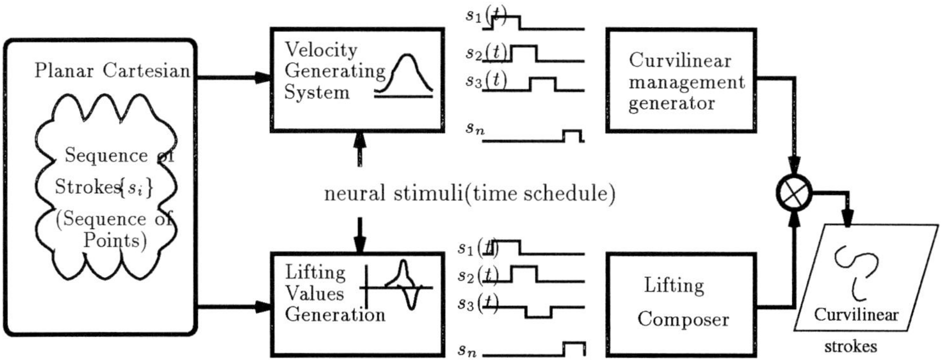

Fig. 3. The scheme of our generation model.

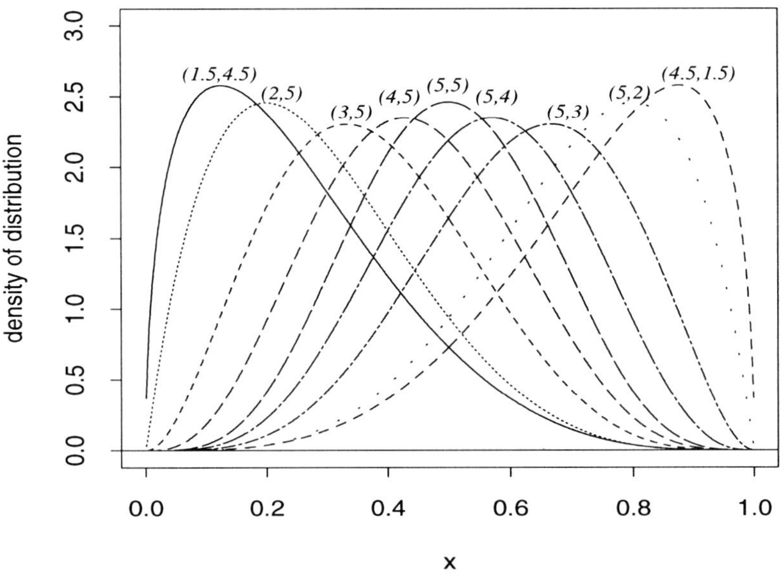

Fig. 4. Beta distribution curve with several (α, β) values.

Let a vector function $\mathbf{V}^{s_i}_{\alpha,\beta}(t)$ denote the velocity of the cursive stroke connecting s_i and s_{i+1}. So we define the final vector $\mathbf{V}^{C}_{\alpha,\beta}(t)$ for the stroke set of $C = \{s_i\}$.

$$\mathbf{V}^{C}_{\alpha,\beta}(t) = \sum_{s_i \in C} \mathbf{V}^{s_i}_{\alpha,\beta}(t)\,. \tag{3}$$

In Fig. 5(b)–(d), we can see the difference in cursive strokes with three different α and β values. The shape of the velocity profile determines the shape of the character.

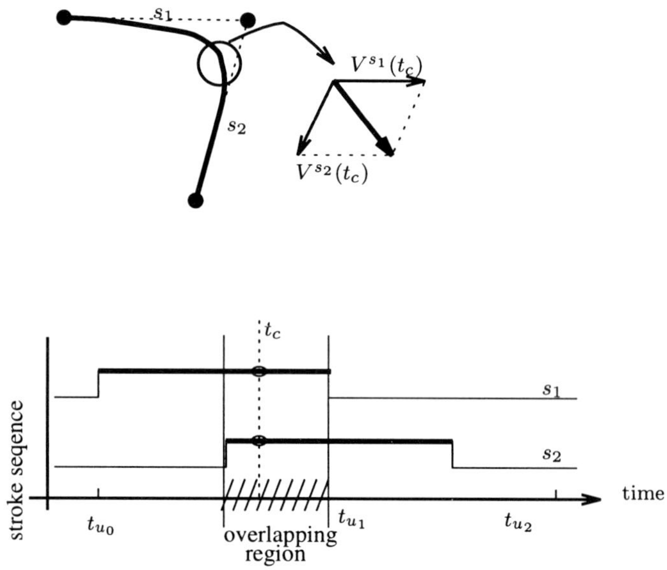

(a) Vector sum of two strokes. The thick line denotes the time interval for activated stroke.

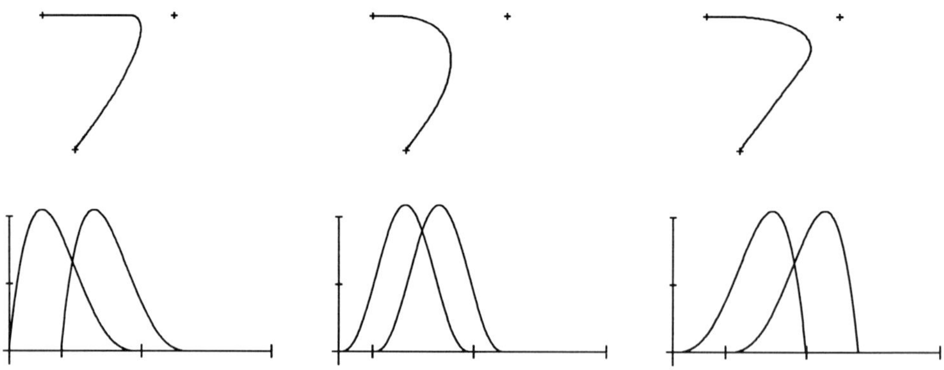

(b) α=2, β=4, overlap = 0.6 (c) α=4, β=4, overlap = 0.75 (d) α=4, β=2, overlap = 0.6

Fig. 5. The segments with different shape parameters.

In the previous section, we explained 11 characteristic parameters for Korean letters handwriting. Since each Korean character consists of several (about 7) disconnected segments, we need to lift the pen tip at least 7 times at a normal writing speed. In fast writing, the number of pen-lifts decreases. Thus, in order to synthesize a realistic handwriting, we have to consider that this pen lifting factor depends on the speed of movement. This movement is also based on a kinematic theory when we write a letter and depends on the shape of the letter. The lifting vector $L^{s_i}(t)$ for a given stroke s_i that determines the starting time of pen-up and the duration time for pen-down is formulated in the following.

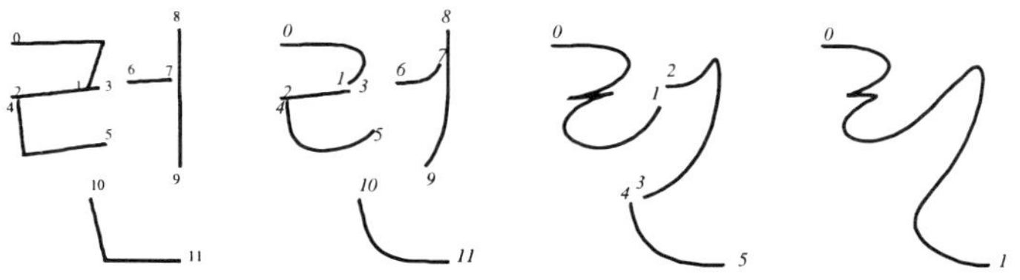

(a) (b) (c) (d)

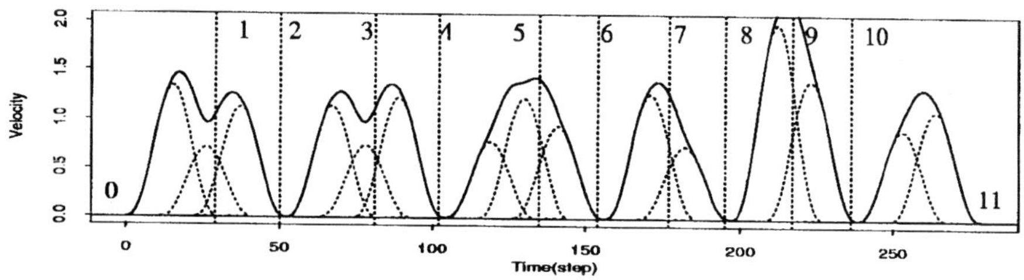

(e) Velocity Profile of (b)

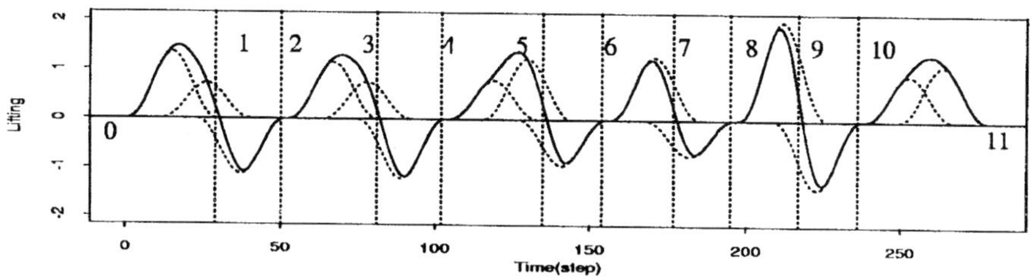

(f) Lifting Profile of (b)

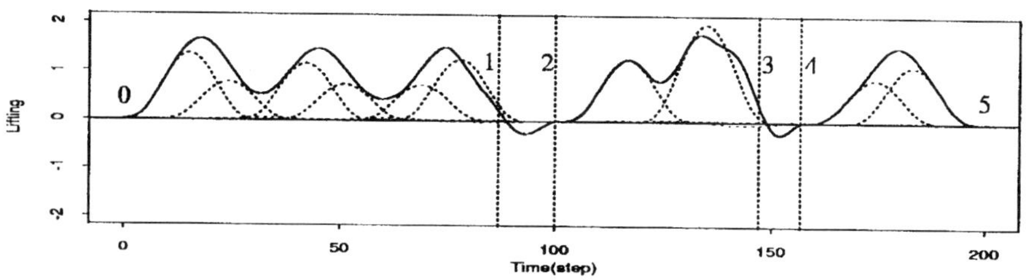

(g) Lifting Profile of (c)

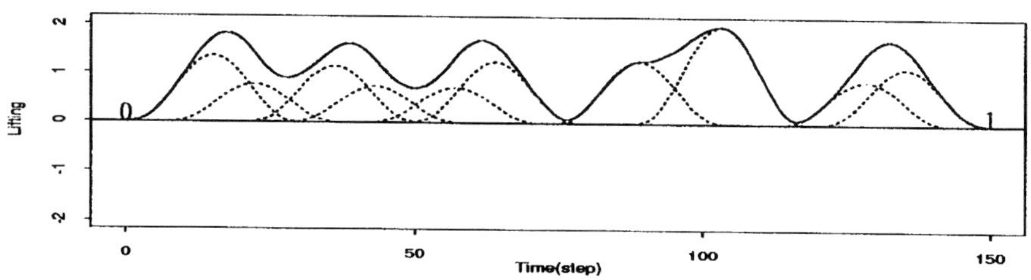

(h) Lifting Profile of (d)

Fig. 6. Cursive stroke generation with velocity and lifting. Each dotted curve denotes the velocity of each stroke, and solid curve is the sum of dotted curves.

$$L^{s_i}_{\alpha,\beta}(t) = l \cdot \frac{|s_i|}{D} \cdot \frac{\Gamma(\alpha+\beta)}{\Gamma(\alpha)\Gamma(\beta)} t^{\alpha-1}(1-t)^{\beta-1}, \qquad 0 \le l \le 1, \tag{4}$$

where l is a constant that controls pen-up/down, and $-1 \le l \le 1$. The relation between the velocity space and the lifting function space can be explained in 3D space which is shown in Fig. 2. Figure 6(a) shows the skeleton font. The different cursive scripts are shown in Fig. 6(b)–(d) and the corresponding lifting velocity profiles are shown in Fig. 6(f)–(h), respectively.

4. IMPLEMENTATION OF HANDWRITING GENERATION SYSTEM

In the previous sections, we described various characteristic parameters and Beta-Velocity model. This section is devoted to generate the handwriting script in practice. Our script generation model $\mathfrak{M}$ can be described formally as follows:

$$O_B = \mathfrak{M}(T, F, V, L, \{P_i\}),$$

where O_B is the final script in PostScript file format, T denotes text input file, F is a skeleton font, V is a Beta-velocity function with α, β fixed and L denotes the pen lifting control curve. $\{P_i\}$ is a set of 11 parameters that are described in Sec. 2.

An overview of our generation system architecture is illustrated in Fig. 3. Input text file contains Korean letter code. As is shown in Fig. 3, we prepared skeleton fonts which consist of the sequence of strokes. Then each character's stroke is converted to the different shape by manipulating the parameters for synthesizing.

4.1. The Basic Font of Generation Model

In writing a specific symbol or character, the shapes that were learned and memorized are recalled, but in actual they are drawn differently according to the individual style and writing speed. It is necessary that the virtual target characters defining the temporal order of the principal targets of the movement, in the case of handwriting, correspond to a simplified representation of the allograph model of a letter. The engram consists of a sequence of points defined in the external space, font file, which will have to be connected by means of translation by a part of the body. The handwriting model should draw the engram of the movement and subsequently generate the corresponding sequence of commands for the neuromuscular system.

Since the Beta-Velocity model requires the virtual target in order to simulate given characters, we prepare a basic skeleton font for the virtual letter target. Since there are no stereo-typed script letters in most oriental languages such as Korean, the skeleton font can be designed as simple as possible.

We prepared two sets of skeleton fonts, since one font set is not enough to simulate lots of different human scripts. The more skeleton font sets prepared, the more natural script could be obtained. Our system has only two font sets for the first-syllable, two font sets for the second-syllable, and one set for the third-syllable.

4.2. Fast Handwriting Generation

The primary purpose of this paper is to show how fast handwriting scripts are controlled and synthesized. In the preliminary version of this work,[1,6] the synthesized handwriting script results were mainly determined by manipulating the control points of the skeleton fonts using simple algebraic B-spline curves.[7] However the B-spline curve did not enable us to control pen speed, since we had to move the physical location of control points to simulate a fast cursive script. Though the synthesized results were similar to real handwriting, it required lots of trial and error parameter adjusting steps, which was an *ad hoc* and troublesome procedure. It should be noted that the previous B-spline cursive model had nothing to do with the neuromuscular network and human motor system.

Our Beta-Velocity model enables to depict the pen tip into 3D space, time, velocity, and lifting vector. Rapid pen tip movement is simulated by overlapping (=adding) of adjacent stroke's velocity, pen-lift vectors of two consecutive strokes. The larger the overlap region is, the faster the pen moves. If two consecutive velocity curves coincide, then the pen moves from the starting control point to the last control point directly without approaching the intermediate control points.

Table 3 shows the control domain (velocity, pen-lift, font shape) of 11 parameters and the main factor of each parameter; for example, we can control the writing speed by (a), (b), (f) and (j) parameters.

5. EXPERIMENTS AND CONCLUSION

We have conducted several experiments to generate a natural handwriting script. The first experiment shows the effect of adjusting α, β variables in Fig. 5. The second experiment shows the difference of handwriting due to the manipulation of the pen lifting velocity in Fig. 6. In our third experiment, we combined five major parameters to give a realistic handwriting. Four handwritings of a Korean word "대한민국" (Republic of Korea) in Table 4 show four different handwriting scripts with 5 varying parameters.

In the fourth experiment, we synthesized one paragraph (the text of the Korea National Anthem). Figures 7(a) shows a synthesized handwriting without parameter control, which is the same as skeleton fonts. Figures 7(b) and (c) show the handwriting script with parameter control of Table 5. In Fig. 7(d), all characters were generated with the least pen lifting.

Synthesizing Korean handwriting requires another methodology compared with simulating western handwriting letters, since the Korean handwriting is composed of many strokes rather than a single curve in western languages. In this paper, in order to obtain the characteristic parameters, we investigated numerous Korean handwriting scripts. Investigating these results, we extracted 11 parameters which control most Korean handwriting. Additionally we proposed a new simulation model, Beta-Velocity in order to consider writing speed, and pen lifting. The

Table 3. Effects of parameters.

Characteristic	Transformation factor
(a) Syllable connect type	V/L^*
(b) Speed	$V^*/L/T$
(c) Shearing	T
(d) Scaling	T
(e) Script noise	T
(f) Dragging	$V/L^*/T$
(g) Segment moving	T
(h) Size of each syllable	T
(i) Box-Transformation	T
(j) Vectorized connection	$V/L^*/T$
(k) Line alignment and spacing	T

V: This parameter controls the velocity of pen movement.
L: This parameter controls the velocity of pen lifting.
T: This parameter translates the control points of a stroke.
$*$: main factor.

Table 4. Resulting scripts with given parameters.

Example	connection type	speed	shearing $(x,\ y)$	α	β
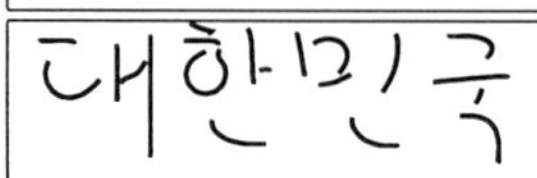	2	0.7	(0.0, 0.0)	4	4
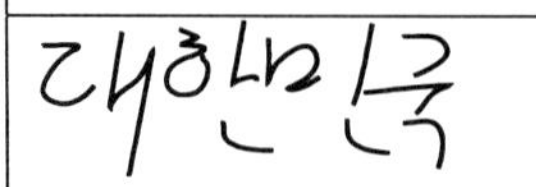	3	0.75	(0.2, 0.0)	3	5
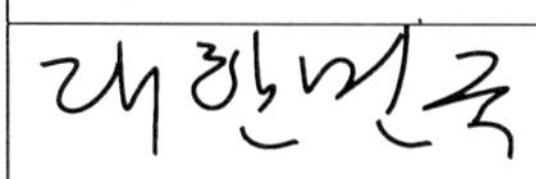	3	0.75	(0.0, 0.2)	5	3
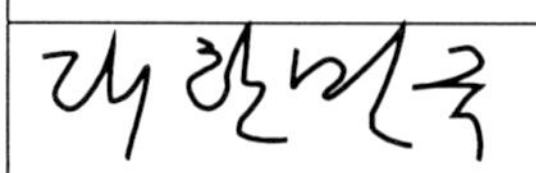	5	0.78	(0.2, 0.0)	2	5
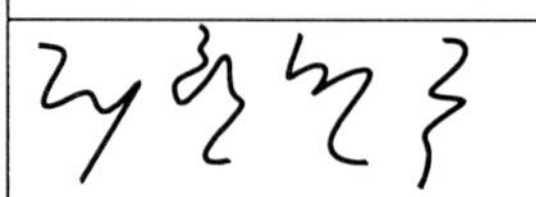	4	0.8	(0.5, 0.0)	5	5

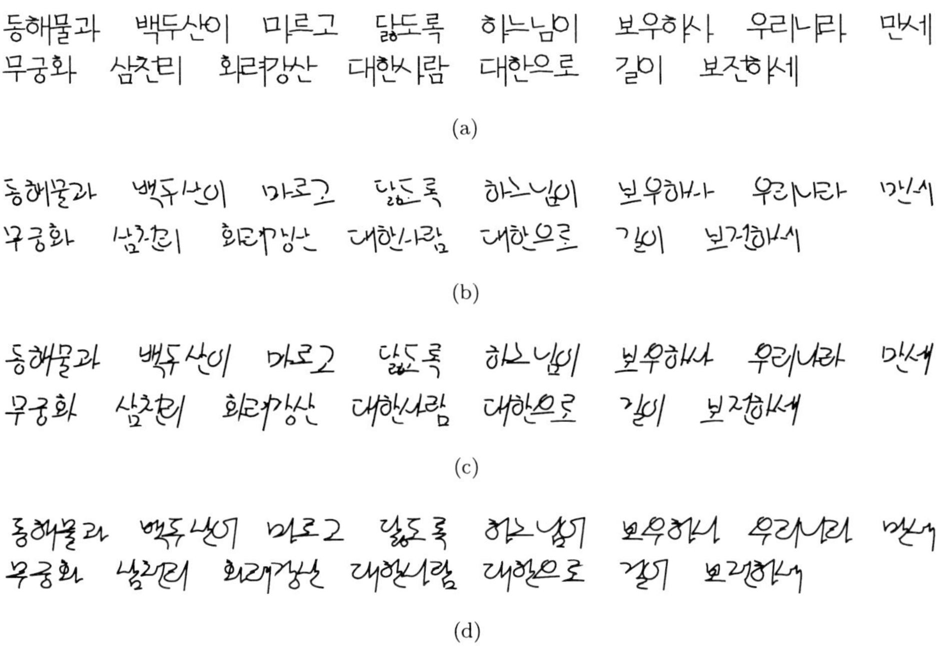

Fig. 7. Four different paragraphs with synthesized scripts.

Table 5. Corresponding parameters used in Fig. 7.

Results	P_1	P_2	P_3	P_4	P_5	P_6	P_7	P_8	P_9	P_{10}	P_{11}
(a)	1	0.3	(0.0,0.0)	(1.0,1.0)	0	0	0	1.0	1.0	0	1.3
(b)	2	0.77	(-0.1,0.15)	(0.9,0.9)	0	0	1	1.3	1.0	0	1.2
(c)	2	0.75	(0.2,0.0)	(1.0,1.2)	10	1	1	1.2	1.0	0	1.4
(d)	5	0.7	(0.1,0.0)	(1.2,1.0)	10	1	1	1.1	1.0	1	1.2

velocity of pen movement was implemented by introducing a beta distribution curve and its overlapping of consecutive strokes.

Experimental results show that the finally synthesized scripts are almost natural. We can generate various types of handwriting by controlling 11 characteristic parameters. Thus, our system enables each user to make his or her own unique script font, namely *customized font script*, that can be used in practice.

The main features of this paper are summarized as follows:

- Parameterizing Korean scripts.
- Synthesizing natural Korean letters considering various aspects of handwriting.
- Generating a large number of handwriting letters to be used as benchmark data set for evaluating automatic character recognition system.[1]
- Establishing one general model for Korean script.
- Enabling each user to build his or her own script font for a word processor.

In the future we will find more parameters to control handwriting minutely. We also have plans to announce a handwriting design system to be used commercially.

REFERENCES

1. H. G. Cho, *A Study on the Standard Data Generation for Performance Test of the Handwritten Hangul Recognition*, Dept. Computer Science, Pusan Nation. Univ., Dec. 1993 (in Korean).
2. E. H. Dooijes, *Analysis of Handwriting Movements*, Ph.D Thesis, Univ. Amsterdam, The Netherlands, 1984.
3. E. H. Dooijes, "The helliscript technique for the digital synthesis of quasi-calligraphic script", *Computer Recognition and Human Production of Handwriting*, World Scientific, 1989, pp. 119–130.
4. W. Guerfali and R. Plamondon, "The delta lognormal theory for the generation and modeling of cursive characters", *Int. Conf. Document Analysis and Recognition*, Aug. 1995, pp. 495–498.
5. S. Kondo, "A model of handwriting process and stroke-structure of character-figures", *Computer Recognition and Human Production of Handwriting*, World Scientific, 1989, pp. 103–118.
6. D. H. Lee and H. G. Cho, "A synthesizing method for handwritten Korean scripts", *Proc. 17th Int. Conf. Computer Processing of Oriental Languages*, April 1997, pp. 180–185.
7. K. J. Maccallum and J. -M. Zhang,"Curve-smoothing techniques using B-splines", *The Comput. J.* **29**, 6 (1986).
8. R. Plamondon, "A model-based dynamic signature verification system", *Fundamentals in Handwriting Recognition*, Springer-Verlag, 1994, pp. 417–434.
9. R. Plamondon "A kinematic theory of rapid human movements, Part I. Movement representation and generation", *Biol. Cybern.* **72** (1995) 295–307.
10. R. Plamondon "A kinematic theory of rapid human movements, Part II. Movement time and control", *Biol. Cybern.* **72** (1995) 309–320.
11. R. Plamondon, "The generation of oriental characters: new perspectives for automatic handwriting processing", *Proc. 17th Int. Conf. Computer Processing of Oriental Languages*, April 1997, pp. 113–120.
12. R. Plamondon and F. J. Maarse,"An evaluation of motor models of handwriting", *IEEE Trans. Syst. Man Cybern.* **19**, 5 (1989).
13. L. R. B. Schomaker, A. J. W. M. Thomassen and H.-L. Teulings, "A computational model of cursive handwriting", *Computer Recognition and Human Production of Handwriting*, World Scientific, 1989, pp. 153–177.
14. A. W. Senior, "Off-line handwriting recognition: A review and experiments", *CUED/F-INFENG/TR105*, Cambridge University Engineering Department, Dec. 1992.
15. B. K. Shin and J. H. Kim, "Hangul handwriting generation using HMMs", *Proc. 7th Conf. Inform. Processing of Hangul and Korean*, Oct. 1995, pp. 152–163 (in Korean).
16. C. C. Tappert, "Online handwriting recognition with hidden Markov models", *in Proc. 5th Handwriting Conf. Int. Graphonomics Society*, Oct. 1991, pp. 204–206.

Do-Hoon Lee received the BS degree in computer science and statistics from Pusan National University, Pusan, Korea, in 1986. He also received the MS and Ph.D degrees in computer science at Pusan National University in 1992 and 1998, respectively. Since 1995, he has been with Department of Computer Engineering, Miryang National University.

His research interests include computer graphics and its application, design of algorithm, data compression, and handwriting model.

Hwan-Gue Cho received the BS degree from Seoul National University in computer science and statistics, Seoul, Korea, in 1984. He also received the MS and Ph.D. degree in computer science at KAIST (Korea Advanced Institute of Science and Technology), Deajon, Korea, in 1986 and 1990, respectively. Since 1990, he has been with Department of Computer Science, Pusan National University. In 1994, he was a visiting scholar at Max-Planck-Institute for Informatics in Saarbruecken. He is also with Research Institute of Computer, Information and Communication.

His research includes computer graphics and its application, computational geometry and graph algorithms. He is currently working on the human animation system.

DIFFERENTIATING BETWEEN ORIENTAL AND EUROPEAN SCRIPTS BY STATISTICAL FEATURES

LOUISA LAM*,†, JIE DING and CHING Y. SUEN

Centre for Pattern Recognition and Machine Intelligence
Concordia University, 1455 de Maisonneuve Blvd. West
Montréal, Québec H3G 1M8, Canada

†*Department of Mathematics, Hong Kong Institute of Education*
10 Lo Ping Road, Tai Po, Hong Kong

Two types of techniques are usually adopted in language differentiation: token matching and statistical analysis. In this paper we present a method which uses a combined analysis of several discriminating statistical features, for the differentiation between European and oriental language scripts. When applied to more than 23 languages, it has proved to be effective in differentiating between documents printed in these different scripts.

Keywords: Script classification, language differentiation, oriental languages, Asian scripts, Chinese characters, Roman scripts.

1. INTRODUCTION

Language identification is a key step in the automatic processing of document images in an international environment. Early determination of the language used in a document has implications in the selection of the proper character recognition algorithm which will also greatly facilitate further processing, such as indexing and translation. Language identification is normally done manually. One can often deduce the language written in a document from its country of origin. If not, language interpreters can be employed to examine the document to determine its language. An automatic language identification approach is needed in environments where the high volume and variety of languages encountered make manual identification impractical. This approach is especially useful as an initial component of systems for processing multilingual documents, for an automatic selection of the appropriate classifier to be used in the further processing of the document.

Research work in language differentiation has been based on two main approaches: one utilizes statistical information (for example Ref. 8), while the other depends on searching for some specific tokens in different languages, such as Ref. 3. Usually the first method is used for gross classification while the second can be used to identify the specific language of a document. In this paper we perform gross classification according to the first approach.

*Corresponding author.

Advances in Oriental Document Analysis and Recognition Techniques (1998) 63–79

In Ref. 8, Spitz proposed a system which can process seven languages: English, French, German, Russian, Japanese, Chinese and Korean. In this system, the differentiation between Asian and Roman scripts is based on the different distributions of vertical locations of upward concavities in the two classes of languages. This difference in distribution arises from a basic difference in structure between these two classes of scripts. Usually, Roman scripts are composed of mostly lower-case characters, and therefore these concavities tend to be concentrated along the baseline and the x-line. On the other hand, Asian scripts are composed of radicals that can be located at any height within the text line, resulting in a more random distribution of upward concavities in these scripts (refer to lines (1) and (3) of Fig. 1).

(1)

(2)

(3)

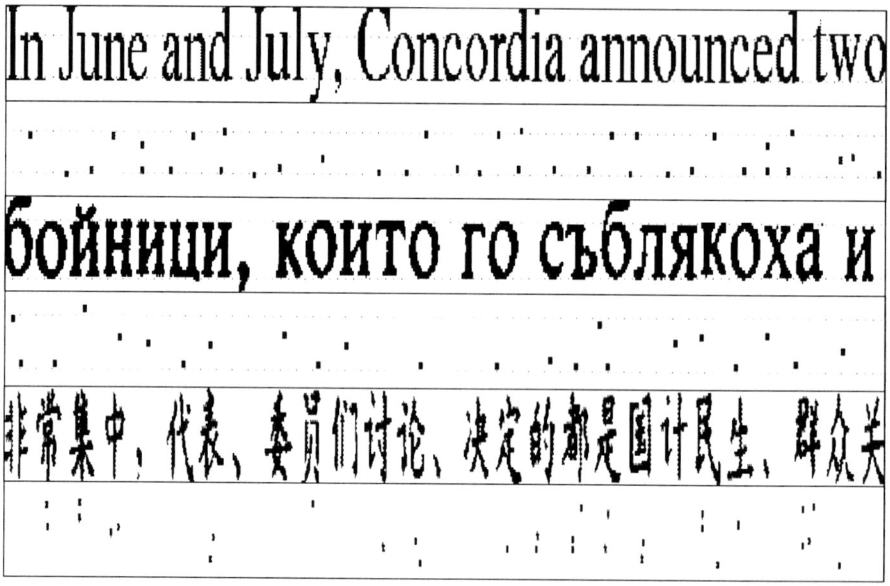

Fig. 1. Upward concavity distributions of several text-lines.

Spitz's system works well within the stated seven languages; however, this reliance on the vertical positions of upward concavities will not work for some other European languages. For example, text-line (2) of Fig. 1 shows a Bulgarian text-line of Cyrillic script, in which the upward concavities cluster near the baseline and some positions between the baseline and the x-line. This distribution is quite different from that of the English text-line shown in (1) of Fig. 1, where upward concavities only cluster near the x-line and the baseline.

In order to handle more languages, in this paper we present a new method for separating two classes of scripts: European (comprising Roman and Cyrillic scripts), and oriental (including Chinese, Japanese and Korean languages). We approach this by performing a combined analysis of statistical features, such as horizontal projection profiles and height distributions of connected components. This method has been applied to test over 20 kinds of European language documents and 3 kinds of oriental language documents. The experimental results are promising. We will discuss the method and present the experimental results in the following sections.

2. METHOD AND IMPLEMENTATION

2.1. Preprocessing

Document images are obtained through scanning and binarization. The preprocessing steps include:

- Noise removal: Since the scanned images are usually not clean, we use the median filter to remove noise.
- Segmentation: We must obtain correctly separated lines before analyzing their characteristics. The Run-Length Smoothing Algorithm (RLSA)[10] has been chosen to segment document images. Horizontal and vertical smoothing are applied separately and two smoothed bitmaps are obtained, then an "AND" operation is used to combine these two bitmaps. Due to the existence of some small gaps in the combined bitmap, an extra horizontal smoothing is performed to remove them. The choice of the parameters is rather uncritical. The values of horizontal and vertical smoothing thresholds should be set to a number of pixels covering the length of long words, whereas the threshold for removing small gaps should be set to cover a few character widths. Shown in Fig. 2 is an example illustrating the segmentation result of applying RLSA.

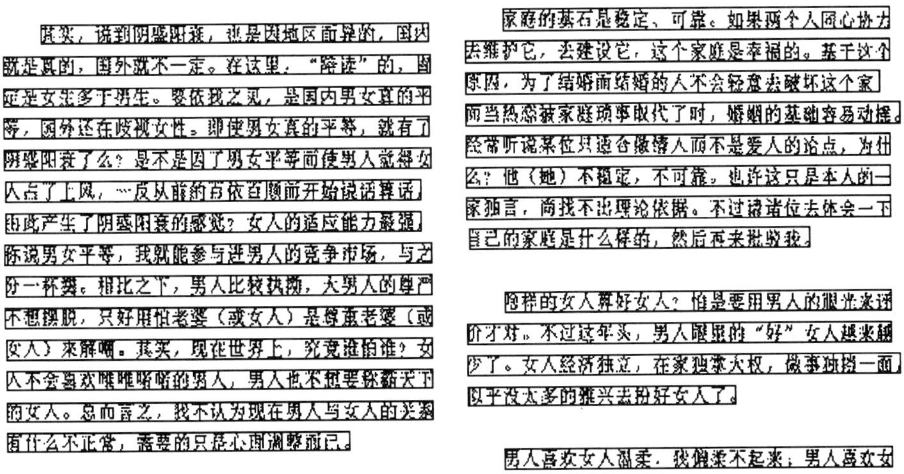

Fig. 2. Segmentation result after applying RLSA.

- Deskewing: a text-line is deskewed along its center of mass. Suppose a text-line has height h and width w, and it contains N black pixels. Then its center of mass $(\overline{x}, \overline{y})$ and the (p, q) order central moments $\mu_{p,q}$ are determined as follows:

$$\overline{x} = \frac{1}{N} \sum_{i=0}^{h-1} \sum_{j=0}^{w-1} x_i \text{ iff } (x_i, y_j) \text{ is black} \tag{1}$$

$$\overline{y} = \frac{1}{N} \sum_{i=0}^{h-1} \sum_{j=0}^{w-1} y_j \text{ iff } (x_i, y_j) \text{ is black} \tag{2}$$

$$\mu_{p,q} = \sum_{i=0}^{h-1} \sum_{j=0}^{w-1} (x - \overline{x})^p (y - \overline{y})^q \tag{3}$$

The orientation of a skewed text-line is defined as the angle of axis of the least moment of inertia,[4] calculated by formula (4). By using this orientation angle θ, a skewed text-line is aligned by the transformations of formula (5), where (x, y) are the coordinates before deskewing, and (α, β) are the coordinates after deskewing.

$$\theta = \frac{1}{2} \tan^{-1} \left(\frac{2\mu_{1,1}}{\mu_{2,0} - \mu_{0,2}} \right) \tag{4}$$

$$\begin{aligned} \alpha &= x \cos\theta \ + y \sin\theta \\ \beta &= -x \sin\theta + y \cos\theta \end{aligned} \tag{5}$$

- Line concatenating: As with any statistical measure, reliability is a function of the sample size. We try to accumulate data from those text-lines containing enough information. However, sometimes all the text-lines in a document may be very short. If this is the case, we need to concatenate several lines into a long one. This is done along their baselines. Inacurracies can occur if we simply concatenate lines along the bottom of bounding boxes. For example, when one line with descenders is to be concatenated with a line having no descenders, the concatenation based on the bottom of bounding boxes will not produce a straight line of text. Shown in (2) of Fig. 3 is the concatenation of the two lines (shown in line (1)) along the bottom of their bounding boxes, while line (3) is the concatenation along their baselines. The difference between the results is clear.

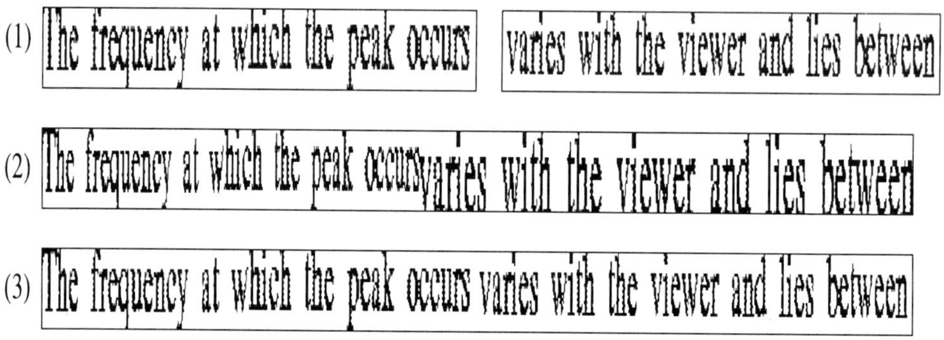

Fig. 3. (1) Two text-lines (2) Concatenation along the bottom of bounding box and (3) Concatenation along the baseline.

- Size normalization: All text-lines are normalized to a given height. We use 64 pixels as the normalized height for all text-lines as we want to express the height of the connected components as accurately as possible and to facilitate further distribution analysis. In order to retain the shapes of the original images, the width of each normalized image is calculated by $nor\_width = w * 64/h$, where h and w represent the height and width of the original image, respectively.

2.2. Separating Oriental from European Scripts

One basic difference between oriental and European languages is that most of the characters in oriental languages are composed of radicals (from 1 to more than 10),[9] which can be located at different heights of the text-line, and these characters are more complex. This is in contrast to the European languages, where each character has at most three connected components and a text-line can be divided into three zones: descenders, lower-case letters and ascenders.

Based on the above difference, several features have been extracted to separate oriental scripts from European ones.

2.2.1. Position of Concavities

The position of concavity points has been used to separate oriental scripts from European ones within several languages in previous works.[6,8] According to Ref. 8, when an image is scanned from its top to the bottom, if two runs of black pixels appear on a single scan line and there is a run on the line below which spans the distance between these two runs, then an upward concavity is formed on the line.

In Ref. 6, the distribution of concavity locations is used as one of the features in distinguishing between these two script groups. This is based on the observation that for Roman languages, the concavity points tend to cluster near the x-line and baseline, which is not the case for oriental scripts. Based on this idea, the numbers of concavities located at different heights are determined for each text-line, after which the locations are normalized by the text-line height. Then the normalized distribution is considered, and the sum n_c of the numbers of concavities located in the two ranges 0.2 to 0.5 and 0.6 to 0.8 are determined. The position 0.2 means 20% below the top of the text-line, and therefore 0.2–0.5 represents the x-line range while 0.6–0.8 represents the baseline range. It is assumed that the regions outside these ranges are occupied by ascenders and descenders of European scripts.

The decision based on this feature is made according to the following criterion. If n_c is greater than 0.8 of the total number of concavities, then the text is classified as European. If n_c is between 0.6 and 0.8 of the total, then it is oriental. No decision is made otherwise.

We applied this method to perform the differentiation in our data sets. In a document, we randomly choose two relatively long text-lines and the decision result is based on the majority decision obtained from the results of these two lines. We only process these longer lines because statistical results are more reliable when based on more information and data. Table 1 shows the results obtained from this method.

Table 1. The results of language classification by concavity location.

Language	# Samples	Recognition rate (%)	Error rate (%)	Reject rate(%)
European	86	55.82	5.81	38.37
Chinese	183	78.14	0.00	21.86
Japanese	89	48.31	5.62	46.07
Korean	166	36.75	0.61	62.65

The results of Table 1 show that the error rate is low, but the rejection rate is high. This agrees with the general result[5] that using an even number for majority vote gives a more reliable result, while it also produces a higher rejection rate when compared to the voting results obtained from using an odd number.

But there are two particular problems with the above decision criteria:

- Those two ranges cannot handle lines containing only capital letters and/or lines without descenders. For each of these two cases, the baseline will move to the range greater than 0.8 of text-line height.
- The above decision criteria cannot separate Cyrillic scripts from oriental ones as it does not consider the concavities lying between those two ranges, which is where concavities tend to accumulate for Cyrillic scripts.

These problems are illustrated in Fig. 4, which shows two text-lines, one Swedish, the other Russian, and their concavity location histograms. The Swedish line does not contain any descenders, and therefore more than 30% of concavity points cluster near its baseline, which is located beyond 0.8 of its line height. In the Russian concavity histogram, 30% of the concavities accumulate in the range of 0.5–0.6. These two lines are misclassified as oriental.

Fig. 4. (1) A Swedish text-line (2) A Russian text-line and (3) Concavity histograms.

Due to the above limitations, the position of upward concavities is used as only one of the four features in the differentiation of European languages from oriental ones within seven languages in Ref. 6. In order to handle a greater variety of languages, we propose a method in the following sections.

2.2.2. Horizontal Projection Profiles

It is well known that one of the most distinctive and inherent characteristics of European languages is the existence of ascenders and descenders as shown in Fig. 5.

This characteristic has often been used in the recognition of words in these languages (for example, Ref. 2). On the other hand, in oriental ideographical languages, each symbol is bounded by a square box and its height is limited within this box. But to represent this feature precisely and to make full use of it are non-trivial problems.

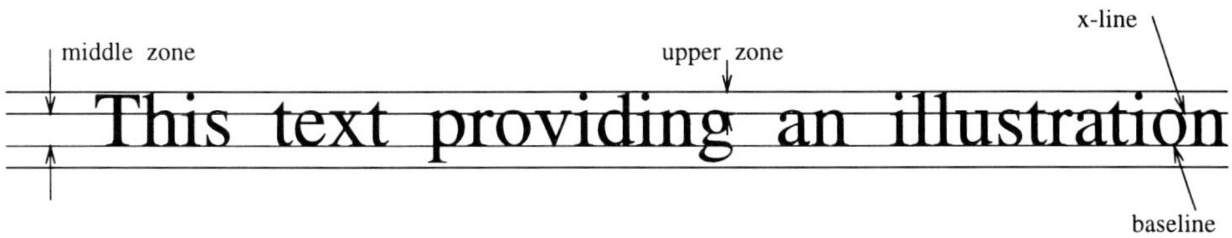

Fig. 5. Reference lines separating three zones.

Based on the study of horizontal projection profiles partially illustrated in Fig. 6, some differences between European and oriental languages are reflected in the following:

1. The location of local maxima at the lower and/or upper ends of the text-line, and
2. Ratio of the area of white region bounded by the two most significant peaks to the area of projection profile.

The first phenomenon is due to the presence of ascenders, descenders, small over-hanging dots (as in "i", "j", etc.) and accent signs (as in "é", "ô", etc.) in European language scripts, which lead to the small local maxima at the two ends of their horizontal projection profiles. For example, in the text line of Bulgarian script shown in the first line of Fig. 6, we can find a small peak at the upper end of the horizontal projection profile. Similarly, we can find small peaks at both ends in the profiles of French and English text-lines from Fig. 6.

The second difference exists because in European languages, long black runs generally occur near the x-line and the baseline, resulting in two significant maxima at these positions. For the other positions along the text-line, the horizontal projections have much lower values. In oriental scripts, the horizontal projections would not contain two such prominent maxima. It is known that oriental characters are denser than European characters and they have more *strokes*, especially more

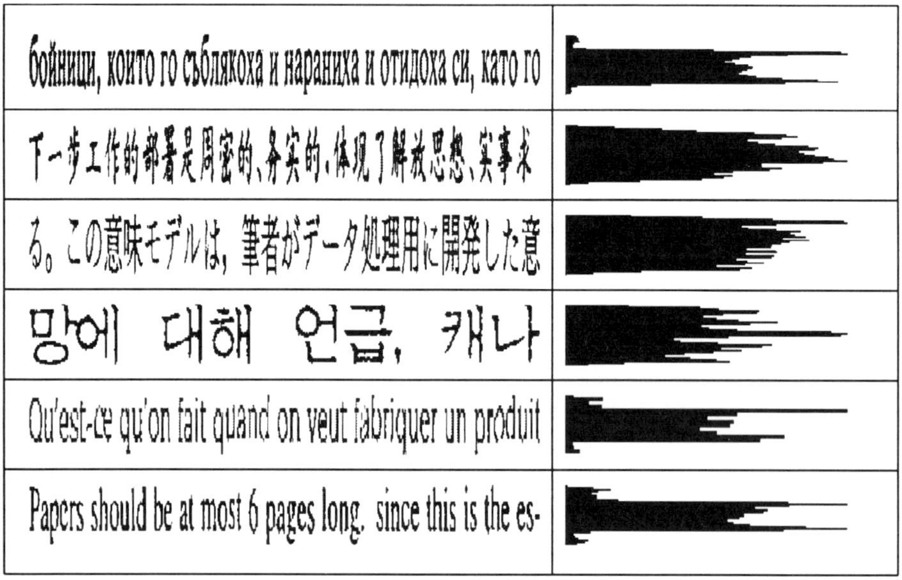

Fig. 6. Several horizontal projection profiles.

horizontal ones. For these reasons, there are more long black runs in an oriental horizontal projection profile than in a European one and they are also more evenly distributed from the top to the bottom of the text-line, which makes the ratio of the white area to the black area smaller.

Consequently, if we consider the white space in the trapezoidal region bounded by the two maximum values (refer to Fig. 7), then the ratio of the white area to the black area is larger in European than in oriental languages.

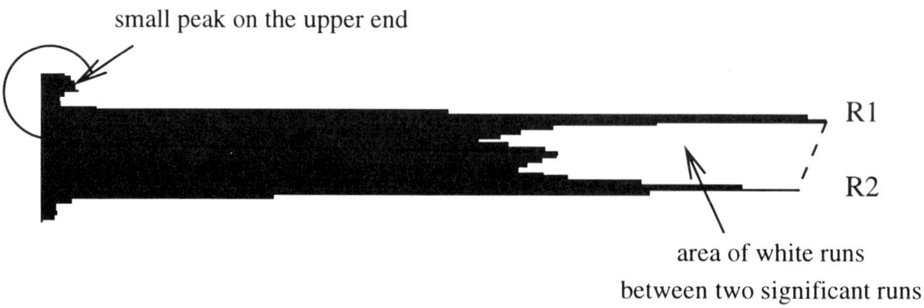

Fig. 7. A horizontal projection profile of a Bulgarian script line.

To calculate the black/white area ratio, a simple method is employed:

1. Find the two maximum runs R_1 and R_2 on the horizontal projection profile.
2. Determine the white area enclosed by R_1, R_2, and the line connecting R_1 and R_2. This is illustrated in Fig. 7.
3. Determine the area of all black runs.
4. Calculate the white/black area ratio.

2.2.3. Height Distributions of Connected Components

As some Cyrillic scripts contain only capital letters, method 1 described in Sec. 2.2.1 for locating the small peak cannot be used to separate such languages from oriental ones. Consequently other features have to be used to differentiate between these languages.

It is known that oriental languages are more complex than European ones. This kind of complexity can be represented by the number of connected components in each character cell. For the 52 lower-case and upper-case letters of the English alphabet, we know that there should be only one connected component in each letter except "i" and "j". Therefore in European scripts, most letters contain only one connected component and none of them should have more than three connected components, whereas many Chinese and Kanji characters have three or more connected components.[1,9] This difference is reflected in the height distributions of the connected components.

For European scripts, the heights of the characters are mainly attributed to three factors:

1. Small accent signs.
2. Lower-case letters with neither ascenders nor descenders.
3. Upper-case letters and lower-case letters with ascenders or descenders.

Figure 8 shows a European text-line and the generated connected components represented by bounding boxes.

Fig. 8. A European text-line and its connected components representation.

For oriental scripts, more than half of the characters consist of two or three connected components and these components can have many different heights, as illustrated by a Chinese text-line and its connected components representation in Fig. 9.

A comparison of Fig. 8 and Fig. 9 suggests that oriental scripts can be separated from the European ones by this difference in the height distributions of their connected components. This is implemented as follows:

1. For a text-line, all the eight-connected components are generated,[7], and the coordinates and the dimensions of the bounding box for each component are determined.

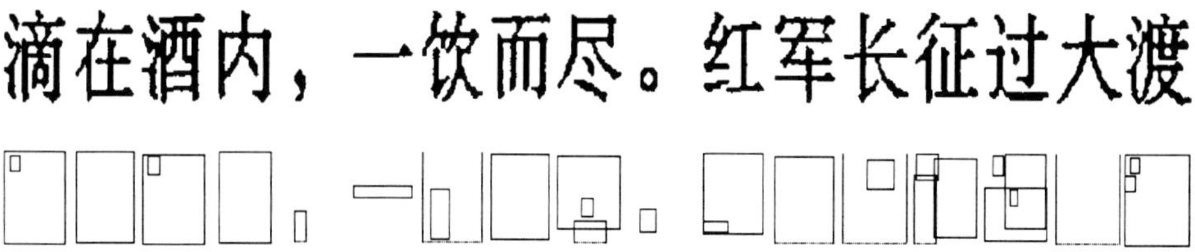

Fig. 9. A Chinese text-line and its connected components representation.

2. The height distribution histogram of the components is constructed. Each value on the x-axis represents a height, which may vary from 1 pixel to the normalized image height. The y-axis shows the populations of components having each height.
3. The numbers and locations of the peaks are used together with other data for analysis.

Figure 10 shows the height distribution histograms of three oriental text-lines (Chinese, Japanese and Korean) and the height distributions of three European text-lines (Polish, French and Russian). It can be seen that the height distributions of European languages show one or two prominent peaks representing factors 2 and 3 of the three factors stated previously, while those of oriental languages are more uniform and the outstanding peaks are located near the full text-line height.

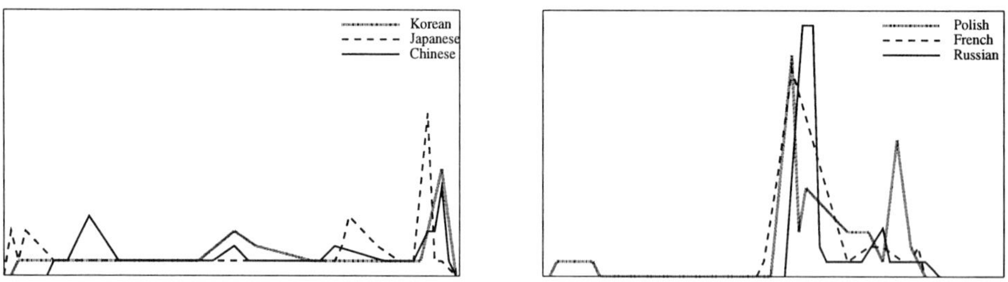

Fig. 10. Components height distribution of oriental and European languages.

We define a prominent peak as a value which is several times larger than the average with an absolute large value. The second condition is to ensure that we select a real prominent peak instead of a trivial one. (If we have a very small average value, several times of this value is still too small for it to be chosen as a prominent peak.)

To search for prominent peaks in a height distribution histogram, the following procedures are adopted:

- Height distribution histogram normalization. The x-axis has already been normalized to 64 pixels and we normalize the y-axis to 50. This value is chosen because we consider fifty components and the maximum possible height population is fifty if all the components have the same height.

- Locate prominent peaks. If a *population* is a prominent peak, then it satisfies the following condition:

$$population \geq MAX(th1 * avg2,\ avg + th2)$$

where *th1, th2* are two thresholds. If there are *N* different component heights in the height distribution histogram, then *avg* and *avg2* are calculated as follows:

$$avg = \frac{1}{N}\sum_{i=1}^{N} population[i]$$

$$avg2 = \frac{1}{M}\sum_{i} population[i],\ \text{iff}\ population[i] < MAX(2avg,\ th3 + avg)$$

where *th3* is another threshold. *M* is the total number of populations for all $population[i] < MAX(2avg,\ th3 + avg)$.

- If prominent peaks cannot be located by the above method, then we take into consideration the two direct left and two direct right neighbors. If *population[i-1], population[i-2]* are the two direct left neighbors of *population[i]* and *population[i+1], population[i+2]* are the two direct right neighbors, then we take *population[i]* as a prominent peak if and only if:

$$\sum_{x=i-2}^{i+2} population[x] \geq MAX(th1 * avg2,\ avg + th2), \tag{6}$$

where the summation is taken over all x for which $population[x] > MIN(avg, avg2 + 2)$.

Besides the number and positions of prominent peaks, we also use several other auxiliary features to analyze the height distribution. In order to represent the relatively uniform height distribution of oriental characters, we consider the variance and the difference between the maximum and minimum values in the remaining data after removing the significant peaks. These two values are smaller in oriental languages due to its uniform distribution.

In summary, the component height distributions of European scripts possess at most three outstanding peaks, representing those three factors stated previously. The heights of oriental scripts are distributed more evenly and a prominent peak occurs near the full text-line height. This is because most oriental characters have a component occupying almost the full text-line height.

2.2.4. Bounding Box Overlapping/Enclosing

Many oriental characters consist of two or more connected components and they are juxtaposed in various ways: right and left, top and bottom, one enclosed within another, etc. In contrast, all European characters have only up to three elements and one component is never contained within another. As shown in Fig. 11, a sample Chinese character which means *nation* has three connected components, two of which are enclosed in a third one. This kind of situation does not occur for characters in European languages.

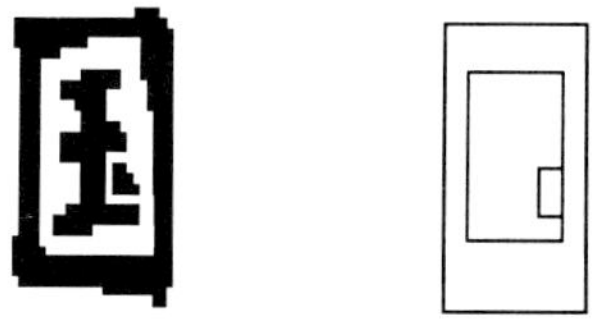

Fig. 11. A sample Chinese character with enclosed structure.

In order to locate the structure of one component enclosed within another in oriental languages, we use the following steps:

- Separate a text-line into characters by using vertical projection profile.
- Generate eight-connected components for each character[7] and use the bounding boxes to represent them.
- Determine if the "one enclosed within another" structure exists in a character as follows:
  Suppose a character contains m connected components CC[i] for $1 \leq i \leq m$, and suppose ul(x_i, y_i) and lr(x_i, y_i) are respectively the coordinates of the upper-left and lower-right corners of the bounding box of CC[i]. If there exist two components CC[i] and CC[j] ($1 \leq i, j \leq m, i \neq j$) such that:

$$\begin{array}{l} CC[j].ul.x_j \leq CC[i].ul.x_i \leq CC[j].lr.x_j, \text{ and} \\ CC[j].ul.x_j \leq CC[i].lr.x_i \leq CC[j].lr.x_j, \text{ and} \\ CC[j].ul.y_j \leq CC[i].ul.y_i \leq CC[j].lr.y_j, \text{ and} \\ CC[j].ul.y_j \leq CC[i].lr.y_i \leq CC[j].lr.y_j \end{array}$$

  then CC[i] is enclosed within CC[j].

2.2.5. Combination of the Features

In previous sections, we have proposed three features to differentiate between the two language groups. Here, we will describe how these features are combined to produce our experimental results.

1. The horizontal projection profile is used to identify some European documents. If we can locate one and/or two small peaks and the white/black area ratio $\geq T1$, then this document is classified as Roman. ($T1$ is a threshold set at 0.38).
2. If no small peak exists and ratio of white/black area $\leq T2$, then the document is classified as oriental. ($T2$ is a low threshold used to filter out some Roman documents.)
3. If neither of the above is satisfied, then we consider the components height distribution. If this distribution shows an oriental tendency, then the document is classified as such. Otherwise,
4. If the components height distribution is Roman-like, then we consider the number e_{bb} of bounding boxes that are enclosed within another. If $e_{bb} < \frac{n_{cc}}{10}$,

the document is classified as Roman; otherwise it is considered to be oriental. (n_{cc} is the number of connected components considered.)

3. EXPERIMENTAL RESULTS

3.1. Datasets

Our images were scanned from books, newspapers, magazines and computer printouts. The oriental images are obtained by scanning at 300 dpi resolution while European documents are scanned at 200 or 300 dpi. The difference in scanning resolution between the two groups of scripts is due to the complexity of oriental scripts, which requires more dots to represent them adequately, compared to European characters.

In our database, there are 86 pages of European documents printed in more than twenty different languages, such as English, French, German, Russian, Italian, etc. For the oriental languages, we have 89 Japanese documents, 166 Korean documents and 183 Chinese documents. Given the large number of languages involved, we have not yet attempted an exhaustive collection of document images in all (or even most) fonts of every language.

3.2. Results

Tables 2–4 show the differentiation results on the basis of one 50-component, two 50-components and three 50-components, respectively. For the last two cases, decisions are made by majority vote of the 2 or 3 sets of 50-components. In our processing, we randomly select a relatively long text-line and if necessary, several lines are concatenated to obtain 50-components. As the generation of one 50-component depends on random selection, we do not rely on the outcome of only one trial. So in the differentiation by using only one 50-component, we test the data set several times and average the results in order to reduce the element of chance.

Note there are only 182 Chinese documents in Table 4, because one document is too short to provide three 50-components. At the present, we are able to differentiate the script of a document as being either European or Asian on the basis of three 50-components and obtain a high recognition rate while maintaining a relatively low error rate. When two 50-components are used, the rejection rate is higher, but 100% reliability is achieved. The voting results obtained also illustrate the theoretical findings published in Ref. 5.

Table 2. The results of language classification by using one 50-component.

Language	# Samples	Recognition rate (%)	Error rate (%)	Reject rate (%)
European	86	97.68	2.32	0.00
Chinese	183	97.27	2.73	0.00
Japanese	89	96.63	3.37	0.00
Korean	166	98.19	1.81	0.00

Table 3. The results of language classification by using two 50-components.

Language	# Samples	Recognition rate (%)	Error rate (%)	Reject rate (%)
European	86	97.68	0.00	2.32
Chinese	183	96.72	0.00	3.28
Japanese	89	97.75	0.00	2.25
Korean	166	98.80	0.00	1.20

Table 4. The results of language classification by using three 50-components.

Language	# Samples	Recognition rate (%)	Error rate (%)	Reject rate (%)
European	86	98.83	1.16	0.00
Chinese	182	99.45	0.55	0.00
Japanese	89	100.00	0.00	0.00
Korean	166	100.00	0.00	0.00

In our experiment, we find that when the quality of a European document image is low and many characters are broken, then its component height distribution may cause the document to be misclassified as oriental script.

Our method is fairly robust in the processing of "mixed" document images (containing a mixture of both language groups), provided that the second language does not occupy more than about 30% of the document image. Errors tend to occur in the classification of an oriental document when more than one third of the 50-components considered actually represent European characters. This is understandable for a method based on statistical features. Using more than one unit of 50 connected components would reduce the probability of encountering unusual occurrences of highly mixed scripts in a document, unless such occurrences are common within the document. In this latter case, it is debatable whether the document can be considered to belong to any one language group. For such documents, it seems clear that multilingual OCR would be more appropriate for processing their contents.

3.3. Comparison with Other Methods

In this section, we compare our work with those presented in Refs. 6 and 8. In Ref. 8, the distribution of vertical concavities is the only feature used to differentiate between oriental and Roman scripts, and this feature is applied to seven languages (Chinese, Japanese, Korean, English, French, German and Russian). As stated in Sec. 1, we developed our method to be applicable to a larger number of language scripts. For example, our data sets also include the Cyrillic script which does not possess the stated characteristics of Roman scripts.

The emphasis of Ref. 6 is on the processing of degraded document images, and the method is applied also to seven different languages: Chinese, English, French,

German, Italian, Japanese and Spanish. Four features are used: (a) position of concavities, (b) distribution of character height, (c) character bounding-box top and bottom profile, and (d) optical density. The classification of a single text-line is based on the majority vote of these four features and the category of the whole document is the result of the majority voting of all text-lines in this document.

Our work is applicable to normal quality documents in 23 language scripts, and we adopt the cascading feature combination method in the identification stage. Our decision is based on the result(s) of 1, 2 or 3 units, where each unit contains 50 connected components of the document image.

The experimental results of our work are not easily compared to those of Refs. 6 and 8 for the following reasons:

- Different document libraries (or data sets) are used.
- The number of languages involved are different.
- The source type of documents are not identical (degraded document images are used in Ref. 6, while normal quality images are used in Ref. 8 and in our work).

In general, the method in Ref. 8 produces accurate results, but it deals with only seven languages. In Ref. 6, more features are used and all text-lines are analyzed in order to classify unoriented and degraded document images. Our method presents some new features that enable us to handle normal quality images for up to 23 languages, and the results obtained are accurate enough for practical usage.

4. CONCLUSIONS

We have proposed a method to differentiate between oriental and European scripts based on the combined analysis of several powerful discriminating features. This method has been implemented and tested on more than 500 documents in 23 languages, and the experimental results indicate that this method is effective and reliable.

ACKNOWLEDGMENTS

This research was supported by the Natural Sciences and Engineering Research Council of Canada, the National Networks of Centres of Excellence program of Canada, and the FCAR program of the Ministry of Education of the province of Québec. The first author is also supported by a research grant from the Hong Kong Institute of Education.

REFERENCES

1. K. Ejiri *et al.*,"Word frequency distribution in Japanese text", *J. Quantitative Linguistics* **1**, 3 (1994) 212–223.
2. D. Guillevic and C. Y. Suen, "Cursive script recognition applied to the processing of bank cheques", *Proc. 3rd Int. Conf. Document Analysis and Recognition*, Montreal, Canada, August 1995, pp. 11–14.

3. J. Hochberg, L. Kerns, P. Kelly and T. Thomas, "Automatic script identification from images using cluster-based templates", *Proc. 3rd Int. Conf. Document Analysis and Recognition*, Montreal, Canada, August 1995, pp. 378–381.
4. A. K. Jain, *Fundamentals of Digital Image Processing*, Information and System Sciences Series, Prentice Hall, 1986.
5. L. Lam and C. Y. Suen, "Increasing experts for majority vote in OCR: Theoretical considerations and strategies", *Proc. 4th Int. Workshop on Frontiers in Handwriting Recognition*, Taipei, Taiwan, December 1994, pp. 245–254.
6. D.-S. Lee, C. R. Nohl and H. S. Baird, "Language identification in complex, unoriented, and degraded document images", *Proc. Int. Association for Pattern Recognition Workshop on Document Analysis Systems*, Malvern, Pennsylvania USA, October 1996, pp. 76–98.
7. C. Ronse and P. A. Devijver, *Connected Components in Binary Images: The Detection Problem*, Research Studies Press, 1984.
8. A. L. Spitz, "Script and language determination from document images", *Proc. 3rd Annual Symposium on Document Analysis and Information Retrieval*, Las Vegas, USA, April 1994, pp. 229–235.
9. C. Y. Suen, "Processing of Chinese and oriental languages", in *Encyclopedia of Computer Science and Technology*, eds. A. Kent and J. G. Williams, vol. 26, Marcel Dekker, Inc., New York, 1992, pp. 333–347.
10. F. M. Wahl, K. Y. Wong and R. G. Casey, "Block segmentation and text extraction in mixed text/image documents", *Comput. Graph. Imag. Process.* **20** (1982) 375–390.

Louisa Lam received the B.A. degree from Wellesley College, MA, USA, and the Ph.D. degree in mathematics from the University of Toronto, Ontario, Canada. She has been conducting research at the Centre for Pattern Recognition and Machine Intelligence at Concordia University, Montreal, Quebec, Canada, in the areas of handwriting recognition, thinning, combination of classifiers, and language differentiation on document images. She is currently an Adjunct Associate Professor with the Department of Computer Science, Concordia University, and the Head of the Department of Mathematics at the Hong Kong Institute of Education, Hong Kong.

Dr. Lam is a member of Phi Beta Kappa.

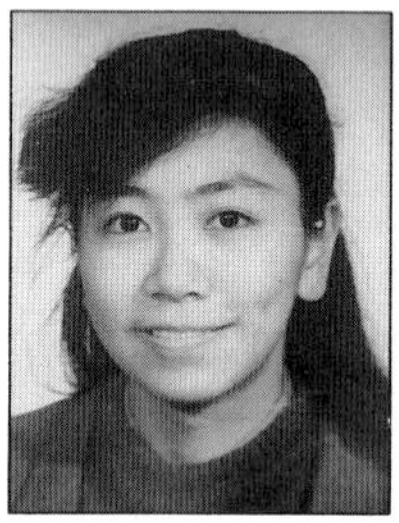

Jie Ding received her M.Eng. degree from Chongqing University, Chongqing, PRC, in 1991. Since September 1994, she has been a graduate student in Computer Science at CENPARMI (Centre for Pattern Recognition and Machine Intelligence) of Concordia University, Montreal, Quebec, Canada.

Ching Y. Suen received an M. Sc. (Eng.) degree from the University of Hong Kong and a Ph.D. degree from the University of British Columbia, Canada.

In 1972, he joined the Department of Computer Science of Concordia University, Montreal, Canada, where he became Professor in 1979 and served as Chairman from 1980 to 1984. Presently he is the Director of CENPARMI, the Centre for Pattern Recognition and Machine Intelligence of Concordia, and the Associate Dean — Research of the Faculty of Engineering and Computer Science.

Prof. Suen is the author/editor of 11 books and more than 250 papers and his current interests include pattern recognition and machine intelligence, character recognition and expert systems, document processing and computational linguistics.

Dr. Suen is an Associate Editor of several journals related to Pattern Recognition and Artificial Intelligence. He founded Computer Processing of Chinese and Oriental Languages, an international journal of the Chinese Language Computer Society in 1983 and served as its Editor-in-Chief for 10 years.

A fellow of the IEEE, IAPR, and the Royal Society of Canada, Prof. Suen is the recipient of several awards, including the 1992 ITAC/NSERC award for outstanding contributions to pattern recognition, expert systems, and computational linguistics.

GRAY-SCALE NONLINEAR SHAPE NORMALIZATION METHOD FOR HANDWRITTEN ORIENTAL CHARACTER RECOGNITION

SANG-YUP KIM and SEONG-WHAN LEE*

Center for Artificial Vision Research
Korea University, Anam-dong, Seongbuk-ku, Seoul 136-701, Korea
E-mail: {sykim, swlee}@image.korea.ac.kr

In general, nonlinear shape normalization methods for binary images have been used in order to compensate for the shape distortions of handwritten characters. However, in most document image analysis and recognition systems, a gray-scale image is first captured and digitized using a scanner or a video camera, then a binary image is extracted from the original gray-scale image using a certain extraction technique. This binarization process may remove some useful information of character images such as topological features, and introduce noises to character background. These errors are accumulated in nonlinear shape normalization step and transferred to the following feature extraction or recognition step. They may eventually cause incorrect recognition results.

In this paper, we propose nonlinear shape normalization methods for gray-scale handwritten Oriental characters in order to minimize the loss of information caused by binarization and compensate for the shape distortions of characters. Two-dimensional linear interpolation technique has been extended to nonlinear space and the extended interpolation technique has been adopted in the proposed methods to enhance the quality of normalized images.

In order to verify the efficiency of the proposed methods, the recognition rate, the processing time and the computational complexity of the proposed algorithms have been considered. The experimental results demonstrate that the proposed methods are efficient not only to compensate for the shape distortions of handwritten Oriental characters but also to maintain the information in gray-scale Oriental characters.

Keywords: Preprocessing, nonlinear shape normalization, two-dimensional nonlinear interpolation, gray-scale nonlinear shape normalization, Oriental character recognition.

1. INTRODUCTION

In recent years, researches on handwritten character recognition are extensively carried out owing to the development of the handwritten character recognition techniques. In handwritten characters, there exist many types of variations, such as position, size, rotation, inclination and shape distortions due to the various writing styles of human beings. In order to compensate for these shape variations of characters effectively, it is indispensable to develop a shape normalization method that converts the image into a normalized one having constant position, size, rotation and inclination.

In general, shape variations of handwritten characters are divided into two classes: linear shape variation and nonlinear shape variation. In the former case,

*Corresponding author.

Advances in Oriental Document Analysis and Recognition Techniques (1998) 81–95

it is possible to compensate for the linear variations including translation, scale, rotation and shear by linear shape normalization (LSN) method, but in the latter case, it is difficult to compensate for the nonlinear variations that are generated unsystematically. In handwritten characters, because of their irregularities and partial distortions in shape, compensating for these unexpected shape variations is much more difficult.

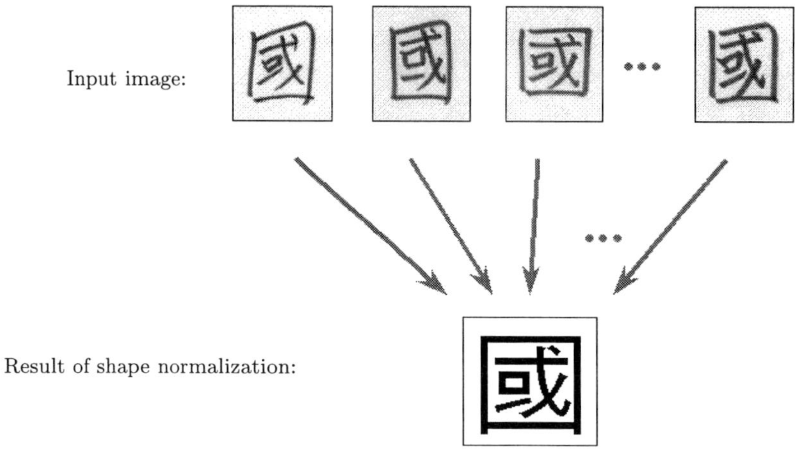

Fig. 1. Ideal shape normalization.

Figure 1 shows an example of ideal shape normalization. The character images that are ideally normalized in shapes can not only reduce the burden of the character recognizer but also increase the performance of the recognition system. However, it is almost impossible to develop such an ideal shape normalization method.

Therefore, the trials for solving this problem have fallen into developing more powerful nonlinear shape normalization methods compensating for the variations of handwritten characters. Recently, several nonlinear shape normalization methods for binary images have been proposed to compensate for the shape variations of handwritten characters.[3,7,8]

All previous nonlinear shape normalization methods have been applied to binary images. Since the binarization of gray-scale data may lose some useful information such as topological features or introduce noise, the nonlinear shape normalization methods for the binary images are not sufficient to compensate for the shape distortions of handwritten characters.

In recent years, some researches for the feature extraction of topographic features from gray-scale data and the segmentation of character images using topographic features in gray-scale data are carried out.[1,2] Therefore, in the case of extracting topographic features from gray-scale characters or recognizing them, it is important to develop gray-scale nonlinear shape normalization techniques which maintain the information of gray-scale characters.

Thus, in this paper, in order to minimize the loss of useful information and to absorb the variations of handwritten Oriental characters, we propose gray-scale nonlinear shape normalization methods.

This paper is organized as follows. Section 2 formulates a basic gray-scale linear shape normalization method and a two-dimensional linear interpolation technique. In Sec. 3, the gray-scale nonlinear shape normalization methods are proposed. In Sec. 4, experimental results are analyzed with the 520 syllables frequently used in Korea. Finally, concluding remarks are discussed in Sec. 5.

2. FORMULATION OF BASIC SHAPE NORMALIZATION METHOD IN GRAY-SCALE

In this section, we formulate the shape normalization method from the two points of view: feature projection and feature density equalization. The former makes feature projection histogram by projecting a certain feature at each point onto the horizontal- or vertical-axes and the latter equalizes feature densities of input image by re-sampling the feature projection histogram and recalculating the gray-scale value.

Consider a gray-scale image $f(i,j)$, $i = 1, 2, \ldots, I$; $j = 1, 2, \ldots, J$. Let $g(m,n)$, $m = 1, 2, \ldots, M$; $n = 1, 2, \ldots, N$, denote the result of shape normalization from input image $f(i,j)$. For the convenient comparison of each method, let $H(i)$ and $V(j)$ denote feature projection functions of a certain feature at each point onto horizontal- and vertical-axes, respectively. Then the feature projection is considered as a procedure that calculates $H(i)$, $i = 1, 2, \ldots, I$ and $V(j)$, $j = 1, 2, \ldots, J$. Feature density equalization transforms input image into normalized image by equalizing the feature densities of input image. Therefore, this step is considered as a procedure that calculates the new position (m,n) and gray-scale value of $g(m,n)$, by resampling the feature projection histogram.

2.1. Linear Shape Normalization in Gray-Scale

Linear shape normalization contains translation, size, rotation and inclination normalization. However, in this paper, we are mainly concerned with size normalization.

2.1.1. Feature projection

Size normalization only depends on the sizes of the input image and the normalized image. Thus, feature projection functions can be simply defined by

$$\begin{aligned} H(i) &= 1 \\ V(j) &= 1 \end{aligned} \tag{1}$$

where, $i = 1, 2, \ldots, I$ and $j = 1, 2, \ldots, J$.

It should be noted that these functions do not depend on the characteristic features of the input image.

2.1.2. Feature density equalization

Using feature projection function $H(i)$ and $V(j)$ of the input image, we calculate the new position (m, n) of the normalized image as follows:

$$m = \sum_{k=1}^{i} H(k) \times \frac{M}{\sum_{k=1}^{I} H(k)}$$
$$n = \sum_{l=1}^{j} V(l) \times \frac{N}{\sum_{l=1}^{J} V(l)} \tag{2}$$

where, $i = 1, 2, \ldots, I$; $j = 1, 2, \ldots, J$; and $m = 1, 2, \ldots, M$; $n = 1, 2, \ldots, N$.

Therefore, the normalized image has equal density of the features. Substituting Eq. (1) into Eq. (2) yields a simple form of size normalization which is given by

$$m = i \times \frac{M}{I}$$
$$n = j \times \frac{N}{J} \tag{3}$$

where $i = 1, 2, \ldots, I$; $j = 1, 2, \ldots, J$; and $m = 1, 2, \ldots, M$; $n = 1, 2, \ldots, N$.

In order to assure the gray-scale values of all pixels of the normalized image, the backward mapping from the normalized image (m, n) to the input image (i, j) is required. We calculate the position (i', j') of the input image corresponding to the position (m, n) of the normalized image as follows:

$$i' = m \times \frac{I}{M}$$
$$j' = n \times \frac{J}{N} \tag{4}$$

where $i' \in [1, I], j' \in [1, J]$.

In Eq. (4), i' and j' may be the fractional values. In binary images, (i', j') may be converted into the integer value by rounding or ceiling, but in gray-scale images, both the calculated position and gray-scale values are equally important. The gray-scale value in every position must be calculated again according to the gray-scale values of the neighboring pixels. Thus, to solve the problem, which is caused by having the fractional value of the position calculated from Eq. (4), the idea of interpolation must be adopted. We adopted a two-dimensional interpolation, not the nearest neighborhood approximation of Ref. 5.

2.1.3. Two-dimensional linear interpolation

Using weighted average of neighboring pixels, gray-scale value of new position can be calculated. The basic idea of two-dimensional interpolation can be defined as follows.

The gray-scale value of position (m, n) is calculated according to the gray-scale values of the neighboring pixels and distance between (i', j') and its neighboring

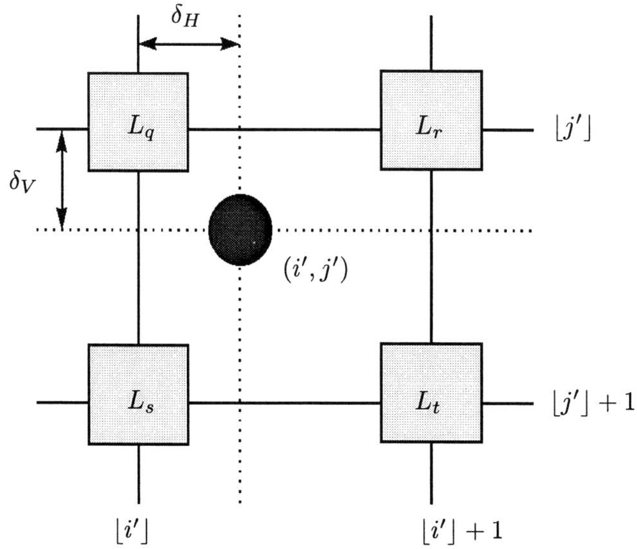

Fig. 2. Two-dimensional interpolation of gray-scale values.

pixels (see Fig. 2). The gray-scale values of the neighboring pixels of (i', j'), q, r, s and t, can be defined as follows:

$$
\begin{aligned}
L_q &= f(\lfloor i' \rfloor, \lfloor j' \rfloor) \\
L_r &= f(\lfloor i' \rfloor + 1, \lfloor j' \rfloor) \\
L_s &= f(\lfloor i' \rfloor, \lfloor j' \rfloor + 1) \\
L_t &= f(\lfloor i' \rfloor + 1, \lfloor j' \rfloor + 1)
\end{aligned} \tag{5}
$$

The horizontal- and vertical distances between (i', j') and $(\lfloor i' \rfloor, \lfloor j' \rfloor)$, δ_H and δ_V, are defined as follows:

$$
\begin{aligned}
\delta_H &= i' - \lfloor i' \rfloor \\
\delta_V &= j' - \lfloor j' \rfloor
\end{aligned} \tag{6}
$$

Finally, the gray-scale value corresponding to the position (m, n) of the normalized images is defined as follows:

$$
g(m, n) = \eta_u + (\eta_d - \eta_u) \times \delta_V \tag{7}
$$

where,

$$
\begin{aligned}
\eta_u &= \delta_H \times (L_r - L_q) + L_q \\
\eta_d &= \delta_H \times (L_t - L_s) + L_s
\end{aligned} \tag{8}
$$

In Eq. (8), η_u and η_d are the interpolated gray-scale values of two upper neighboring pixels and two lower neighboring pixels, respectively. By Eq. (7), the vertically interpolated gray-scale value can be obtained. Figure 3(b) shows an example of the linear shape normalization using two-dimensional linear interpolation technique.

3. PROPOSED NONLINEAR SHAPE NORMALIZATION METHODS IN GRAY-SCALE

In this section, the gray-scale nonlinear shape normalization (GNSN) method will be proposed according to the characteristic features in the feature projection step.

3.1. GNSN Based on Gray-Scale Density

This method uses the accumulated gray-scale values of pixels in the input image. It uses the gray-scale density as a characteristic feature of the input image.

3.1.1. Feature projection

Accumulated gray-scale values of pixels in the input image are obtained by projecting the gray-scale values in the input image onto horizontal- or vertical-axes during the scanning of the input image from left to right or top to bottom.

$$H(i) = \sum_{j=1}^{J} f(i,j) + \alpha_H$$
$$V(j) = \sum_{i=1}^{I} f(i,j) + \alpha_V \tag{9}$$

where α_H and α_V are constants.

The meaning of constants α_H and α_V will be discussed in the next section, but they are supposed to be 0 here.

3.1.2. Feature density equalization

The feature density equalization step is to calculate the new position and the gray-scale value of the new position by re-sampling. Generally, the backward mapping from normalized image to the input image is needed in order to be assured of the gray-scale values of all pixels of the normalized image.

Let us consider (i', j') as the position of the input image corresponding to (m, n) of the normalized image. The adjacent upper left position (i_q, j_q) can be obtained by the calculation using feature projection histogram. The position (i_q, j_q) is defined as follows:

$$i_q = \max\{i | \sum_{k=1}^{i} H(k) \le m \times \frac{\sum_{k=1}^{I} H(k)}{M}\}$$
$$j_q = \max\{j | \sum_{l=1}^{j} V(l) \le n \times \frac{\sum_{l=1}^{J} V(l)}{N}\} \tag{10}$$

where $i = 1, 2, \ldots, I$; $j = 1, 2, \ldots, J$; $m = 1, 2, \ldots, M$; $n = 1, 2, \ldots, N$, and $i_q \in [1, I]$; $j_q \in [1, J]$.

Therefore, the gray-scale values of neighboring pixels of Eq. (5) can be redefined as follows:

$$\begin{aligned} L_q &= f(i_q, j_q) \\ L_r &= f(i_q + 1, j_q) \\ L_s &= f(i_q, j_q + 1) \\ L_t &= f(i_q + 1, j_q + 1) \end{aligned} \tag{11}$$

The linear interpolation technique which is used for LSN method is not suitable to obtain a better quality normalized image as in Fig. 3(c) because the nonlinear normalization process is performed in the feature histogram space. Thus, the nonlinear interpolation technique for gray-scale nonlinear shape normalization method is required.

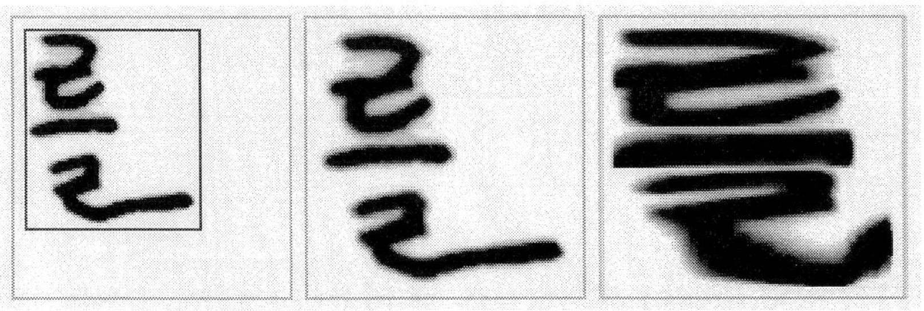

(a) (b) (c)

Fig. 3. Gray-scale shape normalization (a) input image, (b) linearly normalized image, (c) nonlinearly normalized image.

3.1.3. Two-dimensional nonlinear interpolation

It is possible to adopt the linear interpolation technique for the linear shape normalization, but in the nonlinear shape normalization, distance between (i', j') and its adjacent pixel (i_q, j_q) in the input image must be recalculated based on not the size of the input image but the feature projection histogram. Therefore, the distance defined in Eq. (6) can be redefined based on the feature projection histogram as follows:

$$\begin{aligned} \delta_H &= \frac{m \times \frac{\sum_{k=1}^{I} H(k)}{M} - \sum_{k=1}^{i_q} H(k)}{\frac{\sum_{k=1}^{I} H(k)}{I}} \\ \delta_V &= \frac{n \times \frac{\sum_{l=1}^{J} V(l)}{N} - \sum_{l=1}^{j_q} V(l)}{\frac{\sum_{l=1}^{J} V(l)}{J}} \end{aligned} \tag{12}$$

Finally, the gray-scale value of the position (m, n) can be recalculated by Eqs. (7), (8) and (12), and the nonlinearly shape normalized image of better quality such as in Fig. 3(c) can be obtained.

3.2. GNSN Based on Line Density by Changes of Gray-Scale Values

This method uses accumulated changes of gray-scale values when they change from high to low.

3.2.1. Feature projection

Accumulated changes of gray-scale values, when they change from high to low, are obtained by projecting the gray-scale values in the input image onto horizontal- or vertical-axes during the scanning of the input image from left to right or top to bottom. The characteristic features of (i,j), $F_H(i,j)$ and $F_V(i,j)$ are defined as follows:

$$F_H(i,j) = \begin{cases} f(i,j) - f(i,j-1) & \\ \qquad\qquad if\ \ f(i,j-1) < f(i,j) \\ 0 & \\ \qquad\qquad if\ \ f(i,j-1) \geq f(i,j) \end{cases}$$

$$F_V(i,j) = \begin{cases} f(i,j) - f(i-1,j) & \\ \qquad\qquad if\ \ f(i-1,j) < f(i,j) \\ 0 & \\ \qquad\qquad if\ \ f(i-1,j) \geq f(i,j) \end{cases} \tag{13}$$

The feature projection functions are defined as follows:

$$H(i) = \sum_{j=1}^{J} F_H(i,j) + \alpha_H$$

$$V(j) = \sum_{i=1}^{I} F_V(i,j) + \alpha_V \tag{14}$$

3.2.2. Feature density equalization

The new position (m,n) and the gray-scale value of the normalized image are calculated through the same process of GNSN based on the gray-scale density.

3.3. GNSN Based on Line Density by Line Interval

This method is designed to improve the GNSN method based on line density. The changes of gray-scale values have been defined as the line density using line interval.

3.3.1. Feature projection

Let $F_H(i,j)$ and $F_V(i,j)$ denote two characteristic features of a pixel (i,j) in an image area. The characteristic features, $F_H(i,j)$ and $F_V(i,j)$, are given by reciprocals of the neighboring stroke distances, respectively (see Fig. 4).

In gray-scale image, the neighboring strokes are not clearly distinguished. Thus, we define the neighboring strokes as follows:

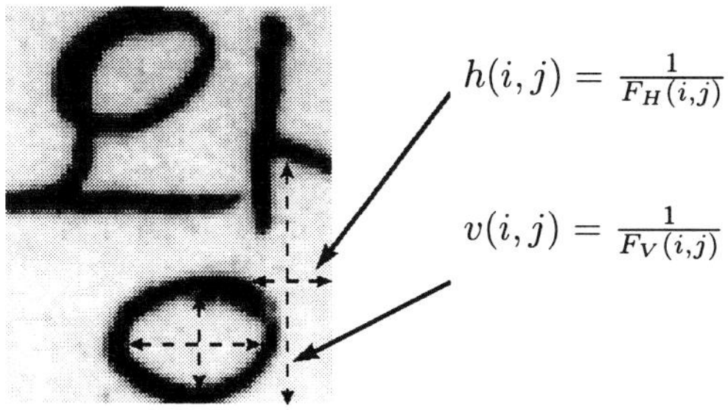

Fig. 4. Characteristic features, $F_H(i,j)$ and $F_V(i,j)$, for GNSN based on line density by changes of gray-scale values.

$$\begin{aligned} P_{H1} &= \max\{i'|i' < i,\ f(i',j) > f(i,j) + T\} \\ P_{H2} &= \min\{i'|i' > i,\ f(i',j) > f(i,j) + T\} \\ P_{V1} &= \max\{j'|j' < j,\ f(i,j') > f(i,j) + T\} \\ P_{V2} &= \min\{j'|j' > j,\ f(i,j') > f(i,j) + T\} \end{aligned} \tag{15}$$

where $T > 0$, T is the threshold of gray-scale value to decide neighboring strokes.

After defining four neighboring strokes of position (i,j), P_{H1} , P_{H2} , P_{V1} and P_{V2}, the line intervals are defined as follows:

$$\begin{aligned} h(i,j) &= P_{H2} - P_{H1} \\ v(i,j) &= P_{V2} - P_{V1} \end{aligned} \tag{16}$$

where $h(i,j)$ is the horizontal distance between left and right neighboring strokes of position, (i,j) and $v(i,j)$ is the vertical distance between upper and lower neighboring strokes of position (i,j).

The characteristic features are defined as follows:

$$\begin{aligned} F_H(i,j) &= \frac{1}{h(i,j)} \\ F_V(i,j) &= \frac{1}{v(i,j)} \end{aligned} \tag{17}$$

And, the feature projection function can be defined as follows:

$$\begin{aligned} H(i) &= \sum_{j=1}^{J} F_H(i,j) \\ V(j) &= \sum_{i=1}^{I} F_V(i,j) \end{aligned} \tag{18}$$

3.3.2. Feature density equalization

In this method, backward mapping technique is also required to be assured of all pixel values of normalized image. Where the position (i',j') of the input image is the corresponding position of the position (m, n) of the normalized image, the neighboring position of (i', j'), q, r, s and t, can be calculated based on the feature projection function. The neighboring position (i_q, j_q) is defined as follows:

$$i_q = \max\left\{ i | A \times \sum_{k=1}^{i} H(k) + i_0 \le m \right\}$$
$$j_q = \max\left\{ j | B \times \sum_{l=1}^{j} V(l) + j_0 \le n \right\} \tag{19}$$

where $i = 1, 2, \ldots, I$; $j = 1, 2, \ldots, J$; $m = 1, 2, \ldots, M$; $n = 1, 2, \ldots, N$, $i_q \in [1, I]$, $j_q \in [1, J]$; i_0 and j_0 denote the starting positions of the normalized image, and A and B are the constants for the normalizing factors.[7]

The remaining steps are the same as with the feature density equalization process of GNSN based on gray-scale density.

Assume that $i_0 = 0$ and $j_0 = 0$, and let

$$A = \frac{M}{\sum_{k=1}^{I} H(k)}$$
$$B = \frac{N}{\sum_{l=1}^{J} V(l)} \tag{20}$$

Then, we can easily observe that Eq. (19) can be deduced to Eq. (10). Therefore, it can be revealed that the feature density equalization in GNSN based on the gray-scale density is the special case of that in GNSN based on the line density by line interval.

4. EXPERIMENTAL RESULTS AND ANALYSIS

The comparison of the proposed shape normalization methods has been made based on the recognition rate, the processing speed and the computational complexity of the proposed algorithms in the feature projection steps. The following methods have been considered:

Method 1: basic linear shape normalization in gray-scale

Method 2: proposed GNSN based on gray-scale density

Method 3: proposed GNSN based on line density by changes of gray-scale values

Method 4: proposed GNSN based on line density by line interval

4.1. Experimental Environments

The proposed methods have been implemented on the Pentium Pro 200MHz PC in Visual C^{++} 4.1 under Windows 95 environment. The handwritten character image data used in our experiments came from 1,000 sets of the most frequently used 520 handwritten Hangul characters having various variations according to the many different writing styles.[4] Figure 5 shows some examples of gray-scale images used in our experiments.

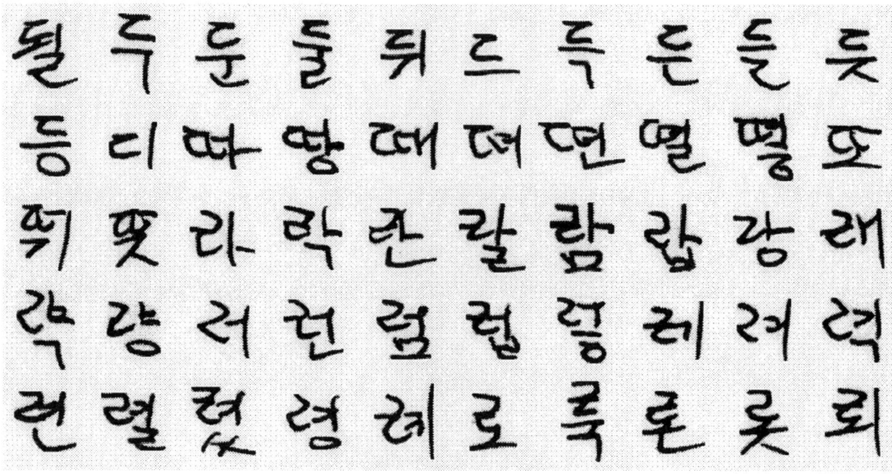

Fig. 5. Examples of gray-scale handwritten Hangul data.

4.2. The Meaning of Constants α_H and α_V

In Sec. 2, the constants α_H and α_V were assumed to be 0. However, in the case of the normalization on the horizontal-axis with GNSN based on gray-scale density, if we assume $\alpha_H = 0$, the center gab in Hangul character "이" is completely contracted owing to the relatively small projected value. This nonlinearity is too strong and unnatural. This phenomenon can be relieved by setting α_V to a positive constant. Constant α_H has the similar meaning to that of α_H. Then if the value of the constant α_H is very large, the effect of projected features is relieved, so the result of the normalization is equivalent to the conventional linear normalization that transforms the rectangle into a square.[3]

4.3. Discussion

Figure 6 shows the results of four different shape normalization methods in the shape of the Hangul character "를" in order to easily compare the differences in each of them.

The reason that the normalized results are not always uniform is attributed to the fact that the NSN method is the space version of the histogram equalization.[8]

In order to verify the efficiency of the proposed methods, the recognition rates, the processing speed and the computational complexity are considered (Table 1). In order to verify the recognition performance, a recognizer based on the principal features which was designed for gray-scale handwritten character recognition[6] is used. From the table, it is evident that the GNSN techniques improve recognition performance and reduce the variations of the handwritten characters.

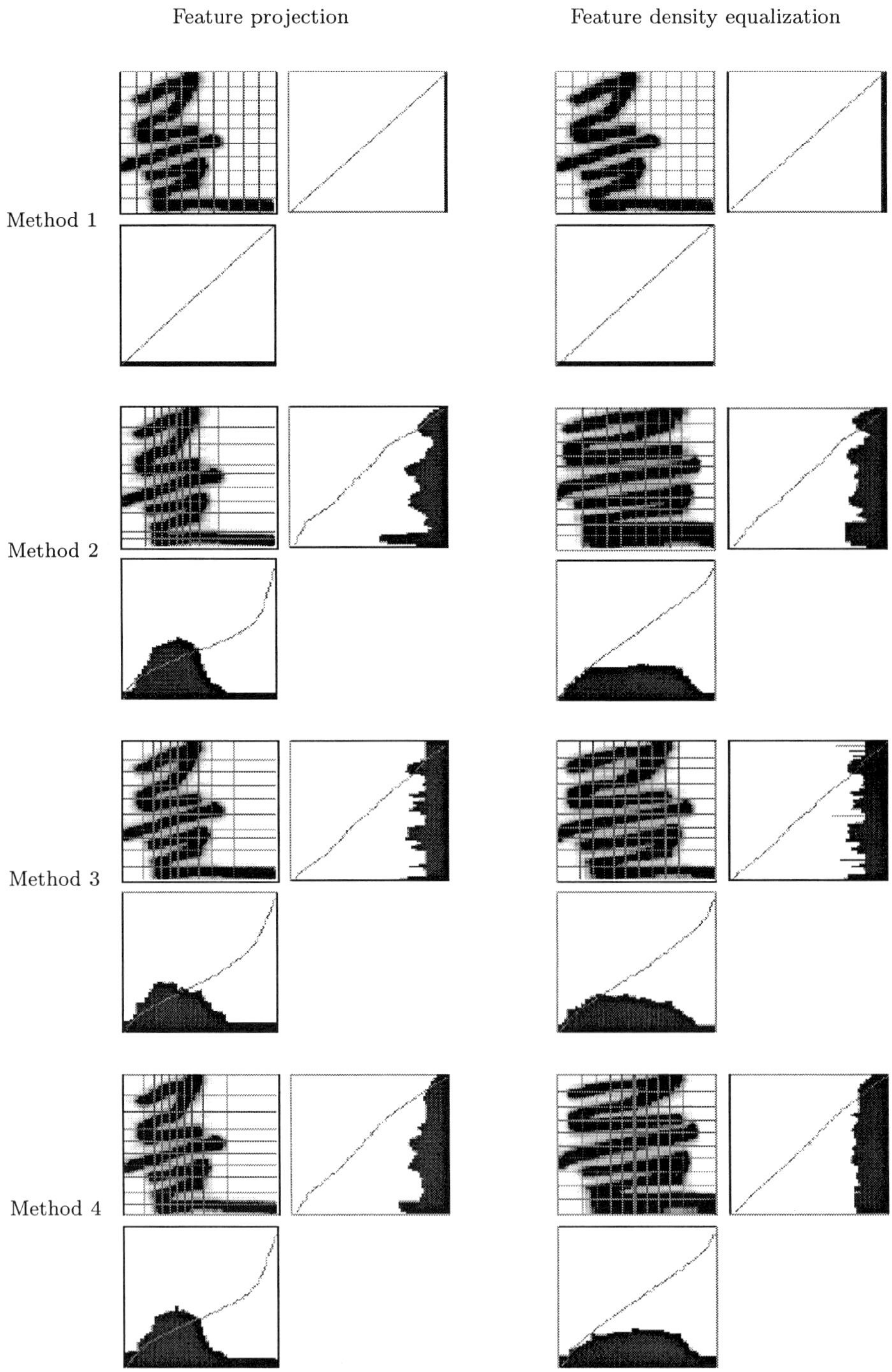

Fig. 6. Examples of feature projection and feature density equalization.

From the point of the recognition rate, Method 4 is the most efficient among several GNSN techniques. Method 2 based on the gray-scale density has relatively high recognition rates, considering the fast processing time.

Table 1. Experimental results of the proposed methods.

Method	Recognition rate	Processing speed (ms/char)	Computational complexity (Feature projection step)
Method 1	85.27	21.70	I + J
Method 2	90.14	22.15	2(I × J)
Method 3	89.02	22.85	4(I × J)
Method 4	91.42	34.84	(I + J + 2)(I × J)

Figure 7 shows the results of four different shape normalization methods. In the shape of the Hangul character "블", a man has a tendency to write the same character differently. This problem of irregular distortions cannot be solved by LSN method (Method 1).

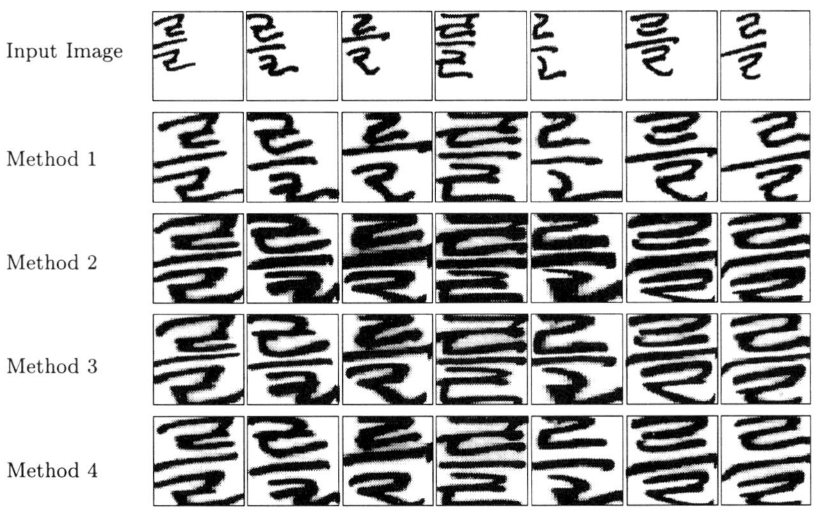

Fig. 7. Examples of gray-scale shape normalization.

According to the characteristics of the gray-scale density (Method 2), this method has the advantage that character shape unbalance is roughly corrected. But the drawback of this method is that the stroke thickness varies with the stroke length.

In Method 3, a local part of the high gray-scale density is expanded and that of the low gray-scale density is shrunk. The merits of this method are that stroke thickness is almost the same and the character shape unbalance is roughly corrected. However, the uniform relocation of the inner strokes is still sticky.

In Method 4, a local part, including the short stroke interval, is expanded and a local part, including the long stroke interval, is shrunk. This method has the advantages that character shape unbalance is roughly corrected and the stroke interval is uniformly normalized.

5. CONCLUDING REMARKS

In general, nonlinear shape normalization methods for binary images have been used in order to compensate for the shape distortions of handwritten characters. However, in most document image analysis and recognition systems, a gray-scale image is first captured and digitized using a scanner or a video camera, then a binary image is extracted from the original gray-scale image using a certain extraction technique. This binarization process may remove some useful information of character images such as topological features and introduce noises to character background. These errors are accumulated in the nonlinear shape normalization step and transferred to the following feature extraction or recognition step. They may eventually cause incorrect recognition results.

In this paper, we proposed nonlinear shape normalization methods for gray-scale handwritten Oriental characters in order to minimize the loss of information caused by the binarization and compensate for the shape distortions of characters. A two-dimensional linear interpolation technique has been extended to the nonlinear space and the extended interpolation technique has been adopted in the proposed methods to enhance the quality of the normalized images.

In order to verify the efficiency of the proposed methods, the recognition rate, the processing time and the computational complexity of the proposed algorithms have been considered. The experimental results indicated that the proposed methods were efficient not only to compensate for the shape distortions of handwritten characters but also to maintain the information in gray-scale Oriental characters.

ACKNOWLEDGEMENT

This research was supported by the 1997 Industry-University Co-Research Fund of Korea Ministry of Information and Communication.

REFERENCES

1. S.-W. Lee and Y. J. Kim, "Direct extraction of topographic features for gray-scale character recognition", *IEEE Trans. Patt. Anal. Mach. Intell.* **17**, 7 (1995) 724–729.
2. S.-W. Lee, D. J. Lee and H.-S. Park, "A new methodology for gray-scale character segmentation and recognition", *IEEE Trans. Patt. Anal. Mach. Intell.* **18**, 10 (1996) 1045–1050.
3. S.-W. Lee and J. S. Park, "Nonlinear shape normalization methods for the recognition of large-set handwritten characters", *Patt. Recogn.* **27**, 7 (1994) 895–902.
4. S.-W. Lee *et al.*, "Design and construction of large-set off-line handwritten Hangul character image database KU-1", *Proc. National Conf. on Hangul Information Processing*, Pusan, Oct. 1997, pp. 152–159.
5. C. A. Lindley, *Practical Image Processing in C*, John Wiley & Sons, 1991.

6. H.-S. Park, S.-Y. Kim and S.-W. Lee, "Gray-scale handwritten character recognition based on principal features", *Proc. 1997 SPIE Conf. Document Recognition(IV)*, San Jose, USA, Feb. 1997, pp. 40–49.
7. J. Tsukumo and H. Tanaka, "Classification of handprinted Chinese characters using nonlinear normalization methods", *Proc. 9th Int. Conf. Pattern Recognition*, Rome, Italy, November 1988, pp. 168–171.
8. H. Yamada, K. Yamamoto and T. Saito, "A nonlinear normalization for handprinted Kanji character recognition — line density equalization", *Patt. Recogn.* **23**, 9 (1990) 1023–1029.

Sang-Yup Kim received the B.S. and M.S. degrees in information engineering from the Korea University, Seoul in 1994 and 1996, respectively. Currently, he is pursuing his Ph.D. degree in visual information processing at the Korea University, Seoul, Korea.

His research interests include image processing, neural networks, and pattern recognition.

Seong-Whan Lee received the B.S. degree in computer science and statistics from Seoul National University, Seoul, Korea, in 1984 and the M.S. and Ph.D. degrees in computer science from the Korea Advanced Institute of Science and Technology in 1986 and 1989, respectively.

He is the Co-Editor-in-Chief of International Journal of Document Analysis and Recognition, and the associate editor of the Pattern Recognition Journal, International Journal of Pattern Recognition and Artificial Intelligence, and Internaitional Journal of Computer Processing of Oriental Languages. He was the Program Chairman of the 17th International Conference on Computer Processing of Oriental Languages and the 6th International Workshop on Frontiers in Handwritten Recognition. He is the General Co-chairman of 3rd International Workshop on Document Analysis Systems, and the Program Co-chairman of the 5th International Conference on Document Analysis and Recognition and 2nd International Conference on Multimodal Interface. He served on the program committees of several well-known international conferences.

He is a senior member of the IEEE Computer Society and a member of the Korea Information Science Society, the Pattern Recognition Society, the International Neural Network Society, and the Oriental Language Computer Society. He is the director of recently-established Center for Artificial Vision Research, Korea University.

His research interests include pattern recognition, document image analysis, computer vision and neural networks.

DISTRIBUTED AUTONOMOUS AGENTS FOR CHINESE DOCUMENT IMAGE SEGMENTATION

JIMING LIU* and Y. Y. TANG

Department of Computing Studies, Baptist University
224 Waterloo Road, Kowloon Tong, Hong Kong

In Chinese document image processing, text and/or graphical block detection serves as an essential step in document layout analysis that in turn permits the effective reasoning about the logical relationships among various text paragraphs and graphical entities for the purpose of document understanding. This paper presents a novel computational paradigm for extracting text/graphic blocks from Chinese document images, which is based on a notion of distributed autonomous agents. The primary features of the agents lie in that they are (1) adaptive to the locality of given images and hence efficient in locating the homogeneous image blocks, (2) reliable in performing image processing as the computation proceeds simultaneously from different image locations, (3) less sensitive to the noise in the given images as the computation disperses gracefully when it is moving away from the homogeneous blocks, and (4) easy to represent in their behaviors and evolvable in their performance. The paper, first of all, describes the formalisms as well as the behavioral characteristics of the agents, which is followed by a demonstration of the agents in detecting document blocks from some real-life images.

Keywords: Autonomous agents, distributed image processing, document segmentation.

1. INTRODUCTION

In view of the increasing needs for processing large volumes of document information, various methods for automatic text segmentation and discrimination have been investigated.[1–3,5,8,9,16–18,25–27] Among them, Hirayama[6] proposed an approach that could isolate text/figure blocks by identifying character strings, grouping text lines with small spacing, and bounding text groups with blocks. Okamoto and Takahashi[19] presented a field-separator based document segmentation approach. Two types of field separators were used to partition a regular document, which included thin black lines and wide or long white spacing. These approaches made explicit assumptions about the text line and column spacing as well as the regularity of the text and figure blocks. Yu *et al.*[29] developed a novel approach to processing unconstrained, irregular documents that allowed for a structural representation of the various document blocks.

As one of the well-known algorithms for region identification, *split-and-merge* makes use of the geometric proximity information to isolate or separate homogeneous regions in an image. The classic formulation of the algorithm builds a quadtree in which the leaf nodes correspond to the homogeneous regions.[21,22] Although it is computationally efficient, it suffers from the limitation of the blind partitioning of the regions during the intermediate segmentation process. There

*Corresponding author. E-mail: jiming@comp.hkbu.edu.hk

Advances in Oriental Document Analysis and Recognition Techniques (1998) 97–118

have been some efforts on improving the adaptiveness of the splitting and merging operations.[20,28] However, most of the existing work focuses on the spatially compact representation of the images in general, and very little has been done to investigate the efficacy of the methodology as well as the particularity of the implementation in the context of the document layout analysis.

Chinese document segmentation is a challenging task in that the paragraphs in such documents may be composed of texts in a variety of fonts in addition to some embedded graphics, and is hence difficult to set a global homogeneity threshold as in conventional image segmentation approaches (e.g. region segmentation based on split-and-merge). One possible way to deal with this difficulty is to apply different operators to the different text blocks catering to the specific changes in the average block intensity gradients, and to do it in such an adaptive way that each operator is only triggered by the desirable locality of the documents.

The goal of this paper is to propose and illustrate an approach to Chinese document segmentation that is in essence developed based on the above-mentioned motivation. In particular, it presents a novel idea of distributed image segmentation based on several classes of autonomous agents, where each class is responsible for the extraction of a specific type of blocks. In extracting the image blocks, the classes of agents will exhibit several reactive behaviors in response to the local condition of the given image. It is due to such reactive behaviors that the adaptability of image segmentation is achieved.

1.1. Organization of the Paper

The remainder of the paper is organized as follows: Sec. 2 describes the essential formalisms as well as the important principles for defining and implementing the agents for document segmentation. Section 3 presents several examples of such agents. Section 4 discusses the main characteristics of the proposed agents approach and compares it with other conventional approaches. Finally, Sec. 5 concludes the paper by highlighting the major contribution of this paper as well as some natural and logical extensions from the present work.

2. THE AGENTS APPROACH

In this section, we provide a description of the proposed agents approach to Chinese document image segmentation. In doing so, we first give an overview of the agents, which is followed by a more detailed presentation of the behavioral control algorithm and the reactive behaviors involved.

2.1. An Overview

The proposed agents for Chinese document segmentation are basically autonomous agents that operate at individual image pixels based on an evaluation of the image intensity at their neighboring regions. In response to the condition as detected within their neighboring regions, the agents will activate some of the following reactive behaviors:

1. Labeling a homogeneous block with feature-markers: Whenever an agent finds that its neighboring region satisfies the specific condition of a homogeneous block, it will place a marker at its present pixel.
2. Generating and distributing new agents based on self-reproduction: At the same time as it places a feature marker, the agent will also self-replicate a finite set of offspring agents within its neighboring region, in a direction as inherited from the self-reproduction direction of its parent and at randomly generated distances.
3. Searching a homogeneous block based on diffusion: Whenever an agent fails to locate a pixel that belongs to the block to be found, it will move to a new location within its neighboring region in a direction as inherited from its parent and at a randomly generated distance.
4. Aging: Each active block-finding agent has a finite life-span; whenever it executes a diffusion behavior, its age will increment accordingly. Once its age is equal to a predefined life-span, the agent will be inactivated and vanish from the image.

The above may be summarized in the form of a schematic diagram that outlines the behavioral reactions of the agents to their local image conditions:

$$\texttt{local\_stimuli} \begin{array}{l} \nearrow \boxed{\texttt{feature-marking}} + \boxed{\texttt{self-reproduction}} \\ \\ \searrow \boxed{\texttt{randomized\_search}} + \boxed{\texttt{decay}} \end{array} \qquad (1)$$

Taking a feature-extraction agent as an example, if the agent of a certain feature sensitive class reaches the desired feature, it will *permanently* "inhabit" at that feature, and proceed to reproduce within its immediate neighboring region. In the present work, we assume that the reproduced offspring inherits all the behavioral characteristics of the parent agents except their ages. As the reproduced agents randomly move away from their current locations, some of them may encounter the desired image features again, and hence the reproduction cycle repeats itself, while others whose ages exceed a certain threshold will vanish.

2.2. Document Images as Agents Environments

A document image is a two-dimensional rectangular grid lattice where each of the 8-connected grids corresponds to an image pixel. In our proposed agents model, this two-dimensional lattice provides an environment for an agent to inhabit and evolve. In this environment, the agent may self-reproduce an offspring, randomly move to adjacent locations, or vanish, in response to the image characteristics of its local neighboring region. In this respect, we regard the behaviors of the agent as being reactive, as they are entirely activated, and hence determined, by the locality of the agent environment.

2.3. An Algorithm for Agent Sensing and Behaving

In the proposed agents model, an agent is designed in such a way that it continuously senses its surrounding environment by evaluating the intensity characteristics of the neighboring pixels, such as their relative contrast, regional mean, and/or regional standard deviation, and determines and executes its behavior according to the results of such a sensory feedback. Here the local image characteristics are also called the *local stimuli* of the agent. In other words, if the evaluation of the local neighboring region shows the local stimuli satisfy a specific behavioral triggering condition, the agent activates its corresponding behavior. Figure 1 presents an algorithm for the behavioral control of agents.

input: A document image of size $U \times V$, in which each pixel has a gray-level value
output: Markers over the detected segment pixels

```
randomly distribute an initial set of agents, {a_i^(0)}, over the image
assign the initial agent set to the active agent set: A ← {a_i^(0)}
while A ≠ ∅ do
  for all current a ∈ A do
    if there exists grandparent(s) a_g of a then
    compute the successful directions for all a_g
      backtrack to find all a_g that have succeeded in finding a homogeneous segment
      update P(Ω)_a and P(Θ)_a, using Eqs. 11 and 12 (to be described later), respectively
    else
      assign P(Ω)_a and P(Θ)_a to uniform distributions
    endif
    if at local triggering stimulus then
      reproduce offspring {a'_v} in direction ω ∈ Ω with P(Ω)_a to a neighboring sector
      of radius κ
      A ← A ⋃{a'_v}
      become immobilized (or leave a marker) at the current location
      A ← A − a
    else
      if age_a = life_span then
        A ← A − a
        remove agent from the image
      else
        diffuse to a neighboring sector of radius κ, in direction θ ∈ Θ with P(Θ)_a
        age_a ← age_a + 1
      endif
    endif
  endfor
endwhile
```

Fig. 1. The agent behavioral control algorithm.

2.3.1. Behavioral triggering conditions

As mentioned in Sec. 2.1, the behaviors of agents are triggered by the local stimuli of the agents whenever the stimuli satisfy certain conditions. In the case of Chinese document segmentation, we utilize the following three types of triggering conditions; namely,

$$\texttt{contrast\_condition}: \; G_{(i,j)\_\text{region}} \in [\lambda_1, \lambda_2] \tag{2}$$

$$\texttt{mean\_condition}: \; \text{mean}_{(i,j)\_\text{region}} \in [M_1, M_2] \tag{3}$$

$$\texttt{std\_condition}: \; \text{std}_{(i,j)\_\text{region}} \in [D_1, D_2] \tag{4}$$

where λ_1, λ_2, M_1, M_2, D_1, and D_2 denote positive constants that are predefined.

To be more specific, the relative contrast stimulus is defined in terms of the following expression:

$$G_{(i,j)\_\text{region}} = \sum_{\|(i,j)-(k,l)\| \leq R_{(i,j)\_\text{region}}} g(i,j,k,l) \tag{5}$$

where

$$g(i,j,k,l) = \begin{cases} 1 & \text{if } \|I(i,j) - I(k,l)\| \leq \delta, \\ 0 & \text{otherwise}. \end{cases} \tag{6}$$

and (i,j) denotes the current location of an agent, and $R_{(i,j)\_\text{region}}$ denotes the radius of the sensing region, i.e. the immediate neighboring region of the agent.

As for the regional mean and the regional standard deviation, the definitions are straightforward, and are respectively listed below:

$$\text{mean}_{(i,j)\_\text{region}} = \frac{1}{N} \sum_{\|(i,j)-(k,l)\| \leq R_{(i,j)\_\text{region}}} I(k,l) \tag{7}$$

and,

$$\text{std}_{(i,j)\_\text{region}} = \sqrt{\frac{1}{N} \sum_{\|(i,j)-(k,l)\| \leq R_{(i,j)\_\text{region}}} \left(I(k,l) - \text{mean}_{(i,j)\_\text{region}}\right)^2} \tag{8}$$

where (i,j) corresponds to the current location of an agent, and N denotes the number of pixels within the agent neighboring region of radius $R_{(i,j)\_\text{region}}$.

2.3.2. Adaptation to image locality

The distributed agents as used in Chinese document segmentation adapt to their local image environments by way of switching in between two behaviors; namely, self-reproduction (SR) of their offspring agents within the local neighboring regions and diffusion (DIFF) to new locations also within such regions. For instance, if an agent detects at an image pixel that its local stimuli satisfy the condition of a certain homogeneous segment, it will reproduce a finite number of offspring agents within its neighboring region in a specific direction. That is,

$$\begin{aligned} \texttt{SR}: \texttt{IF}\; R_{(i,j)\_\text{region}} &\equiv \text{triggers}\; \texttt{THEN}\; a^t(i,j) \\ &\Longrightarrow \{a'_v(\omega, \tilde{r}) \mid v = 1, 2, \cdots, q;\; \omega \in \Omega;\; \tilde{r} \leq R_{(i,j)\_\text{region}}\}^{t+1} \end{aligned} \tag{9}$$

where ω and $\tilde{r}$ denote the selected direction that corresponds to one of the evenly divided directional sectors in Ω and the distance for placing an offspring agent, respectively.

This self-reproduction behavior effectively enables the newly created offspring to be distributed near the pixel location that meets the homogeneous definition, and therefore increases the likelihood of further segment detection.

Figure 2(a) illustrates the self-reproduction behavior of an agent. The direction vectors of self-reproduction by the agent (and subsequently by its offspring) depend on an updating mechanism as described in Sec. 2.3.4.

2.3.3. Biased randomized search

As can be noted in the preceding section, some of the created offspring may not immediately find a pixel location of the homogeneous segment. In such a case, these agents will exhibit a reactive behavior of diffusion by moving to a new location within the neighboring region of its previous location in a specific direction. The diffusion behavior may be formally represented as follows:

$$\begin{aligned} \texttt{DIFF} : \texttt{IF}\ R_{(i,j)\_\text{region}} &\neq \text{triggers}\ \texttt{AND}\ \text{age} < \text{life\_span}\ \texttt{THEN}\ a^t(i,j) \\ &\Longrightarrow a^{t+1}(\theta, \tilde{d}), \theta \in \Theta, \tilde{d} \leq R_{(i,j)\_\text{region}} \end{aligned} \tag{10}$$

where θ denotes the selected direction of diffusion that corresponds to one of the evenly divided directional sectors in Θ, and $\tilde{d}$ denotes the distance of diffusion.

As illustrated in Fig. 2(b), in the attempt to search for a new location of the homogeneous segment, the diffusion behavior may be viewed as a randomized positional mutation in that the length of diffusion is randomly generated as long as it falls within the neighboring region. However, this search behavior is subject to the following two biases: (1) The movement direction is statistically computed based on those of the parent agents that have previously succeeded in finding the homogeneous segment, and (2) the searching agents remain to be close to the location of their parent despite subsequent diffusion motions. In this respect, the diffusion behavior is essentially a biased randomized search behavior that plays an important role for the agents to find the pixels of homogeneous segments within the two-dimensional lattice.

2.3.4. The behavioral evolution of agents

In the above discussion, we mentioned that the directions for the agent self-reproduction and diffusion are determined from the directions of the successful parent agents. Such a mechanism for the direction selection constitutes the essential means for evolving agent behaviors from "high-fitness" (i.e. successful) agents. In what follows, we provide the details on the computational scheme involved.

First, let us suppose that a grandparent agent $a_i^{(g-1)}$ of generation $g-1$ has produced a set of parent agents $\{a_{ij}^{(g)}\}$. This set further produces the offspring of generation $g+1$, as denoted by $\{a_{ijk}^{(g+1)}\}$. In such a case, we will update the

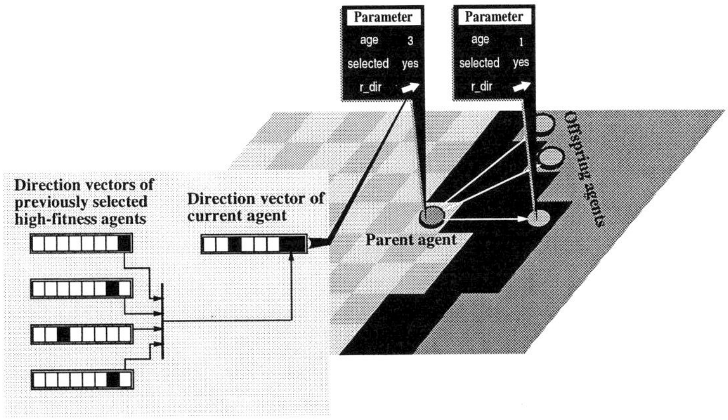

(a)

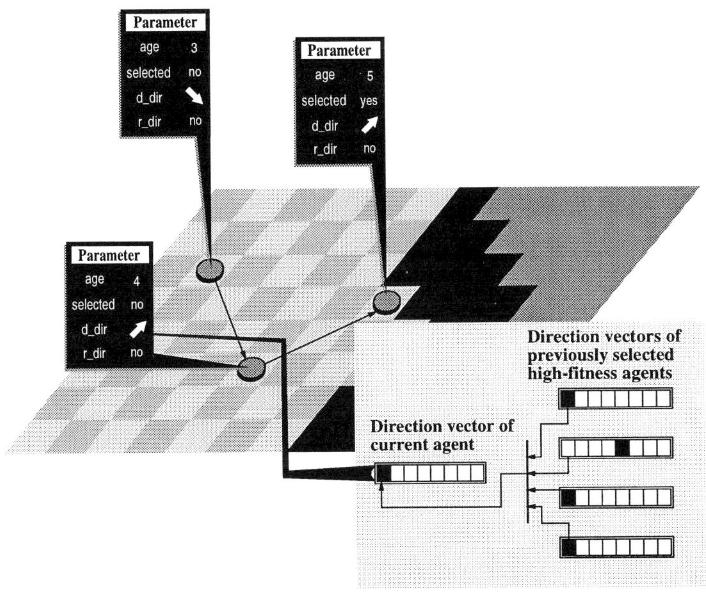

(b)

Fig. 2. An illustration of agent self-reproduction and diffusion behaviors. (a) The asexual self-reproduction of an agent is triggered by the external stimuli in the environment as computed from the density distribution of their neighboring pixels of certain gray-level intensity values. The process of self-reproduction and diffusion repeats during the evolution of the agent population. (b) An agent of age 3 diffuses to its neighboring region of the two-dimensional lattice. After each diffusion step, the age of the agent will be incremented by one. The process of diffusion provides a chance for the agent to search the pixels of homogeneous segments from the locations of its parent. Here the directions of self-reproduction and diffusion are determined from the direction vectors as computed from those of previously selected high-fitness parent agents (see Sec. 2.3.4).

directions of self-reproduction and diffusion by the agent $a_{ijk}^{(g+1)}$ from those of the successful agents in $\{a_{ij}^{(g)}\}$ and $\{a_{ijk}^{(g+1)}\}$. Here we define the notion of a successful parent agent in terms of whether or not the agent has detected a homogeneous segment.

Before we present the updating mechanism for computing self-reproduction and diffusion directions, we will introduce a formalism called *direction vector*. The direction vector of an agent specifies the *probability* of success in locating a homogeneous segment pixel, if the corresponding direction sector is chosen for the respective behavior.

Next, we denote the probabilities as associated with the direction sectors ω and θ, respectively, for self-reproduction and diffusion by agent $a_{ijk}^{(g+1)}$ as $p(\omega)$ and $p(\theta)$, and derive them in the following two steps:

1. **Retrieving parent agents:** Backtrack to find all $a \in \{a_{ij}^{(g)}\}$ and $\{a_{ijk}^{(g+1)}\}$ that have been successful; and
2. **Updating direction vectors:** For all the found parent agents, compute:

$$p(\omega \in \Omega)_a = \frac{O_\omega}{\sum_{\forall i} O_i} \tag{11}$$

and,

$$p(\theta \in \Theta)_a = \frac{N_\theta}{\sum_{\forall i} N_i} \tag{12}$$

where

Ω: the set of possible directions for agent self-reproduction,
Θ: the set of possible directions for agent diffusion,
O_i: the number of agents reproduced by their parents from direction i, and
N_i: the number of agents that have diffused to the local stimulus from direction i.

The above formulas generate the probability distributions for the self-reproduction and diffusion directions by way of calculating the percentage of occurrences.

2.3.5. Agent convergence

According to the behavioral control algorithm as given in Fig. 1, when an agent encounters a pixel pertaining to a homogeneous segment, it will leave a marker to signify that the current pixel belongs to a segment satisfying a certain homogeneity criterion. This can also be expressed as follows:

$$\texttt{MARK} : \texttt{IF } R_{(i,j)\_\text{region}} \equiv \text{triggers } \texttt{THEN } a^t(i,j) \Longrightarrow \alpha^{t+1}(i,j) \tag{13}$$

where (i,j) denotes the current location of an agent, and α denotes a marker as left by the agent.

The number of markers as for labeling a particular segment will gradually increase from zero at the beginning to a fixed constant at the end when all the pixels of this segment are found and then labeled by active agents. During the course when the number of markers is approaching a steady state, the active agents that fail to find a homogeneous segment after several designated steps will also vanish from the document image environment. The latter is controlled by the age of an agent. That is, if the age of the agent exceeds its life-span, it will abort further segment-searching movements in the two-dimensional lattice environment. This reactive behavior may be represented with the following expression:

$$\texttt{DEATH}: \texttt{IF}\ R_{(i,j)\_\text{region}} \neq \text{triggers}\ \texttt{AND}\ age \equiv \text{life\_span}\ \texttt{THEN}\ a^t(i,j) \Longrightarrow \text{null} \quad (14)$$

In our proposed agents approach to Chinese document segmentation, death or vanishing behavior is necessary in order for agents to avoid endless trial-and-error and hence reduce the wasteful computation to as minimal as possible.

3. EXPERIMENTAL VALIDATION

The preceding section has provided a model of the agents covering their behavioral control algorithm as well as their reactive behaviors. During the representation, we also paid special attention to the global dynamics of the agents, including those of the offspring, active agents and markers, during the course of region segmentation, and noted that these dynamics are essential in optimizing (i.e. bringing down) the computational costs. Such global dynamics are readily manifested through a collection of individual agents with the reactive behaviors of self-reproduction, diffusion, marking and vanishing. As a validation of the proposed approach, in this section we shall present some experiments in which real-life Chinese document images have been used and tested with the proposed agents approach. For each of the images, we shall describe how various classes of homogeneous region searching agents are defined, and examine a series of intermediate steps of the agent computation in order to understand at a global level how the agents-based segmentation actually works.

3.1. The Segmentation Task

Figure 3 presents a 260×300 256-gray-level digital document image, which was used as the grid lattice for our agents. This image contains a large font document heading, followed by several paragraphs of small font texts and one inserted graphical illustration. The objective of this segmentation task was to isolate the above-mentioned components of the document from its background. In doing so, we would like to distinguish the texts from the graphical illustration, and further the large font texts from the small font texts. Here we were particularly interested in the regions where various components might be located; the exact sizes as well as the exact shapes of the graphical objects were not our concern. Such a segmentation of various document components would serve as an important pre-processing step for the further logical analysis of the identified components as well as the understanding of the document.

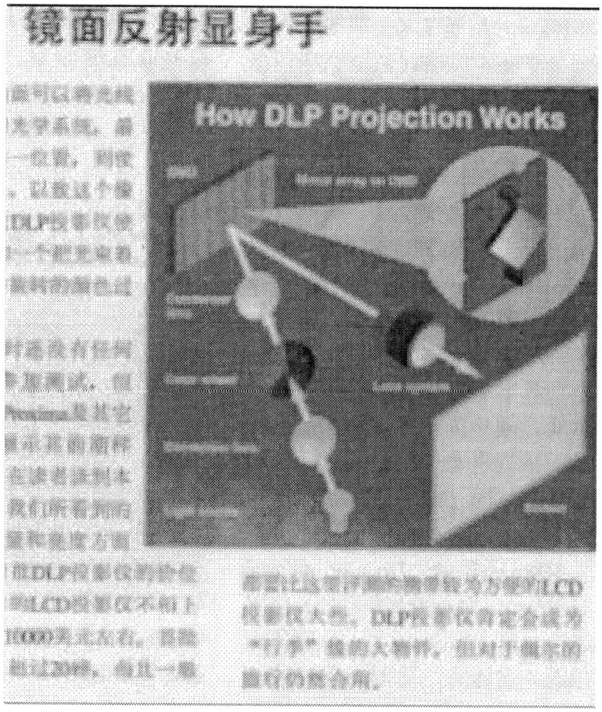

Fig. 3. The gray-level document image to be segmented.

3.2. The Agents

In handling this particular task, we developed four classes of agents that simultaneously co-existed and co-evolved in the given image. These four classes are:

Class 1: to extract small font text region (`life_span`= 10);

Class 2: to extract large font text region (`life_span`= 10);

Class 3: to locate the graphical region (`life_span`= 12); and

Class 4: to highlight the background (`life_span`= 3).

where the `life_span` of each agent class was set in view of the general requirement for the biased randomized searching; the greater the `life_span` the greater the positional mutation would be in searching for a homogeneous location.

In order to show the effects of the parameter setting on the final outcomes of segmentation, in what follows we present the experimental results as obtained under two sets of conditions corresponding to two sets of agent triggering conditions; namely:

Triggering condition set 1: Agents with a small sensing region:

Class 1:

$$G_{(i,j)\_\text{region}=5\times5}\,|_{\delta=20} \in [0,19] \tag{15}$$
$$\text{mean}_{(i,j)\_\text{region}=5\times5} \in [181,230] \tag{16}$$
$$\text{std}_{(i,j)\_\text{region}=5\times5} \in [3,5] \tag{17}$$

Class 2:

$$G_{(i,j)\_\text{region}=5\times5}\,|_{\delta=60} \in [6,17] \tag{18}$$
$$G_{(i,j)\_\text{region}=5\times5}\,|_{\delta=60} \neq 15 \tag{19}$$
$$\text{mean}_{(i,j)\_\text{region}=5\times5} \in [120,170] \tag{20}$$
$$\text{std}_{(i,j)\_\text{region}=5\times5} \geq 3 \tag{21}$$

Class 3:

$$G_{(i,j)\_\text{region}=5\times5}\,|_{\delta=15} \geq 20 \tag{22}$$
$$\text{mean}_{(i,j)\_\text{region}=5\times5} \in [0,129] \tag{23}$$
$$\text{std}_{(i,j)\_\text{region}=5\times5} \in [0,2) \tag{24}$$

Class 4:

$$\text{mean}_{(i,j)\_\text{region}=9\times9} > 218 \tag{25}$$
$$\text{std}_{(i,j)\_\text{region}=9\times9} < 1 \tag{26}$$

Triggering condition set 2: Agents with a larger sensing region:

Class 1:

$$G_{(i,j)\_\text{region}=9\times9}\,|_{\delta=67} > 77 \tag{27}$$
$$G_{(i,j)\_\text{region}=9\times9}\,|_{\delta=20} < 70 \tag{28}$$
$$\text{mean}_{(i,j)\_\text{region}=9\times9} \in [181,245] \tag{29}$$
$$\text{std}_{(i,j)\_\text{region}=9\times9} \in [2,5] \tag{30}$$

Class 2:

$$G_{(i,j)\_\text{region}=11\times11}\,|_{\delta=83} < 99 \tag{31}$$
$$G_{(i,j)\_\text{region}=11\times11}\,|_{\delta=107} < 110 \tag{32}$$
$$\text{mean}_{(i,j)\_\text{region}=13\times13} \in [140,220] \tag{33}$$
$$\text{std}_{(i,j)\_\text{region}=13\times13} \geq 3 \tag{34}$$

Class 3:

$$G_{(i,j)\_\text{region}=5\times5}\,|_{\delta=15} \geq 20 \tag{35}$$
$$\text{mean}_{(i,j)\_\text{region}=5\times5} \in [0,129] \tag{36}$$
$$\text{std}_{(i,j)\_\text{region}=5\times5} \in [0,2) \tag{37}$$

Class 4:

$$\text{mean}_{(i,j)\_\text{region}=9\times 9} > 218 \tag{38}$$

$$\text{std}_{(i,j)\_\text{region}=9\times 9} < 1 \tag{39}$$

In both experiments, an initial group of around 300 agents from each class was randomly distributed in the two-dimensional grid lattice. The number of offspring that could be reproduced by a parent agent was set to 8.

3.3. Experimental Results

What follows presents the experimental results obtained under the aforementioned two experimental conditions.

3.3.1. Agents with a small sensing region

Figure 4 gives several snapshots of the active agents as well as the agent markers during the course of distributed segmentation. In the figure, the marker regions are shown as the simultaneously enlarging darker regions, whereas the active agents may be identified from the small dots in the image and/or the layers of the region boundaries.

From the beginning of execution until the ages of the first batch of agents reached their life-span, marker regions grew considerably fast, as many of the diffusing active agents found the locations of certain homogeneous regions, and at the same time also generated new active agents as a result of continuous self-reproduction. Hence the largest number of active agents would be found at the time when the first batch of the agents vanished. From Fig. 4, it can be readily noted that a significant number of active first-class agents were diffusing within the small font text region. This has been confirmed from the recorded population changes of individual agent classes as shown in Fig. 5(a).

The active agents generated during the initial period played an important role in region growing. As shown in Fig. 5(b), large proportions of the markers for the different regions were in fact generated during this period (e.g. $t = 0 \sim 12$). In the following period (e.g. $t = 13 \sim 25$), the remaining locations of the homogeneous regions were found by some of those active agents, while others that were unsuccessful had started to vanish.

Figure 6 shows a representation of the segmented regions for the given document image, which was obtained at time 70 when all the populations of agents and markers were stabilized. Four types of regions were marked; namely, the heading texts, the small font text lines, the graphical illustration region, and the large background region. Note that several white regions were left out that corresponded to the small space in between the text lines and the graphical components. The smaller white dots could further be removed if so desired.

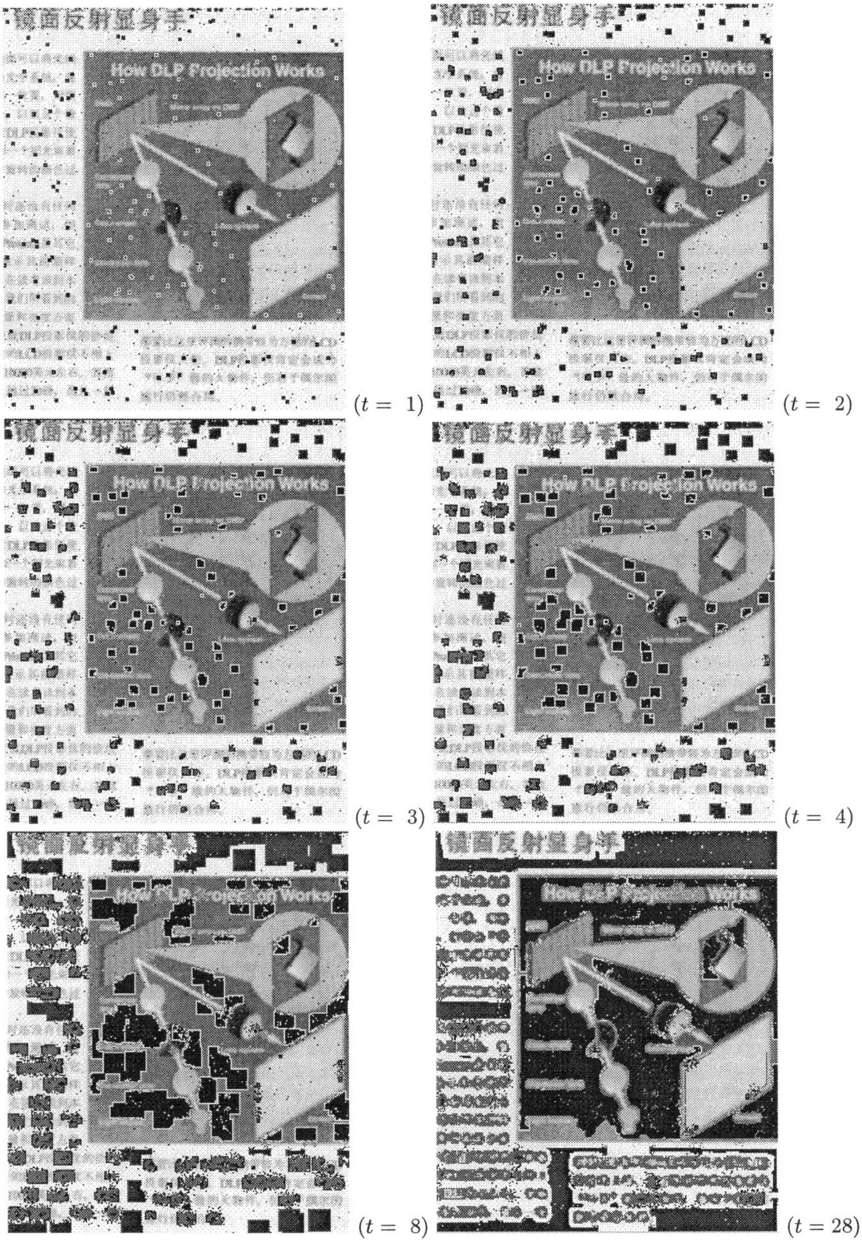

Fig. 4. The extraction of regions from the originally given image based on the proposed four classes of agents. Note that the triggering condition for the behaviors of an agent is computed from its 8-connected neighbors of a 5×5 region. The snapshots show the evolution of the agent population as well as their markers over the two-dimensional lattice at time 1, 2, 3, 4, 8, and 28, respectively.

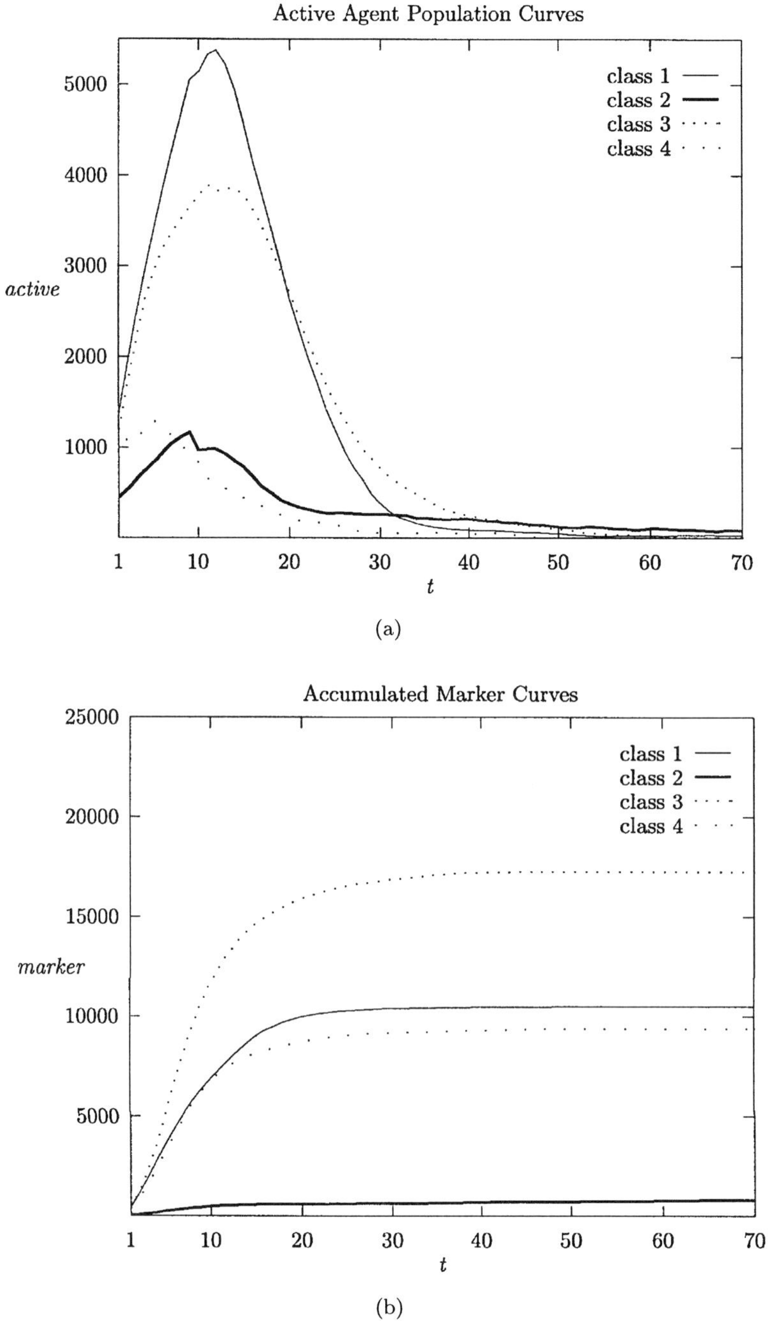

Fig. 5. (a) The population changes of active small-sensing-region agents in the two-dimensional lattice over the entire period of evolution. (b) The homogeneous region markers as generated by the small-sensing-region agents over the entire period of evolution.

Fig. 6. The final segmentation result based on agents with a small sensing region.

3.3.2. Agents with a larger sensing region

This experiment was aimed to show the effect of enlarging the agent sensing region on the segmentation performance. For the sake of comparison, Figs. 7–9 provide a series of agent snapshots, agent population curves, marker curves, and final segmentation result, respectively.

Since in this case the behavioral triggering conditions were computed from within a larger neighboring region, adjacent locations in the given image were more likely to satisfy homogeneity criteria. Therefore, homogeneous region markers grow relatively faster than the preceding case, as shown in Fig. 7 (when $t = 4, 10, 20$), and are also better connected, as shown in Fig. 9. For the same reason, the active agents would require fewer diffusion steps in order to locate a certain homogeneous region. This is particularly apparent in the case of the first-class agents for handling less connected texts, where the active agents readily marked a larger homogeneous region for the small font texts without much searching. Hence, if we compare the population curve of the first-class agents in Fig. 8(a) with the one in Fig. 5(a), we can immediately notice that the number of diffusing agents (i.e. accumulated active agents during the initial period) is relatively smaller.

From Fig. 8(b), we also note that the number of homogeneous region markers as generated by the first-class agents became stabilized at about time 20, while the overall steady segmentation was achieved at time 40 — the final result at time 40 is given in Fig. 9.

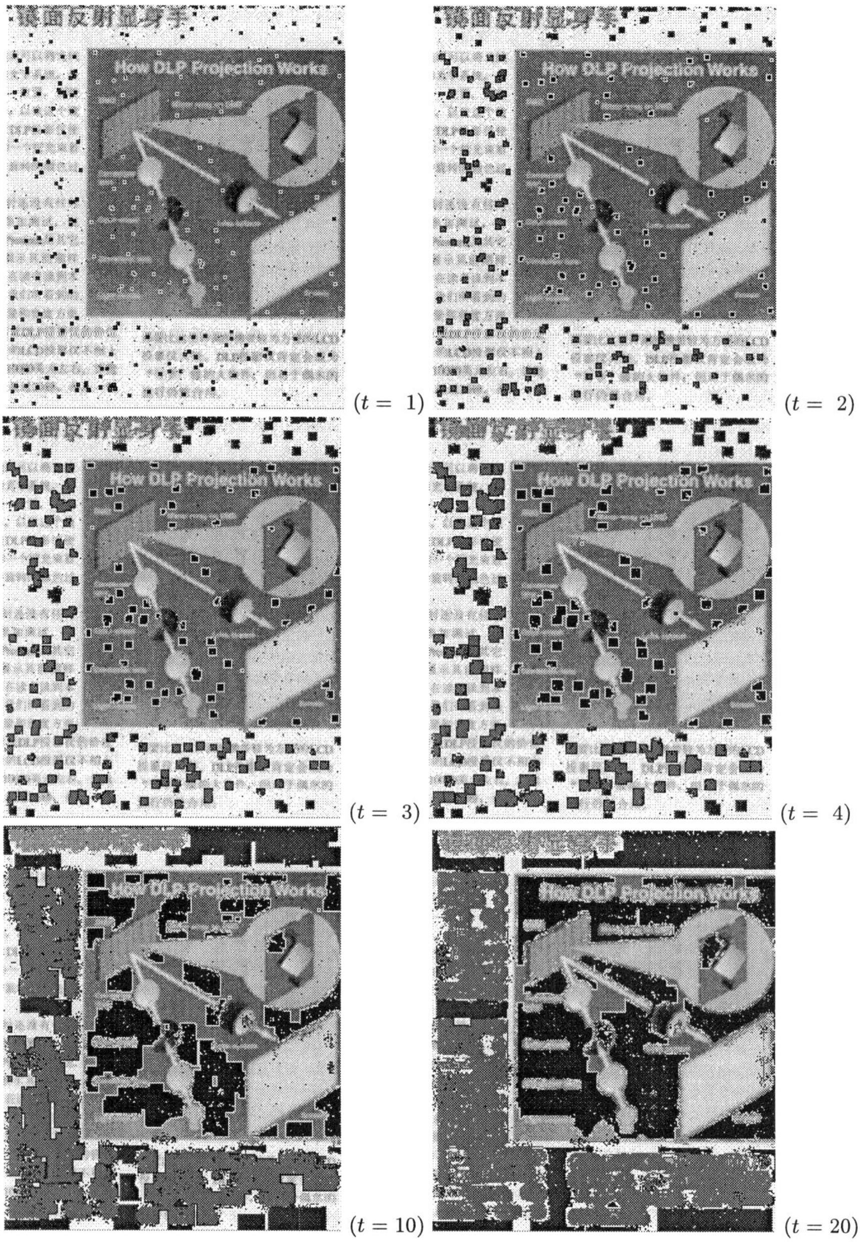

Fig. 7. The extraction of regions from the originally given image based on the proposed agents. Note that the triggering condition for the behaviors of an agent is computed from its 8-connected neighbors of a 9×9 or 11×11 region. The snapshots show the evolution of the agent population as well as their markers over the two-dimensional lattice at time 1, 2, 3, 4, 10, and 20, respectively. After time 20, the majority of markers had been generated.

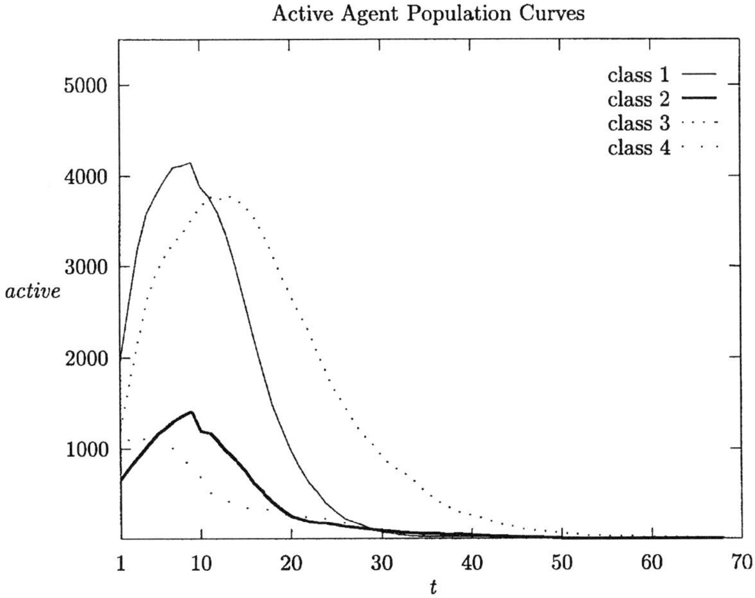

(a)

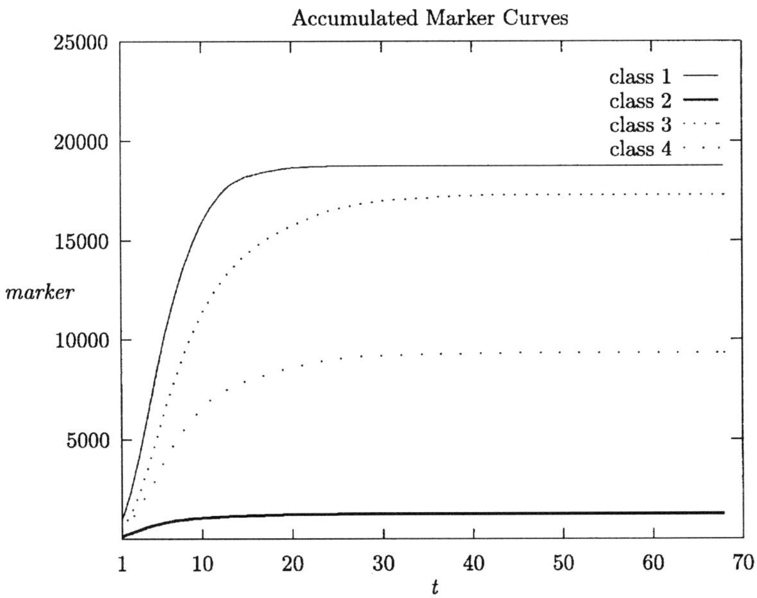

(b)

Fig. 8. (a) The population changes of active larger-sensing-region agents in the two-dimensional lattice over the entire period of evolution. (b) The homogeneous region markers as generated by the larger-sensing-region agents over the entire period of evolution.

Fig. 9. The final segmentation result based on agents with a relatively larger sensing region.

4. DISCUSSIONS

In this section, we provide several general remarks about the performance of the proposed agents approach, based on the earlier descriptions of the agents model and its experimental validation.

4.1. The Characteristics of Agents

In addition to the earlier-mentioned validation example, we have also tested the agents-based document segmentation approach with a number of real-life images that contain different types of regions, namely, (a) texture-like regions, (b) small and localized regions, (c) large complex-shaped regions, (d) regions of varying homogeneity, and (e) connected narrow regions. From the experimental results that we have obtained, we can readily note the following characteristics of agents:

1. At any time, the active agents sense and react to only a small number of pixel locations, and use these locations as seed samples to decide whether or not a certain region contains a homogeneous segment to be searched for.
2. If the region is found not to contain a homogeneous segment, the agents will no longer visit it again after the current active agents abort their searching. In other words, the agents that seek to find one particular segment tend not to visit other types of homogeneous segments.

3. The population of the agents that seek to find a certain homogeneous segment tends to grow exponentially in the regions that contain such a segment.

4.2. A Comparison with Conventional Segmentation Approaches

In conventional region growing approach, image regions are found by gradually growing a seed region from one pixel to another. Since this approach heavily depends on the connectivity of the regions, it could be slowed down in dealing with complex-shaped or less connected regions. In our present approach, we allow a successful agent to self-reproduce and then distribute its offspring within a local region. Hence, the region growing will not be limited to a one-to-one "propagation", but instead, it embarks on a one-to-many exponential growth. It is because of such a distribution that the efficiency of segmentation is not affected by the local connectivity of the segment region.

Another commonly-used segmentation approach is split-and-merge, in which image regions/subregions are continuously divided and evaluated, and adjacent homogeneous regions are simultaneously merged. One major difference between this approach and ours lies in that the former repeatedly performs the homogeneity testing over the subdivided regions and therefore one local region can be checked several times. Furthermore, the resulting merged segments would largely depend on the way in which the splitting operation is performed and how the homogeneity criterion is defined, hence it could be very coarse to represent complex segments, whereas in our approach both segment variations and the locality of the individual segments are well respected. In the split-and-merge approach, since only one homogeneity criterion is defined for the operations, it is sometimes quite difficult to fine-tune (i.e. to trade-off) the parameters in order to separate the segments while eliminating false segmentation due to image noises.

In addition to the above, another important feature of the proposed approach consists in that input document images can be analyzed in a distributed way, which is quite natural for parallel implementation and processing. In the case of parallel processing, the time complexity and efficiency of the proposed approach may be measured in terms of the number of steps required for the agents to concurrently extract all the homogeneous regions, as may be observed from Figs. 5(b) and 8(b).

4.3. Relation to Previous Work

Generally speaking, distributed agents as a model for computation is a newly-explored area of research that studies the emergent behaviors in a lattice of finite automata in which autonomous agents react locally according to a set of behavioral rules.[4,10–14] Shanahan[23] investigated a class of evolutionary automata in which a population of agents evolves in a microworld of square grid locations. The characteristics of Shanahan's evolutionary automata consist in that a sequence of states in the microworld can be non-deterministically generated by repeatedly executing four local procedures. Tamayo and Hartman[24] applied computational agents to model reaction-diffusion systems from which interesting space-time patterns reminiscent of chemical turbulence, solitons and self-excited oscillations can be constructed and observed.

The self-reproduction and diffusion scheme of the proposed agents may also be viewed as analogous to one of the operations commonly used in Genetic Algorithm,[7,15] namely, *mutation*. From the point of view of evolutionary computation, our approach utilizes certain sensitive locations as a selection screening constraint; agents that have high fitness are selected while those that have low fitness gradually disperse and vanish in space and time due to decay.

5. CONCLUSION

In this paper, we described a novel approach to Chinese document image segmentation that drew upon distributed autonomous agents. We experimentally examined the evolution of agents in digital image environments. As shown in our experimental validation, when the internal behavioral parameters, such as λ values, were tuned to particular values, interesting phenotype of the agents can readily be observed which corresponded to the locations of various segments in the images. In particular, the proposed approach is capable of exhibiting several important features; namely, adaptability to image locality, ability to segment the image with different homogeneity criteria, and the reliability to find the homogeneous text/graphical blocks. At the same time, the behaviors of agents are easy to represent and straightforward to implement. One of the immediate extensions as well as improvements based on our present work would be to investigate the possibility of automatic mechanisms for agents to gradually evolve optimal behavioral parameters such as the number of offspring and life-span. This may be viewed as the meta-evolution of the agents. Other future work would consist of in-depth, quantitative comparisons with some existing approaches and a detailed time-complexity analysis for the proposed distributed approach.

ACKNOWLEDGEMENT

This work has been supported by a Hong Kong Baptist University Faculty Research Grant.

REFERENCES

1. L. Abele, F. Wahl and W. Scheri, "Procedures for an automatic segmentation of text graphic and halftone regions in document", *Proc. 2nd Scandinavian Conf. Image Analysis*, 1981, pp. 177–182.
2. R. G. Casey, D. R. Ferguson, K. M. Mohiuddin and E. Walach, "An intelligent forms processing system", *Mach. Vision Appl.* **5**, 3 (1992) 143–155.
3. G. Ciardiello, M. T. Degrandi, M. P. Poccotelli, G. Scafuro and M. R. Spada, "An experimental system for office document handling and text recognition", *Proc. 9th Int. Conf. Pattern Recognition*, 1988, pp. 739–743.
4. F. Dellaert and R. D. Beer, "Toward an evolvable model of development for autonomous agent synthesis", *Artificial Life IV: Proc. 4th Int. Workshop on the Synthesis and Simulation of Living Systems*, eds. R. A. Brooks and P. Maes, The MIT Press, Cambridge, MA, 1994, pp. 246–257.

5. F. Esposito, D. Malerba, G. Semeraro, E. Annese and G. Scafuro, "An experimental page layout recognition system for office document automatic classification: an integrated approach for inductive generalization", *Proc. 10th Int. Conf. Pattern Recognition*, 1990, pp. 557-562.
6. Y. Hirayama, "A block segmentation method for document images with complicated column structures", *Proc. 2nd Int. Conf. Document Analysis and Recognition*, Oct. 20–22, 1993, Tsukuba Science City, Japan, pp. 91–94.
7. J. Holland, *Adaptation in Natural and Artificial Systems*, Univ. Michigan Press, 1975.
8. N. Hagita, I. Masuda, T. Akiyama, T. Takahashi and S. Naito, "Approach to smart document reader system", *Proc. CVPR'85*, 1985, pp. 550–557.
9. E. G. Johnston, "Short note: printed text discrimination", *Comput. Graphics Imag. Process.* **3**, 1 (1974) 83–89.
10. C. G. Langton, "Self-reproduction in cellular automata", *Physica* **D10** (1984) 135–144.
11. C. G. Langton, "Studying artificial life with cellular automata", *Physica* **D22** (1986) 120–140.
12. C. G. Langton, "Artificial life", in *Artificial Life: Proc. Interdisciplinary Workshop on the Synthesis and Simulation of Living Systems*, Los Alamos, New Mexico, Addison-Wesley, Redwood City, CA, 1988, pp. 1–47.
13. M. W. Lugowski, "Computational metabolism: Towards biological geometries for computing", in *Artificial Life: Proc. Interdisciplinary Workshop on the Synthesis and Simulation of Living Systems*, Los Alamos, New Mexico, Addison-Wesley, 1988, Redwood City, CA, pp. 341–368.
14. P. Maes, "Modeling adaptive autonomous agents", *Artificial Life* **1** (1994) 1–2.
15. H. Muhlenbein, "How genetic algorithms really work: I. mutation and hillclimbing", *Parallel Problem Solving from Nature 2*, eds. R. Manner and B. Manderick, North Holland, 1992.
16. G. Nagy, "A preliminary investigation of techniques for the automated reading of unformatted text", *Commun. ACM* **11**, 7 (1968) 480–487.
17. G. Nagy, "Towards a structured-document-image utility", *Proc. SSPR90*, 1990, pp. 293–309.
18. Y. Nakano, H. Fujisawa, O. Kunisaki, K. Okada and T. Hananoi, "A document understanding system incorporating with character recognition", *Proc. 8th Int. Conf. Pattern Recognition*, 1986, pp. 801–803.
19. M. Okamoto and M. Takahashi, "A hybrid page segmentation method", *Proc. 2nd Int. Conf. Document Analysis and Recognition*, Tsukuba Science City, Japan, Oct. 20–22, 1993, pp. 743–748.
20. D. K. Panjwani and G. Healey, "Markov random field models for unsupervised segmentation of textured color images", *IEEE Trans. Patt. Anal. Mach. Intell.* **17**, 10 (1995) 939–954.
21. T. Pavlidis, *Algorithm for Graphics and Image Processing*, Computer Science Press, Maryland, 1982.
22. I. Pitas, *Digital Image Processing Algorithms*, Prentice Hall, New York, 1993.
23. M. Shanahan, "Evolutionary automata", *Artificial Life IV: Proc. 4th Int. Workshop on the Synthesis and Simulation of Living Systems*, eds. R. A. Brooks and P. Maes, The MIT Press, Cambridge, MA, 1994, pp. 387–393.
24. P. Tamayo and H. Hartman, "Cellular automata, reaction-diffusion systems and the origin of life", *Artificial Life: Proc. Interdisciplinary Workshop on the Synthesis and Simulation of Living Systems*, Los Alamos, New Mexico, Redwood City, CA, Addison-Wesley, 1988, pp. 105–124.
25. J. Toyoda, Y. Noguchi and Y. Nishimura, "Study of extracting Japanese newspaper article", *Proc. 6th Int. Conf. Pattern Recognition,* 1982, pp. 1113–1115.

26. S. Tsujimoto and H. Asada, "Understanding multi-articled documents", *Proc. 10th Int. Conf. Pattern Recognition*, 1990, pp. 551–556.
27. K. Y. Wong, R. G. Casey and F. M. Wahl, "Document analysis system", *IBM J. Res. Develop.* **26**, 6 (1982) 647–656.
28. X. Wu, "Image coding by adaptive tree-structured segmentation", *IEEE Trans. Inf. Theory* **38**, 6 (1992) 1755–1767.
29. C. L. Yu, Y. Y. Tang and C. Y. Suen, "Document architecture language (DAL) approach to document processing", *Proc. 2nd Int. Conf. Document Analysis and Recognition*, Tsukuba Science City, Japan, Oct. 20–22, 1993, pp. 103–106.

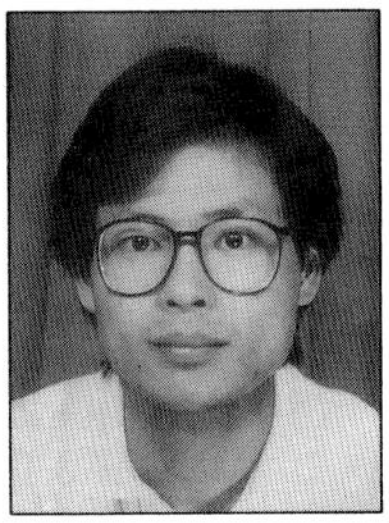

Jiming Liu received the M.A. degree in educational technology from Concordia University, Montreal, Canada, and the M.Eng. and Ph.D. degrees both in electrical engineering from Centre for Intelligent Machines (CIM) at McGill University, Montreal, Canada.

Dr. Liu worked for several years at Canadian R. & D. firms and government labs, prior to joining HKBU in 1993. Dr. Liu is currently an Associate Professor of computer science at Hong Kong Baptist University (HKBU). The primary themes of Dr. Liu's research work are in the areas of autonomous agents and systems, machine learning, and robotics.

Dr. Liu is a member of IEEE Computer Society, and IEEE Robotics and Automation Society, and ACM.

Y. Y. Tang received the B.S. degree in electrical and computer engineering from Chongqing University, Chongqing, China, the M.Eng. degree in electrical engineering from the Graduate School of Post and Telecommunications, Beijing, China, and the Ph.D. degree in computer science from Concordia University, Montreal, Canada. He is presently an Associate Professor in Department of Computing Studies at Hong Kong Baptist University, and Senior Researcher in the Centre for Pattern Recognition and Machine Intelligence, Concordia University. He is a Honorary Lecturer at the University of Hong Kong, an Advisory Professor at Beijing University of Posts and Telecommunications, Chongqing University and Shengyang Institute of Aeronautical Engineering, China. His current interests include wavelet theory and applications, pattern recognition, image processing, document processing, artificial intelligence, parallel processing, Chinese computing and VLSI architecture.

Dr. Tang has published more than 130 technical papers and is the author/co-author of 9 books on subjects ranging from electrical engineering to computer science. He also serves as a reviewer for many journals and international conferences. He is a Senior Member of IEEE.

INK MATCHING OF CURSIVE CHINESE HANDWRITTEN ANNOTATIONS

DANIEL P. LOPRESTI and MATTHEW Y. MA*

Panasonic Information and Networking Technologies Laboratory
Panasonic Technologies, Inc., 2 Research Way, Princeton, NJ 08540, USA

PATRICK S. P. WANG

College of Computer Science
Northeastern University, Boston, MA 02115, USA

JILL D. CRISMAN

Department of Electrical and Computer Engineering
Northeastern University, Boston, MA 02115, USA

In this paper, we discuss the notion of treating electronic ink as first class data without attempting to recognize it by presenting two different variations of approximate ink matching (AIM) for searching ink data. We also illustrate a pen-based electronic document annotating and browsing system and methods for searching handdrawn personal notes employing the described matching schemes. Adapting from the *Learning by Knowledge* paradigm, we propose a semantic matching network that applies semantics of Chinese language early in the process of ink matching. Finally we evaluate several key components in our entire ink matching network via experiments. Preliminary experimental results show the approximate ink matching algorithms perform well, despite the informal and highly variable nature of Chinese handwriting. Our experiments also show some promising results on semantic matching and the feasibility of our semantic matching architecture.

Keywords: Approximate ink matching, semantic matching, electronic ink matching, Chinese handwritten annotations, radical extraction.

1. INTRODUCTION

In Chinese office automation systems, the input of Chinese characters into the computer is a bottleneck. It has been reported that efficient input methods for Chinese characters were proposed and utilized,[19] and more than 100 Chinese characters per minute can be input using a keyboard. However, these input methods are mostly for trained typists; they are too complicated for an ordinary person to learn.

With the advancement of computer technology and input devices such as the stylus, the next generation of pen computers and PDA's has a lot of potential. Handwriting recognition, however, has proved to be a more difficult problem than most people first anticipated. The use of stylus in a pen computing system brings many advantages, it need not be limited to the input for handwriting recognition as this is a very difficult task especially when there is a wide variation in the way people write. Nakagawa *et al.*[14] presented the concept of lazy recognition which is the notion that constantly presenting recognition results to the user (often with errors that the user is forced to correct) interferes with the creative process

*Corresponding author. E-mail: mma@research.panasonic.com

Advances in Oriental Document Analysis and Recognition Techniques (1998) 119–141

of writing. Even if HWX accuracy were 100%, it might still bother the user to replace his/her handwriting with text as it is recognized.

Along these lines, it is possible to do handwriting recognition completely in the background (without showing the results to the user) and then use this for retrieval. However, one potential problem with this approach is that the user receives no immediate feedback, and the handwriting recognition might be doing a very bad job and the user will not realize this until he/she tries to do retrieval.

Instead of handwriting recognition, some research has been done on electronic ink matching, including Lopresti and Tomkins's earlier work.[8] Similar research can also be found in the work of Poon *et al.*[16] and Reynolds *et al.*,[17] but no applications were identified. Manmatha *et al.* has done some work in handwriting matching,[10] but mainly on scanned (off-line) images instead of electronic (on-line) ink. Pavlidis *et al.*[15] has used shape metamorphosis to recognize on-line handwritten patterns, but this is limited to singly connected shapes.

Our work on electronic ink matching is based on the notion of treating electronic ink as "first class" data. The idea is to take electronic ink as a temporal sequence of pen strokes — without attempting to recognize it. Efficient search algorithms based on approximate string matching are then used for matching the query ink sequence with the previously stored ink sequences in a database. This idea was later extended to searching lengthy handwritten notes for keywords ("word spotting").

In this paper, we explore the application of these ideas to searching Chinese handwritten annotations in a pen-based document browser. Then, we describe the approximate ink matching (AIM) algorithm that is being used in the application. Using such an approach, some of the difficult tasks encountered in handwriting recognition such as low accuracy rates due to the variation in writing styles can be avoided.

While our AIM algorithm matches handwriting based on strokes without trying to recognize it, a human, on the other hand, might take a different approach. As illustrated in Fig. 1, when a human tries to match two pieces of handwriting, he/she first tries to identify semantics i.e. radicals in the Chinese language, then match these semantics. Radicals are small structural parts that form a character. They are basic elements of semantics in Chinese, and they usually have their own meanings.

Based on this concept, we extended our ink matching algorithm to be able to identify radicals in the Chinese language contained in handwriting. These extracted radicals will then be used to "classify" the entries in the annotation database. When a query is entered by the user, only items with relevant radicals in the database will be searched, thus speeding up the existing ink matching by reducing the size of the problem. By identifying the radicals in handdrawn Chinese annotations, we can also convert ink into a sequence of computer codes that represent basic elements of Chinese language — radicals. This process does not involve a large vocabulary and hence is far less complicated than traditional HWX, but can be suitable for our application of matching ink annotations. This matching scheme is called *semantic matching*.

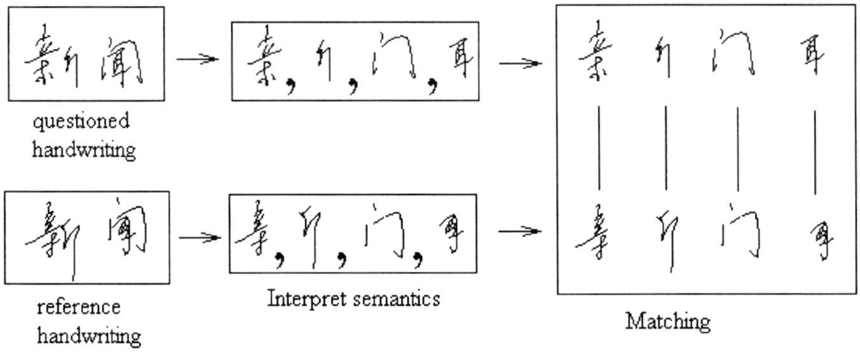

Fig. 1. Use of semantics when matching two pieces of handwriting in Chinese.

Semantic matching employs the same concept of extracting radicals used by most handwriting recognition techniques, but it is not doing handwriting recognition. Semantic matching is an encouraging idea in improving existing ink matching for Chinese handwriting, especially cursive handdrawn annotations. It is also a good example of *Learning by Knowledge* paradigm[23] in processing Chinese handwriting, in which accumulated knowledge is being iteratively used.

The remainder of this paper is organized as follows. In Sec. 2, we provide an overview of the Chinese ink annotation application. Section 3 describes in detail our approximate ink matching (AIM) algorithm. Section 4 describes our ongoing research in semantic matching and illustrates some interesting results. Section 5 discusses a systematic procedure for evaluating the performance of ink matching. Finally, in Sec. 6, we give our conclusions.

2. OVERVIEW OF THE INK ANNOTATION SYSTEM

Annotation is a useful and important operation for handling documents. A quick survey of the desk of an average office worker will turn up many pieces of paper that contain handwritten notes, items that have been circled to indicate their importance, text that has been "edited" by crossing it out, etc. Clearly, any system that attempts to duplicate the familiarity of paper-based document handling must include provisions for user-entered annotations. Most importantly, these annotations should be searchable.

Unfortunately, the search options provided in current document management systems are mostly text-based. Usually text-based descriptions of the documents are either extracted from the scanned documents using document image analysis and OCR techniques, or entered manually by the user using a keyboard. Such search techniques cannot be used for handdrawn annotations created by non-text based input devices, such as a pen.

The text-based search technique itself also has some limitations in real applications. For example, developing similar systems for Chinese-based documents proves to be a challenge. Unlike most western languages, Chinese does not have a fixed alphabet set. Instead, it has a much larger character set than ASCII. Consequently, entering Chinese characters into a computer is a time-consuming task since no simple keyboard is available. Also, the large character set makes Chinese character recognition, either printed or handwritten, more difficult than, say, English OCR.

In this section, we describe an ink annotation tool that is advantageous over a keyboard in a document system. This is particularly important for a Chinese document system which, on a Chinese keyboard, is hard to implement. Our goal is to provide simplicity and ease of use when the users write, so that even someone with little computer background should feel as comfortable using our software as writing annotations on paper documents.

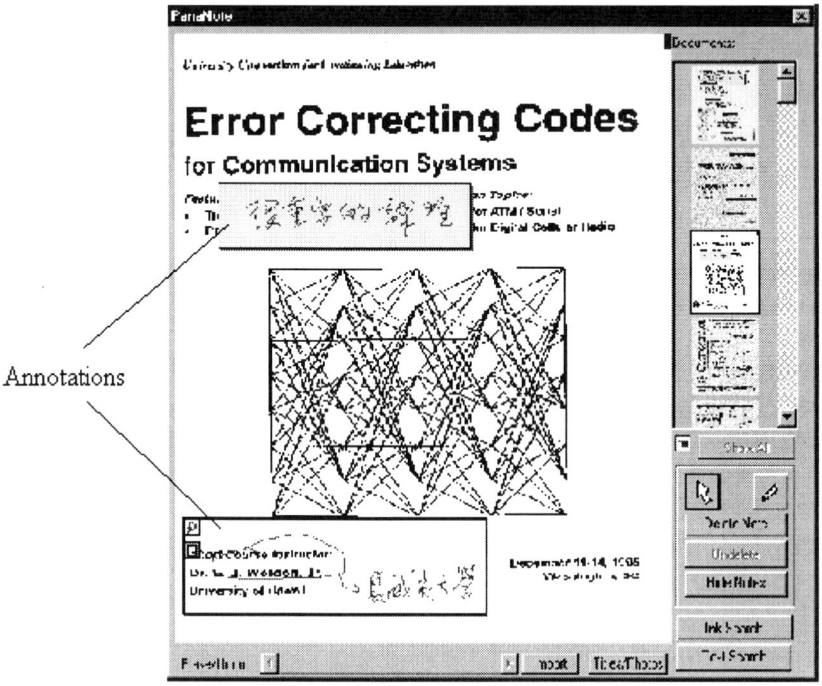

Fig. 2. Annotations are written directly on a document.

As illustrated in Fig. 2, scanned documents can be browsed and annotations can be written directly on a document. Once the annotation is written, it can be highlighted, moved, hidden, deleted or changed to a "stick-on" note with a yellow background. Multiple annotations can exist on the same document page, each having its own mode: hidden or displayed to the user. Ink editing capability is also integrated in the annotation control panel.

The annotation software also provides a search tool which allows users to write a query and search for a previously written annotation. The search algorithm (AIM) we use is based on the assumption that people write differently, but they normally write in a consistent way. As illustrated in Fig. 3, four users were asked to write

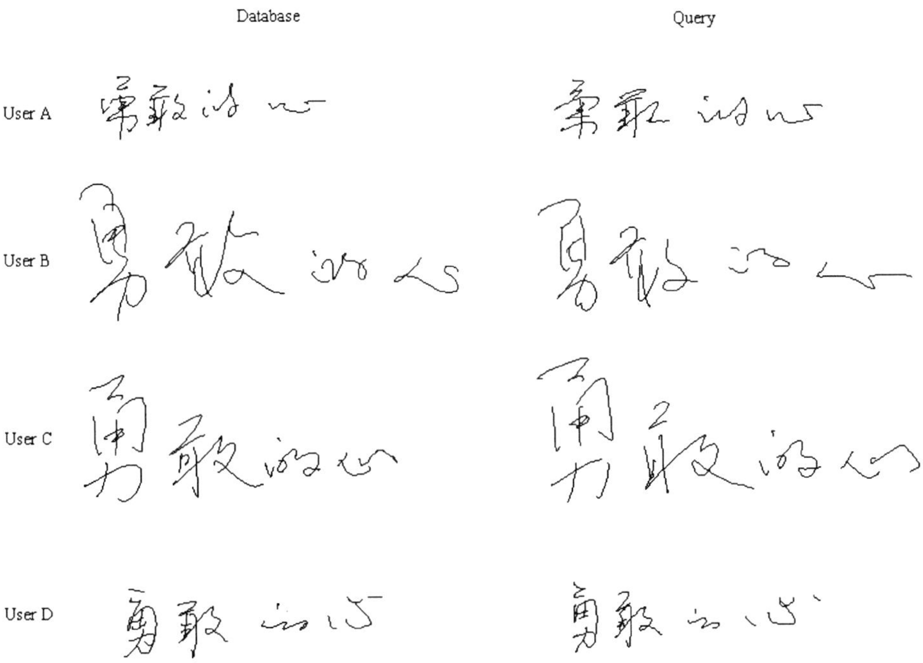

Fig. 3. Handwriting is highly personal. It does, however, exhibit significant self-consistency.

the same annotation twice, at different times. By looking at one column, we can see that four people write differently; looking at each row, we can see that each user writes consistently.

AIM uses a fuzzy search technique. Unlike exact match, AIM never rejects a search query. It always gives results by sorting them, so the best match is shown first and the worst is shown last. A user interface (as shown in Fig. 4) is provided to let users go through each annotation in the order of rank. Therefore, if the best match is not the anticipated match, users can still see the rest of the top hits immediately so they can quickly decide which one is exactly what they want. Clicking on the selected annotation will display the associated document (i.e. the document that the annotation is written on) to the user.

As seen in Fig. 4, an ink query for "important" in Chinese yields matches on "important news", "very important", "a very important course", "important meeting", etc. This is called word spotting. The word spotting capability in AIM allows subsequence matching — a shorter query to be matched to a region contained in a longer database entry. Again, this capability is not just limited to languages, it can also be used to match graphical annotations. Figure 5 illustrates the word spotting concept. The word spotting in AIM has the benefit of retrieving not only the desired annotation itself, but also related annotations.

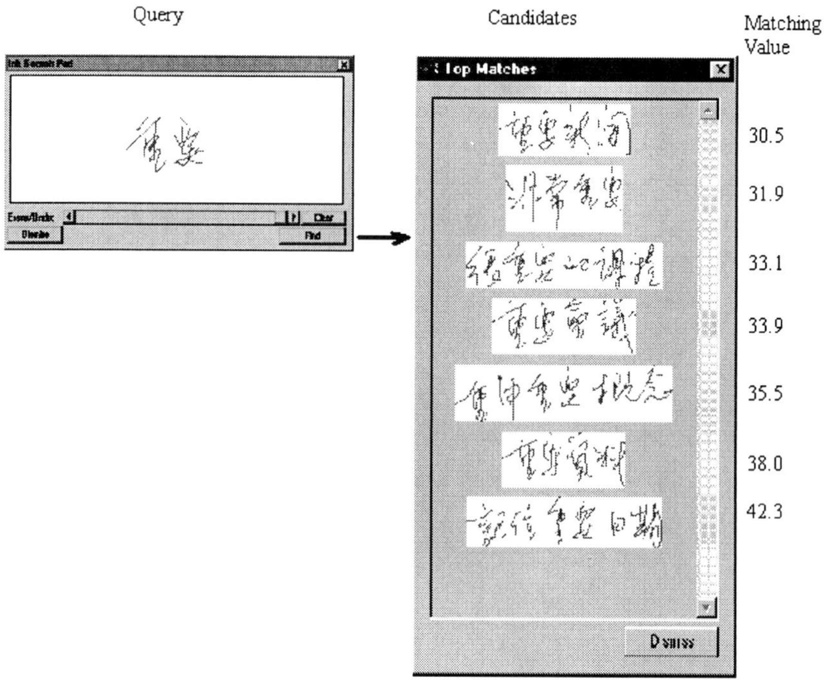

Fig. 4. A ranked list of top matches is returned to the user.

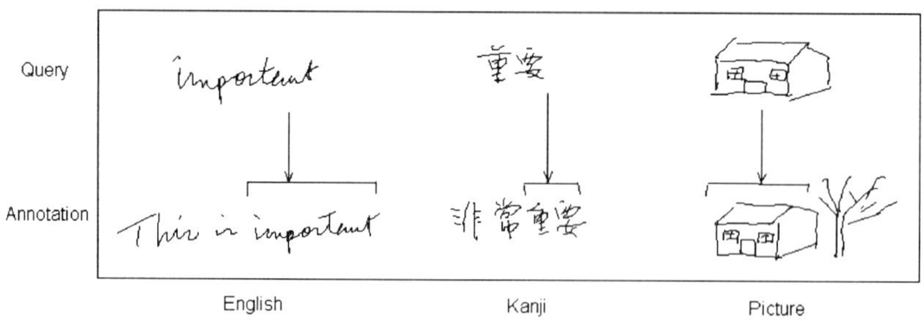

Fig. 5. "Word" spotting (subsequence matching).

3. APPROXIMATE INK MATCHING

The approximate ink matching algorithm (AIM) that was used in the above described ink annotation system was developed to perform matching at the pen-stroke level. This approach has the advantage of allowing the user to do well against a broad range of handwriting, including some so poor that it is effectively illegible. The same algorithm can be used in both English and Chinese, irregardless of source language. The algorithm applies dynamic programming with a recurrence similar to that used for string edit distance, but with a different set of operations and

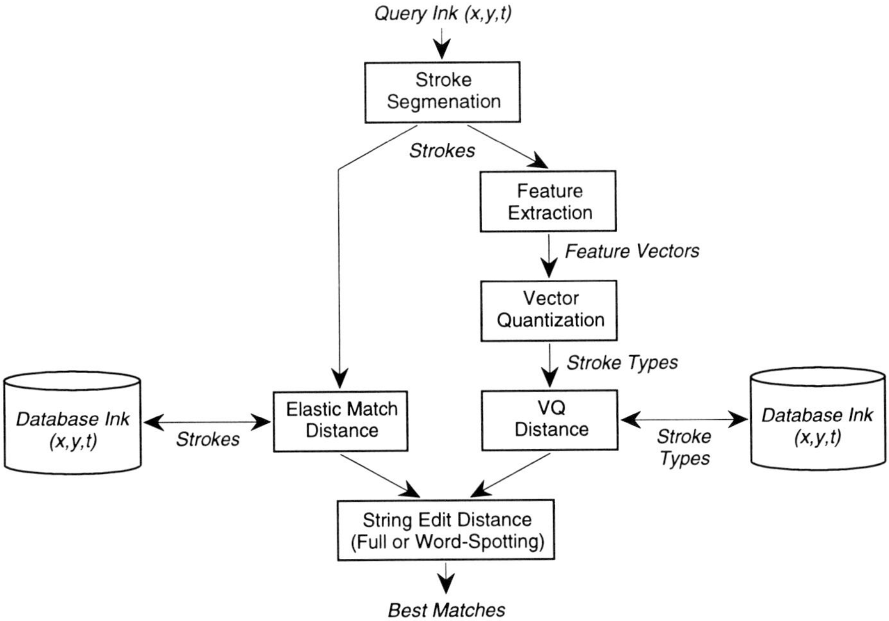

Fig. 6. Overview of the ink search algorithm.

costs. The top-level organization of the ink search algorithm is shown in Fig. 6. The details of the algorithm will be described in the following.

3.1. Stroke Segmentation

Ink consists of a sequence of points representing the movement of the stylus when the user is writing. First, the incoming points are grouped into strokes. Currently we break each stylus movement from "pen-down" to "pen-up" at local minima of the y values and segment into strokes.

3.2. Elastic Distance/VQ Distance

There are two variations of the algorithm as shown in Fig. 6. One is elastic matching which is based directly on segmented strokes. The elastic matching works directly with raw ink stroke thus does not need training. The other is VQ matching which extracts 13 features used by Rubine in the context of gesture recognition[18] from each stroke and forms a 13-dimensional feature vector, then classifies the feature vectors into one of 64 different stroke types. From then on, the ink sequences are represented as strings of stroke types. This particular feature set seems to do well at discriminating single strokes and can be updated efficiently as new points arrive. The VQ codebook was computed from a small sample of handwriting and the same VQ codebook can be used for all users. The details of the vector quantization on strokes were described in our earlier work.[7,8] The cost functions for the edit distance, which will be described later, are then calculated based on the segmented strokes (elastic) or classified stroke types (VQ).

3.3. Edit Distance

In the last phase, we compute the edit distance between the stroke sequence associated with the query ink and the pre-computed sequence for the reference ink. Let $S = s_1 s_2 \ldots s_m$ and $T = t_1 t_2 \ldots t_n$ be the two strings (in our case ink sequences) where s_i and t_i represent strokes, and let $d(S,T)$ be the minimum cost of any sequence of basic operations that transforms S into T. Determining $d(S,T)$ can be implemented by a dynamic programming recurrence:

$$d_{i,j} = \min \begin{cases} d_{i-1,j} & + c_{\text{del}}(s_i) \\ d_{i,j-1} & + c_{\text{ins}}(t_j) \\ d_{i-1,j-1} & + c_{\text{sub}}(s_i, t_j) \end{cases} \qquad 1 \le i \le m,\ 1 \le j \le n \qquad (1)$$

where $d_{i,j}$ is the distance between the first i symbols of stroke sequence S and the first j symbols of stroke sequence T. Note that $d(S,T) = d_{m,n}$. c_{del}, c_{ins}, and c_{sub} are costs associated with three basic operations as in the traditional case [22]: (1) delete a stroke; (2) insert a stroke; (3) substitute one stroke for another.

In our implementation, two operations, split and merge, were added in the VQ algorithm to account for imperfections in the stroke segmentation algorithm. We build a merge table that contains information of the form "an average stroke of type α merged with an average stroke of type β results in a stroke of type γ". Only two adjacent strokes are considered for merging. The costs for split/merge as well as the other system parameters are illustrated in Table 1. The scale parameters w's were from the training process based on the small sample set of handwriting in order to obtain normalized operation costs and optimal performance. However, as will be mentioned later in this paper, how to obtain these parameters that work best for Chinese handwriting is one of our future tasks.

Table 1. Cost parameters in approximate ink matching.

Parameters	Elastic	VQ
c_{del}	w_{del} * length of stroke, $w_{\text{del}} = 1$	w_{del} * length of stroke type, $w_{\text{del}} = 1.1$
c_{ins}	w_{ins} * length of stroke, $w_{\text{ins}} = 1$	w_{ins} * length of stroke type, $w_{\text{ins}} = 0.45$
c_{sub}	w_{sub} * Euclidean distance between two strokes, $w_{\text{sub}} = 1$	w_{sub} * Mahalanobis distance between two stroke types, $w_{\text{sub}} = 1$
c_{merge}	N/A	w_{merge} * length of merged stroke type, $w_{\text{merge}} = 2.2$
c_{split}	N/A	The cost of a split from stroke δ to strokes α and $\beta = w_{\text{split}} * \gamma$, where $\gamma =$ distance from δ to *merge*(α, β), $w_{\text{del}} =$ 1.1

Figure 7 shows a detailed trace of our matching on a stroke level using elastic ink matching. The upper writing is the query while the lower is the reference database item. Each stroke is represented by a bounding box. Strokes that are matched

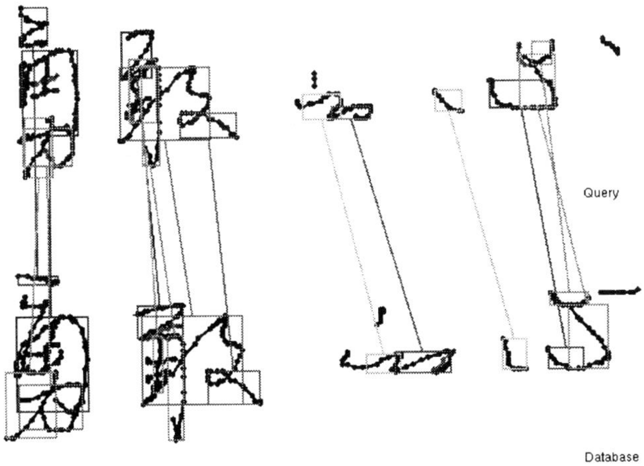

Fig. 7. Trace for the edit distance comparison between the query and the database item in question.

between the query and the database are connected by a line. From this figure we can see that every stroke in the query is matched to the correct one in the database.

Approximate ink matching works directly on the raw ink strokes, so it can be readily applied to the annotation system that we have described in Sec. 2. As will be described in the next section, approximate ink matching can also be combined with the semantics of Chinese language and thus construct a semantic matching scheme in order to improve the raw ink-based matching.

4. SEMANTIC MATCHING

Our work on electronic ink matching is focusing on the user-entered annotations in a document system. This task specially requires dealing with informal cursive handwriting. The structure and semantics of the Chinese language make it unique in dealing with the problems of matching. The semantics embedded in Chinese plays an important role in the human learning process. On the other hand, semantics should also be employed in the recognition of Chinese characters.

In this section, we discuss the concept of Chinese handwriting matching that uses semantics in a *Learning by Knowledge* paradigm. We illustrate that semantics can be used not only in character recognition or linguistic processing, but also in the early process such as segmentation. Our ongoing research on semantic matching consists of two areas: one is identifying radicals from handwriting and using this radical information to speed up the matching process; another is exploring the matching between handwriting and typed texts via radicals.

4.1. Semantic Matching Scheme

Learning by Knowledge is a new methodology presented by Wang,[23] in which old, existing knowledge can be accumulated and iteratively used to enforce and help learn new knowledge via a feedback system, as illustrated in Fig. 8. Wang has

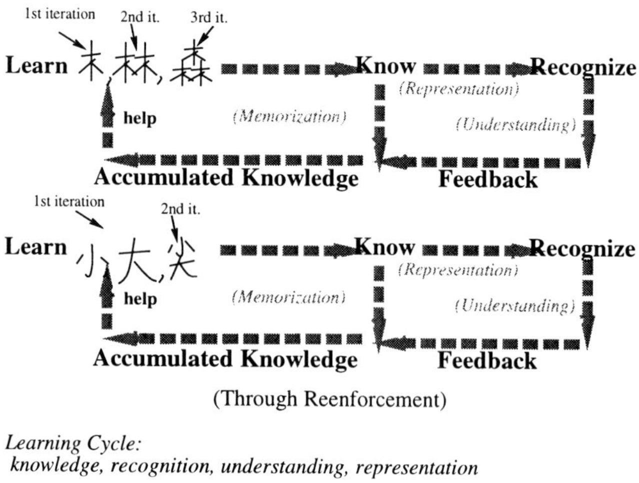

Fig. 8. Learning by knowledge in pattern recognition with examples.

shown that this methodology can be used in the understanding and recognition of Chinese characters via a semantic network.

We have applied semantics in the *Learning by Knowledge* diagram and constructed a semantic matching network as illustrated in Fig. 9. The main steps include pre-processing, character segmentation, radical extraction, classification and matching. As can be seen, our semantic knowledge base was obtained from a learning process (training) and can then be applied in the early processing stage. This would help eliminate unwanted candidates via classification, which in turn speeds up the recognition (matching) process. The knowledge learned from semantics may also convert handwriting to computer coded representation of radicals and thus make handwriting searchable by typed text query.

Our method of "learning by knowledge" and "semantic matching" adapted from Wang[23] has advantages over the others in the literature, for example, "learning by rote" according to Ausubel *et al.*,[1] where in a learning process, new information is being added to the process's learning structure without establishing any relationship with the concepts already existing in the knowledge of the learner. A slightly better way of learning was proposed later by Millward,[11] known as "meaningful learning" by which new information is roughly related to the relevant concepts already existing in the knowledge structure of the learner.

In the remainder of this section, several details of semantic matching will be described. Pre-processing and character segmentation were described in our previous work.[9] Similar work can also be found elsewhere.[13,20]

4.2. Radical Extraction

Radicals in the Chinese language are small structural parts that form a character. A radical can be a character itself, or can only go with another radical in a character. The extraction of radicals from segmented characters is a non-trivial task. Almost

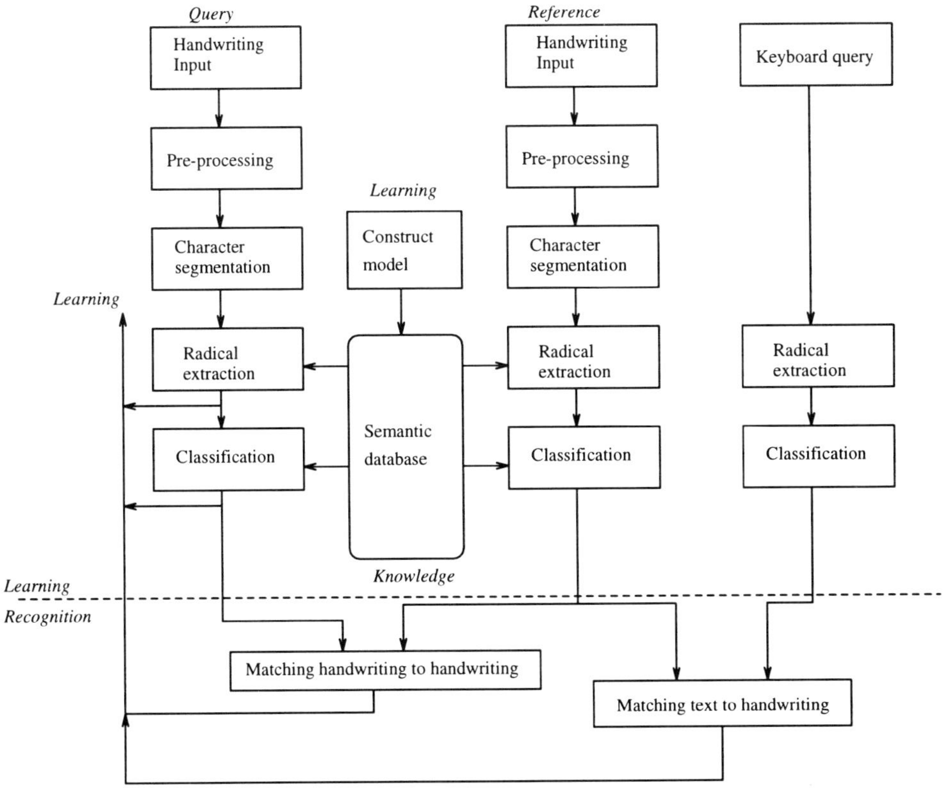

Fig. 9. Diagram of semantic matching.

any Chinese handwriting recognition system has to deal with the extraction of radicals or similar information. Some systems[3,4,6,12,25–27] extract feature stroke segments and then form them into radicals. This method would most likely fail on informal cursive Chinese handwriting since there are so many variations of writing feature strokes in cursive Chinese. Some OCR systems extract radicals based on the one assumption that there exist gaps between radicals. This again can not apply to free-format Chinese handwriting. Radicals are often connected together within a character for cursive handwriting and thus makes the extraction difficult.

On the other hand, temporal order of strokes are often preserved in on-line handwriting. Almost every Chinese character embeds a particular order of strokes for writing. This order is taught when a child learns how to write. As personal writing styles change, this temporal order may change. But one person normally writes in a consistent way, he/she writes in the same order every time he/she writes the same character. This applies to radicals as well.

The semantic database (also called radical database) consists of a set of basic radicals, which are generated through a training process. The number of samples that need to be collected for training is small since the number of basic radicals in Chinese is very small (200 or so) in comparison to the large number of Chinese characters (3000 or so) that are commonly used.

The same elastic matching algorithm (implemented with word spotting) combined with layout detection is used to extract radicals. Word spotting is used to match a radical to a character that contains this radical. However, because radicals contain much fewer strokes than a character or an annotation, this makes the elastic matching less reliable than working on the entire annotation. The layout detection of radicals is based on the fact that a particular radical can only reside at a known location within a character. For instance, Cheng and Hsu[2] classified radicals into seven layouts. We divide the bounding box of each character into $3 \times 3 = 9$ equal size regions and calculate the number of stroke points each region contains. As shown in Fig. 10, the number of stroke points in each region form a sequence of 9 numbers. This is called *radical layout profile.*

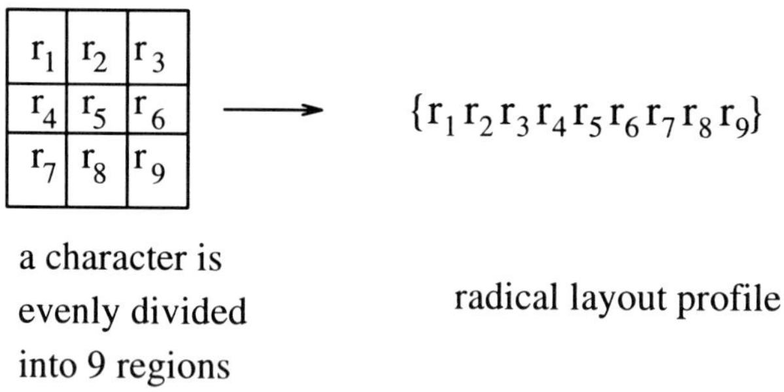

Fig. 10. The definition of radical layout profile.

When the semantic database is generated, the layout profile for each radical can be pre-computed. In the implementation, every input character is matched partially with the limited number of radicals in the semantic database. The returned list of top ranked radicals are then traced back to the original input character in order to compute the layout profile for the radical candidate. The similarity between this newly computed layout profile and the pre-computed profile for the extracting radical is then calculated. Let $P_R = r_1r_2r_3r_4r_5r_6r_7r_8r_9$ be the normalized layout profile (by its maximum value) for a radical in the semantic database, and $P_T = t_1t_2t_3t_4t_5t_6t_7t_8t_9$ be the normalized profile for the traced radical stroke. The similarity measure is defined as:

$$S = c(P_R, P_T) - d(P_R, P_T),$$

whereas $c(P_R, P_T)$ is the correlation expressed as:

$$c(P_R, P_T) = \sum_{i=1}^{9} r_i t_i.$$

and $d(P_R, P_T)$ is the distance which adds a penalty to the overall similarity measure.

It is defined as:

$$d(P_R, P_T) = \sum_{i=1}^{9} (r_i - t_i)^2.$$

The similarity values are used to fine tune the order of top ranked extracted radicals. That the distance is greater than the correlation yields a negative similarity, and this value will be eliminated in sorting the ranks. Since the number of radicals in the semantic database is limited, the matching time on a fast computer will be small. Figure 11 illustrates an example of radical layout profile and its similarity to the profile for the radical model.

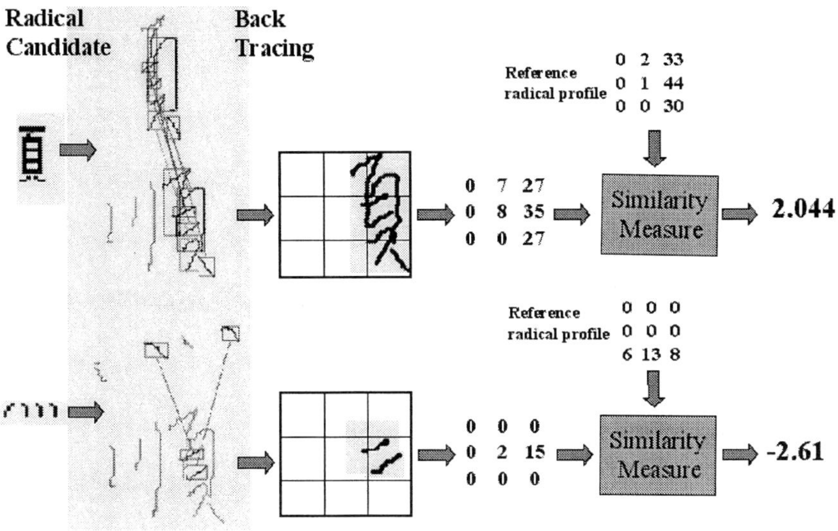

Fig. 11. An example of radical detection, radical layout profile and similarity measure.

As shown in Fig. 11, when radicals in the semantic database are matched against a questioned character by computing the minimum distance, the elastic matching with word spotting tries to find the best location that the radical fits into within the character. This location can be traced back in the ink matching algorithm in order to compute the radical layout profile. With the similarity measure, correctly located radicals yield a higher value than those that are not.

4.3. Classification

We use the results from the radical extraction to obtain the most likely candidates and thus reduce the range of searching. First, each character is represented by its extracted radical number: X or NULL if there are no known radicals contained in the character, or X_1, X_2 if two radicals are extracted. Each handwritten annotation is then represented by a sequence of radical numbers. An example is illustrated in Fig. 12, which is excerpted from the famous poem by the famous Chinese poet

Li Po. (This famous poem has been used as the book cover of *Document Image Analysis* edited by Bunke *et al.*)

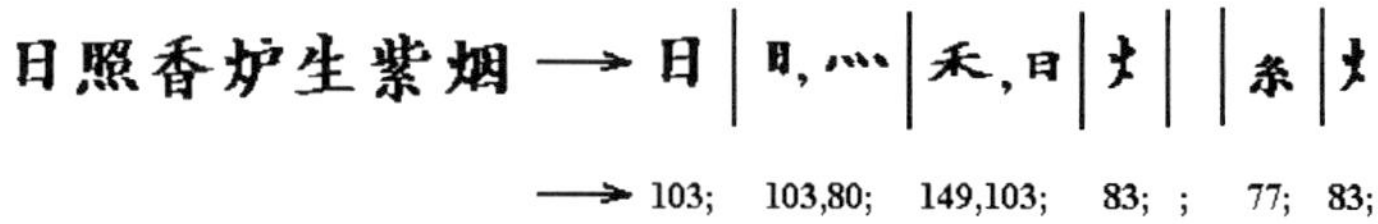

Fig. 12. Radical representation of annotations.

The size of the reference data can be reduced via a classification procedure in order to identify the most likely candidates. Each reference annotation is coded with a sequence of radical numbers by using radical extraction. When each query comes into the system, it is also converted into a radical code sequence via the radical extraction. Edit distances are then computed on the sequence of radical codes between the query and each item in the reference database using dynamic programming. The items in the reference database with the least distances can be selected as the most likely candidates. The time for computing edit distance is significantly less than that required for matching ink strokes (1 : 40) since the selection of the most likely candidates is working on the sequence of the extracted radical codes — a significant reduction of information from raw ink strokes. The number of most likely candidates to be selected is a system parameter, it will be discussed more in Sec. 5.

Similar to the dynamic programming procedure in AIM, we have three basic operations in computing edit distances for radical codes: insertion, deletion and substitution. Instead of working on strokes, we now work on characters. Currently, the cost of insertion and deletion is assigned to be a constant. The cost of substitution is determined by the number of occurrences that a radical code in one character does not exist in the other. For instance, if the two characters to be substituted are encoded as: $c_1 = 1, 3$ and $c_2 = 3, 17$, then the substitution cost is 2. If $c_1 = 1, 3$ and $c_2 = 14, 17$, then the substitution cost is 4. As can be seen, currently all the radicals are of equal weight in computing the cost.

4.4. Matching

To make the matching more reliable, each annotation in the most likely candidate list will be matched against the query annotation using the same approximate ink matching as described earlier in this paper, and a top match list is generated. As illustrated in Fig. 9, the matching could be applied to both ink versus ink query and ink versus typed text query, although the feasibility of matching typed text is still under exploration.

5. EXPERIMENTAL EVALUATIONS

An experimental procedure was developed to systematically evaluate the components of the semantic matching network. The entire semantic matching scheme is still under construction since it is comparatively new. However, the experimental results that will be described in this section show encouraging results.

In our experimental procedure, several issues have to be addressed and the performance (feasibility) has to be evaluated. They are:

- Approximate ink matching — AIM can be used stand-alone in our ink annotation application. It is also a core technique that is used by the radical extraction.
- Radical extraction — The key component in the semantic matching network.
- Classification — The classification for selecting most likely candidates has to allow false/missed radical extraction.

5.1. Data Collection

For our experiments, we collected 200 Chinese annotations — movie titles that are translated into Chinese. A graphical user interface (shown in Fig. 13) was built to make the collection of handwriting easier. The content of the entry is displayed to prompt the user to write with a stylus in the white rectangular area. Clicking the "Next" button will automatically save the annotation and prompt the user for the next entry.

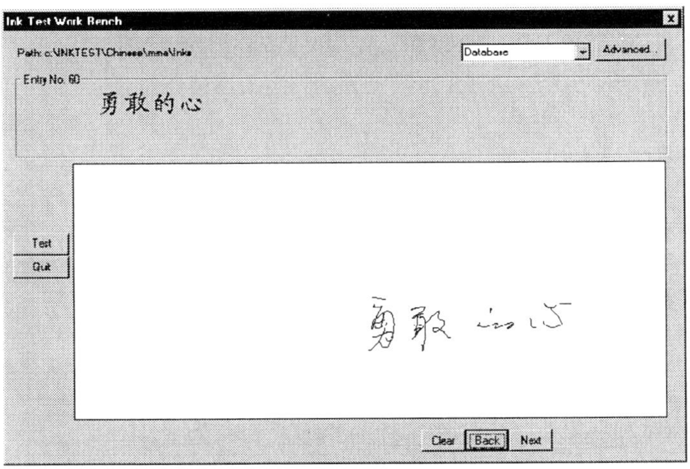

Fig. 13. An ink collection tool.

Four candidates were asked to write 200 Chinese annotations twice. They first wrote 200 annotations and these data were stored as a reference ink database. Then they wrote the same 200 annotations again after a period of time, these data were stored as ink queries.

5.2. Evaluation of Approximate Ink Matching

In our experiment, we allow each of the ink queries to match against all 200 annotations in the reference ink database. Since the contents of these two sets of data are known, we would know in advance what results we should expect. Each matching will yield a list of 200 values, each representing the distance between one item in the reference ink database and the query. These distances are then sorted out and a rank number is given to each item.

When it comes to evaluating the retrieval performance of AIM, as for any IR system, visualization can also play an important role in improving the system interactive recall/precision as stated by Veerasamy *et al.*[21] The top match list as shown in Fig. 4 in our ink annotation system effectively displays the relevance judgement to the user without any burden on the processing time. In evaluating AIM performance, we will observe how the retrieval rate changes with the number of top matches returned.

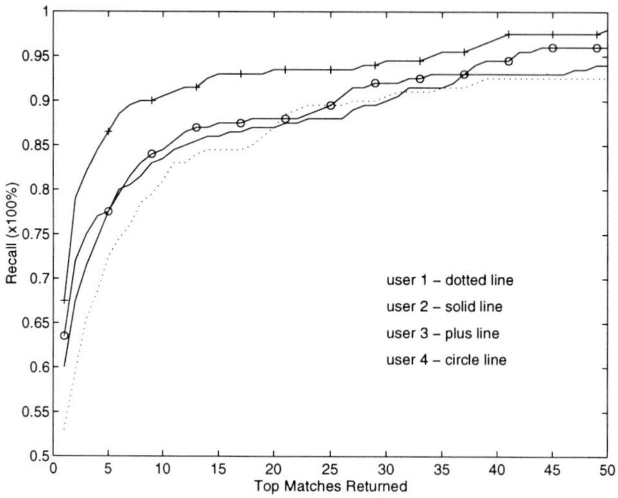

Fig. 14. VQ matching: Recall versus number of top matches returned for four users (represented by solid, "+" and "o" and "*" lines, respectively).

We have experimented with both the VQ ink matching algorithm and elastic ink matching algorithm on the four data sets that we collected. Figures 14 and 15 show the recall for each individual writer using the VQ and elastic ink matching versions, respectively. The entire charts show recall as a function of the number of top matches returned. Although our experiments are run on a small test database, it is a promising result that for VQ ink matching algorithm, about 62% recall can be achieved at the first hit. This number will be 80% if the top 5 matches are viewed, which accounts for only 2.5% of the entire database. The VQ ink matching runs at about 2 seconds per query on a DEC Alpha workstation for our database. The performance is improved significantly in the elastic algorithm. About 92% recall is achieved at the first hit, this number will increase to 96% with the top 5 matches. The speed for the elastic ink matching is 160 seconds per query. As can be seen, the elastic ink matching algorithm is more reliable than the VQ algorithm, yet the computation time is high.

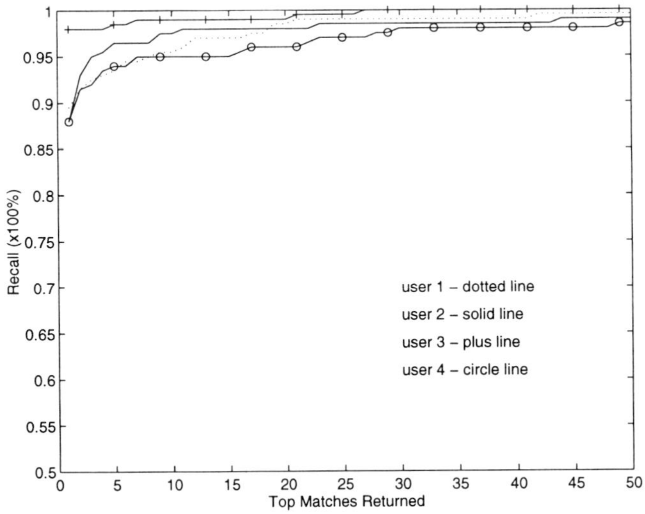

Fig. 15. Elastic matching: Recall versus number of top matches returned for four users (represented by solid, "+" and "o" and " * " lines, respectively).

5.3. Evaluation of Radical Extraction

The radical extraction algorithm uses word spotting elastic matching combined with layout detection. To evaluate this, the data was obtained from running on a small radical database which consists of the 45 most frequently used radicals as identified by Xiao and Dai.[24] The radical extraction then runs on each item in our pre-selected ink database (consisting of characters that contain these frequently used radicals) against each radical. The recalls for radical extraction with and without using layout detection are illustrated in Fig. 16. As can be seen, the performance of the radical extraction significantly improves once the radical layout is being used. Although we are still in the process of improving radical extraction and developing more robust and sophisticated algorithms, this result looks promising.

5.4. Evaluation of Classification

In classification, each character is converted to a radical representation or NULL if no known radicals are contained in the character. This is an information reduction at a rate of 3000 (characters) to nearly 200 (common radicals) or even less. An evaluation procedure was developed in order to test the feasibility of classification that relies on such information reduction.

In our experiment, we extracted the radicals manually from 200 annotations in our previously collected database (translated movie titles in Chinese) and constructed a sequence of radical codes for each item. In this encoding process, we used the nearly 200 radicals listed in the radical index table in the Chinese-English Dictionary[5] and 45 frequently used radicals identified by Xiao and Dai[24] respectively. Again, from 0 to 2 radical numbers are coded for each character. English

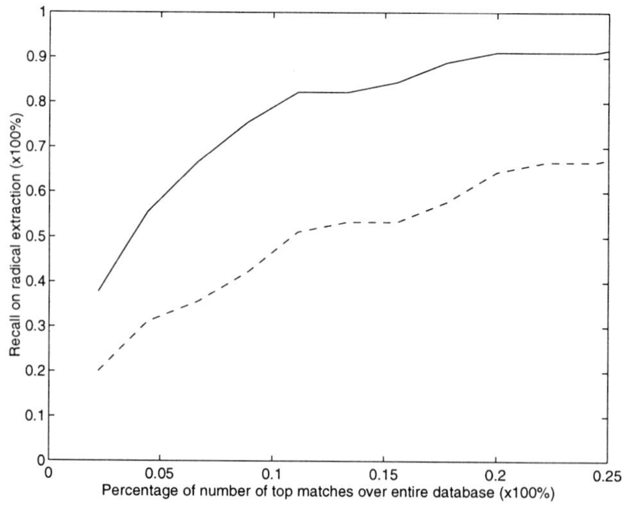

Fig. 16. Recall on radical extraction with (solid line) and without (dashed line) radical layout detection.

letters and punctuations are ignored and simply coded as NULL. These manually extracted radical sequences only simulate the ideal case when all radicals are extracted perfectly. However, as will be described later in this section, we have to allow for false or missed extraction of radicals.

In experiments, each radical coded annotation is compared with all other items in the entire database and a list of edit distances are computed using dynamic programming. By scanning each annotation at its edit distance, we obtain the number of hits at each distance from 0 to the maximum distance. Figure 17 shows the average number of hits a query can get within a specific distance from 0 to the maximum.

In Fig. 17, we can interpret the distance axis as the margin for the missing of radicals in the radical extraction. As the missed/incorrect radical rate increases, the distance increases, thus a higher number of hits occurs, which means there are greater number of most likely candidates within the database. The saving of computation time by classification depends on the number of most likely candidates that have to be selected for the subsequent ink matching. At a given edit distance, a lower value in the number of hits means more discrimination power for the classifier, thus the fewer number of most likely candidates are selected for subsequent ink matching which in turn yields better savings in computation time.

Furthermore, the time savings for computation time for semantic matching is upper-bounded by the horizontal line in Fig. 17.[a] The area below the line indicates a net savings. The encouraging findings from this experiment is that under the

[a]The timing is computed based on the fact that each query takes 160 seconds to match the entire database (200 titles), the radical extraction takes about 30 seconds for an average 5 character long annotation, and the classification time (computing edit distance for radical code sequences) is approximately 4 seconds per query.

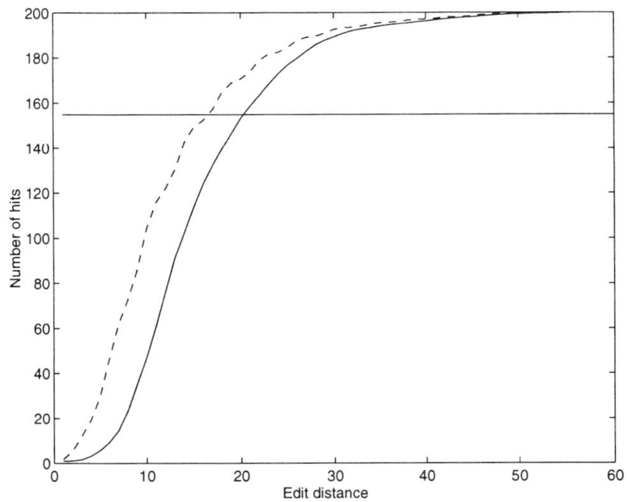

Fig. 17. Average number of hits per query versus distance. Solid line represents near 200 radical indice being used for encoding a character, dashed line represents 45 radical indice being used.

upper bound line, the classifier does have tolerance which allows for miss/incorrect radical extraction.

Also shown in Fig. 17 is that the overall performance gain from the semantic matching depends on the distance threshold, which in turn is determined by the performance of the radical extraction. When fewer radicals are used for character encoding (e.g. 45 suggested by Xiao and Dai[24]), the savings in computation time for the final ink matching is not as good as using 200 radicals. However, this makes the radical extraction less time consuming and more reliable. To obtain the optimal number of radicals, the selection of representative radicals and the distance threshold on the selection of the most likely candidates (classification) are all challenging tasks for the training process.

6. CONCLUSIONS

In this paper, we described ink matching techniques that can be used for Chinese annotation search in a document system. Our ink annotation system allows a user to write notes anywhere on a page, and then later search for them as an aid to information retrieval. We have also given some experimental results on running the ink matching algorithm on Chinese annotations. We also performed systematic evaluations on several key components of our current system which are still under development. The experimental results show that our basic approximate ink matching performs well on cursive Chinese handdrawn annotations with 92% recall for the first hit, and 96% recall for the top five matches returned. The experimental evaluations further show some promising results on the radical extraction and classification along our line of semantic matching.

However, we think there are several ways in which the techniques we have described can be improved. Although the current semantic matching network uses semantics of Chinese for matching cursive handdrawn annotations, the fundamental matching technique of our system — approximate ink matching (AIM) — was developed previously for a language independent environment. Therefore, a more complicated training procedure can be developed for the Chinese language and system parameters can be adapted to work better for Chinese handwriting. For instance, strokes are currently segmented at local minima of the y values. This is generally good for a system with mixed writing in Chinese and English. However, our informal test shows that the choice of segmentation algorithm may have a significant impact on Chinese and English ink matching.

Further improvement can be explored in the selection of features in the VQ version of the algorithm. The feature set we use is generally good for common gestures, it may not be the best one for Chinese. This seems likely since Chinese is stroke based, the angles of strokes are particularly important. Changing slightly the slope of a single stroke in a character can change the meaning of the word. Other system parameters such as the weights for VQ features, and the scaling factors for the basic costs in dynamic programming procedure may also be fine tuned through an empirical training process.

Finally, as stated in this paper, we are also doing further research on semantic matching. The extraction of radicals does not have to be perfect as illustrated in Sec. 4. However, the reliability of the radical extraction does affect the performance of the entire system. The number of radicals and the selection of radicals may be obtained from a training process as this is a component of *Learning by Knowledge.* Some radicals are more immune to noise, while others are not. The careful selection of the radicals to be used can increase the performance of radical extraction and thus the overall matching.

The ink matching scheme we proposed is more sophisticated than the conventional "syntactic" methods without the contextual information,[11,23] it requires more memory and a backtracking procedure. More work needs to be done in the future to overcome these difficulties. A larger dictionary (lexicon) and more intelligent inferencing and reasoning would also be helpful.

7. ACKNOWLEDGMENT

The authors of this paper would like to thank Andrew Tomkins for his early work of approximate ink matching and the staff at the Panasonic Information and Networking Technologies Laboratory for their generous help with the experimental evaluation.

REFERENCES

1. D. P. Ausubel, J. D. Novak, and H. Hanesian, *Educational Psychology: A Cognitive View*, 2nd ed., HRW, New York, 1978.
2. F. Cheng and W. Hsu, "Research on Chinese OCR in Taiwan", *Character and Handwriting Recognition*, ed. P. S. P. Wang, World Scientific, 1991, pp. 139–164.

3. S.-L. Chou and W.-H. Tsai, "Recognizing handwritten Chinese characters by stroke-segment matching using an iteration scheme", *Character and Handwriting Recognition*, ed. P. S. P. Wang, World Scientific, 1991, pp. 175–197.
4. D. Deng, K. P. Chan and Y. Yu, "Handwritten Chinese character recognition using spatial gabor filters and self-organizing feature maps", *Proc. ICIP*, vol. III, Austin, Texas, November 1994, pp. 940–944.
5. Department of English, Beijing Inst. Foreign Languages, *A Chinese-English Dictionary*, Beijing Business Publishing House, 1985.
6. J. Liu, W. K. Cham and M. M. Y. Chang, "Stroke order and stroke number free on-line Chinese character recognition using attributed relational graph matching", *Proc. 13th ICPR*, August 1996, pp. 259–263.
7. D. Lopresti, M. Ma and J. Zhou, "Approximate ink matching of Chinese handwritten annotations", *Proc. 17th Int. Conf. Computer Processing of Oriental Languages*, Hong Kong, April 1997, pp. 95–100.
8. D. Lopresti and A. Tomkins, "On the searchability of electronic ink", *Proc. 4th Int. Workshop on Frontiers in Handwriting Recognition*, 1994, pp. 156–165.
9. M. Ma, P. Wang, D. Lopresti and J. Crisman, "Semantic matching of free-format Chinese handwriting", *Proc. 17th Int. Conf. Computer Processing of Oriental Languages*, Hong Kong, April 1997, pp. 107–111.
10. R. Manmatha, C. Han, E. M. Riseman and W. B. Croft, "Indexing handwriting using word matching", *Proc. 1st ACM Int. Conf. Digital Libraries*, 1996, pp. 151–159.
11. R. B. Millward, "Models of concept formation", *Aptitude, Learning, and Instruction*, eds. R. E. Snow *et al.* L. Erlbaum Assoc. Hillsdale, NJ, 1980.
12. L. Mui, A. Agarwal, A. Gupta, and P. S. P. Wang, "An adaptive modular neural network with application to unconstrained character recognition", *Document Image Analysis*, eds. H. Bunke, P. S. P. Wang and Baird, World Scientific, 1994, pp. 193–208.
13. H. Murase, "On-line recognition system for free-format handwritten Japanese characters", *Character and Handwriting Recognition*, ed. P. S. P. Wang, World Scientific, 1991, pp. 207–220.
14. M. Nakagawa, K. Machii, N. Kato and T. Souya, "Lazy recognition as a principle of pen interfaces", *INTERCHI93 Adjunct Proc.*, 1993, pp. 89–90.
15. I. Pavlidis, R. Singh and N. P. Papanikolopoulos, "An on-line handwritten note recognition method using shape", *Proc. Int. Conf. Document Analysis and Recognition*, 1997, pp. 914–918.
16. A. Poon, K. Weber and T. Cass, "Scribbler: A tool for searching digital ink", *Companion Proc. CHI*, 1995, pp. 252–253.
17. D. Reynolds, D. Gupta and R. Hull, "Architectures for efficient scribble matching", *Proc. 4th Int. Workshop on Frontiers in Handwriting Recognition*, 1994, pp. 488–495.
18. D. Rubine, "Specifying gestures by example", *Comput. Graphics* **25**, 4 (1991) 329–337.
19. J.-W. Tai, "Some research achievements on Chinese character recognition in China", *Character and Handwriting Recognition*, ed. P. S. P. Wang, World Scientific, 1991, pp. 199–206.
20. C. C. Tappert, "Speed, accuracy, and flexibility trade-offs in on-line character recognition", *Character and Handwriting Recognition*, ed. P. S. P. Wang, World Scientific, 1991, pp. 79–96.
21. A. Veerasamy and R. Heikes, "Effectiveness of a graphical display of retrieval results", *Proc. 20th ACM SIGIR Conference on Research and Development in Information Retrieval*, 1997, pp. 236–245.
22. R. A. Wagner and M. J. Fischer, "The string-to-string correction problem", *J. Assoc. Comput. Machinery* **21**, 1 (1974) 168–173.

23. P. S. P. Wang, "Learning, representation, understanding and recognition of words — an intelligent approach", *Fundamentals in Handwriting Recognition*, ed. S. Impedovo, Springer-Verlag, 1994, pp. 81–112.
24. X.-H. Xiao and R.-W. Dai, "On-line handwritten Chinese characters recognition directed by components with dynamic templates", *Proc. 17th Int. Conf. Computer Processing of Oriental Languages*, Hong Kong, April 1997, pp. 89–94.
25. S. L. Xie and M. Suk, "On machine recognition of hand-printed Chinese characters by feature relaxation", *Patt. Recogn.* **21**, 1 (1988) 1–7.
26. K. Yamamoto and A. Rosenfeld, "Recognition of handprinted Kanji characters by relaxation method", *Proc. 6th ICPR*, Munich, 1982, pp. 395–398.
27. K. Yamamoto and H. Yamada, "Recognition of handprinted Chinese characters and Japanese cursive syllabary", *Proc. 7th ICPR*, Montreal, 1984, pp. 385–388.

Daniel Lopresti received his A.B. in mathematics from Dartmouth College in 1982, and his Ph.D. in computer science from Princeton University in 1987. From 1986 until 1991, he was an Assistant Professor in the Department of Computer Science at Brown University. He joined Panasonic Technologies in 1991, leading the Carbon Project there until 1997. Currently he is a Member of the Technical Staff at Bell Labs Research, Lucent Technologies.

His research interests include document analysis, information retrieval, and pen computing.

Matthew Y. Ma is currently a senior research engineer at Panasonic Information and Networking Technologies Laboratory at Panasonic Technologies, Inc. He is also a Ph.D candidate (expected Jan. 1998) at the Dept. of Electrical & Computer Engineering, Northeastern University. He received the M.S. in Electrical and Computer Engineering from State University of New York at Buffalo and the B.S. degree in Electronics Information from Tsinghua University, Beijing. Before he joined Panasonic in 1995, Mr. Ma worked as an engineer and senior research engineer at several research and industrial institutions including National Laboratory of Pattern Recognition at Chinese Academy of Sciences, Maryland Advanced Development Laboratory and NASA Goddard Space Flight Center.

His primary research interests include document image processing, pen-based processing and recognition techniques and human computer interaction in pen-computing.

Patrick S. P. Wang is an IAPR Fellow, tenured full professor of computer science at Northeastern University, research consultant at MIT Sloan School, and adjunct faculty of computer science at Harvard University Extension School. He received his Ph.D. in C.S. from OSU, M.S. in I.C.S. from Georgia Institute of Technology, M.S.E.E. from National Taiwan University and B.S.E.E. from National Chiao Tung University. He was on the faculty at University of Oregon and Boston University, and senior researcher at Southern Bell, GTE Labs and Wang Labs prior to his present position. Dr. Wang was elected Otto-Von-Guericke Distinguished Guest Professor of Magdeburg University of Germany, Fall 1996.

In addition to his research experience at MIT AI Lab, Prof. Wang has been visiting professor and invited to give lectures, do research and present papers in a number of countries in Europe, Asia and many universities and industries in the USA and Canada. Dr. Wang has published over 120 technical papers and 16 books in Pattern Recognition, A.I. and Imaging Technologies and has three OCR patents by US and Europe Patent Bureaus. As IEEE senior member, he has organized numerous international conferences and workshops and served as reviewer for many journals and NSF grant proposals.

Prof. Wang is currently founding Editor-in-Charge of Int. J. of Pattern Recognition and A.I., and Editor-in-Chief of Machine Perception & Artificial Intelligence by World Scientific Publishing Co. and elected chair of IAPR-SSPR (Int. Asso. of P.R.). In addition to his technical interests, Prof. Wang has also written many Chinese poems and articles on Verdi, Puccini, Bizet, and Wagner's operas, and Mozart, Beethoven, Schubert and Tchaikovsky's symphonies, and on Li Po and Tu Fu's poems.

Jill D. Crisman is an associate professor and director of Robotic and Vision System Laboratory at Dept. of Electrical & Computer Engineering, Northeastern University. She received her Ph.D. degree in Electrical and Computer Engineering from Carnegie Mellon University in 1990 and the MS and BS degrees in Electrical Engineering from the University of Pittsburgh. Her primary research interest is the integration of high-resolution perception and computer vision into the control of robotic systems.

Dr. Crisman is an elected member of the IEEE Robotics and Automation Society Administrative Committee. She serves as an Associate Editor of the IEEE Robotics and Automation Society Magazine and as an Editor for the IEEE PAMI Newsletter. She has served on the Technical Program Committees for various robotics and computer vision conferences and has served on proposal review panels for the National Science Foundation. She has been the Chair for the Boston Chapter of the IEEE Robotics and Automation Society since 1994.

ON-LINE HANDWRITTEN CHINESE CHARACTER RECOGNITION DIRECTED BY COMPONENTS WITH DYNAMIC TEMPLATES

XUHONG XIAO*

Intelligent Systems Lab., SAS, Nanyang Technological University
Nanyang Avenue, Singapore 639798
E-mail: xuhong@uranus.sas.ntu.ac.sg

RUWEI DAI

Institute of Automation, Chinese Academy of Sciences
P.O. Box 2728, Beijing 100080, China
E-mail: dai@ht.rol.cn.net

Structural matching has been recognized as a promising approach for on-line Chinese character recognition. In order to reduce its great computational complexity and improve its performance, people have been seeking for ways to direct the matching of a whole character by the result of partial matching. In this paper, the authors proposed 45 basic components for 3,755 categories of daily-used Chinese characters to direct the stroke segment matching of whole characters. Since they are always located at either the beginning or the end of the stroke segment string of characters, these components are easy to be extracted and separated from other parts of a character. Besides, in our approach, the reference templates of these components are extracted dynamically from the corresponding segment string of characters when a specific matching is carried out. This strategy avoids building multiple templates for the components of the same kind but at different places of characters. The experiments show that the segment matching computation has been reduced greatly without reducing the correctness of matching.

Keywords: On-line character recognition, structural matching, component directed, dynamic templates.

1. INTRODUCTION

With the development of compact computers and the recent advance of combining tablets and flat display, on-line handwritten Chinese character recognition spurs renewed interests as a real time recognition approach. Under the condition that the recognition performance of block style writing is almost good enough for practical application, people have turned to the recognition of free handwriting with stroke order deviations and stroke number variations. Although some existing systems claim to handle the problem of stroke connection well,[5] while some others solve the problem of stroke order deviation,[2] almost no system solves these two problems simultaneously. To build a robust recognition system for free handwritten Chinese characters, much is desired in these two aspects.

Looking back at the previous approaches for cursive on-line Chinese character recognition, it seems prevalent to recognize on-line characters by extracting its structural primitives, such as stroke segments, key points, etc. and compare them

*Corresponding author.

Advances in Oriental Document Analysis and Recognition Techniques (1998) 143–157

with known templates by structural matching algorithm. We argue that it will remain the predominant way for on-line character recognition. But it does not mean the existing strategy is perfect, on the contrary, there exist some well-recognized problems in this strategy. For example, first, structural matching approaches are often computationally complex, and the complexity increases greatly with the increase of the primitive numbers and the linkage of primitives in patterns. Secondly, when there are many primitives in two patterns under comparison, essential local differences of pattern structures are most likely neglected due to the global likeness of the patterns, resulting in the failure of the discrimination of similar characters. Thirdly, for the comparison of complex structures, such as those of some very complex Chinese characters, the alignment of the corresponding primitives is very time-consuming and difficult, especially when the patterns are greatly distorted, for example, when there are both stroke order deviations and stroke connections in the characters.

One promising way to solve the above problems is the structural analysis directed by partial component detection, which breaks down a Chinese character with complex structure into several components with more stable, simpler structures. Since these components are imperative for an *ad hoc* character, the recognition process of the character turns to detecting its components and the relations among these components, step by step. The advantage of this strategy is twofold. First, the scope of the alignment and comparison of primitives are narrowed down to simply the basic components from the global character structure, thus reduce the computational complexity. Secondly, the recognition accuracy increases accordingly for two reasons. One is that the local differences of characters become prominent in simple components. The second reason is that some confusing candidates are first ruled out after the detection of structurally stable basic components, therefore reducing the confusion of different character classes caused by stroke order deviation and stroke connection. Although there are thousands of Chinese characters with volatile handwriting forms, the number of basic components is very limited, and the internal relations of these components are simple and stable. So, it is hopeful to reduce the effects of writing variation on recognition results and to acquire a better recognition performance in this way, but how to exactly extract such components and how to induce matching by them remain unresolved.

In this paper, a new viewpoint of components is applied and a practical extraction strategy is proposed. The underlying basis of it is that there are some components in the Chinese characters that almost all people habitually write at the beginning or end of the writing of characters, and in relatively stable stroke order. For instance, when writing character "啊", people write component "口" before other parts, and when writing character "利", people always write component "刂" in the end. Therefore, the authors have used head and tail components selected with special care according to the result of experiments and *a priori* knowledge of Chinese handwriting to direct the structural matching, and have proposed the concept of dynamic template as well as the strategies for the extraction and matching of dynamic templates.

The overall recognition system is improved from our previous systems[7] and adopts a multi-stage model. At the first stage, the feature matching approach, which has been successfully used in off-line character recognition, is used to pre-classify characters and to provide several candidates for each input. At the second stage, the structural matching between the input and its candidates provided by the first stage is directed by the matching of chosen components. When a basic component has been detected in the input, only the classes containing the component are considered as possible candidates and are qualified for further structural matching. The rest in the candidate list are ruled out, so that the matching computation is greatly reduced, and the errors caused by stroke connection or stroke order variation is reduced to some extent. Because these chosen components always emerge at the beginning or end of a character, their detection is very easy. In the following sections, the system model, the building of the component templates and the matching strategy will be described in detail.

2. GENERAL CONSIDERATION

In order to make full use of static information of on-line handwritten characters, the authors once designed a recognition system which pre-classified an input character by statistical feature matching and further recognized it through structural matching of attributed stroke segment strings.[7] The pre-classification process provided several candidates for the input, while the structural matching process compared one by one the stroke segment string of the input with the templates of the candidates provided by pre-classification. The final recognition result was synthesized from the results of the previous two procedures. The second procedure, structural string matching, was a key part of the system. It mainly had the following three weaknesses: First, a Chinese character is usually composed of several strokes, local distortions of one stroke will probably affect attributes of other stroke segments and thus affect the matching result. The more stroke segments there are, the greater the influence is. Secondly, when there are too many stroke segments, local disparity will be obscure among similar structures, which consequently leads to the recognition error of structurally similar characters, such as “拔” and “拨”. Thirdly, segment by segment matching is very time-consuming, especially when the length of the string is long. If we can partition a character into several components and confine the matching process in each separated component, the computation will be greatly reduced, and because the structure of each component is relatively simple, the correct rate of matching will thus increase.

To direct the Chinese character structural matching by parts or components has long been a goal that researchers have been seeking for. At the end of 1980, Liu *et al.* proposed a heuristic compulsive matching approach directed by templates.[3] Let us give more details of Liu's approach to make our consideration more understandable.

In their approach, the stroke segment lists were arranged in different writing orders, such as top-down (td) order, left-right (lr) order, middle-right (mr) order, left-middle (lm) order etc., character roots (a kind of stable, fixed components) were extracted from these lists and compared with their templates respectively according to the structure of the character. For example, for character "落" in Fig. 1, its segment strings of left-right order and top-down order are as follows respectively:

$$lr = s_1 s_2 s_4 s_5 s_6 s_3 s_7 s_8 s_9 s_{10} s_{11} s_{12} s_{14} s_{13},$$

$$td = s_1 s_2 s_3 s_4 s_7 s_8 s_9 s_{10} s_5 s_6 s_{12} s_{11} s_{13} s_{14},$$

where s_j corresponds to the jth segment in Fig. 1.

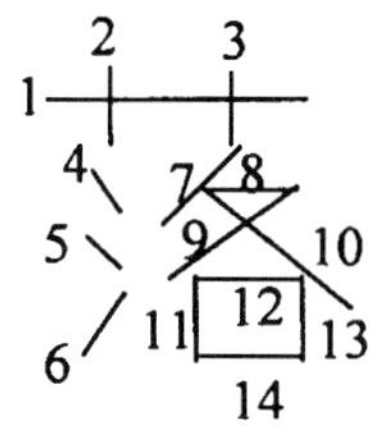

Fig. 1. Segments of character "落".

The grammar description of character "落" is: 艹 ma 氵 lr 夂 ud 口. When matching was carried out, stroke segment sublist "$s_1 s_2 s_3$"was first extracted from the top-down ordered list to match with the template of "艹" because the relation between "艹" and "洛" was top-down, and the segment sublist "$s_1 s_2 s_3$" was deleted from the whole segment lists after matching was successfully done. Thus, sublist "$s_4 s_5 s_6$" came to the head of the list of left-right order and was extracted to match with the template of "氵" since the relation between "氵" and "各" was left-right. This process iterated until all the components were detected. Obviously, it was very difficult to acquire stable stroke segment lists for each character, taking into account the distortion of handwriting. Besides, the accurate structural relationship of components consisting in characters was the prerequisite of Liu's approach. But no existing methods can be applied to extract such information accurately and automatically, nor is it practical to teach the computer such knowledge "hand by hand", considering the astronomical number of Chinese characters.

Another kind of component detection approaches[1] built one or more common templates for each component and searched components from the different positions of a character. The advantage of them is that little knowledge about character structure of a specific class is required. The main obstacle exists in that when a component locates at different positions of the different characters, the attributes of its primitives, such as size, or even topological relations, vary. Therefore, it is very difficult to depict a component with a unique template, multiple templates are usually necessary. A way to make automatic component detection easy and accurate must be found before component directing structural matching is conducted.

From intensive analysis, we find that there are some stable components or roots at the beginning or end of the writing (no matter who the writer is) of most Chinese characters, and they can be easily extracted from the whole writing due to their position particularity. With this in mind, 45 components, which have stable stroke order in different writing styles and are always located at the beginning or end of stroke segment lists, are proposed to direct the structural matching for 3,755 daily-used Chinese characters. The frame of the whole system is described in Fig. 2.

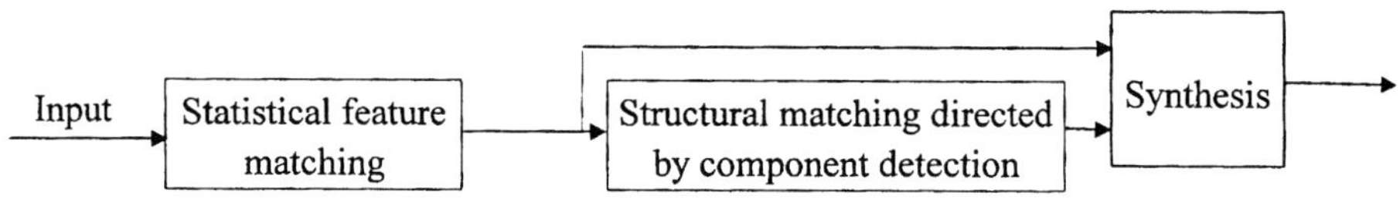

Fig. 2. Frame of the on-line Chinese character recognition system.

What is different from our previous system is the structural matching process. That is, the input is no longer compared with the templates of all candidates provided by the statistical feature matching, but are matched with part of them according to the result of component detection. The structural matching process first examines what kind of basic components are included in the candidates provided by the statistical feature matching, then dynamically extracts the templates of the components included by the candidates and detects them one by one from the input until a basic component is positively detected or all the possible components are traversed. If the input is detected to contain a certain basic component defined, further comparison with those candidates including the same component is carried out and their matching result is combined with the result of the statistical feature matching to get the final recognition result.

3. BUILDING OF DYNAMIC COMPONENT TEMPLATES

The component selection process mainly complies with the following principles:

1. The components must be either at the beginning or at the end of the writing of a character. Those at the beginning of the writing are called head components, while those at the end of the writing are called tail components.
2. The discriminating capability of these components must be as large as possible. The discriminating ability of a component is greatly relevant to two factors:
   (1) degree of being confused with others, and
   (2) frequency of emergence in characters.

   The lesser the degree of confusion with others in a component, the more suitable it is to be the basic component that we want. As to the effect of frequency of emergence, it depends. Generally speaking, the higher the frequency, the better. But if it is embraced by too many characters, a component will probably appear in all the candidates provided by the pre-classification process for the input in terms of our system. Consequently, it provides little guidance for structural matching in the sense that no candidates can be ruled out according to it.

3. The number of chosen basic components must be moderate. If too few components are defined, they can hardly be detected in the input due to their low emergence frequency. Hence, little direction can be provided. In contrast, if too many components are chosen, these components will probably get confused with each other, and their detection will be time-consuming.
4. The writing of these components must be relatively stable for different people. Otherwise, the error of component detection will increase due to the limitation of matching approach, and this consequently leads to recognition errors. In our selection, we have given more consideration to the stroke order.

Based on the above principles, the knowledge of the structures of Chinese characters and trial-and-error tests are required for the selection of basic components. After many experiments, the authors selected 45 components and their total emergence frequency among 3,755 daily-used Chinese characters amounts to 2,106, over 56%. It is worth mentioning that they are still effective if the number of character classes increases, and few other components need adding, for Chinese characters are composed of limited basic components although their total number is enormous. Table 1 shows their indexes assigned by the authors with particular intention, contents and emergence frequencies in 3,755 daily-used Chinese characters of the First National Standard Library.

In Table 1, the components indexed 0–2 are tail components, and the others are all head components. Some components, such as "辶" "亻" and "忄" are not included although they frequently emerge in Chinese characters. This is because the writing order of component "辶" is very unstable, some people are used to writing it at the beginning of characters, others like to write it in the end, and its stroke order is varied from person to person. The reason for not selecting components "亻" and "忄" is that they are easily confused with other components in Table 1 and their discriminating abilities are small since their frequencies are too high.

3.1. Dynamic Templates of Components

When a component appears in different characters, its size, relative position and even the shape, such as the ratio of the length of a stroke to the whole, will probably vary, which will accordingly give rise to the difficulty in building templates suitable for the detection of the component at any unknown positions. One way to overcome this problem is to design multiple, fixed templates for one component at different positions of the characters. But it is not only troublesome to build so many templates but also storage consuming, furthermore, we can hardly take account of all the structural variants of the handwritten characters. In this paper, a dynamic extraction strategy is applied. That is, the templates of a component are no long fixed beforehand, but extracted from the templates of the whole characters dynamically when the matching process takes place. The character samples used to train the system are written in block style and with normal (habitual, consistent with established rules) stroke order, so that the stroke numbers

Table 1. Number, content and frequency (freq.) of components.

Index.	Content	Freq.	Index	Content	Freq.	Index	Content	Freq.
0	刂	50	15	走	10	30	土	53
1	灬	22	16	马	24	31	山	25
2	页	30	17	雨	17	32	王	33
3	扌	215	18	车	25	33	户	7
4	氵	213	19	石	48	34	尸	32
5	木	133	20	阝	42	35	汹	44
6	竹	44	21	彳	25	36	广	35
7	禾	42	22	火	43	37	贝	23
8	钅	77	23	纟	75	38	巾	11
9	衤	20	24	目	26	39	又	14
10	礻	13	25	月	71	40	口	199
11	米	22	26	日	51	41	门	22
12	耳	13	27	女	52	42	讠	86
13	舟	12	28	犭	28	43	辶	44
14	虫	31	29	饣	20	44	穴	19

for each selected component are fixed as regards to the training samples. To be specific, first, a standard stroke segment string template is built for each character by the approach that will be elaborated in Sec. 3.2. Then, a look-up table is designed to store the standard stroke numbers of the selected components, as well as the component attributes of each character indicating the component it contains (the definition of the component attribute of a character will be defined in Sec. 3.3). When recognition of an input is carried out, the pre-classifier based on the statistical features provides several, say M (in our case, $M = 10$) possible candidates from the character pools, the component detection process is then constrained to detect the components contained by the candidates, with it in mind that the input belongs to the same class as one of the candidates. If a candidate contains a certain component, the component is extracted exactly from the reference template of the candidate class according to its stroke number, and we call it a dynamic template of the component, which is only effective to this *ad hoc* matching process. The building of the dynamic template frees us from building multiple templates for each component and makes it possible for the component detection to direct the structural matching of the whole characters.

3.2. Production of Reference Templates of Whole Characters

The production of reference templates is one of the most difficult problems for structural matching approach. The most popular and simplest way is to select one of the reference samples as the template. But the result of this method is far from satisfying according to our experiments. The main reason is that no single sample is the statistically best one. In order to get better results, our reference template production follows two steps:

1. For each character class, select one of the best samples from its sample set as the initial template according to the matching cost (the algorithm will be introduced in Sec. 4.3) between it and the other samples.
2. Register the correspondence between the stroke segment primitives of the standard template and those of other samples in the sample set, one by one, and modify the attributes of each segment of the template in the following way:
   Let *Attr* be one of the attributes of the template segment, *Atts* be the counterpart of the sample segment being considered, the modified value of *Attr* is:

$$Attr = (m \times Attr + Atts)/(m + 1)\,, \tag{1}$$

   where m is the number of modification times. Figure 3 displays the selected initial template of some characters, and Fig. 4 shows their final templates.

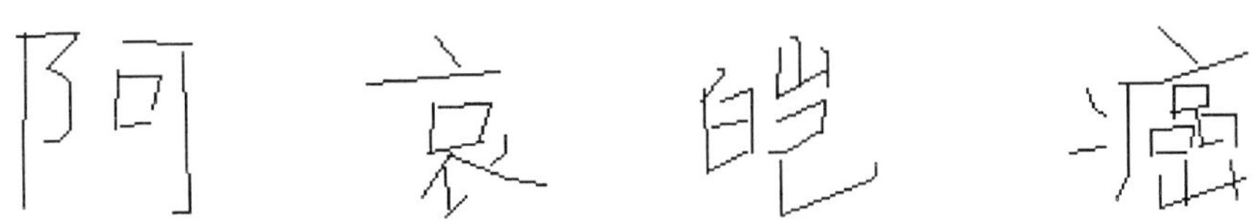

Fig. 3. Initial templates of four characters.

Fig. 4. Final templates corresponding to Fig. 3.

3.3. Definition of the Component Attribute of a Character

How to determine whether a character contains a certain component? This problem is solved according to the component attributes of the characters. For each character, a component attribute is defined. If it contains a certain component, the component attribute is set to be equal to the index (defined in Table 1) of the component, or else, the attribute is set to be -1. In cases where more than one component is included in a character, which often happens, the attribute is set to be equal to the index with the smaller value. For instance, character "热" contains both component "扌" and "灬", since the index of the component "灬" is smaller than that of "扌", the component attribute of the character "热" is set to be the index of the "灬", i.e. it is equal to 1. The main reason for doing so is that the index of the components are defined with care beforehand in case some components might embrace others or be similar to others. For example, component "日" contains "口". The indexes of these components are so defined that those with the larger values will never embody those with the smaller values, and the detection of components must begin from the components with the smallest index among the candidates. When a component is successfully detected, the component detection process ends. This guarantees that the detection of a component cannot be hampered by the detection of simpler components which the correct component contains.

4. STRUCTURAL MATCHING DIRECTED BY COMPONENTS

Suppose that the ith candidates provided by the pre-classification process is $w_i(i = 1, 2, M)$, if w_i includes a certain component (i.e. its component attribute is not equal to -1), denote the component by a_i, then the structural matching process directed by the component detection is as follows (shown in Fig. 5): First, sort the candidates in terms of their component attributes so that the non-negative attributes are in ascending order (those with the negative attributes are listed rather at the end). Then, from the beginning to the end of the candidate list, extract one by one the corresponding component from the standard template and match it with the initial component segment string (defined in Sec. 4.1) extracted from the input until the matching cost c_i is less than the predefined threshold th, which means the detection succeeds, and the component detection process will end. In this case, rule out the segments of the component from the segment string of the input according to the pairwise matching result, and then compare the residual part of the input with the counterparts of the candidates embracing the detected component and record their matching costs. If no component is successfully detected, compare one by one the whole segment string of the input with the templates of all candidates and record their costs. The matching costs are finally synthesized with the result of preclassification to get the final recognition result.

4.1. Component Extraction and Segment Reordering

Because the stroke numbers of the standard templates of characters and their components are normally stable, it is fairly straightforward to separate components

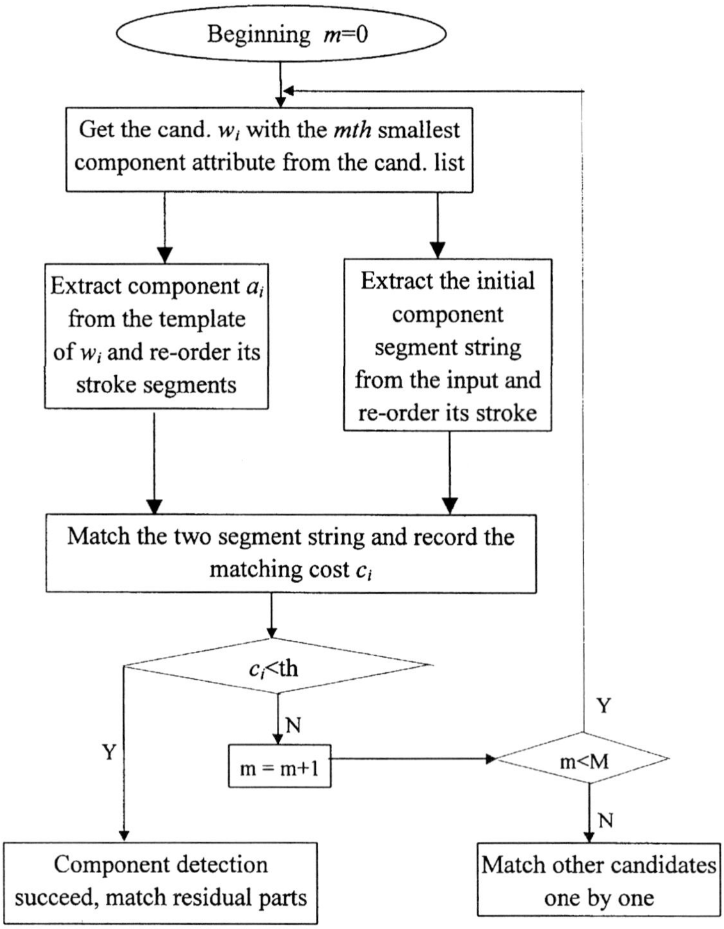

Fig. 5. Structural matching process directed by the component.

from the standard templates. As for the input samples, the situations are quite different. Due to the possible stroke connection and stroke order variation (rare cases), the number of strokes of an input component may be less than that of the standard one, so that the component extraction of the input samples is not so direct, and a dynamic extraction strategy is used in this paper.

In most cases (except for the case that much spurious noise exits), the stroke number of the input component will be less than its standard value, so the N strokes at the beginning (for the head component) or the end (for the tail component) of a character are extracted, letting N be the standard stroke number of the component to be extracted, to guarantee that such a substroke string absolutely embraces the expected component. Then these extracted strokes are divided into stroke segments and these segments are arranged sequentially in terms of the writing order to form the initial segment string. Linking the end point of each stroke with the starting point of its successive stroke, a pseudo-stroke segment is inserted to correspond to the possible stroke connective segment. Although special care has been taken in the component selection so that basic components usually have stable stroke order, stroke order deviation is still possible for some special writings. In order to overcome the errors brought about by the possible change of stroke order, the stroke segments are reordered according to the following rules:

1. If the position relation between two segments is left-to-right or upper-to-below, the left (or upper) segment should be arranged before the right (or below) one. For example, in Fig. 6, the relation between the segment l_1 and the segment l_4 is left-to-right, and the relation between l_8 and l_6 is upper-to-below, then l_1 should be put before l_4, and l_8 before l_6.
2. If the relation between the two segments is not obviously left-to-right or upper-to-below, to say, their relation is left down or right top, they are arranged in the writing sequence. For example, segment l_4 are right $*$ ($*$ stands for indefinite relation) to segment l_8 in Fig. 6, then l_4 is before l_8 in light of the writing order.

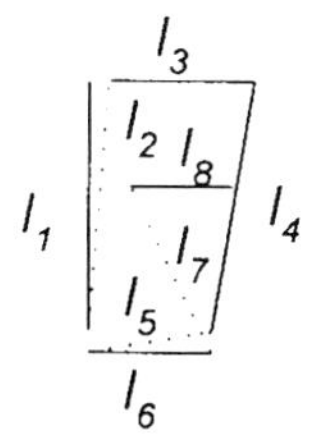

Fig. 6. Stroke decomposition of character "日".

According to the above rules, the stroke segment list of character "日" is $l_1l_2l_3l_4l_8l_7l_5l_6$. In this way, no matter in what stroke order a component is written, the order of its stroke segments is aligned in the end. It is worth mentioning that the first consideration of the re-ordering algorithm is the writing order, therefore, the algorithm is only effective for the minor adjustment of the stroke segments of the basic components which are relatively stable in terms of the stroke order. The possibility and the convenience of such a reordering algorithm was based on the fact that the structures of the components are relatively simple.

4.2. Extraction of Residual Part

Residual part is referred to the substring of the stroke segment string with those consisting of the detected component removed. Obviously, the extraction of the residual part is just as simple as the extraction of component for standard templates. So this section is mainly related to the extraction of the residual part from the input characters.

Due to the stroke connection, there possibly exist some segments belonging to the residual parts in the initial segment string of the components of the input. To get a complete residual part, the starting stroke (for characters containing head component) or ending stroke (for characters containing tail component) must be accurately relocated after component detection. During the component matching process, the one to one paired relationship among segments of the input and standard templates is recorded, so that the residual parts can be separated according to the pairing relation after the component matching is done.

After the component is detected from the input, rank the segments of the input in accordance with the writing order, with each segment containing a pointer linking to its paired segment in the standard template of the component, and a null pointer is given to those without any association with segments of the standard template. Then, for the head component, search the segment string of the input from the end to the beginning until the segment associated with one in the template (and their matching cost is less than the threshold th_1) is met. Those segments before it comprise the component. Likewise, for the tail component, search its segment string from the beginning to the end until a segment with an appropriate pairing segment of the template is met. Those segments behind it consist of the component. Remove the component from the segment string of the input, and the remainder is the so-called residual part.

4.3. Structural Matching Algorithm

For each segment, the following attributes are extracted:

1. (x_i, y_i): Coordinates of the center of the ith segment,
2. l_i: Length of the ith segment,
3. θ_i: Direction of the ith segment, denoted by the angle between the segment and the horizontal line,
4. X_i: Rank of the x-coordinate of the ith segment,
5. Y_i: Rank of the y-coordinate of the ith segment,
6. C_{ij}: Croxssing count in the jth scanning direction of the ith segment ($j =$ 1, 2, 3, 4). j is the order of the scanning directions shown in Fig. 7.

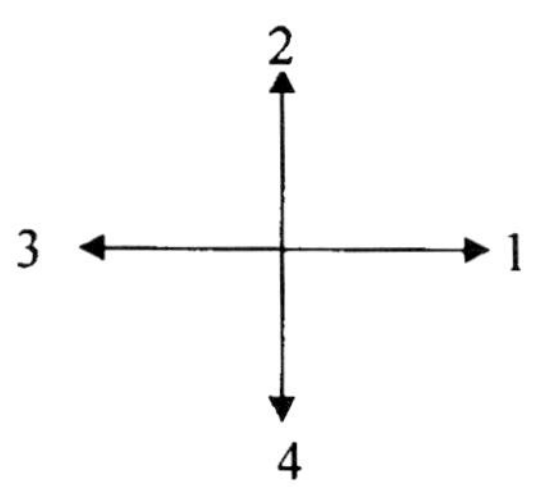

Fig. 7. Four scanning directions.

As regards to the components, since their stroke orders are relatively stable, we have used the dynamic programming matching approach with some editing operations.[5] For the residual parts, we have applied quasi-relaxation matching strategy[8] instead since their stroke orders may be irregular, the calculation of the matching cost is as follows.

Let the attribute set of the ith segment of the input be

$$S_i = \{x_i^s, y_i^s, l_i^s, \theta_i^s, X_i^s, Y_i^s, C_{i1}^s, C_{i2}^s, C_{i3}^s, C_{i4}^s\}, \tag{2}$$

the attribute set of the jth segment of the template be

$$R_j = \{x_j^r, y_j^r, l_j^r, \theta_j^r, X_j^r, Y_j^r, C_{j1}^r, C_{j2}^r, C_{j3}^r, C_{j4}^r\}, \tag{3}$$

then, for the individual segment pair (S_i, R_j), the matching cost is:

$$\text{FinalC}(S_i, R_k) = \text{IniC}(S_i, R_k) + |l_i^s - l_k^r| + |x_i^s - x_k^r| + |y_i^s - y_k^r|, \tag{4}$$

where

$$\text{IniC}(S_i, R_j) = |X_i^s - X_j^r| + |Y_i^s - Y_j^r| + \sum_{k=1}^{4} |C_{ik}^s - C_{jk}^r| + f(\theta_i^s - \theta_j^r),$$

and

$$f(\theta_i^s, \theta_j^r) = \begin{cases} 5.0 * |\theta_i^s - \theta_j^r|/\pi & |\theta_i^s - \theta_j^r| < \pi/2 \\ \infty & |\theta_i^s - \theta_j^r| \geq \pi/2 \end{cases} \tag{5}$$

The total matching cost between the input and the template is:

$$\text{TotalC} = \sum \text{FinalC}(S_i, R_k) + \text{InsertC} + \text{DeleteC}. \tag{6}$$

Since the segments of the input and those of the template do not correspond one-to-one, there probably exist some segments in both the input and the template which do not have any correspondences in their counterparts; they are called unmatched segments. The second item in Eq. (6) denotes the cost produced by the unmatched segments of the input. The third item denotes the cost produced by the unmatched segments of the template. The cost produced by an unmatched segment is proportional to the length of the segment.[6]

5. EXPERIMENTAL RESULTS

In our experiments, 35 sets of block writing samples from the first National Standard (3,755 categories for each set, totally 131,425 samples) were used to train the system and build the standard templates. And another three sets of moderate writing (partly cursive, some stroke order variation and writing slant) were used to test the performance of the system. The pre-classification process by feature matching provided 10 candidates for each input. In order to test the effects of the structural matching directed by the components, the authors carried out experiments from the following aspects:

1. Influence of dynamic templates. First, for each component, one standard template was built from character samples including it, and the correct rate of component detection was only 89%, while the correct rate is as high as 98% using the dynamic templates.
2. Computation complexity. Using the approach in this paper, a character was structurally matched with 5.1 candidates on the average, the matching computation was reduced almost 50% compared with complete matching in our previous system, which obviously must compare the input with the 10 candidates provided by the pre-classifier.
3. Recognition performance. The recognition rate of the system is 93.9%, remaining almost the same with our previous system. The main reason is that although the immunity to the shape distortion and stroke order variation is increased by using the component guidance, the errors led by the failure of the component detection increase correspondingly since the correct rate of it is not 100%. The other reason is that the accumulative correct rate of pre-classification is only 97%, which becomes the bottleneck for performance enhancement.

6. CONCLUSIONS

Upon the basis of the integration of feature matching and structure matching, a novel structural matching strategy directed by the component detection is proposed in this paper. The definition and the use of head or tail components in directing residual part matching greatly reduce the computational complexity of the algorithm. And the building of dynamic templates for the components and the dynamic extraction of the components greatly increase structural matching accuracy. With the development of recognition technology, the advancement in recognition may come from the combination of the handwriting generation process modeling and techniques of artificial intelligence. From this respect, the strategy in this paper is also enlightening for other recognition problems.

ACKNOWLEDGMENT

This work is mainly based on the first author's doctorate degree project in the Institute of Automation, Chinese Academy of Sciences.

REFERENCES

1. R. W. Dai, J. Wang and J. Tian, *Intelligent System Metasysthesis* (in Chinese), Zhejiang Scientific Press, 1995.
2. Y. J. Liu and R. W. Dai, "A method of line segment ordering by character structure for on-line handwritten Chinese character recognition", (in Chinese), *Acta Automatica Sinica*, 1988, pp. 10–17.
3. Y. J. Liu and J. W. Tai, "The theory and practice of on-line Chinese character recognition", (in Chinese), *J. Chinese Inf. Process.* **2**, 4 (1988) 18–30.
4. K. Raman *et. al.*, "Document image analysis: An overview of techniques for graphics recognition", *Pre-Proc. Int. Workshop on Syntactic and Structural Pattern Recognition*, 1990, pp. 192–230.

5. Y. T. Tsay and W. H. Tsai, "Attributed string matching by split-and-merge for on-line Chinese character recognition", *IEEE Trans. Patt. Anal. Mach. Intell.* **15**, 2 (1993) 180–185.
6. H. Tsai and S. S. Yu, "Attributed string matching with merging for shape recognition", *IEEE Trans. PAMI* **7**, 4 (1995) 453–462.
7. X. H. Xiao, "On-line handwritten Chinese character recognition by merging image features with dynamic information", *Proc. 2nd China-Korea Joint Symp. Oriental Language Processing*, 1996, pp. 65–70.
8. X. H. Xiao and R. W. Dai, "On-line Chinese signature verification by matching dynamic and structural features with a quasi-relaxation approach", *Pre-Proc. 5th Int. Workshop on Frontiers in Handwriting Recognition*, 1996.

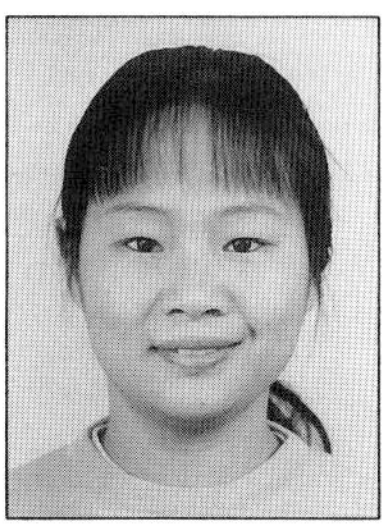

Xuhong Xiao received the B.S. degree in electronics engineering and information science from the University of Science and Technology of China in 1992, and the Ph.D. degree from the Institute of Automation, Chinese Academy of Sciences. She is now a post doctoral fellow of Nanyang Technological University, Singapore.

Her research interests include document analysis, character recognition, handwriting verification and artificial intelligence.

Dai Ruwei graduated from Beijing University in 1955, and worked at the Chinese Academy of Sciences. From 1980 to 1982, he was a visiting scholar at the School of Engineering, Purdue University. He has published more than 150 articles in China and abroad. He was elected to be a member of the Chinese Academy of Sciences in 1991. He is the chief editor of the Chinese Journal of Pattern Recognition and Artificial Intelligence.

His research interests are pattern recognition and artificial intelligence.

A RELIABILITY DESIGN METHODOLOGY FOR CHINESE CHARACTER RECOGNITION

Y. S. HUANG*

Application Software Department
Computer and Communication Research Laboratories
Industrial Technology Research Institute, Taiwan

K. LIU and C. Y. SUEN

Centre for Pattern Recognition and Machine Intelligence
Concordia University, Canada

Y. Y. TANG

Department of Computing Studies
Hong Kong Baptist University, Hong Kong

This paper proposes a novel method which enables a Chinese character recognition system to obtain reliable recognition. In this method, two thresholds, i.e. *class region threshold* R_k and *disambiguity threshold* A_k, are used by each Chinese character k when the classifier is designed based on the nearest neighbor rule, where R_k defines the pattern distribution region of character k, and A_k prevents the samples not belonging to character k from being ambiguously recognized as character k. A novel algorithm to derive the appropriate thresholds A_k and R_k is developed so that a better recognition reliability can be obtained through iterative learning. Experiments performed on the ITRI printed Chinese character database have achieved highly reliable recognition performance (such as 0.999 reliability with a 95.14% recognition rate), which shows the feasibility and effectiveness of the proposed method.

Keywords: Reliable recognition, OCR, competitive learning, rejection.

1. INTRODUCTION

The ultimate goal of a pattern recognition system is to make a correct decision for every input pattern. However, unless the encountered problem is simple and straightforward, there always exist some patterns for which it is difficult or even impossible to make the right decision. Therefore, for those patterns, it is preferable that the recognition system rejects them and then let human experts process them manually. If the system does not reject an uncertain pattern and instead makes a wrong decision, then probably this error will cause severe damage to the corresponding application or subsequently, a lot of effort is required to locate this error and fix it.

Obviously, to a recognition system, the extra cost caused by making wrong decisions should be as low as possible. From this point of view, it becomes essential that only the highly confident patterns are recognized and the uncertain ones are

*Corresponding author. E-mail: huang@autumn.ccl.itri.org.tw
Mailing address: W300 CCL/ITRI Bldg. 51, 195-11 Sec. 4, Chung Hsing Rd., Chutung, Hsinchu, Taiwan 310.

Advances in Oriental Document Analysis and Recognition Techniques (1998) 159–172

rejected.[4,6] In this paper, a novel recognition criterion is proposed and an iterative competitive learning for deriving better recognition reliability is also presented below.

The structure of this paper is as follows. Section 2 defines the symbols used and discusses the previous reliable decision making strategies. Section 3 further illustrates the drawbacks of such symbols. Section 4 proposes a novel reliable recognition scheme with an effective threshold update approach which can derive better thresholds through an iterative learning process. Section 5 describes the experimental results by applying the proposed approach to the ITRI printed Chinese character database, and by using the learned thresholds, the rejection performance of the ITRI non-Chinese symbol set. Finally, Sec. 6 draws conclusions and points out future research directions.

2. PROBLEM AND PREVIOUS TECHNOLOGY

Let S be a pattern space which consists of K mutually exclusive sets $S = C_1 \cup \cdots \cup C_K$, each C_k, $i \in \Lambda = \{1, \cdots, K\}$ representing a set of specified patterns called a class (e.g. $K = 10$ for numeral recognition). x denotes the feature vector of an input pattern and r_k denotes the representative prototype of class k. $e(x) = \{m_k(x) |\ \forall k\ (1 \le k \le K)\}$ means that a classifier e assigns an input x to each class k with a measurement value $m_k(x)$. A measurement may be a distance, a similarity, or a confidence. For the sake of simplicity, $m_k(x)$ is regarded as a distance in the following discussion, that is $m_k(x) = D(x, r_k)$ where D is a distance function. Let M, S and I denote the nearest, the second nearest, and the ground-truth classes, respectively. Therefore,

$$D(x, r_M) = \min_{k=1}^{K} D(x, r_k),$$

and

$$D(x, r_S) = \min_{k=1 \text{ and } k \neq M}^{K} D(x, r_k).$$

The classification of a pattern is a function of $e(x)$, that is $m_1, \cdots, m_K$. In the most trivial case, the classification is based on the minimum distance,[2] and x is recognized in class M no matter how abnormal the pattern could be. However, for certain applications (e.g. check recognition systems[1,3]), it could be better not to make a decisive classification if the pattern is unclear or ambiguous, instead a pattern should be rejected if it is either close to more than one class or does not look similar to any class at all.

The first attempt on making reliable decision is to impose a disambiguity threshold[7] in the decision criterion as

$$\text{class\_of}(x) = \begin{cases} M, & \text{when } D(x, r_M) = \min_{k=1}^{K} D(x, r_k) \\ & \text{and } D(x, r_S) - D(x, r_M) > A; \\ \text{rejected}, & \text{otherwise.} \end{cases} \tag{1}$$

This equation specifies that a definite decision is made only when the difference value between the distances of an input sample to its second nearest class S and to its first nearest class M is larger than a disambiguity threshold A; otherwise no decisive opinion is made and this sample is rejected. In other words, threshold A is set to reject those samples close to more than one class.

Sometimes, improper character segmentation or various kinds of noises may result in non-character patterns[a] and they are inputted to a recognition system as normal character patterns are done. It is desirable that no identification to such characters is made and instead these patterns should be rejected. In other words, only x is close enough to its nearest class M, it is recognized, otherwise it is rejected. For this purpose, a class region threshold R is adopted so that a precise recognition will be made only when $D(x, r_M)$ is smaller than R; otherwise x is regarded as a non-character and is rejected. Therefore, a criterion for rejecting non-character patterns[5] would be

$$\text{class\_of}(x) = \begin{cases} M, & \text{when } D(x, r_M) = \min_{k=1}^{K} D(x, r_k) \text{ and } D(x, r_M) < R; \\ \text{rejected}, & \text{otherwise.} \end{cases} \tag{2}$$

Ideally, a recognition system is expected to detect both ambiguous[b] and non-character patterns. Accordingly, a criterion for rejecting both of them[5] is further proposed as

$$\text{class\_of}(x) = \begin{cases} M, & \text{when } D(x, r_M) = \min_{k=1}^{K} D(x, r_k) \text{ and } D(x, r_M) < R \\ & \text{and } D(x, r_S) - D(x, r_M) > A; \\ \text{rejected}, & \text{otherwise.} \end{cases} \tag{3}$$

3. DRAWBACK OF PREVIOUS TECHNIQUES

It is obvious that the minimum distance criterion will not reject patterns even when they are far from all feature prototypes or they look similar to several classes. The decision criterion adopting Eq. (2) indeed considers the rejection of non-character patterns, but quite often it will still make wrong decisions for those ambiguous ones. Only the decision criterion adopting Eq. (3) can reject both non-character patterns and ambiguous patterns. Therefore, the decision criterion adopting Eq. (3) in general produces a more reliable decision than the other two.

Still, one major drawback exists in Eq. (3), that is, it uses only one A and one R so that the two thresholds are not sensitive to the different classes. This results in either too much rejection or too much misrecognition. For example, if A is small, then ambiguous samples may be misrecognized; but if A is large, samples tend to

[a] Traditionally, non-character patterns mainly are incomplete characters, touching characters, and noise blobs. However, it is surely desirable to reject all non-Chinese patterns if they are applied to a Chinese character recognition system. In such a sense, non-character patterns indeed contain all patterns which are not included in the current recognition domain even if they are noises, or partial or complete characters.

[b] In this paper, patterns close to more than one class are denoted as ambiguous patterns.

be rejected even when they are not ambiguous. As another example, if R is small, then a few samples belonging to a scattered class will be rejected, but if R is large, then the non-character patterns close to a compact class will be recognized as this class negligibly.

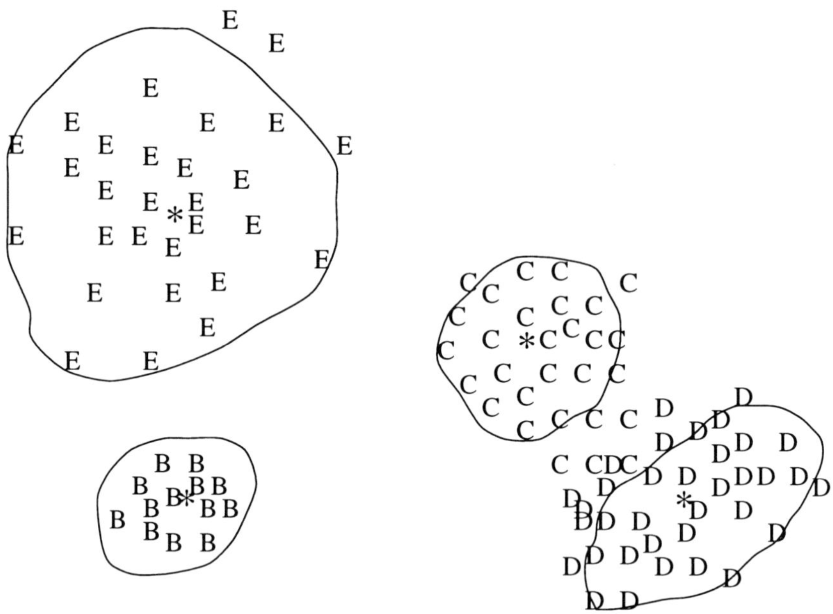

Fig. 1. A four-class (B,C,D,E) distribution of patterns. The centroid of each class is marked by symbol *, and the reliable recognition region of each class is indexed by a solid line for conceptually visual inspection.

Figure 1 shows a pattern distribution of four classes. In this figure, each member of the class k ($k \in \{B, C, D, E\}$) is denoted by symbol k. Visually, classes B and E are neighbors, and class E is much scattered than class B, and classes C and D are overlapping each other such that the samples of the two classes are impossible to be separated fully. With the assumption that all patterns of both classes B and E are recognized correctly under a current distance measurement, if A is small, then some members of either class C or class D will be misrecognized; however, if A is large, a few patterns belonging to either class E or class B will be unnecessarily rejected. With the consideration of non-character patterns, if R is small, then a few samples of class E will be rejected; however if R is large, then some non-character patterns close to class B will be misrecognized as class B.

Therefore, a new recognition criterion needs to be designed, which takes the factors of compactness and ambiguity of the different classes into consideration. This can be achieved by equipping each class k with its own class region and disambiguity thresholds (i.e. R_k and A_k for $1 \leq k \leq K$). Using Fig. 1 as example, R_A should be much larger than R_B, and both A_C and A_D should be large.

4. A NOVEL RELIABLE RECOGNITION CRITERION AND ITS PARAMETER LEARNING

A new recognition criterion with high reliability is proposed here

$$\text{class\_of}(x) = \begin{cases} M, & \text{when } D(x, r_M) = \min_{k=1}^{K} D(x, r_k) \text{ and } D(x, r_M) < R_M \\ & \text{and } D(x, r_S) - D(x, r_M) > A_M; \\ \text{rejected}, & \text{otherwise.} \end{cases} \tag{4}$$

In this approach, each class k consists of its own disambiguous threshold A_k and class region threshold R_k. In general, the more scattered a class is, the larger its region threshold will be. Also, the more an ambiguous class is distinguishable from other classes, the larger its disambiguous threshold should be. A process to compute A_k and R_k effectively for each class k is designed in the next section.

The initial values of R_k and A_k are computed by the following equations

$$R_k = a * \frac{\sum_{i=1}^{N_k} D(x_i^k, r_M)}{N_k} \tag{5}$$

and

$$A_k = b * \frac{\sum_{i=1}^{N_k} (D(x_i^k, r_S) - D(x_i^k, r_M))}{N_k} \tag{6}$$

where a and b are two predefined constants, N_k is the total number of training samples of class k, and x_i^k is the ith training sample of class k. Descriptively, the initial R_k is a times of the average distance between the training samples of class k and their individual corresponding nearest classes, and the initial A_k is b times of the average difference between the distances of the training sample of class k to the second nearest class S and to the nearest class M.

Obviously, the initial R_k and A_k are in general different for different classes of k. However, the initial R_k and A_k are not optimal because they are computed from the training patterns of the class k alone, without considering the influence of the other classes. Therefore, they should be updated based on competitive learning by taking all classes into consideration. To this end, a novel threshold update rule is proposed with the basic concept: "*When a decision based on the minimum distance is incorrect and the current pattern is not rejected by Eq. (4), then both R_M and A_M should be updated properly; also, if a pattern is rejected by its own R_I and A_I, the two thresholds should be updated too*". This concept is further mathematically formulated as follows:

IF $\quad M = I$, and

$\quad D(x, r_M) < R_M$, and

$\quad D(x, r_S) - D(x, r_M) > A_k$

THEN $\quad$ No thresholds are updated;

ELSE Thresholds of classes M and I are updated as

For class I

$$\triangle R_I = \begin{cases} \alpha * [D(x, r_I) - R_I], & \text{if } R_I < D(x, r_I); \\ 0, & \text{otherwise.} \end{cases}$$

$$\triangle A_I = \begin{cases} \alpha * [(D(x, r_S) - D(x, r_I)) - A_I], & \text{if } A_I > D(x, r_S) - D(x, r_I); \\ 0, & \text{otherwise.} \end{cases}$$

and,

for class M and $M \neq I$

$$\triangle R_M = \begin{cases} \beta * [D(x, r_M) - R_M], & \text{if } R_M > D(x, r_M); \\ 0, & \text{otherwise.} \end{cases}$$

$$\triangle A_M = \begin{cases} \beta * [(D(x, r_S) - D(x, r_M)) - A_M], & \text{if } A_M < D(x, r_S) - D(x, r_M); \\ 0, & \text{otherwise.} \end{cases}$$

where α and β are two monotonically decreasing functions, their values are gradually decreased with the increment of the epoch iteration number. In general, $0 \leq \alpha$ and $\alpha < \beta$. Interestingly, the proposed threshold update rule has a similar form to the famous LVQ prototype update rule,[9] and they are both competitive learning rules. This threshold update rule states that if the first choice of an input pattern is correct and this pattern is not rejected, then no thresholds are updated; otherwise, thresholds of classes M and I will be updated so that the thresholds of the genuine class I can accept the input pattern. Meanwhile, if the first choice is wrong, then the thresholds are updated in order to reject this pattern by reducing R_M if its original value is too large, and enlarging A_M if its original value is too small to reject this pattern. The larger value β intrinsically corresponds to a higher recognition reliability because in such a situation R_M and A_M are more likely to reject a pattern. An easy and useful approach to stop the learning process is to observe the recognition performance after each learning iteration. If the performances within several iterations are almost the same, then the learning process can stop accordingly.

5. EXPERIMENTS

The proposed algorithm has been implemented on a SUN SPARC 20 workstation in C. The experimental data come from the ITRI[c] printed Chinese character data base which contains 5401 daily-used Chinese characters and the ITRI non-Chinese pattern data base containing digits, upper-case and lower-case alphabets, and other common symbols. Each Chinese character contains about 120 samples collected from the three most popular fonts (Ming, Kai, and Bold) used in Taiwan, and the odd-number samples are used to construct class prototypes and derive the optimized

[c]Industrial Technology and Research Institute is a government-support organization in Taiwan.

disambiguity and class region thresholds of each class, and the even-number samples are used to test the recognition reliability performance. All samples of the non-Chinese are used for testing the rejection performance of Table 1 which shows all symbols and their collected sample numbers of the ITRI non-Chinese symbol data set.

Table 1. Symbols and sample numbers of the ITRI non-Chinese data set, where "sym" denotes symbol and "s_no" represents the total number of samples of a certain symbol.

sym	s_no	sym	s_no	sym	s_no	sym	s_no	sym	s_no	sym	s_no
!	94	&	22	#	28	$	94	%	58	&	88
'	22	(	94	)	94	*	58	+	40	,	22
-	22	.	52	/	200	0	200	1	200	2	200
3	200	4	200	5	200	6	200	7	200	8	200
9	200	:	94	;	94	<	22	=	40	>	22
?	94	@	22	A	200	B	200	C	200	D	200
E	200	F	200	G	200	H	200	I	173	J	200
K	200	L	200	M	200	N	200	O	200	P	200
Q	124	R	200	S	196	T	200	U	200	V	200
W	200	X	200	Y	200	Z	200	[	74	\	22
]	71	^	22	-	22	'	22	a	200	b	200
c	200	d	200	e	200	f	200	g	200	h	200
i	200	j	200	k	200	l	200	m	200	n	200
o	200	p	200	q	200	r	200	s	200	t	200
u	200	v	200	w	200	x	200	y	200	z	200
{	22	|	22	}	22	~	22				

In order to investigate the efficiency of the proposed method, several experiments have been conducted. The first one is to observe the recognition performances to the training data after each two epoch training iterations. The purpose of this experiment is to evaluate whether the proposed threshold update rule can learn from the training data and improve the recognition reliability. The second experiment is to test the recognition performance on both the training and testing data sets by using different β values in different training processes. Decisions made by traditional approaches are also implemented for performance comparison. In the third experiment, the trained Chinese character recognition system is applied to the ITRI non-Chinese symbol data set, and the purpose is to verify the rejection ability on the trained thresholds. In all the three experiments, features consisting of gradient, loci, and peripheral[10] are first extracted from each input pattern and are formed into a feature vector x. Then the distances between x and the pre-constructed character

Table 2. The recognition performance of the training data set with 30 iterations and β is set to 10, only the results of odd-number iteration are listed.

iteration no	recognition rate	error rate	reliability
1	0.966254	0.001645	0.998300
3	0.969438	0.001072	0.998896
5	0.969163	0.001044	0.998924
7	0.968992	0.001035	0.998933
9	0.968763	0.000991	0.998978
11	0.968732	0.000942	0.999029
13	0.969163	0.000932	0.999039
15	0.970662	0.000880	0.999094
17	0.975160	0.000871	0.999108
19	0.978488	0.000793	0.999190
21	0.979445	0.000815	0.999169
23	0.980250	0.000731	0.999255
25	0.980802	0.000759	0.999277
27	0.980696	0.000700	0.999287
29	0.980368	0.000647	0.999340

Table 3. The recognition performance of the training data set with 30 iterations of different β.

β	recognition rate	error rate	reliability
1	0.993395	0.002454	0.997536
5	0.982654	0.000998	0.998986
10	0.979340	0.000626	0.999361
30	0.973921	0.000387	0.999603
50	0.971325	0.000335	0.999657
100	0.965467	0.000223	0.999769

Table 4. The recognition performance of the testing data set with 30 iterations of different β.

β	recognition rate	error rate	reliability
1	0.963590	0.002348	0.997569
5	0.951410	0.000888	0.999067
10	0.947689	0.000708	0.999253
30	0.941693	0.000587	0.999377
50	0.939084	0.000559	0.999405
100	0.93290	0.000466	0.999500

prototypes[8] are calculated. Due to the extremely large number of Chinese characters, each Chinese character consists of only one feature prototype. After the distance computation, Eq. (4) is applied to derive the final recognition decision. So far, there is little effort spent on obtaining the best values of the parameters a, b and α. Here, their values are just set as $a = 2$, $b = 0.2$ and $\alpha = 1$, and the termination criterion of the learning process is reached simply by performing 30 epoch iterations.

Table 2 lists the recognition performances of the first experiment with $\beta = 10$. Obviously, it shows that the recognition reliability is constantly increased with the increment of the iteration number. This reveals the learning ability of the proposed threshold update rule. Tables 3 and 4 list respectively the recognition performances of the training and testing data with different β in the second experiment. Interestingly, it shows perfectly that the recognition reliability of both data is indeed improved when β is increased. This manifests that with the proposed approach by using different values of β different degrees of recognition reliability can be obtained. This is a very important property which ensures that this method can be applied to different reliability-sensitive applications. To further investigate the superiority of the proposed approach, decisions made by traditional methods in Eqs. (1)–(3) are also performed individually. Through experiments, symbol R is best chosen to be the summation of the average $D(x, r_M)$ and three times of the average standard deviation of $D(x, r_M)$ of all learning samples. Similarly, symbol A is chosen to be the substraction value of the average $D(x, r_S) - D(x, r_M)$ and three times of the average standard deviation of $D(x, r_M) - D(x, r_M)$ of all learning samples. Represented by mathematical formulation, symbols R and A become

$$m = \frac{\sum_{k=1}^{K} \sum_{i=1}^{N_k} D(x_i^k, r_M)}{\sum_{k=1}^{K} N_k}$$

$$V = \sum_{k=1}^{K} \sum_{i=1}^{N_k} (D(x_i^k, r_M) - m)^2$$

$$S = \sqrt{\frac{V}{\sum_{k=1}^{K} N_k}}$$

$$A = m + 3 * S$$

and

$$Dm = \frac{\sum_{k=1}^{K} \sum_{i=1}^{N_k} D(x_i^k, r_S) - D(x_i^k, r_M)}{\sum_{k=1}^{K} N_k}$$

$$DV = \sum_{k=1}^{K} \sum_{i=1}^{N_k} (D(x_i^k, r_S) - D(x_i^k, r_M)) - Dm)^2$$

$$DS = \sqrt{\frac{DV}{\sum_{k=1}^{K} N_k}}$$

$$R = Dm - 3 * DS$$

where N_k is the total number of training samples of class k, and x_i^k is the ith training sample of class k. With testing data, the decisions made in Eqs. (1)–(3) are (97.50%, 0.53%), (95.50%, 0.44%) and (93.53%, 0.08%), respectively where in each brace pair the first parameter denotes the recognition rate and the second parameter denotes the error rate. Comparing with Table 4, it is shown that the proposed method has better performance than the traditional ones.

Table 5. The individual error rate of each ITRI non-Chinese data symbol recognized by the trained Chinese thresholds performed in the second experiment with $\beta = 10$, where err-r denotes the error rate. Two symbols + and − are particularly displayed by enlargement in a bold type font.

sym	err-r	sym	err-r	sym	err-r	sym	err-r	sym	err-r	sym	err-r
	0.000	"	0.000	#	0.000	$	0.000	%	0.000	&	0.000
'	0.000	(	0.000	)	0.000	*	0.000	**+**	0.525	,	0.000
-	0.000	.	0.000	/	0.000	0	0.000	1	0.000	2	0.000
3	0.000	4	0.000	5	0.000	6	0.000	7	0.000	8	0.000
9	0.000	:	0.011	;	0.000	<	0.000	=	0.000	>	0.000
?	0.000	@	0.000	A	0.010	B	0.000	C	0.000	D	0.065
E	0.000	F	0.000	G	0.000	H	0.000	I	0.023	J	0.000
K	0.000	L	0.000	M	0.025	N	0.000	O	0.000	P	0.005
Q	0.000	R	0.000	S	0.000	T	0.000	U	0.000	V	0.000
W	0.000	X	0.000	Y	0.095	Z	0.010	[	0.000	\	0.000
]	0.000	^	0.000	**—**	0.409	'	0.000	a	0.000	b	0.000
c	0.000	d	0.000	e	0.000	f	0.000	g	0.000	h	0.000
i	0.000	j	0.000	k	0.005	l	0.000	m	0.000	n	0.000
o	0.000	p	0.000	q	0.000	r	0.000	s	0.000	t	0.000
u	0.000	v	0.000	w	0.000	x	0.000	y	0.005	z	0.000
{	0.000	|	0.000	}	0.000	~	0.000				

Finally, in the third experiment, Table 5 lists the error rate of each non-Chinese symbol with the trained Chinese thresholds when $\beta = 10$. The total error rate is 0.59% with a 99.4% rejection rate. This performance is indeed very encouraging. After analyzing the errors, it is found that many of them come from the two symbols "+" (52.5% in error) and "–" (40.9% in error). However, recognizing the samples of the symbols "+" and "–" into Chinese should not be counted as error because they do exist as "*ten*" and "*one*" in Chinese. Since the character features are normalized in width and height in the feature extraction stage, it is impossible to distinguish these two symbols from Chinese by considering only the distance in the feature space. Other information such as the geometric and semantic information should be taken into consideration so that the recognition system can decide whether the pattern "+" means *plus* in symbols or *ten* in Chinese, and pattern "–" means *minus* in symbols or *one* in Chinese. In fact, it is reasonable to take samples of these two symbols out of the non-Chinese data set, then the error rate is only 0.37% and the other 99.6% of the samples is rejected. From the above experimental results, it can be concluded that the proposed method is rather effective in arriving at highly reliable decisions.

6. CONCLUSION

This paper proposes a novel approach to design highly reliable Chinese character recognition systems. In this approach, each Chinese class consists of two thresholds, class region threshold and disambiguity threshold. A large class region threshold corresponds to a scattered class, and a small disambiguity threshold corresponds to a considerable overlap between the corresponding class and some other classes. An iterative threshold update rule has been proposed so that better thresholds from the reliability point of view can be derived through a character learning stage. Experiments performed on the ITRI printed Chinese character database consisting of 5401 daily-used Chinese characters have shown that through learning the number of misrecognized samples is reduced and the recognition reliability is constantly increasing. Also, by adopting different values of parameter β, different recognition reliabilities can be produced. Furthermore, the trained system has shown a very prominent rejection ability to the ITRI non-Chinese symbol set which illustrates the usability of this method.

So far, this method can be applied directly to the recognition system with one feature prototype for one character class. It is essential to extend the decision making and the threshold update methods to the situation where multiple feature prototypes of one character class exist. Most importantly, more effort should be devoted to elaborate the proposed threshold update rule based on the optimization theory so that the superiority of this method can be further guaranteed theoretically. One plausible approach to the last issue is to design a meaningful and differential error function with variables only related to the different class thresholds. Thus, to derive the minimal value of the error function corresponds to deriving the best reliability thresholds. Currently, we are working in this direction.

ACKNOWLEDGEMENTS

The authors would like to thank the reviewers' precious comments which have made this paper more clear and complete.

REFERENCES

1. A. Agarwal, A. Gupta, K. Hussein and P. S. P. Wang, "Bank check analysis and recognition by computers", *Handbook of Character Recognition and Document Image Analysis*, World Scientific Publishing Company, 1997, pp. 623–651.
2. J. Bryant, "A fast classifier for image data", *Patt. Recogn.* **22**, 1 (1989) 45.
3. R. Casey, D. Fergueson, K. Mohiuddin and E. Walach, "Intelligent forms processing system", *Machine Vision and Application* **5** (1992) 143–155.

4. C. K. Chow, "Recognition error and reject tradeoff", *Proc. 3rd Annual Symp. Document Analysis and Information Retrieval*, University of Nevada, Las Vegas, USA, 1994, pp. 1–8.
5. L. P. Cordella, C. D. Stefano, F. Tortorella and M. Vento, "A method for improving classification reliability of multilayer perceptrons", *IEEE Trans. Neural Networks* **5**, 5 (1995) 1140–1147.
6. T. M. Ha, "An optimum class-selective rejection rule for pattern recognition", *Int. J. Pattern Recognition Artificial Intelligence* **10**, 4 (1996) 349–363; *Proc. 13th Int. Conf. Pattern Recognition*, Vol. 2 Track B, Vienna, Austria, 1996, pp. 75–80.
7. Y. S. Huang, K. Liu and C. Y. Suen, "The combination of multiple classifiers by a neural network approach", *Int. J. Pattern Recognition and Artificial Intelligence* **9**, 3 (1995) 579–597.
8. Y. S. Huang *et al.*, "A simulated annealing approach to construct optimized prototypes for nearest-neighbor classification", *Proc. 13th Int. Conf. Pattern Recognition*, Vol. 4 Track D, Vienna, Austria, 1996, pp. 483–487.
9. T. Kohonen, "The self-organizing map", *Proc. IEEE* **78** (1990) 1468–1480.
10. L. T. Tu *et al.*, "Recognition of handprinted Chinese character by feature matching", *Proc. 1991 1st National Workshop on Chinese Character Recognition*, Taiwan, 1991, pp. 166–175.

Yea-Shuan Huang graduated in 1994 from Concordia University, Canada. Currently, he works for Computer and Communication Laboratory of Industrial Technology and Research Institute and he is the leader of man machine interface project.

His research interests include image processing, pattern recognition, and neural networks.

Ching Y. Suen received an M.Sc. (Eng.) degree from the University of Hong Kong and a Ph.D. degree from the University of British Columbia, Canada.

In 1972, he joined the Department of Computer Science of Concordia University, Montreal, Canada, where he became Professor in 1979 and served as Chairman from 1980 to 1984. Presently he is the Director of CENPARMI, the Centre for Pattern Recognition and Machine Intelligence of Concordia, and the Associate Dean — Research of the Faculty of Engineering and Computer Science.

Prof. Suen is the author/editor of 11 books and more than 250 papers and his current interests include pattern recognition and machine intelligence, character recognition and expert systems, document processing and computational linguistics.

Dr. Suen is an Associate Editor of several journals related to pattern recognition and artificial intelligence. He founded Computer Processing of Chinese and Oriental Languages, an international journal of the Chinese Language Computer Society in 1983 and served as its Editor-in-Chief for 10 years. A fellow of the IEEE, IAPR, and the Royal Society of Canada. Prof. Suen is the recipient of several awards, including the 1992 ITAC/NSERC award for outstanding contributions to pattern recognition, expert systems, and computational linguistics.

Ke Liu received the B.S. degree from Nankai University, China in 1982, and the M.S. and Ph.D. degrees from Nanjing University of Science and Technology, China, in 1985 and 1989, respectively. He served as an Assistant Professor and Associate Professor in the Nanjing University of Science and Technology from 1989 to 1993, where he has been a Professor since April 1993. He was a visiting scientist at Robot Laboratory, Ecole Superieure d'Ingenieurs en Genie Electrique, Roune, France from 1992 to 1993 and a Canada International Fellow at CENPARMI, the Centre for Pattern Recognition and Machine Intelligence of Concordia, University of Canada, from 1993 to 1995. He has joined CENPARMI as a senior researcher since October 1995 and the Faculty of Engineering and Computer Science of Concordia University as an Adjunct Professor since June 1996.

He has published over 70 scientific and technical papers in international journals and conferences. He was the winner of the Outstanding Chinese Ph.D/M.S Degrees Recipient Award by the Government of P.R. China in 1991, and was one of fifty winners of the Third Fok Ying Tung Education Prize for the youth professors (below age 40) of the all universities in P.R. China in 1992. He was awarded a 1993–1995 Canada International Fellowship by the Natural Sciences and Research Council of Canada in 1993.

Dr. Liu's interests are in the areas of pattern recognition, computer vision, neural network, image processing and their applications in handwriting recognition, document image analysis, facial image recognition, speech recognition, multimedia, internet computing, etc.

Yuan Y. Tang received the B. S. degree in electrical and computer engineering from Chongqing University, Chongqing, China, the M. Eng. degree in electrical engineering from the Graduate School of Post and Telecommunications, Beijing, China, and the Ph.D. degree in computer science from Concordia University, Montreal, Canada. He is presently an Associate Professor in Department of Computing Studies at Hong Kong Baptist University, and Senior Researcher in the Centre for Pattern Recognition and Machine Intelligence, Concordia University. He is a Honorary Lecturer at the University of Hong Kong, an Advisory Professor at Beijing University of Posts and Telecommunications, Chongqing University and Shengyang Institute of Aeronautical Engineering, China. His current interests include wavelet theory and applications, pattern recognition, image processing, document processing, artificial intelligence, parallel processing, Chinese computing and VLSI architecture.

Dr. Tang has published more than 130 technical papers and is the author/co-author of 9 books on subjects ranging from electrical engineering to computer science. He also serves as a reviewer for many journals and international conferences. He is a Senior Member of IEEE.

TYPEFACE IDENTIFICATION FOR PRINTED CHINESE CHARACTERS

YI-HONG TSENG, CHI-CHANG KUO and HSI-JIAN LEE*

Department of Computer Science and Information Engineering
National Chiao Tung University, Hsinchu, Taiwan, R.O.C.

In this paper, we propose a methodology for identifying typefaces of printed Chinese characters in documents. Three kinds of features, *stroke width means, stroke width variations*, and *aspect ratio*, are first used to classify character typefaces as: Black, Li, Kai-Round, or Ming-Song. Each of the last two groups contains two typefaces. *Vertical/horizontal stroke width ratios* are used to distinguish between the Ming and Song typefaces and *accumulative pixel ratio* to distinguish between the Kai and Round typefaces. Six different typeface feature distributions measured from 5401 printed Chinese characters are considered, and a trapezoid-shaped membership function is constructed for each distribution. Based on these membership functions, we determine what typeface each input character belongs to using a two-level decision tree. To increase the identification rate, the typeface of a certain character is adjusted according to the typeface identification results of the front and the next characters. In the character recognition system, we use two statistical features: *crossing counts and contour directional counts.* We achieved an 89.87% typeface identification rate in our experiments, and a 95.60% character recognition rate.

Keywords: Typeface identification, stroke width means, stroke width variations, aspect ratio, vertical/horizontal stroke width ratio, accumulative pixel ratio, typeface adjustment, crossing count features, contour directional features.

1. INTRODUCTION

To access information from printed documents effectively, various automatic document entry systems are needed to handle the different layouts.[1] In general, Chinese document characters occur in one of the six typefaces, Ming, Song, Li, Kai, Black, and Round. If we use character models of known typefaces to recognize characters printed in other typefaces, the recognition accuracy will be very poor due to different characteristics. In order to obtain higher recognition rates for documents printed in different typefaces, we identify document typefaces before recognizing characters.

Six examples of the Chinese character "李" are shown in Fig. 1. Characters in different typefaces have different widths, lengths, directions, shapes, and so on. If we use models of a certain typeface to recognize characters printed in other typefaces, recognition results are very poor as shown in Table 1. Thus, typeface characteristics significantly affect the accuracy of character recognition.

*Corresponding author. E-mail: hjlee@csie.nctu.edu.tw.

Advances in Oriental Document Analysis and Recognition Techniques (1998) 173–190

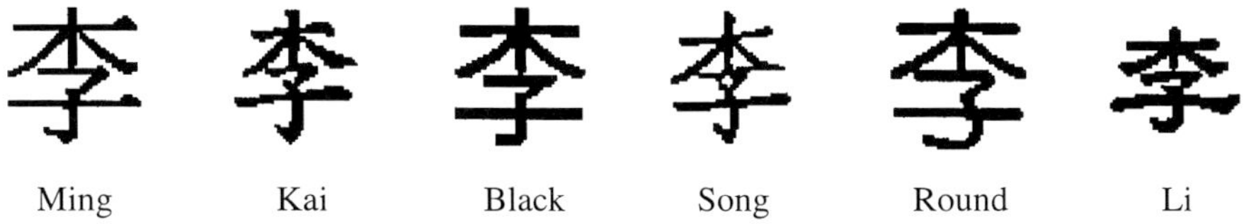

Fig. 1. One character in different typefaces.

Table 1. Printed Chinese character recognition results using different typesfaces. (Test sample = 5401 characters)

Reference typefaces / Test typefaces	Song	Li	Kai	Round	Ming	Black
Song	**97.50%**	59.05%	82.34%	30.40%	57.91%	48.69%
Li	59.03%	**93.75%**	48.43%	41.10%	54.98%	63.87%
Kai	78.34%	41.06%	**98.33%**	15.66%	29.14%	24.22%
Round	45.65%	55.43%	26.95%	**95.83%**	86.64%	93.63%
Ming	67.26%	61.90%	41.80%	83.05%	**98.75%**	87.08%
Black	57.46%	69.57%	48.65%	91.63%	87.41%	**97.33%**

According to our observations and analysis, some characteristics among different typefaces are listed in the following:

1. 99% of the characters in the Li typeface are "fat" characters. Most characters in the Ming, Round and Black typefaces are more or less square. 98.5% of the characters in the Song typeface are narrow or square.
2. Stroke width variations in the Kai and Li typefaces are greater than those in the Round and Black typefaces. Moreover, character stroke widths in the Black typeface are thicker than those in the Round typeface.
3. Characters in the Black typeface have corners at the ends of strokes, as shown in Fig. 2(a). Characters in the Ming typeface have thinner horizontal strokes than their vertical strokes, and small protrusions occur in the right-hand sides of the horizontal strokes, as shown in Fig. 2(b).

Few studies have considered identification of typefaces for printed Chinese characters. Fan[3] proposed a method based on stroke width correlations to identify Chinese character typefaces automatically. He detected the variant in the tails of horizontal strokes since tail shapes of different typefaces were not the same. Under the assumption that the typefaces of all characters in a text-block were the same, the character typeface of the text-block was identified from all horizontal strokes

(a)

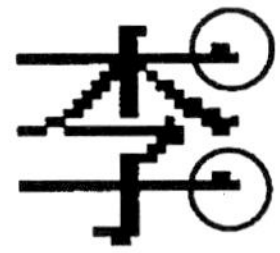

(b)

Fig. 2. (a) Corners at the ends of character strokes in a Black typeface "只"; (b) two protrusions in a Ming typeface "李".

extracted from all characters in the text-block. However, in documents such as business cards and forms, text-blocks may contain very few characters and characters may have different typefaces. Fan's method will obtain less accurate identification rate.

Jou *et al.*[5] suggested a data compression algorithm to model Chinese character patterns and a scheme based on this model to recognize typefaces. They used 10,000 Chinese characters in the same typeface to obtain their model. Character typefaces were finally determined by the model that yielded the largest compression ratio. They concluded that the correct typeface was the one with the largest compression ratio. Anyway, the compression ratio is not a reliable feature since the differences among the compression ratios were not significant enough. Furthermore, their method can only be used to identify a sufficiently large collection of characters with the same typeface.

Tseng and Tsai[10] recognized typefaces using Fourier spectrum features and a back-propagation neural network. An input character image was transformed into the frequency domain using the Fourier transform, and the Fourier amplitude spectra were then divided into non-overlapping square blocks. Spectrum feature vectors were derived from the mean amplitudes of the square blocks. A back-propagation neural network classifier was then used to recognize the printed Chinese character typefaces. Since the Fourier amplitude spectra were different for characters in the same typeface, their approach was used only to identify the character typeface of known characters.

In our paper, we intend to identify the typeface of each individual unknown character. We use five statistical features to differentiate structural differences among characters in different typefaces. Since we count the features from the outer regions of input patterns, we can obtain more stable features. The five features are also calculated from 5401×6 Chinese characters in six typefaces to obtain stable feature values. To further improve the identification rate, we adjust the typefaces of certain characters by considering three consecutive three characters, instead of characters in a whole paragraph. Hence, this system can be applied to the documents such as forms and business cards whose text-blocks have a small number of characters in the same typeface.

The remainder of this paper is organized as follows. Section 2 describes the five statistical features for typeface identification. Section 3 develops a typeface identification process using a decision tree. Section 4 explains typeface adjustment and character recognition. Section 5 reports on experimental results, and presents some discussion. Section 6 gives our concluding remarks.

2. STATISTICAL FEATURES FOR TYPEFACE IDENTIFICATION

The printed Chinese character database used by our system contains the six typefaces that are used most frequently, and each typeface contains 5401 Chinese characters. The six typefaces are Ming, Song, Li, Kai, Black, and Round. To identify the typeface of an input character, we observe and analyze some characteristics of the characters printed in different typefaces. The five kinds of features used to identify character typefaces are defined and explained in the following sections.

2.1. Stroke Width Means

The average stroke width is a useful characteristic for distinguishing among typefaces. For instance, the average stroke widths of Ming or Song characters are smaller than those of Black characters. Often, the central areas of complex characters are blurred because many strokes overlap. In order to obtain more accurate average stroke widths, we ignore character central areas and consider only the black pixels in the outer areas of scanned image patterns. Input images are first divided into 8×8 sub-regions. The outer regions are then selected for feature extraction; these are shown shadowed in Fig. 3.

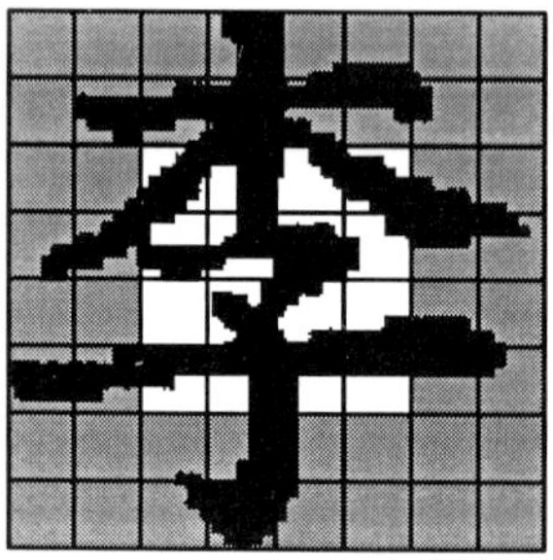

Fig. 3. Shadowed regions are used for feature extraction.

Chinese characters are composed of strokes in four directions: horizontal, vertical, diagonal and inversely diagonal directions. For each black pixel i, we compute the run lengths of black pixels horizontally, vertically, diagonally and inversely diagonally. The four run lengths are denoted as H_length_i, V_length_i, D_length_i, and ID_length_i, as shown in Fig. 4. The stroke width w_i of the black pixel i is the minimum of these four lengths, that is,

$$w_i = \min(H\_length_i, V\_length_i, D\_length_i, ID\_length_i)\,.$$

The mean of character stroke widths is the average width of all black pixels, and is represented as: $m = \frac{1}{n}\sum_{i=1}^{n} w_i$, where n is the number of black pixels in the outer areas.

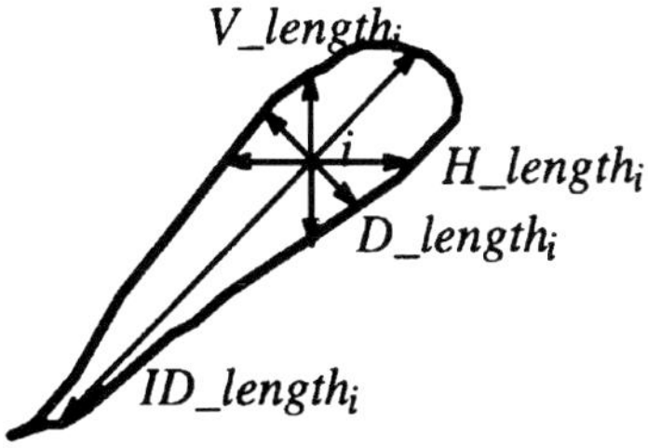

Fig. 4. Four lengths of black runs in four directions for black pixel i.

To make this feature more reliable, the stroke width means obtained from the input patterns are adjusted according to the character sizes. Let the size of a training sample be $A_{old} \times A_{old}$ and the test character $A_{new} \times A_{new}$. The mean of stroke widths m is calculated from the test character and the adjusted value m' is $m \times \frac{A_{old}}{A_{new}}$. The value of m' is employed to compare with the six distributions of the mean stroke widths in Fig. 5.

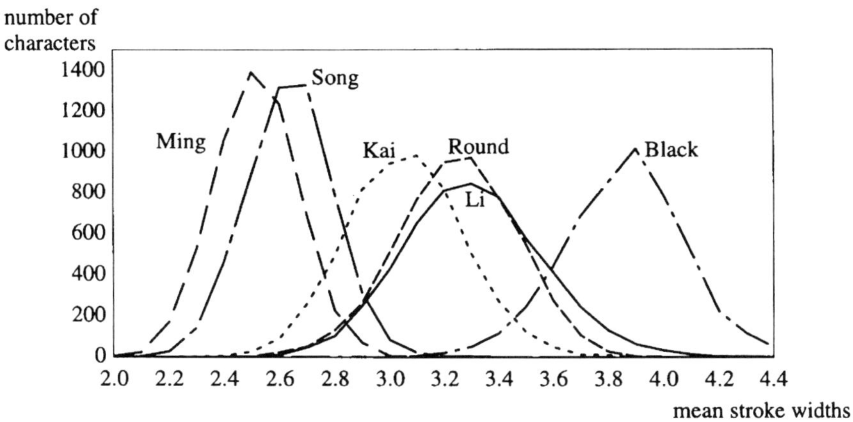

Fig. 5. Distributions of mean stroke widths.

2.2. Stroke Width Variations

The changes of stroke widths can be used to separate the Ming, Kai, and Li typefaces from other typefaces. Ming characters have almost the same stroke widths, except at the right ends of the horizontal strokes. To measure this feature, we also consider black pixels in the outer areas of the image patterns. The variations in stroke widths in characters are defined as

$$\sigma^2 = \frac{1}{n}\sum_{i=1}^{n}(m - w_i)^2 \,,$$

where n is the number of black pixels in the outer areas, m is the mean stroke width and w_i is the stroke width in the black pixel i. The distributions of this feature obtained from 5401 character samples in six different typefaces are shown in Fig. 6.

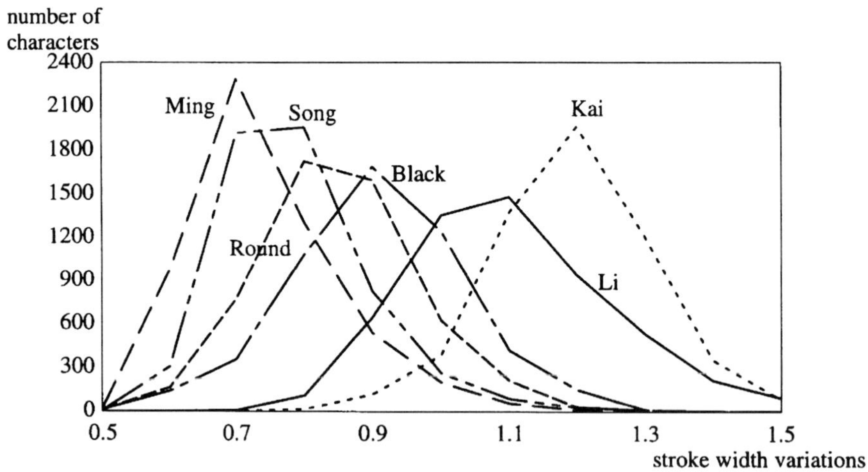

Fig. 6. Distributions of the stroke width variations.

2.3. Aspect Ratio

Although Chinese characters in most typefaces are generally square, characters in the Li typeface are almost flat. Hence, the degree of squareness can be used for typeface identification. Squareness is measured according to the aspect ratio, which is defined as $AR = \frac{CW}{CH}$, where CW and CH denote the character width and character height, respectively. Figure 7 depicts the distributions of this feature among six different typefaces. Figure 7 shows that the Li typeface has a larger aspect ratio and the Song typeface has a smaller one.

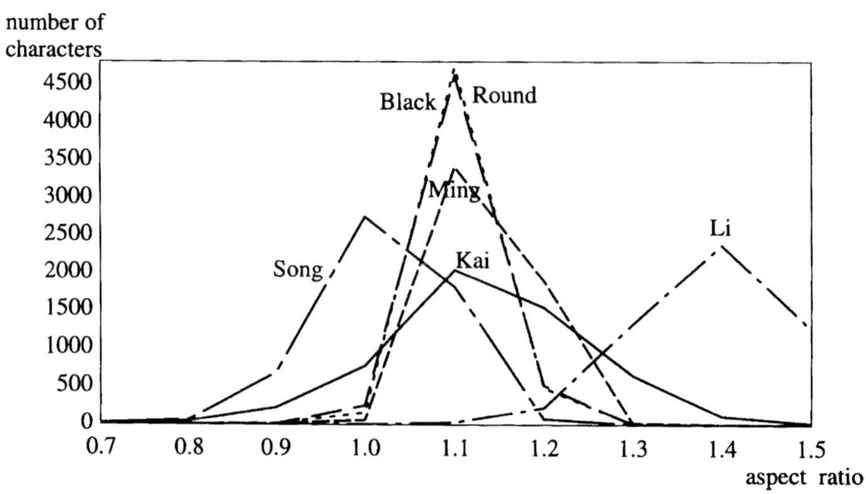

Fig. 7. Aspect ratio distributions.

2.4. Vertical/Horizontal Stroke Width Ratio (VHSWR)

Using the preceding three features to identify the printed Chinese character typefaces, we can divide the six different typefaces into four groups: Black, Li, Kai-Round, and Ming-Song. That is, each of the last two groups contains two typefaces. In order to further distinguish among the typefaces, other features need to be used to separate the Ming typeface from the Song typeface and the Kai typeface from the Round typeface. In general, horizontal and vertical strokes in Song characters have almost the same average widths, and the horizontal strokes are thinner than the vertical strokes in Ming characters. In other words, the average horizontal stroke widths are smaller than the average vertical stroke widths for most Ming characters.

There have been many studies on the skew detection of documents or text-blocks. These methods are based on the Hough transform, projection based approaches and the Fourier transform. In this paper, we assume that all test characters are extracted from deskewed documents. Then the feature, vertical/horizontal stroke width ratio, can be used to distinguish between Ming and Song typefaces. Also a small rotation angle can be tolerated according to our experiments.

The projection method is used to determine the horizontal and vertical stroke widths. All black pixels of images are projected on the horizontal axis and the vertical axis. Pixels are removed from the source images when the projection histograms are below a given threshold. Figure 8 shows an example of projecting character image on the vertical and horizontal axes. The average horizontal stroke width W_{hor} and the average vertical stroke width W_{ver} are calculated using only images consisting of horizontal or vertical strokes, respectively.

(a) (b) (c)

Fig. 8. Examples of image projection (a) source images; (b) vertical strokes; and (c) horizontal strokes.

We define the stroke width ratio as $R_{\text{sw}} = \frac{W_{\text{ver}}}{W_{\text{hor}}}$. The larger R_{sw} is, the more likely the character is to be from the Ming typeface. The R_{sw} distributions for the Ming and Song typefaces are shown in Fig. 9.

2.5. Accumulative Pixel Ratio (APR)

In order to distinguish the characters from the Kai-Round typeface group, we note that the stroke widths change in the different positions in the Kai characters, but

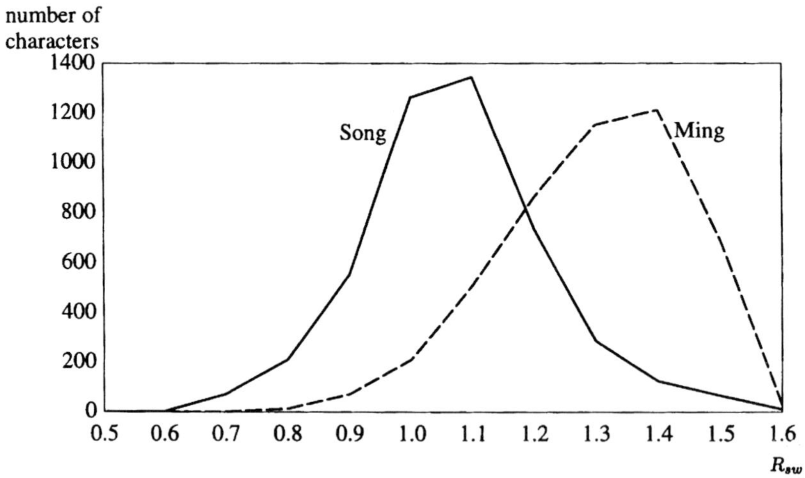

Fig. 9. Distributions of the feature R_{sw}.

remain constant in the Round characters. We count the stroke width distributions for all black pixels and record the three stroke widths that appear most frequently. Let w_1, w_2, and w_3 denote the three stroke widths, and P_1, P_2, and P_3 be their respective frequencies. That is, there are P_i black pixels of stroke width w_i, where $i = 1, 2$, or 3. The accumulative pixel ratio is defined as $R_{\mathrm{ap}} = \frac{P_1+P_2+P_3}{TP}$, where TP is the total number of pixels in a character image. If stroke widths are consistent, such as with characters in the Round typeface, the value of R_{ap} will be larger than that for characters with varying stroke widths, such as with characters in the Kai typeface. Figure 10 shows the R_{ap} distributions for the Kai and Round typefaces.

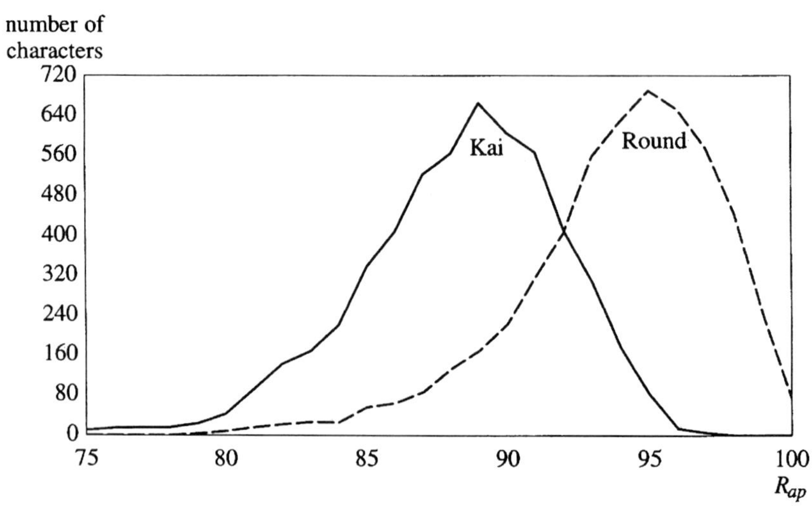

Fig. 10. Distributions of the feature R_{ap}.

Blurred areas, small components, broken characters and interfering strokes are the noise we find frequently in character images. In our system, we extracted statistical features from outer regions instead of the more blurred central areas. We also removed isolated pixels by mask filtering and the small connected components by comparing to a threshold. The four features, except the aspect ratio, in our system are relative to the run-lengths in the four main directions: vertical, horizontal, diagonal, and inverse diagonal. The broken characters and interfering strokes will affect the identification accuracy. However, the four features were extracted from all black pixels in the outer regions of the character images, and thus the effect from broken images and interfering strokes can be reduced.

3. TYPEFACE IDENTIFICATION USING A DECISION TREE

The distribution of features extracted from 5401 Chinese characters printed in six different typefaces appears as normal distribution, and each probability density function (pdf) represents the probability of the respective typeface. Since the feature distributions of certain typefaces may overlap those of other typefaces, the probability density function can be generalized such that the values assigned to elements of the universal set fall within the specified ranges and indicate the membership grades of these elements in the set. Larger values denote higher degrees of set membership. Such a function is called a *membership function*, and the set defined by it a *fuzzy set*.[5]

Triangular and bell-shaped membership functions are often used to represent fuzzy numbers. The former is inadequate at representing the probability density function correctly. The latter can describe the probability density function precisely. A curve-fitting method is used to obtain the bell-shaped membership function, which is usually a rather difficult procedure. Another membership function frequently used to approximate the probability density function is the trapezoid-shaped function, which can be implemented more easily and yields results that approximate the function more accurately. We use a trapezoid-shaped function and the least-square line-fitting method[7] to construct the membership function. In our system, the trapezoid-shaped function is defined as follows.

$$f(x;\alpha,\beta,\gamma,\delta,\theta)=\begin{cases} 0 & \text{when } x<\alpha \text{ and } x>\delta \\ \dfrac{(\alpha-x)\theta}{\alpha-\beta} & \text{when } \alpha\le x\le\beta \\ \theta & \text{when } \beta\le x\le\gamma \\ \dfrac{(\delta-x)\theta}{\delta-\gamma} & \text{when } \gamma\le x\le\delta \end{cases},$$

where $x \in \mathbb{R}$, the real numbers.

The meanings of the five parameters are illustrated in Fig. 11.

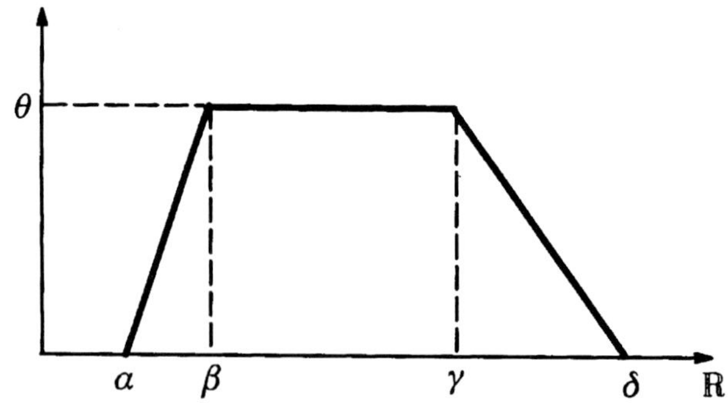

Fig. 11. Trapezoid-shaped functions $f(x;\alpha,\beta,\gamma,\delta,\theta)$.

Assume that n sample points $\langle x_1, a_1\rangle$, $\langle x_2, a_2\rangle, \ldots, \langle x_n, a_n\rangle$ are obtained from the distribution of features, where $x_i \in \mathbb{R}$ for each $i \in \mathbb{N}_n$, and a_i is the value of the probability density function for x_i. The least-square line-fitting method obtains the function $f(x;\alpha_0,\beta_0,\gamma_0,\delta_0,\theta_0)$ at which the square-error cost function

$$E = \sum_{i=1}^{n} [f(x_i;\alpha,\beta,\gamma,\delta,\theta) - a_i]^2$$

reaches its minimum. Since the values $f(x)$ do not need to be in [0, 1] for some $x \in \mathbb{R}$, the function $f(x)$ cannot be taken directly as the membership function $A(x)$. We convert $f(x)$ to $A(x)$ for each $x \in \mathbb{R}$ using the formula

$$A(x) = \max[0, \min(1, f(x; a_0, \beta_0, \gamma_0, \delta_0, \theta_0))] \qquad \text{for all } x \in \mathbb{R}\,.$$

Since there are five kinds of features for each typeface, we obtain $30(= 6 \times 5)$ membership functions from the feature distributions using the least-square line-fitting method. The decision tree for typeface identification is shown in Fig. 12. For an input character pattern, we can calculate the membership grades according to the features extracted from the input pattern and the trained membership functions. The membership grade represents the probability that the input character is from a certain typeface. The former three features, stroke width means, stroke width variations, and aspect ratio, are used to distinguish among the four groups of typefaces. We sum up the three membership grades obtained from these three features and select the typeface group with the highest score as the candidate group at the first level. If the relatively indistinguishable groups, Kai-Round and Ming-Song, are selected, other identification procedures are activated using other features at the second level.

Table 2 shows the experimental typeface identification results using only the three above-mentioned features. In this table, the Black and Li typefaces were identified with a higher degree of accuracy, but there was some confusion

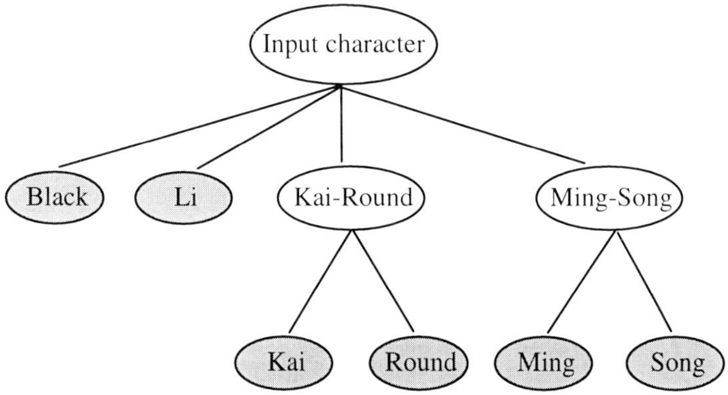

Fig. 12. The decision tree for typeface identification.

between the Kai and Round, and between the Ming and Song. When an input character is classified as Kai or Round at the first level, the vertical/horizontal stroke ratio feature is used to distinguish between these two typefaces. If Ming or Song is selected at the first level, the accumulative pixel ratio is used. The typeface identification results using the two-level decision tree are shown in Table 3.

Table 2. Experimental typeface identification results at the first level.
(Test sample = 5401 characters)

Test typefaces \ Reference typefaces	Song	Li	Kai	Round	Ming	Black
Song	**84.56%**	0.02%	3.26%	0.62%	**11.54%**	0.00%
Li	1.1%	89.89%	4.77%	1.18%	0.1%	2.96%
Kai	2.09%	3.70%	**78.41%**	**12.66%**	1.03%	2.11%
Round	5.09%	0.13%	**10.47%**	**75.06%**	1.13%	8.12%
Ming	**11.28%**	0.02%	2.36%	2.11%	**84.21%**	0.02%
Black	0.12%	0.09%	2.85%	7.33%	0.13%	89.48%

4. TYPEFACE ADJUSTMENT AND CHARACTER RECOGNITION

The typeface identification system diagram is shown in Fig. 13. A recognition system for printed Chinese characters is usually used with the automatic document reader. In most printed Chinese documents, the typefaces of characters in the same paragraph are usually the same. If a character is classified as being from a certain typeface, the typeface classifications of neighboring characters may strengthen the classification reliability or change the typeface classification of the character.

Table 3. Experimental typeface identification results using the two-level decision tree. (Test sample = 5401 characters)

Test typefaces \ Reference typefaces	Song	Li	Kai	Round	Ming	Black
Song	**92.94%**	0.02%	3.26%	0.62%	**3.16%**	0.00%
Li	1.1%	89.89%	4.77%	1.18%	0.1%	2.96%
Kai	2.09%	3.70%	**86.70%**	**4.37%**	1.03%	2.11%
Round	5.09%	0.13%	**3.72%**	**81.81%**	1.13%	8.12%
Ming	**3.97%**	0.02%	2.36%	2.11%	**91.52%**	0.02%
Black	0.12%	0.09%	2.85%	7.33%	0.13%	89.48%

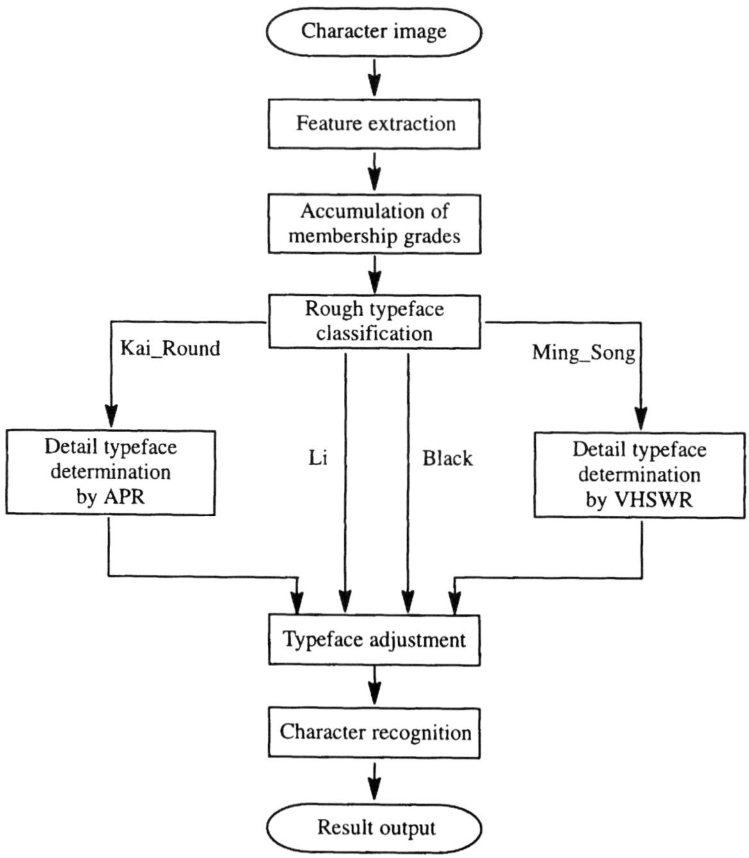

Fig. 13. System diagram of typeface identification.

In order to increase the accuracy of typeface identification, the preceding and succeeding characters are considered when identifying character typefaces. Let $Typeface_i(C_j)$ denote the $Typeface_i$ membership grade for character C_j. The adjusted membership grade is

$$Typeface_i'(C_j) = c_1 \times Typeface_i(C_j) + c_2 \times Typeface_i(C_{j-1}) + c_2 \times Typeface_i(C_{j+1}),$$

where C_{j-1} and C_{j+1} are the characters preceding and following C_j; c_1 and c_2 are constants. In our experiments, c_1 was set at 1.0 and c_2 at 0.7. An example of the typeface adjustment is given in Table 4.

Table 4. Revision of membership grade for typeface adjustment.

Test typefaces \ membership grades	$Typeface(C_{j-1})$	$Typeface(C_j)$	$Typeface(C_{j+1})$	$Typeface'(C_j)$
Song	0.20	0.24	0.32	0.604
Li	0.37	0.19	0.29	0.652
Kai	**0.78**	0.45	**0.86**	**1.598**
Round	0.38	**0.74**	0.43	1.307
Ming	0.11	0.24	0.2	0.457
Black	0.21	0.19	0.39	0.61

Techniques used for optical character recognition (OCR)[2,4,8] can be roughly grouped into two categories: structural methods and statistical methods. Structural methods represent characters as combinations of structural units, usually called *primitives*. Relaxation, dynamic programming and other techniques are then applied to match the input characters with all reference character models. Statistical methods consider a character as a whole 2-D image and extract sets of features from this character image. A classifier is then used to match features extracted from the input character image with those of the reference character images.

In this study, we evaluated some statistical features: *stroke count features*,[11] *contour pixel count features*[12] *contour directional features*,[13] *Oka's cellular features*,[9] *peripheral background area features*,[12] *crossing count features*[12] and *projection features*.[6] We used two among them to implement our OCR system. The first feature we selected was the *crossing count feature* (*CCF*). A 2-D character image was first decomposed uniformly into 8 sub-regions in both horizontal and vertical directions. After splitting the character image into horizontal and vertical strips, we extracted the *CCF*s from each strip. Four uniform scan lines were defined in each strip and the numbers of strokes CC_k that intersected each scan line k were counted. The crossing count feature is then defined as

$$f_i = \sum_{k=1}^{4} CC_k, \qquad i = 1, 2, \ldots, 16\,.$$

The second feature we selected was the *contour directional feature* (CDF). This feature represents the number of contour points in the four main directions: horizontal, vertical, diagonal and inversely diagonal directions. A 3×3 window was used to define the feature pattern. Since strokes differ widely in width, only feature patterns located on stroke boundaries were considered. Input character images were also segmented uniformly into 8×8 sub-regions, the total dimension of this feature vector was $8 \times 8 \times 4 = 256$.

The feature vector u_k of the reference character k stores the CDF from dimension 1 to dimension 256 and the CCF from dimension 257 to dimension 272. The distance between the feature vector x of the input character and the kth reference character is defined as:

$$Distance_k = \sum_{i=1}^{256} \left[\frac{(x_i - u_{ki})^2}{\sigma_{ki}} + c \times \log(\sigma_{ki}) \right] + w \times \sum_{i=257}^{272} (x_i - u_{ki})^2\,,$$

where σ_i is the standard deviation of the dimension i, and c and w are constants.

5. EXPERIMENTAL RESULTS

Our typeface identification system was implemented in C language on a Sun Sparc-10 workstation. Test images were obtained using a Umax Vista S-8 color scanner at 300 dpi (dots-per-inch). In order to evaluate typeface identification performance, we selected three pages of text documents; one of them is shown in Fig. 14. Each had 1500 Chinese characters in six different typefaces. Table 5 shows the results of character recognition without using the typeface identification. Note that the number of reference character models is 5401×6. Due to the large number of models, the average recognition rate in this case was high (96.86%), but the execution time was rather long (10.76 sec/character).

If a character model is defined for six typefaces, the number of models is only 5401. Since differences in the six typefaces were not considered, the recognition rate was reduced to 91.80%, as shown in Table 6, and the average execution time was 1.53 sec/character. The experimental results when the typeface identification was used before character recognition, are shown in Table 7. The identification rate represents the ratio of the number of characters identified correctly to the total number of test characters. The recognition rate indicates the ratio of the number of characters recognized correctly to the total number, 1500, of test characters without concern for the typeface identification performance. In our experiments, the identification rate was 82.20%, the recognition rate was 94.13%, and the execution time was 1.98 sec/character. After typeface adjustment, the final identification rate was

Fig. 14. Some of the printed Chinese characters used for testing in experiments.

Table 5. Experimental character recognition results using 5401 × 6 reference models.

Typeface	Song	Li	Kai	Round	Ming	Black	Total
Recognition rate (%)	97.50	93.75	98.33	95.83	98.75	97.33	96.86

Table 6. Experimental character recognition results using 5401 reference models.

Typeface	Song	Li	Kai	Round	Ming	Black	Total
Recognition rate (%)	90.42	88.75	92.08	92.50	93.75	93.00	91.80

Table 7. Experimental typeface identification results and character recognition without typeface adjustments.

Typeface	Song	Li	Kai	Round	Ming	Black	Total
Identification rate (%)	85.25	83.50	79.58	76.25	85.00	83.33	82.20
Recognition rate (%)	96.67	91.25	88.75	95.42	96.67	95.67	94.13

Table 8. Experimental typeface identification and character recognition results using typeface adjustments.

Typeface	Song	Li	Kai	Round	Ming	Black	Total
Identification rate (%)	93.33	90.83	87.08	85.42	92.08	90.33	89.87
Recognition rate (%)	97.08	92.91	92.92	95.42	97.50	97.00	95.60

89.87%, the recognition rate was 95.60%, as shown in Table 8, and the execution time was 2.02 sec/character.

6. CONCLUSIONS

A typeface identification system for printed Chinese characters has been presented in this paper. Chinese characters in printed documents generally occur in one of the six typefaces: Ming, Song, Li, Kai, Round, and Black. In order to increase character recognition accuracy, we identify typefaces before conducting character recognition and match input character images with reference character models of the same typeface.

We measure probability distributions of features for these six typefaces and use these features to classify character typefaces. Membership functions are constructed to represent the fuzzy numbers for the distribution of each feature. In order to obtain higher typeface identification rates, we propose a two-level decision tree. Three features, the stroke width means, the stroke width variations, and aspect ratio, are used at the first level. Input characters are classified as belonging to one of the four typeface groups: Black, Li, Kai-Round, and Ming-Song. The two other features, vertical/horizontal stroke-width ratio and accumulative pixel ratio, are used for further typeface identification.

To further improve the identification rate, a contextual heuristic is used. Since neighboring characters usually appear in the same typeface in printed documents, we adjust the typeface classifications of certain characters by considering the typefaces of the three consecutive characters. Experimental results show that a typeface identification rate of 89.87% was achieved along with a character recognition rate of 95.60%.

In the printed character recognition system, the memory required to store features for 5401 characters in six typefaces is very large. We must load these features into the memory before recognizing unknown patterns. Reducing the need for so much memory, and speeding-up the recognition time are important issues for further study. Furthermore, a printed document may use characters from more than six typefaces. The typeface identification of Chinese characters when more than six typefaces are used is also left for future work.

REFERENCES

1. T. Akiyama and N. Hagita, "Automated entry system for printed documents", *Patt. Recogn.* **23** (1990) 1141–1154.
2. F. H. Cheng and W. H. Hsu, "Research on Chinese OCR in Taiwan", *Int. J. Pattern Recognition and Artificial Intelligence* **5**, 1&2 (1991) 139–164.
3. K. C. Fan, "Document analysis and lossless reproduction (II)", Technical Report, National Science Council, R.O.C., 1995, p. 7.
4. V. K. Govindan and A. P. Shivaprasad, "Character recognition — a review", *Patt. Recogn.* **23**, 7 (1990) 671–683.
5. I. C. Jou, Y. G. Chau, R. H. Ju and J. Y. Lee, "Modeling for Chinese character patterns", *Proc. CVGIP*, Taiwan, R.O.C., 1994, pp. 131–134.
6. S. H. Kim and J. I. Doh, "Off-line recognition of Korean scripts using distance matching and neural network classifiers", *Proc. 3rd ICDAR*, August, 1995, pp. 34–37.
7. G. J. Klir and B. Yuan, "Fuzzy sets and fuzzy logic", Prentice Hall Inc., 1995.
8. G. Nagy, "Chinese character recognition: a twenty-five-year retrospective", *Proc. ICPR*, 1988, pp. 163–167.
9. R. Oka, "Handwritten Chinese–Japanese characters recognition by cellular feature", *Proc. 6th Int. Conf. Pattern Recognition*, IEEE, October 1991, pp. 783–785.
10. H. H. Tseng and W. H. Tsai, "Chinese character font recognition using Fourier spectrum features and back-propagation neural network", *Proc. CVGIP*, Taiwan, R.O.C., 1996, pp. 206–213.
11. J. Tsukumo and K. Asai, "Machine printed Chinese and Japanese characters recognition method and experiments for reading Japanese pocket books", *IEEE Comput. Soc. Conf. Computer Vision and Pattern Recognition*, 1986, pp. 162–167.
12. L. Tu *et al.*, "Recognition of handprinted Chinese characters by feature matching", *Int. Conf. Computer Processing Chinese and Oriental Languages*, 1991, pp. 154–157.
13. C. H. Tung, *A Study of Handwritten Chinese Text Recognition*, Ph.D. dissertation, Dept. Comp. Sci. & Info. Engr., National Chiao Tung University, Taiwan, R.O.C., 1994.

Yi-Hong Tseng received the B.S. degree in applied mathematics from the National Chung Hsing University, Taichung, Taiwan, in 1992, and M.S. degree in computer science and information engineering from the National Chiao Tung University, Hsinchu, Taiwan, in 1994. He is now a Ph.D. candidate in the Department of Computer Science and Information Engineering, National Chiao Tung University, Taiwan.

His research interests are in the areas of image processing, pattern recognition, and document analysis.

Chi-Chang Kuo received the B.S. and M.S. degrees in information engineering and computer science from the Feng Chia University, Taichung, Taiwan, in 1990, and the National Chiao Tung University, Hsinchu, Taiwan, in 1996, respectively. He is now a researcher at the Electronic Data Processing Center, Directorate General of Budget Accounting and Statistics, the Executive Yuan.

His research interests are in the areas of pattern recognition and image processing.

Hsi-Jian Lee received the B.S., M.S. and Ph.D. degrees in computer engineering from National Chiao Tung University, Hsinchu, Taiwan, in 1976, 1980, and 1984, respectively. Since 1981 he has been in the Department of Computer Engineering, National Chiao Tung University, and since August 1989 he has been a professor. He is also a Deputy Director at Microelectronic and Information Research Center (MIRC) since January 1997.

He is now the president of the Oriental Language Computer Society (OLCS), the editor-in-chief of the International Journal of Computer Processing of Oriental Languages (CPOL), and an associate editor of the International Journal of Pattern Recognition and Artificial Intelligence, and Pattern Analysis and Applications. He has been a member of the executive committee of the Chinese Society on Image Processing and Pattern Recognition.

He was responsible for the 1992 R.O.C. Computational Linguistic Workshop and 1993 R.O.C. Conference on Computer Vision, Graphics, and Image Processing. He was the program chair of the 1994 International Computer Symposium and the Fourth International Workshop on Frontiers in Handwriting Recognition (IWFHR). In 1997, he was a winner of the award for ten outstanding information persons of R.O.C. In 1992–94, he was a winner of the award for outstanding researchers of the National Science Council, R.O.C. He is a member of Phi Tau Phi.

His current research interests include document analysis, optical character recognition, image processing, pattern recognition, digital library and artificial intelligence.

A SELF-ORGANIZING HIERARCHICAL CLASSIFIER FOR MULTI-LINGUAL LARGE-SET ORIENTAL CHARACTER RECOGNITION

HEE-SEON PARK

Software Center, Samsung Electronics Co., Ltd.,
Apkujong Bldg., 599-4 Shinsa-dong, Kangnam-ku, Seoul 135-120, Korea

HEE-HEON SONG

Department of Computer Engineering Education, Andong National University
Songchon-dong, Andong, Kyongbuk 760-749, Korea

SEONG-WHAN LEE*

Center for Artificial Vision Research, Korea University
Anam-dong, Seongbuk-ku, Seoul 136-701, Korea
E-mail: swlee@image.korea.ac.kr

In this paper, we propose a practical scheme for multi-lingual, multi-font and multi-size large-set Oriental character recognition using a self-organizing hierarchical neural network classifier. In order to absorb the variation of the character shapes in multi-font and multi-size characters, a modified nonlinear shape normalization method based on dot density was introduced, and also to represent the different topological structures of multi-lingual characters effectively, a hierarchical feature extraction method was adopted. For coarse classification, a tree classifier and SOFM/LVQ based classifier which is composed of an adaptive SOFM coarse-classifier and an LVQ4 language-classifier were considered. For fine classification, a classifier based on LVQ4 learning algorithm has been developed.

The experimental results revealed that the proposed scheme has the highest recognition rate of 98.27% for testing data with 7,320 kinds of multi-lingual classes and the time performance of more than 40 characters per second on 486DX-2 66MHz PC.

Keywords: Multi-lingual character recognition, Oriental character recognition, SOFM, LVQ4, language classifier.

1. INTRODUCTION

For a long time, significant research efforts have been devoted to character recognition which is used to translate human-readable documents into machine-readable codes. In spite of the considerable attempts to build practical character recognition systems, it is still a very challenging problem.[8] One of the main reasons is that the general documents contain multi-font and multi-size characters as well as multi-lingual characters, such as Korean, Chinese, and Japanese characters, English alphabets, numerals, and some special characters especially seen in Oriental countries. And, the differences in their shapes do not seem to simplify the recognition problem.

*Corresponding author.

Advances in Oriental Document Analysis and Recognition Techniques (1998) 191–208

In the past several years, many investigators have tried to tackle these problems, and some neural network based recognition systems have been successfully applied to practical recognition problems with good results.[3,11] However, most of them are used to recognize small-set characters, such as the English alphabets and numerals. Although there were also some recognition schemes for multi-font and multi-size large-set characters, such as the Korean, Chinese, and Japanese characters, and so forth, most were only developed to recognize unilingual languages[1] and the system had limitations in learning abilities due to large-set classes. Also, the speed of learning and recognition was very low. Therefore, a new practical scheme is indispensable for effectively recognizing multi-lingual, multi-font, and multi-size large-set Oriental characters.

In this paper, we propose a new practical scheme for the recognition of the multi-lingual, multi-font, and multi-size large-set Oriental characters using a self-organizing hierarchical classifier. In order to improve the recognition speed and performance, a hierarchical feature extraction method is presented. The overview of the proposed recognition scheme is shown in Fig. 1.

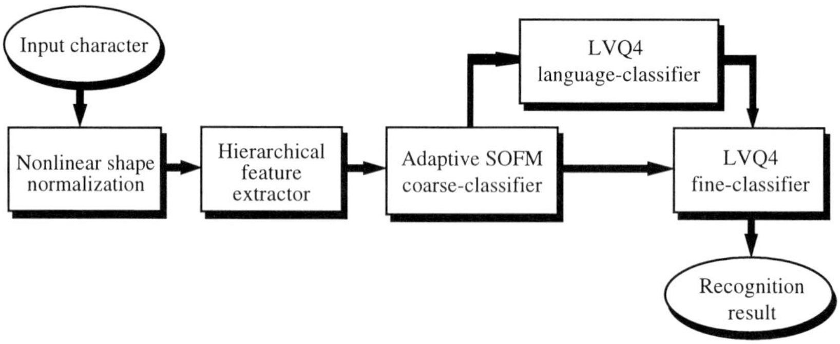

Fig. 1. Overview of the proposed recognition scheme.

In the next section, a nonlinear shape normalization method based on the dot density method is introduced. In Sec. 3, various feature extraction strategies based on the hierarchical concept are presented in order to improve the performance of the classifier. In Sec. 4, a tree coarse-classifier and an adaptive SOFM coarse-classifier combined with LVQ based language-classifier are proposed. For fine classification, an LVQ4 fine-classifier is introduced. Section 5 presents experimental results for the multi-lingual, multi-font, and multi-size large-set Oriental character recognition. Finally, the concluding remarks are discussed in Sec. 6.

2. SHAPE NORMALIZATION

Conventionally, the purpose of the linear shape normalization is to convert the image into one having constant position and size. However, linear shape normalization is insufficient for characters with various kinds of fonts and sizes because of their irregularities, partial distortions, the differences in shape and the mechanical property of the scanner.

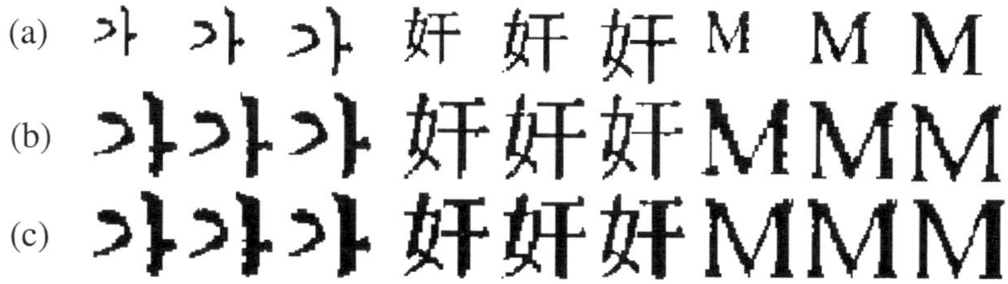

Fig. 2. Comparison of LSN with NSN: (a) Input character, (b) LSN, (c) NSN based on dot density.

In this paper, we use nonlinear shape normalization based on dot density for the purpose of overcoming these problems.[6] Figure 2 shows a comparison between nonlinear shape normalization method (LSN) based on dot density and the linear shape normalized method (NSN). The nonlinear shape normalization based on dot density is invented by Yamashita *et al.*[12] Its basic idea is that the number of black dots in the input character is used as a characteristic feature. However, if the conventional nonlinear shape normalization is applied for some characters, such as 'I', 'l', '1', '-', '_', '[', and ']' samples, their normalized images are mostly filled with black pixels as shown in Fig. 3(a). In order to overcome this problem, we modified the conventional nonlinear shape normalization method by using the information of width and height, and obtained the effective result as shown in Fig. 3(b).

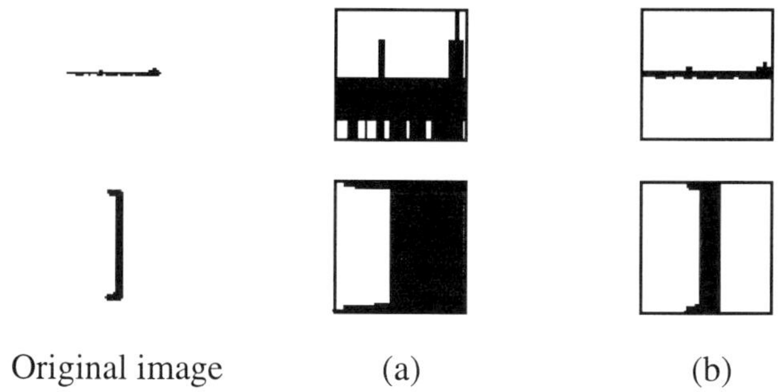

Fig. 3. Examples of nonlinear shape normalization: (a) Conventional nonlinear shape normalization, (b) Modified nonlinear shape normalization.

3. HIERARCHICAL FEATURE EXTRACTION

By investigating the structural characteristics of multi-lingual characters, we find that some characters are very simple, while others are very complicated. Moreover, there are many mutually similar characters which differ from each other by only one point or stroke, especially Korean and Chinese characters.

In order to effectively represent the different topological structures of the multi-lingual large-set Oriental characters, we propose a hierarchical feature extraction method. According to the strategy mentioned above, we define hierarchical features as follows:

Let G represent a normalized input character, and $F_r(\cdot)$ a certain transform function of r-order, where r = 0, 1, 2, 3. Then, $F_0(G) = G$ is defined as the zero-order feature of G, and actually it is the normalized input character of G itself. $F_1(G)$, $F_2(G)$, and $F_3(G)$ are defined as the first, second, and third-order features of G, respectively. The first-order feature will be used by adaptive SOFM coarse-classifier and the second- and third-order features will be used by LVQ4 language-classifier or LVQ4 fine-classifier.

In this section, we present three kinds of hierarchical features which represent the different topological structures in the different classification levels: mesh feature, overlapping CDC (Contour Directional Code) feature, and directional feature by Kirsch mask.

3.1. Mesh Feature

In general, mesh feature has been used for character recognition due to its simplicity and good performance. Also, it is more suitable for the nonlinear shape normalization based on dot density among others because it is actually based on the number of black pixels. Figure 4 shows how the hierarchical mesh feature is extracted from the normalized input character.

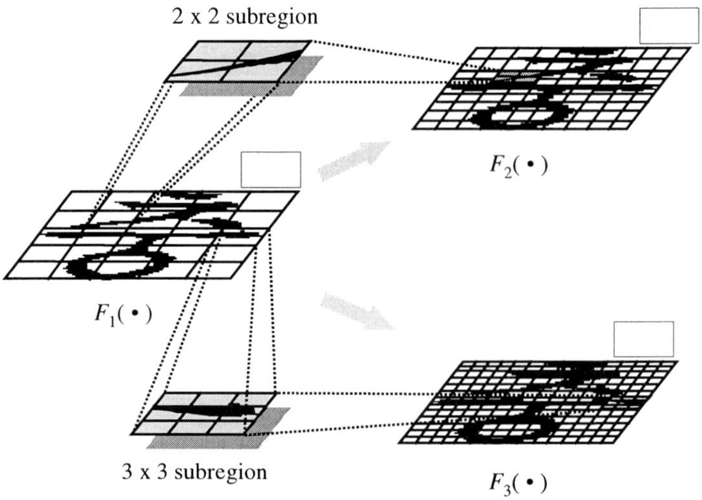

Fig. 4. Hierarchical mesh feature.

The first-order feature $F_1(\cdot)$ of the proposed hierarchical mesh feature is extracted as follows: A normalized input character is divided into $N \times N$ subregions of equal size. Then, the total number of black pixels in each subregion is accumulated. Totally, $N \times N$ elements of the first-order mesh feature are extracted from the normalized input character. In the extraction of the second-order feature $F_2(\cdot)$ and the third-order feature $F_3(\cdot)$, each subregion divided into $N \times N$ subregions by the first-order feature extraction is again divided into $r \times r$ subregions. In other words, the total number of black pixels in each subregion is calculated, and $r^2 \times N^2$ elements of the second- and third-order features are extracted.

3.2. Overlapping CDC Feature

Another feature considered, overlapping CDC feature, is extracted as follows: Firstly, the contour directions of the normalized characters are detected by contour tracing algorithm[9] as shown in Fig. 5. Then, we can obtain four direction codes such as the horizontal (H), vertical (V), right-diagonal (R) and left-diagonal (L) from the normalized input character by tracing the relative locations of the current pixel. Secondly, the normalized input character is divided into $N \times N$ subregions. We consider the overlapping subregions in order to absorb the variation caused by the positional translation and the mechanical properties of the scanner.

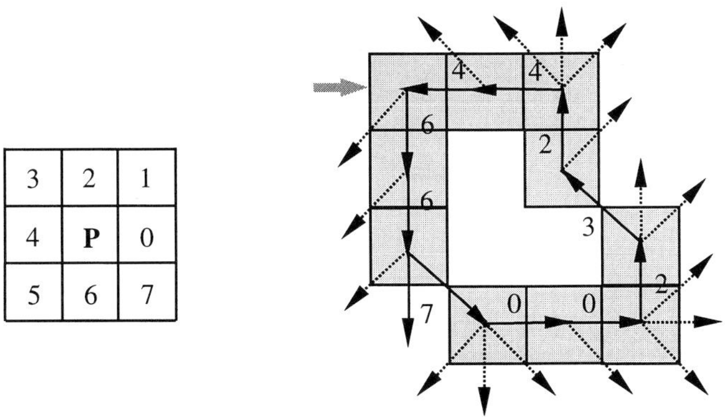

(a) (b)

Fig. 5. Contour tracing: (a) Relative locations of pixels with respect to a pixel P, (b) A simple example of contour tracing.

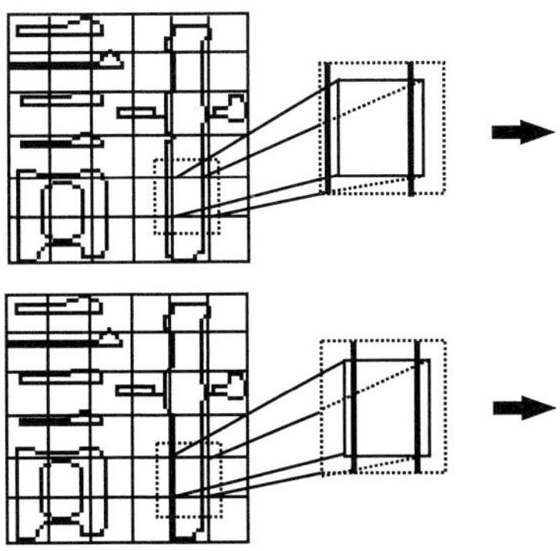

direction	value
H	0
V	28
D	0
R	0

direction	value
H	0
V	28
D	0
R	0

(a) (b)

Fig. 6. Overlapping CDC feature: (a) Two character images with the same overlapping CDC, (b) Direction code histograms of an extended subregion in (a).

As shown in Fig. 6, when the histogram of a local contour direction code is calculated, the overlapping subregions contribute their direction values to the histograms of the related local subregions. And the quantity of each direction code within an extended subregion is accumulated.

The first-order overlapping CDC feature $F_1(\cdot)$ is extracted by using just the horizontal and the vertical direction codes for each subregion and contains totally $2 \times N^2$ elements. We obtain $4 \times N^2$ elements of the second- and third-order overlapping CDC features, $F_2(\cdot)$ and $F_3(\cdot)$ by adding right-diagonal and left-diagonal direction codes to the horizontal and vertical direction codes used in the first-order feature.

3.3. Directional Feature by Kirsch Mask

We also consider the directional feature based on the Kirsch edge detector.[10] Nonlinear edge enhancement algorithm is as follows:

$$\mathrm{Grad}(i,j) = \max\{1, \max_{k=0}^{7} |5S_k - 3T_k|\}, \tag{1}$$

where

$$S_k = A_k + A_{k+1} + A_{k+2}, \tag{2}$$

$$T_k = A_{k+3} + A_{k+4} + A_{k+5} + A_{k+6} + A_{k+7}. \tag{3}$$

In Eq. (1), $\mathrm{Grad}(i,j)$ is the gradient of the pixel (i,j) and A_k $(k = 0, 1, \cdots, 7)$ are eight neighbors of pixel (i,j) defined as shown in Fig. 7.

A_0	A_1	A_2
A_7	(i, j)	A_3
A_6	A_5	A_4

Fig. 7. Definition of eight neighbors of pixel (i,j).

We calculate the directional features for the four directions as follows:

$$\begin{aligned}
\mathrm{Grad}(i,j)_H &= \max(|5S_0 - 3T_0|,\ |5S_4 - 3T_4|)\\
\mathrm{Grad}(i,j)_V &= \max(|5S_2 - 3T_2|,\ |5S_6 - 3T_6|)\\
\mathrm{Grad}(i,j)_R &= \max(|5S_1 - 3T_1|,\ |5S_5 - 3T_5|)\\
\mathrm{Grad}(i,j)_L &= \max(|5S_3 - 3T_3|,\ |5S_7 - 3T_7|)
\end{aligned} \tag{4}$$

Figure 8 shows the directional values extracted from a normalized input character by the Kirsch mask described in Eq. (4). As a final feature extraction step, each feature map is compressed to the $N \times N$ feature map. The first-order directional feature by the Kirsch mask, $F_1(\cdot)$, is extracted by using just the horizontal directional feature $\mathrm{Grad}(i,j)_H$ and the vertical directional feature $\mathrm{Grad}(i,j)_V$ in each compressed subregion, and contains totally $2 \times N^2$ elements. Also, we obtain $4 \times N^2$ elements of the second- and third-order directional features, $F_2(\cdot)$ and $F_3(\cdot)$, by adding the right-diagonal and left-diagonal direction features $\mathrm{Grad}(i,j)_R$

and $\text{Grad}(i,j)_L$ to the horizontal and vertical direction features $\text{Grad}(i,j)_H$ and $\text{Grad}(i,j)_V$ used in the first-order feature.

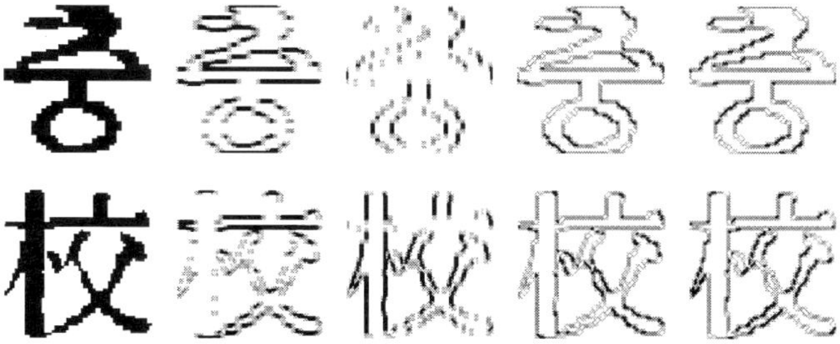

(a) (b) (c) (d) (e)

Fig. 8. Directional feature by the Kirsch mask: (a) Normalized image, (b) Horizontal feature, (c) Vertical feature, (d) Right-diagonal feature, (e) Left-diagonal feature.

4. PROPOSED SELF-ORGANIZING HIERARCHICAL CLASSIFIER

In this section, we propose a robust self-organizing hierarchical classifier for the multi-lingual, multi-font and multi-size large-set Oriental character recognition. That is, we consider a coarse-classifier which can play an important role in reducing the number of candidates to be recognized and a fine-classifier which can discriminate similar characters effectively.

4.1. Coarse-Classifier

Generally, the coarse classification method is used to classify large-set characters into several small groups of candidates for recognition. This is a typical clustering problem. To solve this problem, we consider two kinds of coarse-classifiers.

4.1.1. Tree coarse-classifier

The tree coarse-classifier is characterized by the fact that an unknown input character is classified into a cluster by using one or more criterion. In this paper, we automatically generate a hierarchical tree coarse-classifier by applying the following technique.[5] In order to select the most separable and stable features used in each internal node of the tree, the Fisher's discriminant (FD) ratio has been used. After calculating the FD values of the input features, we select the first N elements of them in decreasing order. Thus, features with more discriminative power on the character family in an internal node are determined. After feature selection, we divide current cluster into some child clusters by using the K-means clustering algorithm and their cluster centers are updated to new values, respectively. After global training on the basis of the given training set, hierarchical tree coarse-classifier in the recognition phase finds the external node by searching the nearest cluster between the input character and the cluster centers with only N separable features in the current internal node. Then, the input character is fed into the fine-classifier corresponding to the current external node.

4.1.2. Adaptive SOFM coarse-classifier and LVQ4 language-classifier

The SOFM learning algorithm was first introduced by Kohonen.[4] It is based on the unsupervised competitive learning in which only one output unit, one per local group of units at time gives the active response to the current input vector. By the SOFM learning algorithm developed by Kohonen, the network can perform unsupervised classification learning, which is based on the clustering of the given training data. The level of activity represents the similarity between the input vector and its associated weight vector, and the standard way of expressing similarity is through a set of distances between a pair of objects.

In the training process, the learning algorithm automatically adapts connected weights to the units in the network such that each unit comes to represent a distinct category of the input vector as shown in Fig. 9.

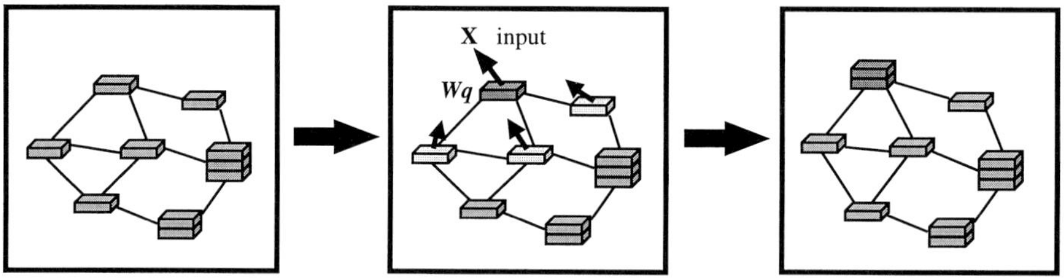

(a) Before adaptation (b) Occurrence of an input data (c) After adaptation

Fig. 9. A typical example of adaptation step of SOFM learning algorithm

After the network is sufficiently trained, each weight vector represents the center of the cluster learned from the training data. The network thus learns the probability distribution of the training data. However, the initial weight vectors in the traditional SOFM learning algorithm have a great influence on the discrimination power of the network. Therefore, we introduce an adaptive SOFM learning algorithm, which has the following advantages over the traditional SOFM algorithm:

(1) It can break the local minimum that the clustering problem may encounter;
(2) the creation operation of the unit enables it to find a better distribution of clusters; and
(3) the initial weights can be assigned at random before training the network.

Let $\mathbf{X}$ be an input sample from the training set. In our case, each element of $\mathbf{X}$ represents the value of the first-order feature $F_1(\cdot)$ obtained from the feature extraction process. Let $\mathbf{W}_j$, $j = 1, 2, \ldots, M$ and $\mathbf{C}_j$, $j = 1, 2, \ldots, M$ be the weight vectors of an adaptive SOFM network and cluster vectors, respectively. Also, let θ_j, $j = 1, 2, \ldots, M$ be the reference-count of ith unit. Then, the proposed adaptive SOFM coarse-classifier is trained as follows:

1. Initialize all weight vectors $\mathbf{W}_j$ of the network with zero and reference-count θ_j with zero.
2. Randomly pick up an input sample $\mathbf{X}$ from the training set and select the nearest weight vector.

$$q = i, \quad D_i < D_j \quad \text{for all } i \neq j \tag{5}$$

where

$$D_j = \| \mathbf{X} - \mathbf{W}_j \|, \quad j = 1, 2, \cdots, M\,. \tag{6}$$

3. Update the selected weight vector according to SOFM adaptation criteria:

$$\mathbf{W}_i(t+1) = \mathbf{W}_i + \eta(t)[\mathbf{X} - \mathbf{W}_i(t)] \quad \text{for all } i \in N_q(t),$$

where $N_q(t)$ is a topological neighborhood of q and $\eta(t)$ is the learning rate. And add 1 to the reference-count θ_q:

$$\theta_q(t+1) = \theta_q(t) + 1.$$

4. If $\theta_q > \beta$ holds, then create a new unit r according to Ref. 2 (Fig. 10):

$$\begin{aligned} \mathbf{W}_r &= \frac{\mathbf{W}_q + \mathbf{W}_f}{2}, \\ \theta_q &= \theta_f = \theta_r = 0, \end{aligned} \tag{7}$$

where f is a unit satisfying

$$\|\mathbf{W}_f - \mathbf{W}_q\| \geq \|\mathbf{W}_i - \mathbf{W}_q\| \quad \text{for all } i \in N_q.$$

5. Repeat Step 2~4 until the number of training iterations, T, is reached.
6. Finally, cluster vectors $\mathbf{C}_i$ are determined by

$$\mathbf{X} \in \mathbf{C}_i \;\; \text{iff} \;\; \|\mathbf{X} - \mathbf{W}_i\| \leq \|\mathbf{X} - \mathbf{W}_j\| \quad \text{for all } j (j \neq i) \tag{8}$$

By investigating the structural characteristics of the multi-lingual characters, we can observe that English alphabets, numerals, and special characters have relatively simple structures, some Korean characters are very complicated, and some Chinese characters have more complex structures than Korean characters. Thus, the separation of Korean characters, Chinese characters, and the other character set is needed to improve the recognition speed and performance. At this point, we propose an LVQ4 language-classifier in the process of designing the coarse-classifier.

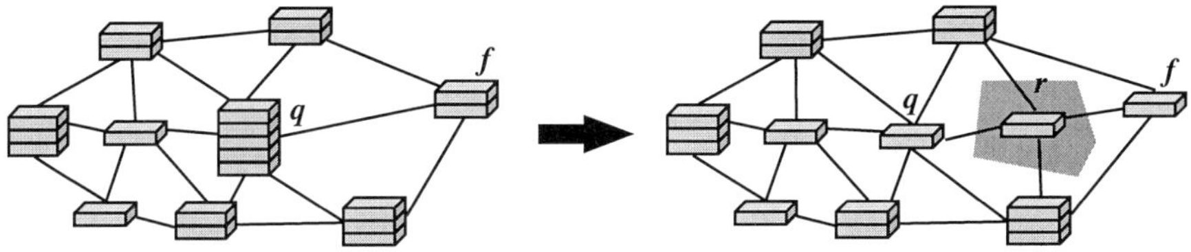

(a) Before creation (b) After creation

Fig. 10. Creation of a new unit.

LVQ is an approach to the approximation of class distributions on the basis of available samples and a supervised learning technique that uses class information to move the optimal reference vectors, so as to improve the quality of the decision regions. Each class is described by one or more reference models, which is properly placed within each class zone such that the decision borders are approximated by the nearest-neighbor rule. Some LVQ learning algorithms were introduced by Kohonen.[4] Among them, the improved LVQ3, so called LVQ4, learning algorithm has shown efficient performance for large-set character recognition.[7] The detailed description of the LVQ4 learning algorithm will be given in the next subsection.

We construct many representative clusters through adaptive SOFM learning algorithm, and each cluster is assigned to the labeled class which is designated as Korean characters, Chinese characters, alphanumeric/special characters, or mixed characters. If a cluster is composed of only a single language, the cluster is directly applied to LVQ4 fine-classifier with the second-order feature $F_2(\cdot)$. And if there exists any mixed cluster, we use LVQ4 language-classifier to reduce further the classification error with the second-order feature $F_2(\cdot)$. Then, each cluster separated by LVQ4 language-classifier is applied to LVQ4 fine-classifier with the third-order feature $F_3(\cdot)$.

4.2. Fine-Classifier

For fine classification, we adopt a classifier based on LVQ4 learning algorithm, which is linked to each cluster resulting from the coarse classification. The adopted LVQ4 fine-classifier is trained by the following LVQ4 learning algorithm:

---

1. Randomly pick up an input sample $\mathbf{X}$ from the training set.
2. Compute distances from the input sample to all reference vectors.

$$D_i = \| \mathbf{X} - \mathbf{m}_i \|, \quad i = 1, 2, \ldots, M . \tag{9}$$

3. Select two reference vectors, $\mathbf{m}_i$ and $\mathbf{m}_j$, that are the two nearest neighbors to $\mathbf{X}$.
4. If $\mathbf{X}$ falls into a zone of values called a window, update the selected reference vectors, $\mathbf{m}_i$ and $\mathbf{m}_j$, according to the adaptation criteria.

The input $\mathbf{X}$ is defined to fall into the window if

$$\min\left(\frac{D_i}{D_j}, \frac{D_j}{D_i}\right) > s. \tag{10}$$

If w is the relative width of the window in its narrowest point, then $s = (1-w)/(1+w)$.

Adaptation criteria:

$$\begin{aligned} \mathbf{m}_i(t+1) &= \mathbf{m}_i(t) - \alpha(t)[\mathbf{X} - \mathbf{m}_i(t)], \\ \mathbf{m}_j(t+1) &= \mathbf{m}_j(t) + \alpha(t)[\mathbf{X} - \mathbf{m}_j(t)], \end{aligned} \tag{11}$$

where $\mathbf{m}_i$ and $\mathbf{m}_j$ are the two closest reference vectors to $\mathbf{X}$, whereby $\mathbf{X}$ belongs to the same class as $\mathbf{m}_j$, but not as $\mathbf{m}_i$. $\alpha(t)$ is the learning rate and it monotonically decreases with time; furthermore $\mathbf{X}$ must fall into the window;

$$\mathbf{m}_j(t+1) = \mathbf{m}_j(t) + \epsilon(t)\alpha(t)[\mathbf{X} - \mathbf{m}_j(t)] \tag{12}$$

for the nearest $\mathbf{m}_j$ to $\mathbf{X}$ regardless of the window, if $\mathbf{X}$, $\mathbf{m}_i$ and $\mathbf{m}_j$ belong to the same class.

$$\mathbf{m}_k(t+1) = \mathbf{m}_k(t) - \epsilon(t)\alpha(t)[\mathbf{X} - \mathbf{m}_k(t)] \tag{13}$$

for $k \in \{i, j\}$, if $\mathbf{X}$, $\mathbf{m}_i$ and $\mathbf{m}_j$ belong to different classes. The optimal value of ϵ depends on the size of the window, being smaller for narrower windows.

5. Repeat step 2~4 until the number of training iteration is reached.

Figure 11 shows the structure of the proposed classifier, which is composed of an adaptive SOFM coarse-classifier, LVQ4 language-classifiers, and LVQ4 fine-classifiers.

5. EXPERIMENTAL RESULTS

In this section, we present experimental results and analyze the performance of the proposed classifier with the various features. Experiments have been carried out on Cray Y-MP super-computer and 486DX-2 66MHz PC.

5.1. Environments

Experiments have been conducted with the data set described in Tables 1 and 2.

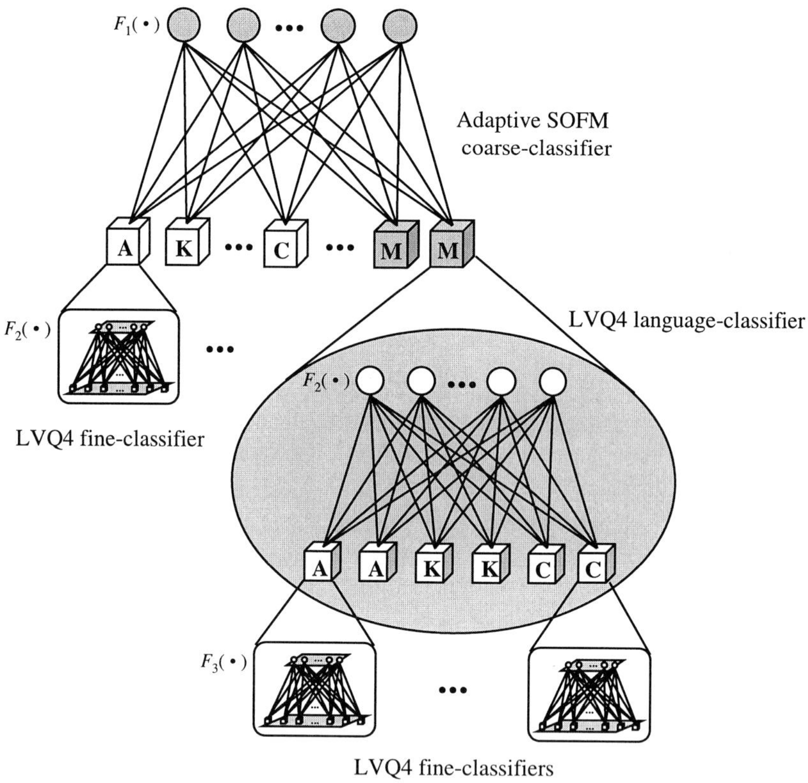

K : Cluster consisting of only Korean characters
C : Cluster consisting of only Chinese characters
A : Cluster consisting of only English alphabets, numerals, and special characters
M : Cluster consisting of mixed characters

Fig. 11. Structure of the proposed classifier.

Table 1. Training data.

Language	Korean characters	Chinese characters	Alphanumeric characters	Special characters
Class	2,350	4,888	52 + 10	20
Font	Myungjo Gothic Goongseo		Times Arial Courier	
Size	8, 10, 12, 14, 16 points			
Resolution	400 DPI			
Samples	2,196,000 samples (20 sets for each font and size)			

Table 2. Testing data.

Language	Korean characters	Chinese characters	Alphanumeric characters	Special characters
Class	2,350	4,888	52 + 10	20
Font	New Myungjo Thick Gothic Middle Myungjo Goongseo		New Times Arial Courier Arial Narrow	
Size	9, 11, 13, 15 points			
Resolution	300 or 400 DPI			
Samples	1,171,200 samples (10 sets for each font and size)			

Figure 12 shows a typical example of the scanned characters for the experiments.

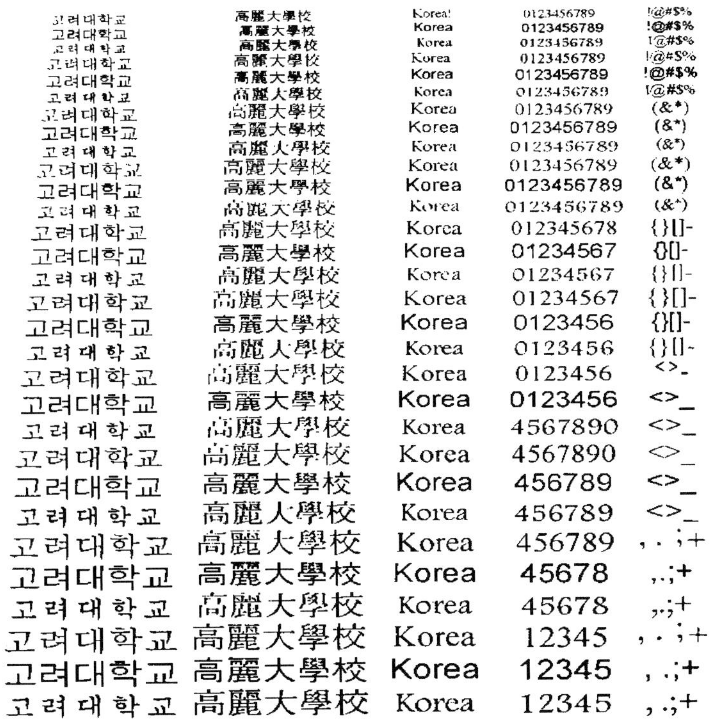

Fig. 12. A typical example of the multi-lingual, multi-font, and multi-size character set.

In order to demonstrate the performance of the proposed scheme, three kinds of hierarchical features and three kinds of classification methods have been considered as follows:

Mesh: mesh feature
CDC: overlapping contour direction code feature
Kirsch: directional feature by Kirsch mask
Method 1: LVQ4 fine-classifier without coarse-classifier
Method 2: tree coarse-classifier + LVQ4 fine-classifier
Method 3: adaptive SOFM coarse-classifier + LVQ4 language-classifier + LVQ4 fine-classifier

5.2. Recognition Experiments

In our experiments, a hierarchical tree coarse-classifier was trained with the branch factor of 2 and the overlapping degree of 0.2. For training the proposed adaptive SOFM coarse-classifier, the learning rate of 0.02 and β of 20,000 have been used. Each language-classifier and fine-classifier was trained by LVQ4 learning algorithm with the learning rate of 0.03, the epsilon of 0.01 and the window size of 0.2.

Owing to the hierarchical structure used in the proposed scheme, the recognition speed has been very much improved as shown in Table 3.

Table 3. Average processing time.

Processing		Time(ms/char)
Normalization		10
Feature extraction	Mesh	2
	CDC	6
	Kirsch	11
Classification	Method 1	363
	Method 2	19
	Method 3	15

In Fig. 13, we demonstrate that the proposed classifier using the adaptive SOFM coarse-classifier combined with the LVQ4 language-classifier has desirable performance. These results show that the proposed adaptive SOFM coarse-classifier combined with the LVQ4 language-classifier has relatively higher performance than the others.

Table 4 shows the recognition rates for the various features and classification methods. This result indicates that the hierarchical mesh feature is relatively superior to the overlapping CDC and Kirsch features. Also, it should be noted that Method 3 has a relatively high performance, considering the fast processing time.

Table 4. Classification accuracy for testing data.

	Classification method		
	Method 1	Method 2	Method 3
Mesh	98.31%	97.07%	98.27%
CDC	97.50%	96.17%	97.32%
Kirsch	97.82%	96.48%	97.48%

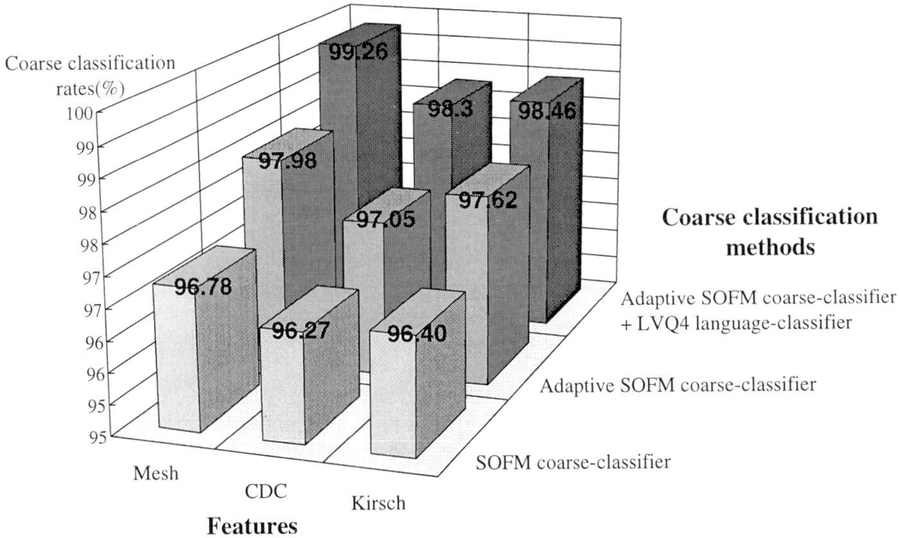

Fig. 13. Comparison of the coarse classification rates.

6. CONCLUDING REMARKS

In general, documents may contain multi-font and multi-size characters, as well as multi-lingual characters, such as the Korean, Chinese and Japanese characters, English alphabets, numerals, and some special characters especially in Oriental countries. However, the previous Oriental character recognition systems were only developed to recognize uni-lingual language, and the system had limitations in the learning ability due to the large-set classes. Also, the speed of learning and recognition was very low. Therefore, a new scheme is indispensable for effectively recognizing multi-lingual, multi-font, and multi-size large-set Oriental characters.

In order to overcome these problems, we proposed a practical high speed recognition scheme using a self-organizing hierarchical classifier. For the purpose of absorbing the variation of the character shapes in the multi-lingual, multi-font, and multi-size Oriental characters, a modified nonlinear shape normalization method based on dot density has been developed. In order to improve the performance of the recognition scheme, a hierarchical feature extraction method has been proposed. The proposed method could represent the different topological structures of the multi-lingual Oriental characters effectively. For coarse classification, a hierarchical tree classifier and a SOFM/LVQ based classifier which is composed of an adaptive SOFM coarse-classifier and a LVQ4 language-classifier have been proposed. For fine classification, a classifier based on the LVQ4 learning algorithm has been adopted.

Experimental results revealed that the proposed hierarchical classifier could effectively discriminate the type of languages from the multi-lingual large-set Oriental characters. And, the proposed scheme could effectively recognize the multi-lingual, multi-font and multi-size large-set Oriental characters with high recognition rates of 98.27% for 7,320 multi-lingual classes of testing data and the time performance of more than 40 characters per second on 486 PC with DX-2 66MHz.

ACKNOWLEDGMENT

This research was supported by the 1997 Industry-University Co-Research Fund of Korea Ministry of Information and Communication.

REFERENCES

1. S. B. Cho and J. H. Kim, "Recognition of large-set printed Hangul (Korean script) by two-stage backpropagation neural classifier", *Patt. Recogn.* **25**, 11 (1992) 1353–1360.
2. B. Fritzke, "Growing cell structures — A self-organizing network for unsupervised and supervised learning", *Neural Networks* **7**, 9 (1994) 1441–1460.
3. S. Kahan, T. Pavlidis and H. S. Baird, "On the recognition of printed characters of any font and size", *IEEE Trans. Patt. Anal. Mach. Intell.* **9**, 2 (1987) 1029–1058.
4. T. Kohonen, "The self-organizing map", *Proc. IEEE* **78**, 9 (1990) 1464–1480.
5. S.-W. Lee, "Noisy Hangul character recognition with fuzzy tree classifier", *Proc. SPIE/IS&T's Conf. Machine Vision Application in Character Recognition and Industrial Inspection*, San Jose, California, February 1994, pp. 127–136.
6. S.-W. Lee and J.-S. Park, "Nonlinear shape normalization methods for the recognition of large-set handwritten characters", *Patt. Recogn.* **27**, 6 (1994) 895–902.
7. S.-W. Lee and H.-H. Song, "Optimal design of reference models for large-set handwritten character recognition", *Patt. Recogn.* **27**, 9 (1994) 1267–1274.
8. S. Mori, C. Y. Suen and K. Yamamoto, "Historical review of OCR research and development", *Proc. IEEE* **80**, 7 (1992) 1029–1058.
9. T. Pavlidis, *Algorithms for Graphics and Image Processing*, Computer Science Press, Rockville, MD, 1982.
10. W. K. Pratt, *Digital Image Processing*, New York, Wiley, 1978.
11. A. Rajavelu, M. T. Musavi and M. V. Shirvaikar, "A neural network approach to character recognition", *Neural Networks* **2**, 5 (1989) 387–389.
12. Y. Yamashita, K. Higuchi, Y. Yamada and Y. Haga, "Classification of handprinted Kanji characters by the structured segment matching method", *Patt. Recogn. Lett.* **1**, 5 (1983) 475–479.

Hee-Seon Park received the B.S. degree in computer science and statistics from Chungbuk National University, Cheongju, Korea, in 1991, and the M.S. and Ph.D. degrees in computer science from Chungbuk National University, Cheongju, Korea, in 1993 and 1996, respectively. Since 1996, she has been working as a senior engineer at Samsung Electronics Co. Ltd., Seoul, Korea.

Her research interests include stochastic modeling, image processing and speech recognition.

Hee-Heon Song received the B.S. degree in computer science from Dongkook University, Seoul, Korea, in 1986, the M.S. degree in computer science from Chungnam National University, Cheongju, Korea, in 1995, respectively.

From 1986 to 1998, he worked as a Senior Researcher at Electronics and Telecommunications Research Institute, Daejon, Korea. In March 1998, he joined the faculty of the Department of Computer Engineering Education, Andong National University, Andong, Korea.

His research interests include neural networks, pattern recognition, and intelligent networks. He is a member of the IEEE Computer Society and a member of the Korea Information Science Society.

Seong-Whan Lee received the B.S. degree in computer science and statistics from Seoul National University, Seoul, Korea, in 1984 and the M.S. and Ph.D. degrees in computer science from the Korea Advanced Institute of Science and Technology in 1986 and 1989, respectively.

In 1987, he worked as a visiting researcher at the Pattern Recognition Division, Delft, the Netherlands. He was a visiting scientist at the Centre for Pattern Recognition and Machine Intelligence, Concordia University, Montreal, Canada, during the winter of 1989 and the summer of 1990. From 1989 to 1994, he was an Assistant Professor in the Department of Computer Science, Chungbuk National University, Cheongju, Korea. In March 1995, he joined the faculty of the Department of Computer Science and Engineering, Korea University, Seoul, Korea, as an Associate Professor.

He was the winner of the Annual Best Paper Award of the Korea Information Science Society in 1986. He obtained the First Outstanding Young ResearcherAward at the 2nd International Conference on Document Analysis and Recognition in 1993, and the First Distinguished Research Professor Award from Chungbuk National Universityin 1994. In 1996, he also obtained the Outstanding Research Award from the Korea Information Science Society. He has more than 120 publications on pattern recognition and neural networks in international journals and conference proceedings, and authored two Korean books: Theory and Practice of Character Recognition, Hongneung Press (1993) and Principles of Pattern Recognition, Hongneung Press (1994).

He is the Co-Editor-in-Chief of the International Journal of Document Analysis and Recognition, and the Associate Editor of the Pattern Recognition Journal, International Journal of Pattern Recognition and Artificial Intelligence, and International Journal of Computer Processing of Oriental Languages. He was the Program Chairman of the 17th International Conference on Computer Processing of Oriental Languages and the 6th International Workshop on Frontiers in Handwritting Recognition. He is the General Co-chairman of 3rd International Workshop on Document Analysis Systems, and the Program Co-chairman of the 5th International Conference on Document Analysis and Recognition and 2nd International Conference on Multimodal Interface. He served on the program committees of several well-known international conferences.

He is a senior member of the IEEE Computer Society and a member of the Korea Information Science Society, the Pattern Recognition Society, the International Neural Network Society, and the Oriental Language Computer Society. He is the Director of the recently-established Center for Artificial Vision Research, Korea University.

His research interests include pattern recognition, document image analysis, computer vision and neural networks.

PRINTED CHINESE CHARACTER SIMILARITY MEASUREMENT USING RING PROJECTION AND DISTANCE TRANSFORM

P. C. YUEN*, G. C. FENG and Y. Y. TANG

Department of Computing Studies, Hong Kong Baptist University
Waterloo Road, Kowloon, Hong Kong

This paper presents a new Chinese character similarity measurement method based on the ring projection algorithm and distance transform. The ring projection algorithm is used to transform a character image with two independent variables into a function of one independent variable in the ring projection space. This representation of character in the ring projection space has been proved to be in orientation and scale invariant. However, this representation will be distorted nonlinearly in the presence of noise. Therefore, common linear metrics such as Euclidean distance, cannot be applied to measure distance. To solve the nonlinear distortion problem, distance transform is proposed as a nonlinear metric. The similarity measurement is performed using the distance transformed image in the ring projection space. A number of Chinese characters are selected to evaluate the capability of the proposed measurement scheme and the results are encouraging.

Keywords: Chinese character recognition, similarity measurement, ring projection, distance transform, nonlinear distortion.

1. INTRODUCTION

Optical character recognition is a key component in automatic document analysis. The recognition of Chinese characters is a complicated task[5] because of two reasons. First, the Chinese character set is very large. There are 3755 characters in the national standard GB2312-80 first level specification and 6763 characters in the second level. Second, there is a high degree of similarity among the character shapes. Many Chinese characters share the same component such as "jia" and "shi" shown in Fig. 1.

For practical applications, the optical character recognition scheme should have the following properties:

- insensitive to orientation and scale of character,
- high accuracy (high discriminating power),
- computationally efficient and,
- insensitive to noise.

In the last twenty years, a lot of research works have been done in the printed Chinese character recognition. Some of the outstanding works include attributed relational graph and constrained connection graph.[5] This approach is insensitive to the orientation and scale of characters and provides a relatively good result. However, this approach is computationally expensive. Along the line, a large tree classifier with heuristic search[9] is developed to reduce the computational load. And

*Corresponding author. E-mail: pcyuen@comp.hkbu.edu.hk

Advances in Oriental Document Analysis and Recognition Techniques (1998) 209–221

Fig. 1. Chinese characters: 'jia' means home, 'shi' means room.

yet, the computational load in matching an unknown character with a reference character is still high.

The horizontal and vertical projection scheme[3] is a fast and simple approach for character recognition. However, it suffers from two limitations: scale and orientation variants. To overcome these limitations, Tang *et al.*[6] proposed a new projection method — Transformation-Ring-Projection (TRP) algorithm. Under TRP, the scaling factor is first determined to normalize the size of the character. The character is represented by a feature vector constructed through ring projection method which is orientation invariant. It has been proved that TRP algorithm is invariant to the scale and orientation of the character. A linear metric (Euclidean distance) is employed to measure the distance between the reference and the unknown characters. Tang *et al.* provide a very good direction in printed Chinese character recognition because the method is orientation and scale invariant, and computationally efficient. However, it is noise sensitive. If the character is contaminated with noise, its representation in the projection space will be distorted nonlinearly.

In view of the limitations in the existing approaches, a new similarity measurement scheme is proposed based on the ring projection algorithm and distance transform. Figure 2 gives the block diagram of the proposed scheme. The scheme consists of two phases, namely, the training phase and the recognition phase. In the training phase, all characters in the domain are presented to the system sequentially. Each character is then represented by a function with one independent variable in projection space using ring-projection algorithm. A distance image based on the function in ring projection space is constructed using distance transform, and the resultant images will be stored in the library. In the recognition phase, the unknown character is first represented in the ring projection space, same process as described in the training phase. The similarity between the unknown character and the reference character is then calculated based on the unknown character's function in ring projection space and the reference character's distance image constructed in the training phase. Details of each step are described in the following sections. This paper assumes that the character to be recognized has been segmented out from the document.

2. REPRESENTATION OF CHARACTERS IN RING PROJECTION SPACE

The ring projection algorithm was developed by Tang *et al.*[6] It is proved that the representation is scale and orientation invariant. The basic idea is to transform a

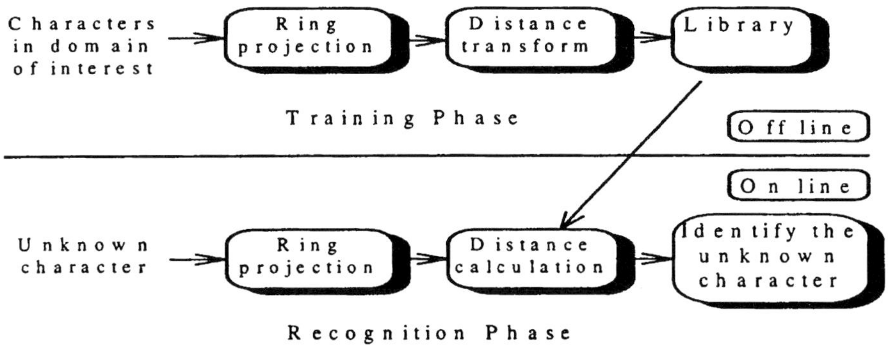

Fig. 2. Block diagram of the proposed similarity measurement scheme.

character image $\mathbf{G[f(x,y)]}$ with two independent variables into a signal with one independent variable in the ring projection space. Suppose $\mathbf{F(I^n)}$ denotes a set of functions with n independent variables. The ring projection algorithm can be represented by an operator $\mathbf{P}$ defined as,

$$\mathbf{P} : G[f(x,y)] \to f(r) \tag{1}$$

where $G[f(x,y)] \in \mathbf{F(I^2)}$ and $f(r) \in \mathbf{F(I^1)}$.

The effect of applying the ring projection algorithm on the binary Chinese character image "jia" (means home) shown in Fig. 3(a), is outlined[7] as follows.

A binary character image can be obtained from its gray scale representation by using the following operation.

$$f(x,y) = \begin{cases} 1 & \text{if } (x,y) \in \wp \\ 0 & \text{otherwise} \end{cases} \tag{2}$$

where domain $\wp$ corresponds to the white region of the character.

The multivariate function $f(x,y)$ can also be viewed as a two-dimensional density function of mass distribution on the plan. From Eq. (2), it is noted that the corresponding density function is a uniform distribution, i.e. the mass is homogeneously distributed over the region $\wp$. From this uniform mass distribution, the centroid of the mass for the region $\wp$, as denoted by $m(x_0, y_0)$ can be calculated. By translating the origin of our reference frame to this centroid, we can obtain the translation invariant property.

Next, let

$$M = \max_{N \in \wp} |N(x,y) - m(x_0, y_0)| \tag{3}$$

where $|N(x,y) - m(x_0,y_0)|$ represents the Euclidean distance between the two points, N and m, on the plane. The scale of the character is then normalized using the value of M.

Further, we transform the original reference Cartesian coordinate into a polar coordinate based on the following relation:

$$\begin{cases} x = r\cos\theta \\ y = r\sin\theta \end{cases} \tag{4}$$

where $r \in [0, \infty]$ and $\theta \in [0, 2\pi)$. Hence,

$$f(x, y) = f(r\cos\theta, r\sin\theta) \tag{5}$$

For any fixed $r \in [0, M]$, the following integral is computed,

$$f(r) = \int_0^{2\pi} f(r\cos\theta, r\sin\theta)d\theta \tag{6}$$

$f(r)$ is equal to the total mass as distributed along the circular rings with center $m(x_0, y_0)$ and radius r, $r \in [0, M)$. Hence the derivation of $f(r)$ is also termed as a ring projection of the planar mass distribution. Owing to the fact that the centroid of the mass is invariant to the rotation and the projection is done along circular rings, the derived one-dimensional pattern is invariant to the rotation of its original two-dimensional pattern. In other words, the ring projection is rotation invariant. In practice, the images to be analyzed by a recognition system are most often stored in discrete format. The discrete representation of $f(r)$ is as follows.

$$f(r) = \sum_{k=0}^{M} f(r\cos\theta_k, r\sin\theta_k)\,. \tag{7}$$

The character in spatial domain is then represented by the function of one independent variable in ring projection space.

The representation of the character "jia", shown in Fig. 3(a) in ring projection space is constructed and displayed in Fig. 3(b). Figure 3(d) shows a character "jia" with different orientation and its ring projection space representation is given in Fig. 3(e). It can be observed that their ring projection space representations (Figs. 3(b) and (e)) are the same.

Figures 4(a)–(c) show the characters "jia" contaminated with different types of noise. Using the ring projection algorithm, their corresponding representations in ring projection space are shown in Figs. 4(d)–(f). Comparing Figs. 4(d)–(f) with Fig. 3(b), it can be seen that the representations of noisy "jia" are distorted nonlinearly.

3. DISTANCE TRANSFORM AND SIMILARITY MEASUREMENT

Section 2 has presented the ring projection algorithm and demonstrated that the representation in the ring projection space will be nonlinearly distorted if the character image in spatial domain is contaminated with noise. In this case, it is not feasible to use linear metric to measure the distance/similarity between the two patterns. In turn, a nonlinear matching technique has to be used. Dynamic programming[4] is a well-known technique for nonlinear matching. However, this technique is computationally expensive. In this section, distance transformation[2] and similarity measurement techniques are proposed to measure the similarity between the two patterns.

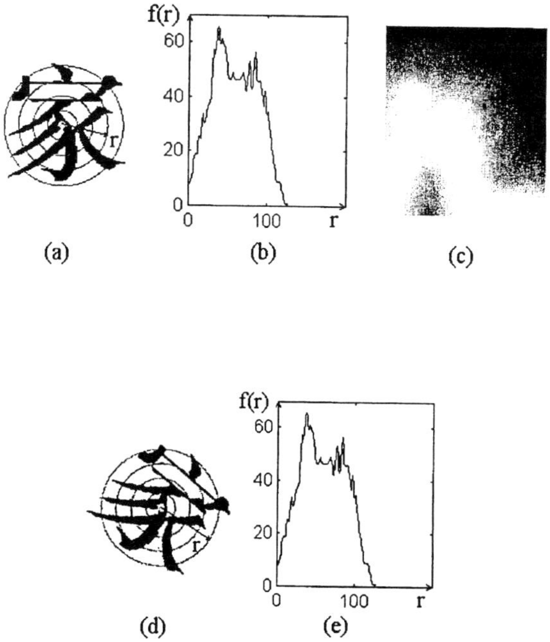

Fig. 3. (a) A Chinese character "jia"; (b) The ring projection space representation of character in (a); (c) The distance image of (b); (d) A rotated Chinese character "jia"; (e) The ring projection space representation of character in (d).

The representation in the ring projection space can be treated as a two-dimensional curve. Each point on the curve is represented by $C(r, f(r))$ which is termed as the feature pixel. The distance transformation converts the feature pixels of the function in ring projection space into a gray level image where all pixels have a value corresponding to its distance to the nearest feature pixel. The created gray level image is called the distance image.

The Weighted Distance Transform[1,2,8] of the function $C(r, f(r))$ in ring projection space is defined as,

$$\begin{aligned} WDT(x,y) &= \min\{D^{ab}(\xi,\eta)\} \\ D^{ab}(\xi,\eta) &= (\xi-\eta)xa + \eta xb \\ \xi &= \max\{|x-i|, |y-j|\} \\ \eta &= \min\{|x-i|, |y-j|\} \end{aligned} \tag{8}$$

where $(i,j) \in (r, P(r))$, $r \in [0, M]$ and $f(r) \in [0, 2\pi M]$.

If $a = 3$ and $b = 4$, it is called the chamfer 3/4 distance transform. According to Ref. 8, the chamfer 3/4 distance can be calculated sequentially by a two-pass algorithm, namely forward and backward passes. First a distance image is created such that each feature pixel is set to zero and each non-feature pixel is set to infinity. The forward pass modifies the distance image as follows,

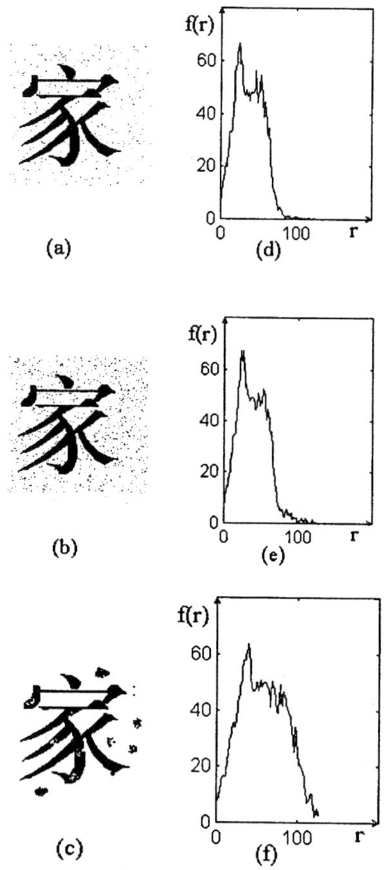

Fig. 4. (a)–(c) Noisy Chinese characters "jia", (d)–(f) their representation in ring projection space.

for $i = 2, \ldots, s$ do

  for $j = 2, \ldots, t$ do

$$d(i,j) = \min(d(i-1,j-1)+4, d(i-1,j)+3, d(i-1,j+1)+4, d(i,j-1)+3, d(i,j)).$$

Similarly, the backward pass is as follows,

for $i = s-1, \ldots, 1$ do

  for $j = t-1, \ldots, 1$ do

$$d(i,j) = \min(d(i,j), d(i,j+1)+3, d(i+1,j-1)+4, d(i+1,j)+3, d(i+1,j+1)+4)$$

where s and t represent the row and column width; $d(i,j)$ is the value of the pixel in position (i,j); $\min(a,b,c,d)$ is the minimum value of (a,b,c,d).

By applying the distance transformation on the ring projection space representation of the character "jia" shown in Fig. 3(b), the distance image can be obtained in Fig. 3(c). In the distance image, the darker the pixel, the greater the pixel value is.

To determine the similarity between the two characters $G_u[f(x,y)]$ and $G_v[f(x,y)]$, we first construct their representations in ring projection space using the ring projection algorithm, say $C_u(r, f_u(r))$ and $C_v(r, f_v(r))$. Applying the distance transform on $C_u(r, f_u(r))$, its corresponding distance image is constructed. Each pixel in the distance image has a value which is proportional to its distance from its current position to the closest feature point. Then each feature pixel on the second pattern $C_v(r, f_v(r))$ is superimposed on the distance image of $C_u(r, f_u(r))$. The degree of similarity between the two curves can be computed from the average of the feature pixels of the second curve on the distance image which is created by the first curve.

An expression for calculating the distance D_a between two pattern $C_u(r, f_u(r))$ and $C_v(r, f_v(r))$ is given by,

$$D_a = \frac{1}{12}\left[\frac{1}{n}\sum_{(i,j)\in C_v(r,f_v(r))} WDT_u(i,j)\right] \tag{9}$$

where n is the total number of pixels in $C_v(r, f_v(r))$ and $WDT_u(i,j)$ is the value of pixel (i,j) in the distance image of $C_u(r, f_u(r))$.

If $f_v(r)$ fits $f_u(r)$ perfectly, the total distance will be zero. That means the two characters, $G_u[f(x,y)]$ and $G_v[f(x,y)]$, are identical. The lesser the similarity between the two characters in spatial domain, the greater will be the deviation of $f_v(r)$ and $f_u(r)$, and also the distance D_a. Finally, the similarity between the two characters is defined by the following expression.

$$S = \frac{1}{1+D_a}, \qquad S \in (0,1]\,. \tag{10}$$

The similarity S ranges from zero to one. If S is equal to one, it indicates that the two characters are identical. The smaller the value of S, the lower the similarity will be.

4. RESULTS

The results presented in this section are divided into three parts. The first part demonstrates the problem of using Euclidean distance as a distance measurement for noisy characters in the ring projection space. The second part shows the capability of the proposed similarity measurement method for Chinese characters. The third part presents the statistical results of the proposed method on a large data set of Chinese characters.

Part I

Refer again to the example shown in Figs. 3 and 4. Using the character in Fig. 3(a) as a reference character and the noisy characters shown in Figs. 4(a)–(c) as unknown characters, and employing Euclidean distance in ring projection space as a distance measurement, the results are tabulated in Table 1. The first entry shows the distance between a noise-free "jia" and the reference character, so the distance is zero. From other results in Table 1, it can be observed that the distance between the reference and the noisy characters are relatively large. The main reason is due to the fact that the ring projection space representation is nonlinearly distorted if the character in the spatial domain is contaminated with noise. Figures 5(a) and (b) show another character "shi" and its representation in the ring projection space, respectively. The Euclidean distance between the characters "shi" and "jia" shown in Fig. 3(a) is calculated and added to Table 1 as well. It is found that the distance between the characters "shi" and "jia" is smaller than that of the noisy "jia" in Figs. 4(a) and (b), corresponding to the second and third entries in Table 1. This example shows that Euclidean distance measurement does not work well in some situations.

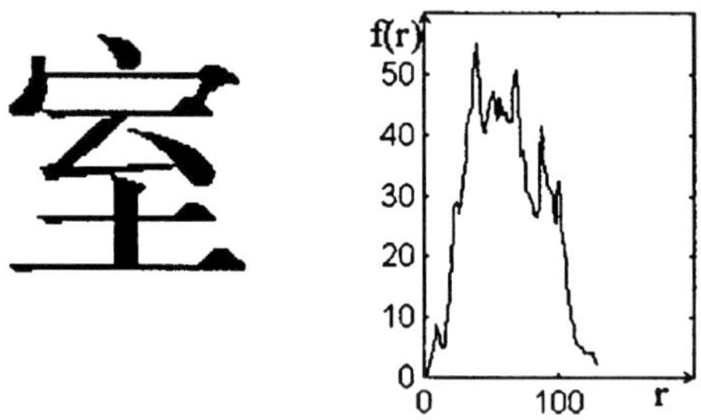

(a) (b)

Fig. 5. (a) Chinese character 室, and (b) the corresponding ring projection space representation.

Part II

To evaluate the capability of the proposed scheme, same testing characters as in Part I are used. Applying the character in Fig. 3(a) to the procedures described in Sec. 3, the distance image of the noise-free character "jia" in the projection space is constructed and shown in Fig. 3(c). Calculating the similarity between the reference character "jia" in Fig. 3(a) and testing characters in Figs. 4(a)–(c) and Fig. 5(a), the pattern of the testing character in the ring projection space is overlaid on the distance image of the reference character. The distance is first calculated using Eq. (9) and the similarity is calculated using Eq. (10). After each testing character has been compared with the reference character, the results are recorded and tabulated in Table 2. As demonstrated in Table 2, even the characters are contaminated with noise, the proposed method provides a correct similarity score which reflects the actual spatial similarity between the two characters.

Another 10 Chinese characters are selected to evaluate the proposed method. The similarity of each character is tested with the rest of nine characters and the results are summarized in Table 3. It can be observed that the proposed scheme reflects the actual spatial character similarity.

Table 1. The Euclidean distance between the reference character 家 and the unknown characters.

Unknown character	Euclidean distance
家	0
家	34.656
家	33.312
家	8.539
室	15.414

Table 2. The distance and similarity between the reference characters 家 and the unknown characters using the proposed method.

Unknown character	Distance D_a	Similarity
家	0	1
家	0.332	0.75
家	0.476	0.70
家	0.347	0.74
室	0.544	0.64

Table 3. Another 10 Chinese characters are selected to evaluate the proposed method. Each entry in the matrix represents the similarity between the characters shown in a row and a column.

	人	八	大	天	矢	失	同	圓	田	鼠
人	1									
八	0.54	1								
大	0.58	0.45	1							
天	0.53	0.47	0.63	1						
矢	0.41	0.39	0.48	0.59	1					
失	0.39	0.43	0.45	0.54	0.65	1				
同	0.41	0.34	0.44	0.37	0.35	0.34	1			
圓	0.30	0.34	0.34	0.33	0.34	0.36	0.45	1		
田	0.33	0.26	0.36	0.33	0.34	0.32	0.40	0.56	1	
鼠	0.30	0.27	0.35	0.35	0.41	0.41	0.36	0.41	0.31	1

(a) Noise free (b) 1% of noise © 5% of noise

(d) 10% of noise (e) 20% of noise (f) 30% of noise

(g) 40% of noise

Fig. 6. Character "de" contaminated with different degrees of noise.

Part III

The objective of this part is to demonstrate the capability of the proposed system on a large data set of Chinese characters. 1600 commonly used Chinese characters with resolution 50×50 are selected. Each character is added with different percentages of noise from 0% to 40%. The noise is added in the following way. 10% of noise means that 10% of the character's pixels are inverted from black to white or vice versa, randomly. In fact, when the percentage of noise is greater than 30%, it cannot be recognized by humans. Figure 6 shows the noisy images of Chinese character "de" contaminated with different degrees of noise.

The accuracy in recognizing the noisy characters using the proposed method is recorded and plotted in Fig. 7. The graph shows that there is no error when the noise power is zero. This result is expected as our representation is orientation and scale invariant. When the noise power increases, the accuracy decreases. When the noise power is less than 5%, the accuracy of the proposed method is higher than 93%. The accuracy falls to 80% when the noise power is increased to 10%. If the noise power is further increased to 40%, the accuracy of the proposed system becomes 20%. In fact, by experience, the contaminated noise power in the scanning process is usually less than 5%.

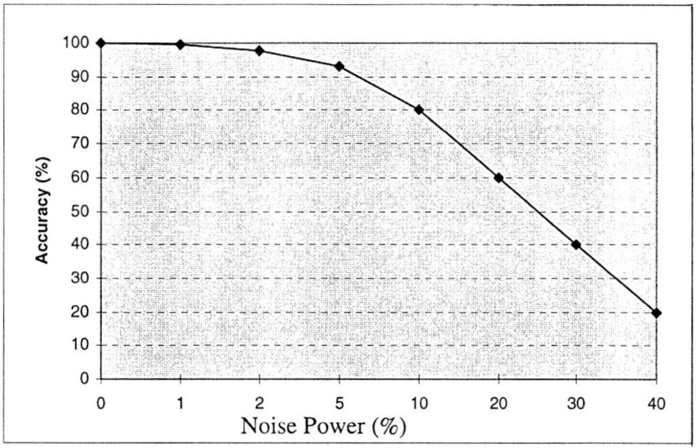

Fig. 7. Performance on noisy images.

5. CONCLUSIONS

A novel printed Chinese character similarity measurement based on the ring projection algorithm and the distance transform has been developed and reported in this paper. The proposed measurement offers the following advantages:

- computationally efficient,
- insensitive to noise,
- high discriminating power; and,
- insensitive to orientation and scale of character.

ACKNOWLEDGMENT

This project was supported by the Faculty Research Grant of the Baptist University. The authors would also like to thank Ms. Joan Yuen for proof reading this manuscript.

REFERENCES

1. D. Borgeors, Another comment on a "Note on distance transformations in digital images", *Image Understanding* **54**, 2 (1991) 301–306.
2. H. C. Liu and M. D. Srinath, "Partial shape classification using contour matching in distance transformation", *IEEE Trans. Patt. Anal. Mach. Intell.* **12**, 11 (1990) 1072–1079.
3. S. Mori, C. Y. Suen and K. Yamamoto, "Historical review of OCR research and development", *IEEE Proc.* **80**, 7 (1992) 1029–1058.
4. H. Sakoe, "Two-level DP matching — A dynamic programming based pattern matching algorithm for connected word recognition", *IEEE Trans. Acoustics, Speech and Signal Processing* **27**, 6 (1979) 588–595.
5. J. W. Tai, "Some research achievements on Chinese character recognition in China", *Int. J. Pattern Recognition and Artificial Intelligence* **5** (1991) 199–206.

6. Y. Y. Tang, H. D. Cheng and C. Y. Suen, "Transformation-ring-projection algorithm and its VLSI implementation", *Int. J. Pattern Recognition and Artificial Intelligence* **5** (1991) 25–56.
7. Y. Y. Tang, H. Ma, B. F. Li, J. Liu and C. Y. Suen, "Dimension-reduction-wavelet (DRW) method for extracting features in character recognition", submitted to *The Fourth Int. Conf. Document Analysis and Recognition*, 1997.
8. P. W. M. Tsang, P. C. Yuen and F. K. Lam, "Classification of partially occluded objects using 3-point matching and distance transformation", *Patt. Recogn.* **27** (1994) 27–40.
9. Q. R. Wang and C. Y. Suen, "Large tree classifier with heuristic search and global training", *IEEE Trans. Patt. Anal. Mach. Intell.* **9**, 1 (1987) 91–102.

P. C. Yuen received his B.Sc. degree in electronic engineering in 1989 from City Polytechnic of Hong Kong, and his Ph.D. degree in electrical and electronic engineering in 1993 from The University of Hong Kong. He is now an Assistant Professor in Department of Computing Studies, Hong Kong Baptist University and honorary lecturer at the Zhongshan University in China.

His major research interests include computer vision, image analysis, human face recognition and pattern recognition.

G. C. Feng received his M.S. degree in bio-mathematics from Zhongshan (Sun Yat-sen) University, China in 1988. Now he is pursuing his Ph.D. degree at Baptist University.

His current interests include pattern recognition and computer vision.

Yuan Y. Tang received the B. S. degree in electrical and computer engineering from Chongqing University, Chongqing, China, the M. Eng. degree in electrical engineering from the Graduate School of Post and Telecommunications, Beijing, China, and the Ph.D. degree in computer science from Concordia University, Montreal, Canada. He is presently an Associate Professor in the Department of Computing Studies at Hong Kong Baptist University, and Senior Researcher in the Centre for Pattern Recognition and Machine Intelligence, Concordia University. He is a Honorary Lecturer at the University of Hong Kong, an Advisory Professor at Beijing University of Posts and Telecommunications, Chongqing University and Shengyang Institute of Aeronautical Engineering, China.

Dr. Tang has published more than 130 technical papers and is the author/co-author of 9 books on subjects ranging from electrical engineering to computer science. He also serves as a reviewer for many journals and international conferences. He is a Senior Member of IEEE.

His current interests include wavelet theory and applications, pattern recognition, image processing, document processing, artificial intelligence, parallel processing, Chinese computing and VLSI architecture.

SEGMENTATION AND RECOGNITION OF CONTINUOUS HANDWRITING CHINESE TEXT

CHEN HONG, GARETH LOUDON*, YIMIN WU
and RUSLANA ZITSERMAN

Apple-ISS Research Center, National University of Singapore
Heng Mui Keng Terrace, Singapore 119597

This article introduces the basic segmentation problems in Chinese handwriting and also several prior work to solve these problems. A new segmentation method is proposed, which is applicable to both on-line and off-line systems for free-format handwritten Chinese character sentences. This method performs basic segmentation and fine segmentation based on the varying spacing thresholds and the minimum variance criteria. The five most probable ways of segmentation are derived from this stage and all the possible segments are extracted and recognized. A lattice is created from all the segments and searched using a viterbi based algorithm to find the most likely character sequence. The algorithm presented in this paper provides large flexibility and robustness to handle free-format continuous Chinese handwriting and is a promising solution for a natural and fast Chinese pen input system. The character accuracy is 85.0% for on-line and 77.4% for the off-line test data.

Keywords: Continuous handwriting recognition, segmentation, Chinese handwriting recognition, language model, lattice.

1. INTRODUCTION

In recent years, the need to improve human-computer interaction has created a great deal of research activities in the area of automatic handwriting recognition. Handwriting traditionally was and still remains a very natural way of communicating between people. This explains why there is a growing demand to extend this method to the area of human-computer interaction. This is especially true when viewed in the context of ideographic languages. It can be argued that in the case of alphanumeric languages the use of a keyboard can be faster than handwriting. However, in the case of ideographic languages (Chinese, Japanese, Korean, etc.) keyboard input requires special training and it is very time-consuming.

The field of handwriting recognition (HWR) can be divided into two major categories: on-line recognition and off-line recognition. Compared with off-line data, the on-line data provides much more information to work with, for example, time ordering of strokes and pen-lifts. An off-line system has to resolve the problem of different pen thickness, stroke intersection, overlapping strokes and the lack of stroke ordering information.

Chinese characters can be written in a neat print style where rules based on the stroke order and number are followed, but are generally written in a more cursive style where the strokes are joined. The main problems for isolated handwritten simplified Chinese character recognition are the large number of characters used (there are about 6000 commonly used Chinese characters), the complexity of the

*E-mail: gareth@krdl.org.sg

Advances in Oriental Document Analysis and Recognition Techniques (1998) 223–232

characters, the character distortion and multiple styles of writing. Also some characters can differ only by a small stroke or mark.

Recognition of continuous handwritten text is even more difficult than that of isolated characters because of the character segmentation issue.

A typical handwriting recognition system, for either on-line or off-line, for free-format and continuous text consists of the following processing stages:

text input → segmentation → recognition → (language model) → result

Segmentation is a process of separating characters from one another. It is a very important step to prepare character data for the recognizer because most recognizers can only deal with isolated characters. A great deal of research work has been done to solve the Chinese character recognition problem[1,3,4,6,7,10] The overall accuracy of a system is determined by both segmentation and recognition.

Several methods[5,12] have been reported for the segmentation of the writing of Roman alphabets. Most of these methods make use of time and spatial information or character shape information provided by the character recognition process. However, Chinese characters are quite different from alphabets. Their structures are more complicated. In addition, our goal is to find a generic algorithm that is applicable to both on-line and off-line systems. Therefore the time-related information such as stroke sequence cannot be used.

1.1. Characteristics of Chinese Handwriting

The following are the characteristics of Chinese handwriting and their related segmentation and recognition problems:

(1) Most Chinese characters consist of more than 2 radicals and any of these radicals can be an individual character in itself. For example, character "明" has two radicals: "日" and "月". Each radical is a meaningful character in itself. This makes segmentation difficult because from a recognition point of view, the result is valid even if a character is mis-segmented into several radicals. Therefore linguistic knowledge is needed to distinguish correct segmentation just as human beings usually group radicals into a character by the meaning and context.

(2) In free-format handwriting, the space between characters and the space between radicals vary considerably. Though it is common for people to leave a larger gap between characters than that between radicals, the spatial information is not reliable.

(3) Writing style varies from person to person; however, for a particular person, the writing style is somewhat consistent. This conclusion is drawn from the observation that the correct segmentation of a sentence is frequently the one where the width of each segment is evenly distributed.

(4) Chinese characters are written either horizontally or vertically. Without losing its generality, the following study focuses on the horizontally written sentences and it can be easily applied to vertically written sentences with only minor modifications.

(1) and (2) tell us that spatial information may be of some help for the segmentation, but should not be the only criteria. (3) gives us a hint that the width of the character is an important factor to consider.

1.2. Prior Work

Some segmentation methods have been proposed to separate Japanese characters which are also ideographic in nature. Though Japanese characters are very similar to Chinese characters, the Japanese are usually more neat in handwriting.

In Ref. 2, Shunji introduced the following stages to split the text string into isolated characters: preprocessing — segmentation of non-touching characters → segmentation of compound characters → segmentation of touching Japanese characters → segmentation of English characters.

In each stage, some hypotheses for character segmentation were generated on the basis of the information obtained in the earlier stages and these hypotheses were verified by the character recognition results. The method is quite effective for the printed document.

Murase[9] proposed another important approach in which character recognition results and grammatical constraints were used for character segmentation. First, all possible character candidates were extracted and recognized. Then, the most plausible sequences of the characters were sought by dynamic programming and they were verified under grammatical constraints. His method is devoted to on-line handwritten character recognition and cannot solve the touching character problem.

In this paper, a new segmentation method is proposed, which is applicable to both on-line and off-line systems for free-format continuous handwritten Chinese text and is intelligent enough to split touching characters. "Free-format" here refers to any style of handwriting, cursive or printed, and there are no rules imposed on the space between the characters.

2. SEGMENTATION ALGORITHM

The segmentation process is broken down into several steps: first, the basic segmentation is done by varying the space threshold. Five possible ways of basic segmentation are obtained from this stage. Then a minimum variance criteria is used to fine tune the possible ways of segmentation recursively. The touching characters are separated and the wrongly separated parts are merged during this stage. The possible ways of segmentation increase as the procedure goes on and are sorted based on the variance criteria. The top five ways of segmentation are selected and combined to form the lattice. Each possible segment in the lattice is fed into a character recognizer. The recognition results and their probabilities are integrated into the lattice. Finally the lattice search engine is utilized to find the overall result for the sentence.

2.1. Basic Segmentation

The basic segmentation is very simple. Five ways of segmentation are obtained by using five different space thresholds. First, project all the data points onto X and Y-axes. Scan the projection from left to right. (It won't affect the method if the projection is scanned from right to left). If a gap is larger than the threshold, mark the gap as a boundary. Vary the threshold value and do the above process again. Once a particular segmentation is decided, the width median of each segment and the width variance are calculated and stored for the next stage process.

Figure 1 shows an example of this basic segmentation with different threshold values.

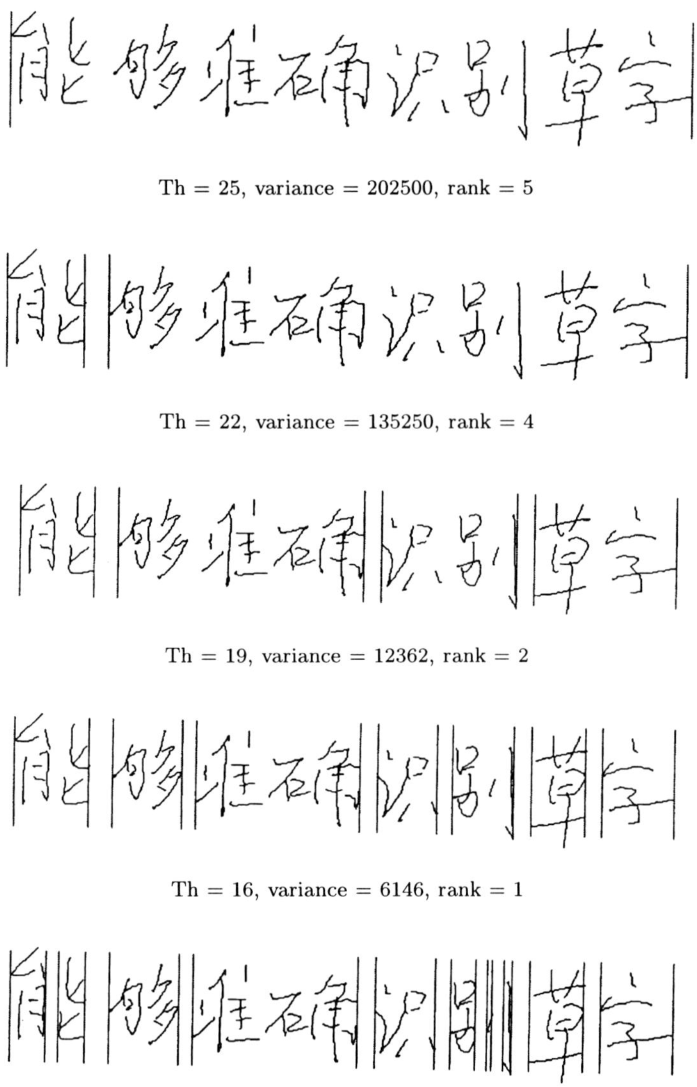

Th = 25, variance = 202500, rank = 5

Th = 22, variance = 135250, rank = 4

Th = 19, variance = 12362, rank = 2

Th = 16, variance = 6146, rank = 1

Th = 13, variance = 13622, rank = 3

Fig. 1. Basic segmentation.

2.2. Fine Segmentation

The basic segmentation is not effective in the case where more than one radical is joined together or the distance between the radicals is too large. In the fine segmentation stage, these problems are solved by splitting joined segments and merging over-segmented parts. Fine segmentation is performed based on the result from the basic segmentation. Five possible ways of basic segmentation are sorted according to the variance. The one with the minimum variance is considered as the closest segmentation to the optimum because the width of each segment is the most evenly distributed. To allow some tolerance, the top two ways with minimum variance are selected to do the fine segmentation.

The basic idea behind the fine segmentation is that if the splitting or merging makes the variance less, it is regarded as a better way of segmentation and is stored.

The following process is repeated until no new segmentation is generated. Each segment is scanned from left to right. If the width of the segment is too small compared with the median, try to combine the segment with the next few segments. Calculate the median and variance of the new segmentation. If the variance decreases, regard the new segmentation as a valid way and store it. Otherwise, ignore the new segmentation. Similarly, if the width of the segment is too large, estimate how many parts the segment should be split into as compared with the median and split the segment. Again, calculate the variance of the new segmentation and decide whether to count it as a new way of segmentation or to discard it.

Figure 2 gives one fine segmentation result which is obtained by splitting one of the segments in segmentation 4 of Fig. 1.

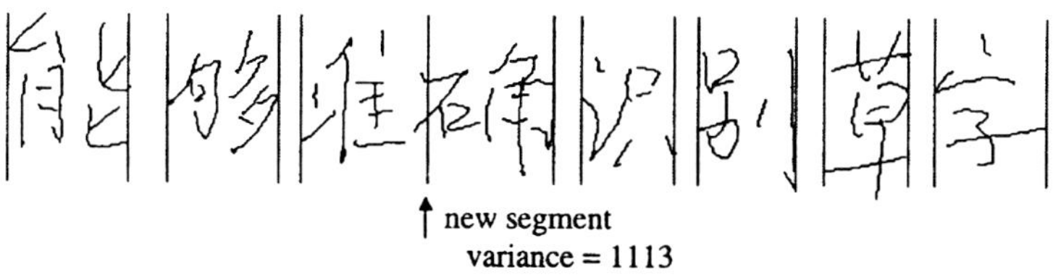

Fig. 2. Fine segmentation.

2.3. Lattice Formation

Segmentations are re-sorted according to the variance criteria and the top five ways are chosen to form the lattice. Then the recognizer and language model are applied to get the overall result for the sentence.

From the 5 ways of segmentation, all the possible segments are extracted and fed into the character recognizer. 50 recognition candidates for each segment are obtained together with their corresponding probabilities. The character recognizer we used here is an on-line recognizer based on discrete hidden Markov models (HMMs). This is proprietary technology developed at the Apple-ISS Research Center. Theoretically, the recognizer can be of any type, on-line or off-line,[7] according to the application.

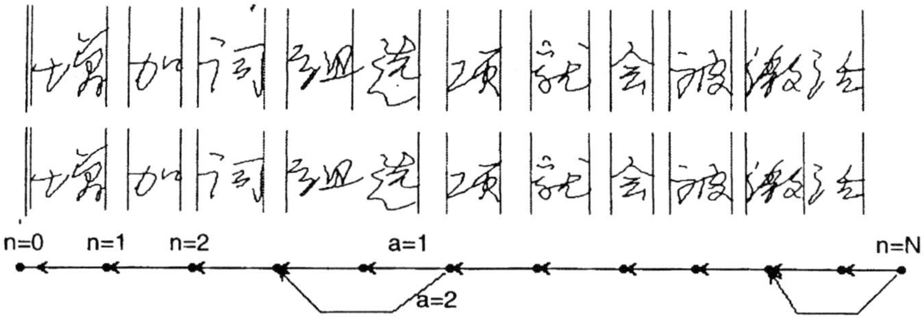

Fig. 3. Lattice generation.

The result of the segmentation and candidate character recognition is expressed in the form of lattice that is a two-dimensional weighted directional graph. A node (n) represents a possible boundary in the basic segmentations; an arc (a) is associated with the candidate characters (i) and the corresponding probabilities ($CP(n, a, i)$) from the recognizer. A sample lattice is shown in Fig. 3. In this simple example, neither basic nor fine segmentations are completely correct. However, by using the lattice engine, the correct segmentation is included in the search paths. So it is possible that this can be recovered.

2.4. Search

To find the most likely sequence of characters from the lattice a search method is used based on the character recognition scores and language model scores. The language model scores describe the likelihood of a character appearing within a specified context. A simple statistical language model is used and is based on the character unigram and bigrams.

The technique used for finding the single best character sequence is based on the Viterbi algorithm.[8,11] There are four basic steps. During the first three stages (the forward pass) an accumulated probability is calculated for each node (n) in the lattice. The fourth stage then traces back through the lattice to find the most likely character sequence.

First we define $\mathrm{ACC}(n, a, i)$ as the best accumulated score (highest probability) along a single path upto the candidate character i in arc a of node n; $\mathrm{NSQ}(n, a, i)$ is the record of the node sequence for the best accumulated score.

(Note that the following parameters are log probabilities to simplify the calculations.)

(i) Initialization of lattice
For node 1:
$\mathrm{ACC}(1, a, i) = \mathrm{CP}(1, a, i) + \text{weight} * \mathrm{U}(1, a, i)$ for $a = 1$ to A, $i = 1$ to I
Where $\mathrm{CP}(1, a, i)$ is the character recognition probability of character candidate i for node 1, arc a; $\mathrm{U}(1, a, i)$ is the unigram probability of the candidate character i for node 1, arc a; A is the total number of arcs for node n; I is the total number of candidate characters for arc a.

(ii) Recursion through the lattice
For nodes $n = 2$ to N:
$\text{ACC}(n, a, i) = \max\,[\text{ACC}(m, b, j) + \text{weight} * (\text{U}(n, a, i) + \text{BI}(n, a, i, m, b, j))] + \text{CP}(n, a, i)$ for $a = 1$ to A, $i = 1$ to I, $b = 1$ to B, $j = 1$ to J
$\text{NSQ}(n, a) = \text{f}(\text{ACC}(n, a, i))$ where $f()$ records the node m and arc b that maximizes $\text{ACC}(n, a, i)$
Where $\text{BI}(n, a, i, m, b, j)$ is the bigram probability of the candidate character i for node n, arc a and the candidate character j for node m, arc b; B is the total number of arcs for node m; J is the total number of candidate characters for arc b.

(iii) Termination of the lattice
$\text{TP}(N) = \max\,[\text{ACC}(N, a, i)]$ for $a = 1$ to A, $i = 1$ to I
$\text{TCC}(N) = g(TP(N))$ where $g()$ records the candidate character that maximizes $\text{TP}(N)$.
Where $\text{TP}(N)$ is the total probability at node N; $\text{TCC}(N)$ is the top candidate character at node N.

(iv) Path backtracing through the lattice
$\text{TCC}(m) = h(TCC(n))$ where $h()$ records the candidate character from the node m and arc b that maximizes $\text{TP}(n)$
At the start of the backtrace $n = N$.
At the end of the backtrace $m = 1$.

3. EXPERIMENTAL DESIGN

Both on-line and off-line data were tested using the segmentation and recognition system described above. Since no common database for Chinese handwritten sentences is available, we did the data collection to do the experiments. Firstly, one hundred on-line sentences were collected on Power Mac7500 using WACOM tablet as the input device. These sentences were written by seven different users with eight characters on average in each sentence. No rules were imposed on the way and the style of writing. Most sentences were written in a very cursive style. Secondly, 39 handwritten sentences, 394 characters in total, were scanned in using HP ScanJet IIp scanner with the resolution of 300 dpi. These characters were written in a neat style but with no restriction on spacing between the characters.

4. EXPERIMENTAL RESULTS

Table 1 gives the experimental results. It is important to note that the on-line and off-line isolated character recognizers, used as part of the system in these experiments, have an accuracy of about 90% and 85% for similar style isolated character writing. As described in the previous sections, an input sentence is firstly segmented using minimum variance criteria and five possible ways of segmentation are obtained. The character accuracy in context without lattice, showed in Table 1, is obtained at this intermediate stage by choosing the most likely segmentation and feeding each segment into the recognizer to get the result. The second result, presented in Table 1, shows the character accuracy in context with the lattice which is the final result from the lattice search.

Table 1. Experiment result.

Accuracy	on-line	off-line
Character in context (without lattice)	70.3%	66.8%
Character in context (with lattice)	85.0%	77.4%

It is difficult to compare the result with other work because no common database for Chinese handwritten sentences is available.

5. DISCUSSION

From the experimental results, it can be seen that the language model helps a great deal in the recognition accuracy. In addition, it was observed that the number of candidates for each segment is critical to the overall speed and accuracy. A smaller number pulls down the accuracy because the correct character may be missed out. In this case, the language model is unable to do anything if the correct character is not included in the candidate list. On the other hand, a larger number of candidates requires more memory and slows down the search speed. Fifty was found to be the optimal number in terms of the accuracy and speed ratio for this application through the experiments. Table 2 presents the comparison result between the number of character candidates and the accuracy for the on-line test set.

Table 2. Number of candidates and the accuracy.

Number of candidates	Character accuracy
20	83.1%
50	85.0%
70	85.5%

The method proposed here is equally applicable to both on-line and off-line systems. The system can be easily customized by plugging in different recognizers since the algorithm does not make use of any time-related information. However, this method only performs segmentation, recognition and linguistic analysis after a whole sentence has been completely written. Therefore, the response time is still not satisfactory for an on-line recognition. Besides, the alphabets and symbols cannot be handled very well as the width of some punctuation and alphabets varies quite significantly.

6. CONCLUSION

Continuous Chinese handwriting recognition has always been a difficult problem because of both segmentation and recognition issues. In this paper, a generic segmentation method based on the minimum variance criteria is described. Combined with a lattice search engine, the algorithm provides large flexibility to handle free-format Chinese handwriting. The experimental result shows that the method provides a promising solution for a natural and fast Chinese pen input system.

Our future work will focus on the improvement of the segmentation algorithm and the recognizer so that the system can still perform segmentation and recognition while users are still writing.

REFERENCES

1. J. C. Anigbogu and A. Belaid, "Hidden Markov models in text recognition", *Int. J. Pattern Recognition Artificial Intelligence* **9**, 6 (1995) 925–958.
2. S. Ariyoshi, "A character segmentation method for Japanese printed documents coping with touching character problems", *Proc. ICPR* (1992) 313–316.
3. M. Y. Chen *et al.*, "Off-line handwritten word recognition using hidden Markov model type stochastic network", *IEEE Trans. Patt. Anal. Mach. Intell.* **16**, 5 (1994) 481–496.
4. M. Y. Chen *et al.*, "Variable duration hidden Markov model and morphological segmentation for handwritten word recognition", *IEEE Trans. Imag. Process.* **4**, 12 (1995) 1675–1688.
5. G. F. Groner, "Real-time recognition of handprinted text", *Proc. FJCC* (1966) 591–601.
6. S. B. Jeng, C. H. Shih *et al.*, "On the use of discrete-state Markov process for Chinese character recognition", *Visual Commun. Imag. Process.* **1360** (1990) 1663–1670.
7. G. Loudon, C. Hong, Y. Wu and R. Zitserman, "The recognition of handwritten Chinese character from paper records", *Proc. IEEE-TECON* **2** (1996) 923–926.
8. Y. Maeda, F. Yoda, K. Matsuura and H. Nambu, "Character segmentation in Japanese hand-written document images", *Proc. ICPR* (1988) 769–772.
9. H. Murase, "Online recognition of free-format Japanese handwritings", *Proc. ICPR* (1988) 1143–1147.
10. R. Nag *et al.*, "Script recognition using hidden Markov models", *Proc. ICASSP* (1986) 2071–2074.
11. L. Rabiner and B. H. Juang, *Fundamentals of Speech Recognition* (Prentice Hall, 1993).
12. C. C. Tappert, "Cursive script recognition by elastic matching", *IBM J. Res. Dev.* **26** (1982) 765–771.

Chen Hong obtained her B.Sc. and M.Sc. in computer science in 1990 and 1993 from Fudan University, Shanghai. She was the winner of GuangHua Award and OMRON Award in 1991 and 1992, respectively. After graduation, she worked as a software engineer for a year in Hua Pu Information Technology Pte Ltd in Shanghai. In January 1995, she joined Singapore Technology Electronics and Engineering Ltd as a development engineer. Chen Hong joined the research and development team of Apple-ISS Research Centre on handwriting recognition in January 1996.

Her research interests include handwriting and speech recognition, multi-modal man machine interaction and digital signal processing. She is currently a member of IEEE.

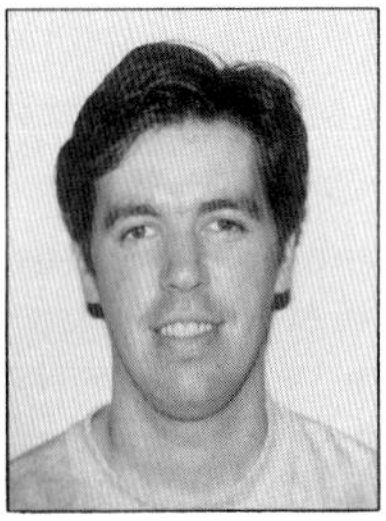

Gareth Loudon received his B.Sc. in electrical and electronic engineering in 1988 and obtained his Ph.D. in 1991, both from the University of Leicester, UK. On completing his Ph.D., he worked for Cegelec Projects Ltd., UK, as a systems design engineer. In May 1993 he joined the Apple-ISS Research Centre, Singapore. He was a member of the speech recognition research team that helped develop Apple's award winning Chinese dictation product (CDK 1.0) and was the project leader for the handwriting recognition research team that helped create the next generation product: Apple's Advanced Chinese Input Suite, which included Chinese handwriting recognition.

He is currently the head of the Asian Interactive Systems Group at the Institute of Systems Science, Singapore. He is a chartered engineer and a member of the IEEE.

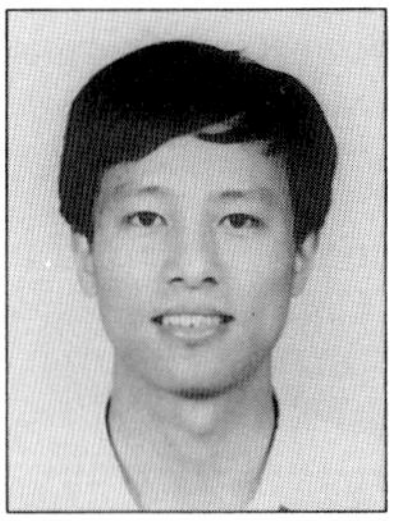

Yimin Wu received the B.Eng. and M.Eng. degrees from the Department of Information and Electronic Engineering from Zhejiang University, Zhejiang, China, in 1985 and 1988, respectively. From 1988–1992, he was a lecturer in the Department of Electronic Engineering, Shenzhen University, Guangdong, China and the following year, he was a visiting scholar in the University of Central Lancashire, Preston, U.K. From 1993–1997, he was a senior software engineer in Apple-ISS Research Centre, Singapore and thereafter he joined the Asian Interactive Systems group, Institute of Systems Science, Singapore.

His research and development interests include handwriting and speech recognition, OCR, and multilingual computing.

Ruslana Zitserman received her M.A. and B.A. degrees in computer science in 1993 and Magna Cum Laude, 1991, from the Boston University, Boston, USA, respectively. She completed her undergraduate education at Boston University, where she studied computer science and East Asian Studies. From 1991 to 1992 she worked as a software developer at Science Applications International Corporation (SAIC).

From 1992 to 1993 she was working as a system administrator at the Centre for Polymer Studies. Ruslana received her M.A. in computer science in 1993. After graduation, she received a scholarship from CCNAA (Co-ordination Council for North American Affairs) to study Chinese at the Mandarin Training Centre, National Taiwan Normal University. She joined the Apple-ISS Research Centre in September 1994.

Her research interests lie in the area of computational linguistics. She is particularly interested in Chinese parsing, grammar construction and machine translation.

NETWORK-BASED APPROACH TO KOREAN HANDWRITING ANALYSIS

BONG-KEE SIN*

Information Retrieval Team, Multimedia Research Labs, Korea Telecom
Wumyon-dong 17, Socho-ku, Seoul 137-792 Korea
E-mail: bkshin@pine.kotel.co.kr

JIN H. KIM

Computer Science Department, Korea Advanced Institute of Science and Technology
Taejon 305-701, Korea
E-mail: jkim@gorai.kaist.ac.kr

It is well known that the stochastic approach using the HMM and dynamic programming-based search is particularly suited to the analysis of time series signals including on-line handwriting. The starting point of this research is a network of HMMs which models the whole set of characters. Then it is followed by the assertion that the HMM for the on-line script can be applied to not only on-line character recognition but also to the handwriting synthesis and even pen-trajectory recovery in off-line character images. The solutions to these problems are based on the single network of HMMs and the single principle of DP-based state-observation alignment. Given an observation sequence, the search for the best path in the network corresponds to the recognition. Given a character model, the search for the best observation sequence corresponds to the handwriting generation. The proposed framework has been shown to work nicely through a set of tests on Korean characters.

Keywords: Character recognition, handwriting generation, pen trajectory recovery, hidden Markov model, Viterbi algorithm, Korean character.

1. INTRODUCTION

Since the first application of computers to character recognition, there have been numerous attempts to model the sources of variabilities and ambiguities in on-line and off-line scripts.[11,21] Historically the first and the most frequently used approach has been based on templates using either fixed length or variable length feature vectors. Although it suffers from closure property and is limited to small vocabulary, this approach achieves reasonable performance in isolated character recognition tasks.[8,20] Structural approach with theoretical roots in formal language theory was in vogue for some time in the past decades,[7] but its use now is limited mainly because of the difficulty in designing good grammars. Recently artificial neural network has become the most widely used tool because of its discrimination power in pattern classification tasks.[10] But the problem is that temporal variations in on-line characters are not modeled effectively by a simple neural network architecture. More recently the Hidden Markov Model (HMM) has been introduced to both on-line and off-line character recognition with success.[9,19] Due to the capability of

*Corresponding author.

Advances in Oriental Document Analysis and Recognition Techniques (1998) 233–249

modeling temporal signals, we consider HMM as a highly suitable tool for the recognition problem.

There are additional problems of interest: the generation or synthesis of on-line character patterns[13,17] and the recovery of on-line information from off-line character images.[3,5] This paper will address mainly the issues of character recognition and generation, and provide just a brief sketch on the last issue.

One of the characteristic features of the proposed approach is the use of HMMs for letters and ligatures, and their networking (unit HMMs) into one big HMM. In the network-based approach, we define a generic problem of script analysis as that of finding jointly the best path and the best observation sequence, using any of the graph-searching or dynamic programming algorithms. If the observation sequence is given, the task is reduced to on-line character recognition. If we have to determine the best observation sequence out of the network model only, the task is reduced to pattern generation or synthesis.

In the rest of the paper, we will first describe the design of a script model using a set of HMMs in Sec. 2. In Sec. 3 we will present script analysis algorithms for recognition and generation, both of which are based on the same technique of dynamic programming. Section 4 presents a set of experimental results for the two problems. Section 5 discusses the unresolved issues of pattern evaluation and pen trajectory recovery. Finally Sec. 6 concludes the paper.

2. HANDWRITING MODEL

While a Latin word consists of a sequence of letters and is written simply from left to right, a Korean character is different in several ways. A Korean character consists of the following three types of letters or graphemes:

C := ㄱ | ㄲ | ㄴ | ㄷ | ㄹ | ··· | ㅎ
V := ㅏ | ㅐ | ㅑ | ㅒ | ㅓ | ㅔ | ··· | ㅣ
Z := ㄱ | ㄲ | ㄳ | ㄴ | ㄵ | ㄶ | ··· | ㅎ

The letters in each class correspond to the initial consonants, vowels, and final consonants respectively of the syllables. Consisting of those three types of sounds, a Korean character represents a syllable by $\mathtt{C} \cdot \mathtt{V} \cdot \mathtt{Z}$ or $\mathtt{C} \cdot \mathtt{V}$. Handwritten character introduces to this definition one or two ligatures ℓ that occur between letters as[19]

$$\mathtt{HandwrittenCharacter} := \mathtt{C} \cdot \ell \cdot \mathtt{V} \cdot \ell \cdot \mathtt{Z} \mid \mathtt{C} \cdot \ell \cdot \mathtt{V}$$

In cursive script, each ℓ pattern is dependent on the shape and position of the preceding and the following letters, called the left and the right contexts, respectively. So we cluster the ligatures based on those contexts, and define a model for each cluster.

Just like the hierarchical definition of a character, we first design individual letter and ligature models using the left-right HMM, (Fig. 1(a)), and then connect them to obtain a character model as shown in Fig. 1(b).[19] Each edge of Fig. 1(b)

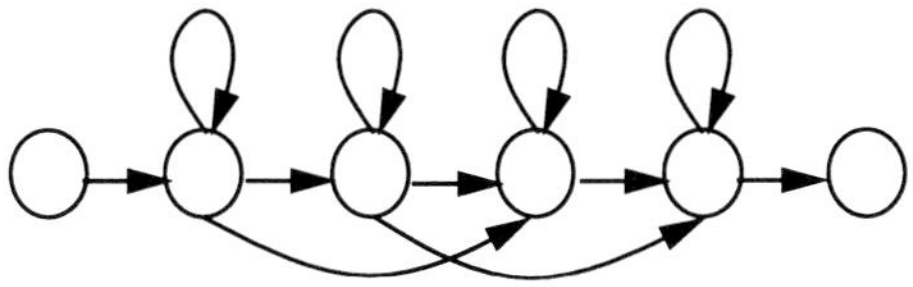

(a)

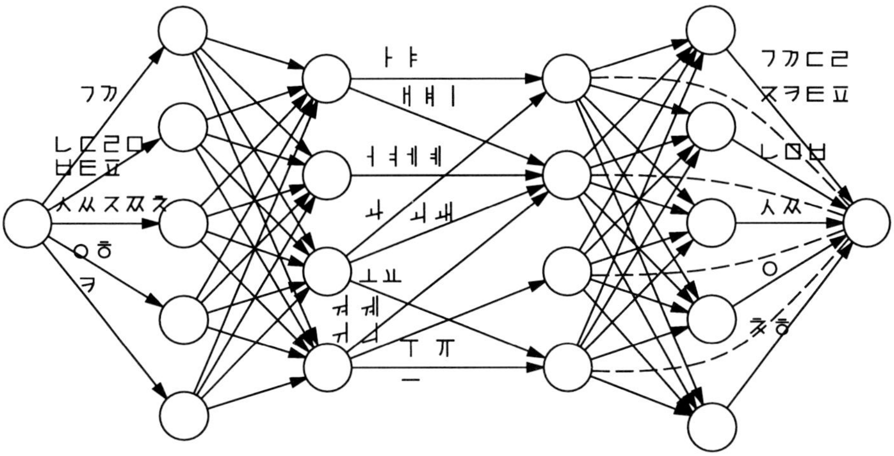

(b)

Fig. 1. (a) The structure of letter or ligature HMMs, and (b) the Korean handwritten character model — *BongNet*.

corresponds to a set of letter HMMs or a ligature HMM. And every legal Korean character corresponds to a unique path in the network.

3. STOCHASTIC INFERENCE

The characteristics of a finite state network (FSN) can be effectively understood with the principle of optimality that constitutes the basis of DP.[2] This section discusses the application of the Viterbi algorithm, a DP, to searching the FSN.

3.1. Inference Architecture

In this section the two stochastic inference algorithms are provided for on-line character recognition and (on-line) character pattern synthesis. The main idea underlying the algorithms is to align an observation sequence to network paths. The immediate goal of inference is the maximization of the joint probability of the observation sequence $X = x_1 x_2 \ldots x_T$ and the state sequence $Q = q_1 q_2 \ldots q_T$. Let $\hat{X}$ and $\hat{Q}$ be the best pair of observation and state sequences, respectively. Then we can write the maximal joint probability given a character model $\mathcal{M}$ as

$$\begin{aligned} P(\hat{X}, \hat{Q} | \mathcal{M}) &= \max_{X,Q} P(X, Q | \mathcal{M}) \\ &= \max_{X,Q,W} P(X, Q | W) P(W | \mathcal{M}) \end{aligned} \tag{1}$$

where W is a network path corresponding to a character. $P(W|\mathcal{M})$ is estimated using a language model. It is independent of the observation sequence, thus it can be estimated separately. $P(X,Q|W)$ is the probability that is estimated efficiently using the Viterbi algorithm, a DP technique. Let $W = W_1 \dots W_k \dots W_K$ be a sequence of HMMs, and let $Q_{1,t}$ be a t-long partial state sequence from the global start node to some state j of some model W_k through $W_1 \dots W_{k-1}$. Let a_{ij}^k be the transition probability from the state i to j of the HMM W_k, and b_j^k the output probability of the state j of the HMM W_k. The probability of the partial path that has the observation sequence $X_{1,t} = x_1 \dots x_t$ at time t while arriving at state j of the kth model W_k is calculated by using the recurrence relation as[22]

$$\delta_t^k(j) = \max_i \delta_{t-1}^k(i) a_{ij}^k b_j^k(x_t), \; t = 1,\dots,T, \; k = 1,\dots,K, \; j = 1,\dots,N \qquad (2)$$

where

$$b_j^k(x_t) \triangleq \begin{cases} b_j^k(o_t) & \text{if recognition task,} \\ \max_v b_j^k(v) & \text{if generation task.} \end{cases}$$

Let us explain each case separately in more detail.

3.2. Stochastic Recognition

In character recognition tasks, we are given an observation sequence O, that is, $X = O$, and the objective is not just maximal probability but the state sequence from which we can recover the letter sequence. Thus, we have two recurrence relations, by removing k in Eq. (2) for convenience,

$$\begin{aligned} \delta_t(j) &= \max_i \delta_{t-1}(i) a_{ij} b_j(o_t) \\ \psi_t(j) &= \arg\max_i \delta_{t-1}(i) a_{ij} b_j(o_t), \end{aligned} \qquad j = 1,\cdots,N, \; t = 2,\cdots,T \qquad (3)$$

where $\psi_t(j)$ stores the index of the state prior to the transition to j. ψ maintains all possible transition history so that, after the forward search, the optimal path can be recovered by back-tracking the chain of ψ.

This method of recognition algorithm dispenses with the explicit letter segmentation which is required in letter-by-letter matching approaches. The optimal segmentation is calculated during the forward pass, and can be obtained by finding in the optimal alignment the observations (or points) at which the model boundaries fall.

3.3. Stochastic Generation

The character generation task can be expressed as the question: *What* is the most likely observation string of this size, e.g. T, that this model can produce? The objective is two fold, the maximizations of the state sequence and the observation sequence. Here the symbol sequence is not given, rather it must be determined using only the knowledge contained in the model. In the current method based on HMMs, the best observation sequence is calculated by choosing locally the best symbols and keeping them in ζ in each state at each time as

$$\begin{aligned} \delta_t(j) &= \max_{i,x} \delta_{t-1}(i) a_{ij} b_j(x) \\ \psi_t(j) &= \arg\max_i \max_x \delta_{t-1}(i) a_{ij} b_j(x) \\ \zeta_t(j) &= \arg\max_x \max_i \delta_{t-1}(i) a_{ij} b_j(x), \\ & \qquad j = 1, \cdots, N, \; t = 2, \cdots, T. \end{aligned} \tag{4}$$

Here δ and ψ are the same as those of the stochastic recognition. ζ maintains the best observation symbol in each state. In the above equations the symbol x is independent of the preceding state, so we can write

$$\zeta_t(j) = [\max_i \delta_{t-1}(i) a_{ij}][\arg\max_x b_j(x)]. \tag{5}$$

In addition, the best observation symbol is fixed given a state j, that is,

$$\zeta_t(j) = [\arg\max_x b_j(x)] = o_j^*. \tag{6}$$

Therefore, the overall computation time is the same as that of the recognition if we store the best symbol in every state before the Viterbi search.

The retrieval of the best sequence of a given length T is similar to that of the segmentation in the recognition algorithm. The best observation sequence can be recovered by following recursively the chain of $\psi_t(j^*)$ and producing the symbols in $\zeta_t(j^*)$. Let q_F be the single final state (or let Q_F be the set of final states) of the model. Then we can write the back-tracking procedure formally as follows.

[Initialization]

$$\begin{aligned} q_T^* &= q_F \text{ (or } \arg\max_{i \in Q_F} \delta_T(i)) \\ x_T^* &= \zeta_T(q_T^*) \end{aligned}$$

[Recursion] $t = T-1, \ldots, 1$

$$\begin{aligned} q_t^* &= \psi_{t+1}(q_{t+1}^*) \\ x_t^* &= \zeta_{t+1}(q_{t+1}^*). \end{aligned}$$

The result becomes the sequence $X^* = x_1^* x_2^* \cdots x_T^*$.

3.4. Extension to HMM Network

The algorithms described in the preceding sections are based on the conventional Viterbi search within a single HMM. But it can also be applied to searching the network of HMMs such as the Hangul character model of Fig. 1(b). The computation performed in the dummy nodes of the network is similar to the maximization done in HMM states. Let T be the length of the observation sequence and

$0 = t_0 \le t_1 \le t_2 \le \cdots \le t_K = T$. By using conditional assumption, we can write

$$
\begin{aligned}
P(\hat{X}, \hat{Q}|\mathcal{M}) &= \max_{X,Q,W} P(X_{1,T}, Q_{1,T}|W_{1,K})P(W_{1,K}|\mathcal{M}) \\
&= \max_{X,Q,W} \prod_{k=1}^{K} P(X_{t_{k-1}+1,t_k}, Q_{t_{k-1}+1,t_k}|W_k)P(W_k|W_{k-1}, \mathcal{M}) .
\end{aligned} \tag{7}
$$

By changing the constants K and T to variables m and t, without the loss of generality, we can write (7) in a recursive form

$$
\begin{aligned}
&\max_{X,Q,W} P(X_{1,t_{m-1}}, Q_{1,t_{m-1}}|W_{1,m-1})P(W_{1,m-1}|\mathcal{M}) \\
&\qquad \times P(X_{t_{m-1}+1,t}, Q_{t_{m-1}+1,t}|W_m)P(W_m|W_{m-1}, \mathcal{M}) .
\end{aligned} \tag{8}
$$

Note that (8) is a form similar to (2). The first term of the maximization corresponds to the accumulated likelihood of matching the initial partial sequence $X_{1,t_{m-1}}$ and a Viterbi path of $W_{1,m-1} = W_1 \cdots W_{m-1}$. The second term may be termed as the output probability of the model, and the last term the probability of inter-model transition or bigram transition. We call the computational process of (8) as the model-wise Viterbi algorithm.

4. EXPERIMENTS

In this section we will see experimental results related to the two problems of on-line recognition of Korean characters and the generation of handwriting.

4.1. Experimental Context

For training the letter and ligature HMMs, we have collected about 52,000 cursive character samples from 58 subjects. Each sample is first preprocessed, resampled into a sequence of equidistant points covering both pen-down and pen-up loci, and are then converted to a chain of sixteen direction codes. The letter and the ligature HMMs are trained by the forward-backward algorithm[1] using the collection of hand-segmented chain codes. The test samples for recognition includes more than eight thousand characters written cursively without any stylistic constraint.

4.2. On-Line Recognition

In the recognition experiments, we have employed a letter-bigram language model whose perplexity is around 5.1. The primary use of the Korean character model has been to recognize the on-line characters. So the HMMs have been fine tuned to the recognition task. After training, we have smoothed the HMM output distribution parameters. In this way we could reduce recognition errors by 46.7%, down from 87.4% correct recognition to 93.3% with the single best candidates. Table 1 shows the recognition rates measured by varying the number of accepted candidates.

The success of a character or a word recognizer, unless it is based on the whole word models, depends on the sequence of letter matching results. This implies the

Fig. 2. Test samples used for recognition.

Table 1. Character recognition rates with varying number of accepted candidates.

Candidates	1	2	3	4	5
Recognition rate	93.30	97.15	97.57	97.75	97.81

need for letter segmentation whether it is explicit or implicit. In our recognizer the letter segmentation is carried out in parallel with the process of recognition, and the optimal result can be obtained after the forward search is finished. Although not necessary for the recognition, the segmentation results are useful for some analytic purposes.

Along the back-tracked path, the time at which the initial state of an HMM was met with for the first time during forward search corresponds to the segmentation point between the letter and ligature HMMs.[19] Figure 3 shows some examples of segmentation results mapped on to the raw handwriting. The segmentation

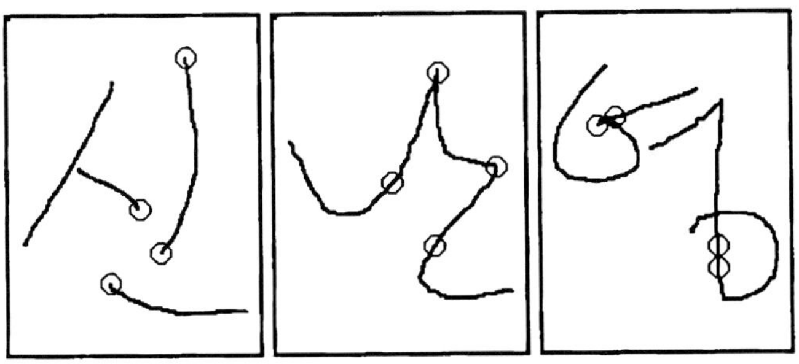

(a) (b) (c)

Fig. 3. Letter segmentation examples: (a) discrete, (b) cursive, and (c) another cursive character with two touches.

points are highly reasonable. The points in Fig. 3(a) are easy to detect by analyzing the stroke shape when discreteness is known, but several other points lying in the middle of locally straight region of strokes (Fig. 3(b) and (c)) are unprecedented in other segmentation-based approaches based on the shape analysis. There being no guiding features around the points, it is next to impossible to find them unless the recognizer is armed with *a priori* character-specific knowledge. In the proposed model, however, it is straightforward and those points are determined in simple probabilistic terms.

The HMMs have a left-right transition structure. Let M be the number of HMMs, $\bar{N}$ the average number of states of an HMM, and l the average number of arcs directly connected to a state. Then the computational requirement for the Viterbi search amounts to $Ml\bar{N}T$ where T is the length of an input sequence. According to the experiments, the preprocessing stage spends only about ten percent of the total computation, and the overall speed of recognition is about two characters per second, which is deemed practical for the real time application.

4.3. Handwriting Generation

Pattern generation using the HMM involves choosing jointly the best observations and the best state sequence. In this task the network model serves as the knowledge base for human handwriting. Here we have to make an active control over the course of transition, and we assume that the length (or size) of the sequence is given.

Fig. 4. A deformed pattern zero('0') generated by a standard HMM.

According to the theory of hidden Markov modeling, the state duration behavior of the standard HMM is far from being accurate. This means that the Markov chain underlying the HMM provides an inaccurate control over the duration in a state, thus unduly emphasizing certain local features (i.e. segment length) as shown in Fig. 4. So we will compare the generation results with those of the two variants of the standard HMM, called state duration HMM (DHMM)[16] and nonstationary HMM (NSHMM).[18] These models explicitly parameterize the state duration behaviors in terms of the state duration PDs and the time-varying state transition probabilities, respectively. They are capable of controlling the local durations so that the global shape is under control.

Figure 5 shows digit patterns from the three types of HMMs. In Fig. 5(a) it is evident that only one local feature is emphasized in each of the ten patterns. Thus

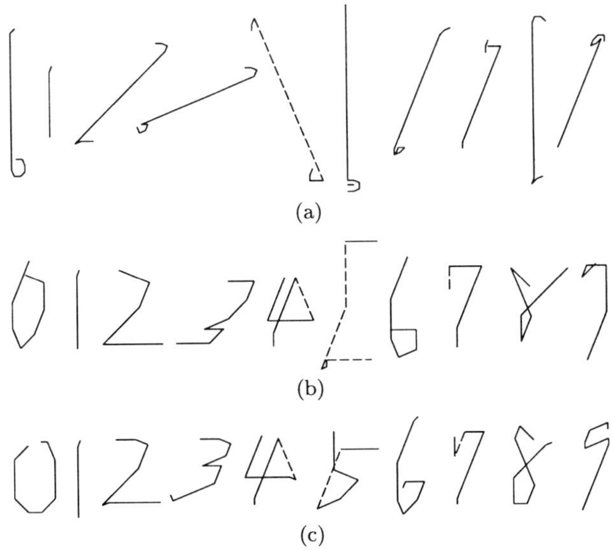

Fig. 5. Digit patterns from (a) HMM, (b) DHMM, and (c) NSHMM.

they are difficult to be read as digits. Among the DHMM outputs shown in Fig. 5(b) slight deformations are observed in the patterns '5', '7', and '9'. But the NSHMM patterns in Fig. 5(c) are considered highly regular and relatively natural. We can make the same overall comments about the Latin alphabet patterns generated from the HMMS in Fig. 6. The size of the patterns were set to the average length of the training samples.

The Hangul character model is a network of the letter and the ligature HMMs. Character patterns can be derived from the network in two ways. First, we can generate individual letter patterns of an appropriate size from the letter HMMs, and concatenate them in order. See Fig. 7(b), each character corresponds to a human-drawn sample in Fig. 7(a). For normal characters the size may be set to the average length of the training samples. In this method of generation, the shape and the size of each letter is fixed, so we have only to concatenate the letters once the set of all the letters are generated and stored in memory. For bigger or smaller characters, each letter can be scaled up or down proportionately.

Another way to generate a character pattern is to choose a single character path in the network as of Fig. 1(b), and then to extract the best symbol sequence out of the character path. Sample results are shown in Fig. 7(c). One problem of this method is determining the relative size of the individual letters. Owing to probabilistic maximization, only one local segment of only one letter may be extended when the corresponding letter model has been overly fitted to the training samples of small variations. This can be seen in the six leftmost characters of Fig. 7(c) where only one horizontal or vertical stroke segment per character is elongated. This result can also be explained by the inaccurate state duration behavior. The other two

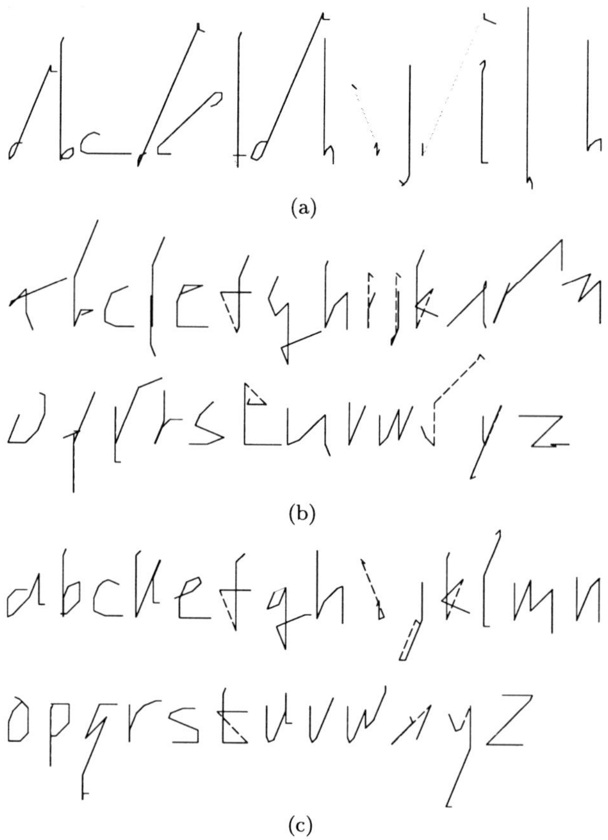

Fig. 6. Latin letter patterns generated by (a) standard HMM, (b) DHMM, and (c) NSHMM. Chain codes were used for the experiment.

HMM variants generate patterns which are readily legible and whose local segments are well-balanced with the global size and shape. However, one problem with the patterns is that the small segments of complex letters do not often appear at all (as in the two characters at the bottom of each set in Fig. 7). This phenomenon is primarily due to the simplistic assumption of output independence

$$P(X = x_1 x_2 \cdots x_N | i) = \prod_{n=1}^{N} b_i(x_n),$$

which ignores the correlation among the sequence of symbols. There are other interpretations such as the unbalanced usage of parameters of a given HMM, that is, the interpretation that there are more transition parameters A than are needed or when compared to the size of B. We believe that more accurate and natural handwriting patterns will be possible when a more rigorous encoding and representation scheme is employed. In fact the study on HMM theory has been concentrated on the observation process than the Markov chain process.[4,14,15] The only rationale for

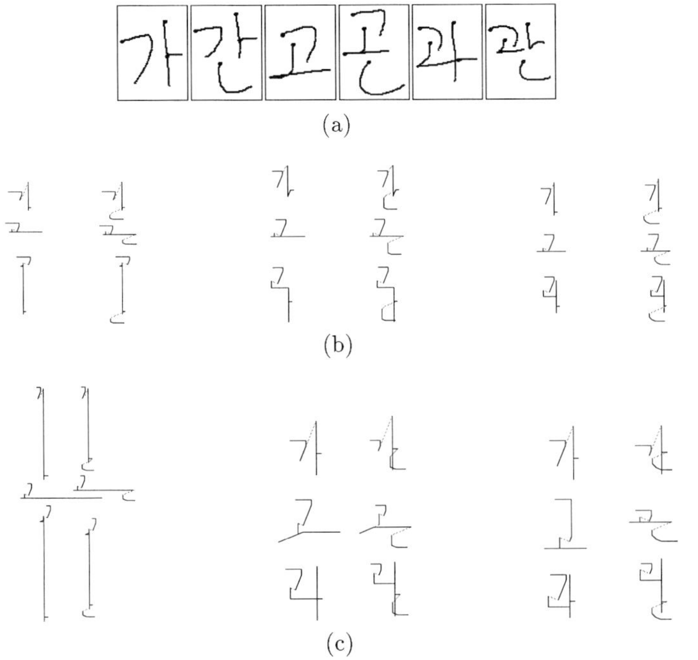

Fig. 7. Korean character patterns generated using standard HMM, DHMM, and NSHMM, from left to right: (a) human-drawn examples for reference, (b) concatenation of letters and ligatures, and (c) generation from character models.

using direction code is that the local shape features are preserved and can simply be restored to the spatial patterns.

In the task of character generation, where the character path is given, the total amount of computation is small compared to that of the recognition task. So the complexity of DHMM and NSHMM search does not pose any trouble, to say nothing of the method of concatenating isolated letters and ligatures.

5. DISCUSSION

5.1. Handwriting Evaluation

In the preceding section we have examined character patterns generated from HMMs. But we have omitted their subjective evaluation. This is because there is no objective measure for evaluating the handwriting quality. The naturalness, readability of script, to be precise, can only be measured qualitatively by human eyes. And in the literature dealing with mechanically generated script, no evaluation has been performed except showing the plausibility of the model or presenting the simple statistics based on a number of subjective opinions.[6,12]

There is another possibility. Let us now replace the human subject with a statistical handwriting recognizer as developed in the preceding sections. If the script model represents accurately the statistical aspects of the handwriting shape, so will be the recognition results based on the model. For instance, when the script of a certain style is accepted with low percentage, it is obvious that the style has little in common with other styles. But when the recognition rate is high, we can safely conclude that the style has a lot in common with the average features representing the training set. One caveat is that the previous explanation is impossible when the script model is incorrect or under-trained. Let us provide a sample result which is considered worth mentioning.

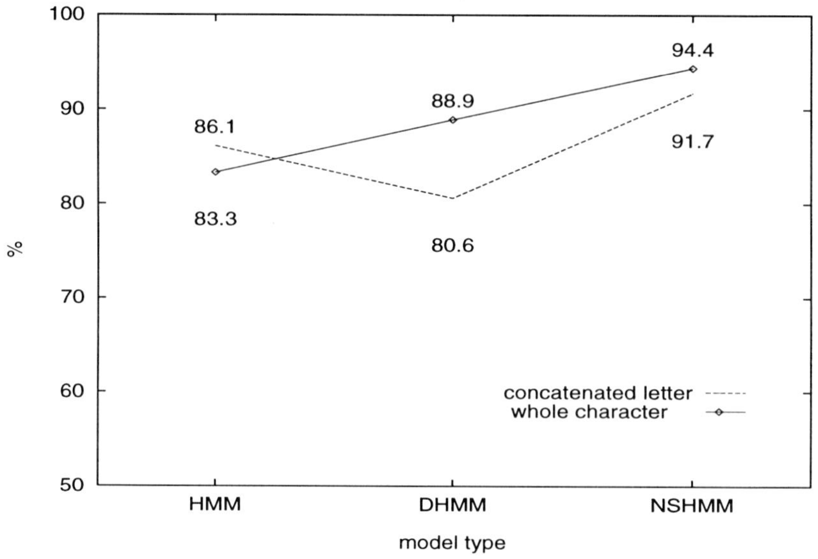

Fig. 8. The recognition rates for the handwriting samples generated in two ways using HMM, DHMM or NSHMM.

Figure 8 is a summary of the test result which is based on the recognizer used in the recognition test. Test samples include six sets of generation samples, each with one of the two generation methods and one of the three HMM types. The figure shows that the recognition rates for the character patterns generated by NSHMM, 94.4% and 91.7% are the highest. Moreover these performance indices are the most comparable to that of the human handwriting recognition rate 93.3% shown in Table 1. This indicates that the NSHMM samples are the most natural and similar to that of human handwriting as far as the recognizer is concerned. (Note that the script model of the recognizer has learned the handwriting patterns of a large number of writers.) On the contrary, it is difficult to interpret the results of the other two HMMs except for the fact that the recognition rates are low. It is primarily due to the complex nature of the probabilistic interactions of the local processes in the sequence of HMMs. Our conjecture is that the low recognition rates are due to the different extents of model optimization in the case of HMMs and the effect of under-training in the case of some DHMMs.

Finally, cross-validation is another technique that can be applied to evaluating handwritings. It is based on the cross-evaluation of character generations with character models each of which is trained using a partition of a given training set. This, however, will not be discussed here because the method measures the difference between two training/generation samples rather than the quality of the generation samples.

5.2. Pen Trajectory Recovery

In the handwriting generation task, the sequence of output symbols were determined according to the output probability distributions. In the following discussion let us consider the case in which the choice is also constrained by the external input signals. The case is about the task of recovering temporal information from off-line character images[5]. In this paper we define the task as that of following the pen trajectory of the black pixels in a given image. Note that each parameter of an HMM describes the local characteristic of the corresponding position in a character. Thus, in principle, we can do better than the blind tracking of pen trajectory if we consult the model during the trace. In this task the model serves as the knowledge base for human handwriting behavior.

The overall computational structure is similar to that of the generation algorithm as given by the recurrence relations in Eq. (4). In the current task the choice of the best symbol sequence is constrained by the configuration of black pixels (Fig. 9) as well as the output PDs of the HMM. Let us suppose that we have followed a pen trajectory, previously at pixel $\mathbf{x}_{t-1}(i)$ in state i at time $t-1$ and we are going to move one step away to some other pixel of a fixed distance. Thus the last output function of (3) can be written as a function of b_j, $\mathbf{x}_{t-1}(i)$ and $\mathbf{u}$ which is a pixel in the neighborhood of $\mathbf{x}_{t-1}(i)$ as

$$b_j(x) = f(b_j, \mathbf{x}_{t-1}(i), \mathbf{u}). \tag{9}$$

We simplify this to be a linear combination of output PD b_j and a pixel evaluation function g as

$$b_j(x) \triangleq \max_{\mathbf{u}} b_j(\theta(\mathbf{u} - \mathbf{x}_{t-1}(i)))\; g(\mathbf{u}) \tag{10}$$

such that

$$\theta(\mathbf{u} - \mathbf{x}_{t-1}(i)) = x \tag{11}$$

for some direction code x. Here $\mathbf{u}$ is a pixel following and in the neighborhood of the pixel $\mathbf{x}_{t-1}$, $\theta()$ is an appropriate direction coding function as described in Fig. 9(a), and $g()$ a normalized convolution operator based on a mask such as in Figure 9(b) for evaluating the next step of pen trajectories. Formally g is defined by

$$g(\mathbf{u}) = \sum_{\mathbf{y} \in \mathcal{N}(\mathbf{u})} w_i I(\mathbf{y}). \tag{12}$$

The mask pattern of g is defined by a neighborhood $\mathcal{N}(\mathbf{u})$ or a set of neighbor pixels around and including $\mathbf{u}$ (see Fig. 9(b)), $I(\mathbf{y}) \in \{0,\ 1\}$(or $[0,1]$ in gray scale images) is a normalized intensity of the pixel at $\mathbf{y}$, and w_i's are the weights of the mask pixels satisfying $\sum_i w_i = 1$.

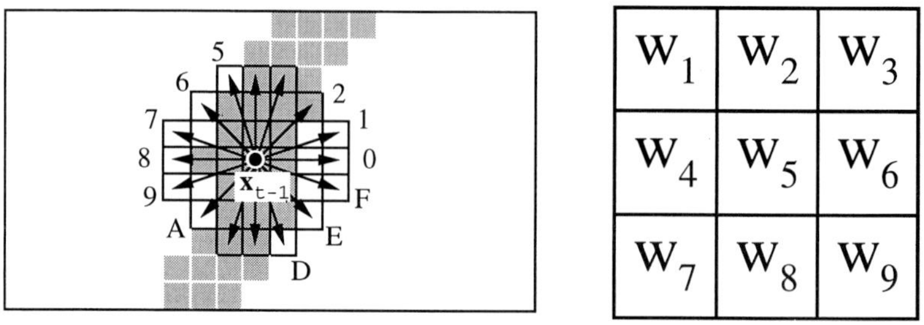

(a) (b)

Fig. 9. (a) Direction encoding function θ of pen trajectory step, and (b) a pixel mask operator defining g.

Using the previous definitions (10), (11), and (12), we can then write the most likely next position $\mathbf{x}_t(j)$ as

$$\mathbf{x}_t(j) = \arg\max_{\mathbf{u}} \max_{i}\ \delta_{t-1}(i)\ a_{ij}\ b_j(\theta(\mathbf{u} - \mathbf{x}_{t-1}(i)))\ g(\mathbf{u}).$$

This is the pixel coordinate which must be maintained separately for the next step of the pen trajectory following. After the forward computation, the best sequence of $\mathbf{x}_t$'s is similarly obtained by tracking back the state sequence using $\psi_t(j^*)$, $t = T, \ldots, 1$ to produce $\mathbf{x}_t(j^*)$'s.

There is one assumption for the above algorithm to work on real samples; the starting point of a trace is assumed to be given, usually in the upper left corner of the image. Although this alone is not without difficulty and ambiguity, we believe that it is possible to locate with high reliability the starting points by using various sources of knowledge and clues from the input images.[11] The forward pass and the back-tracking of the modified Viterbi algorithm is very similar to those in Sec. 3.3.

Figure 10 shows sample final results, the starting point marked by a white dot. It is surprising that the trajectory includes the pen-up moves corresponding to an alternate set of direction codes. For the recovery of pen trajectory of Hangul characters, the character model *BongNet* was used. In Fig. 10(b) the numbers denote the state indices of the letter and ligature HMMs: The first seven arrows along the writing sequence correspond to the initial consonant letter HMM, the next three arrows to the ligature HMM, the next five to the vowel letter HMM, and so forth. Due to the incorrect modeling of the state duration and the imperfect output probability distribution, the preference for the early forward transitions is obvious at the end of the second/upper ligature. This affected the trajectory at the initial part of the vowel, the L-shaped segment in the upper right quadrant.

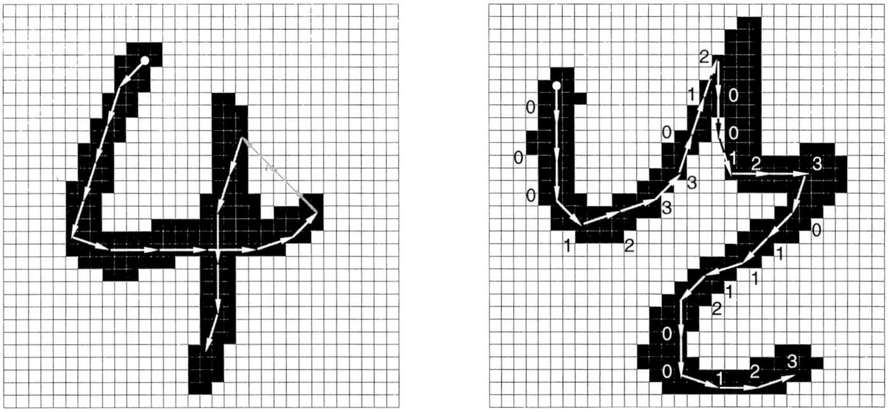

(a) (b)

Fig. 10. (a) Examples of pen trajectories using an isolated HMM and (b) the character network of Sec. 2(b).

The recovery system used in the above experiment is not complete *per se* in that the prototype system incorporates several assumptions: the knowledge of the starting point of trace, the size of the image and the step, the form of heuristic convolution operator g, and so on. According to further tests with the above assumptions, a large part of the trajectory errors were due to the Markovian assumption. Other errors came from the rigid step size and direction that often force the system to choose boundary pixels or even white pixels beyond the inked loci. These problems can possibly be solved by the use of duration-aware HMMs and some elaborations to guide the choice of 'safe' pixels. These works and a rigorous analysis of the method are left for future study.

6. CONCLUSION

The variabilities of time-sequential on-line handwriting can be effectively modeled using the tool of HMM. Using HMM network-based models, it has been shown that we can not only recognize input characters, but also generate handwriting patterns characteristic of humans and possibly recover the lost temporal information from off-line character images. The generated patterns presented in this paper may not be considered similar to those of humans. But we believe that the HMMs reproduced the statistically human aspect of character shape, and that the HMMs will reproduce highly human characters when a more sophisticated data coding scheme is employed.

REFERENCES

1. L. E. Baum, T. Petrie, G. Soules and N. Weiss, "A maximization technique occurring in the statistical analysis of probabilistic functions of Markov chains", *Ann. Math. Stat.* **41**, 1 (1970) 164–171.
2. R. Bellman, *Dynamic Programming*, Princeton: Princeton Univ. Press, 1957.

3. G. Boccignone, A. Chanese, L. P. Cordella and A. Marcelli, "Recovering dynamic information from static handwriting", *Patt. Recogn.* **26**, 3 (1993) 409–418.
4. L. Deng, "A stochastic model of speech incorporating hierarchical nonstationarity", *IEEE Trans. Speech Audio Process.* **1**, 4 (1993) 471–474.
5. D. S. Doerman and A. Rosenfeld, "Recovery of temporal information from static images", in *Proc. IEEE Comp. Soc. Conf. CVPR*, Urbana, 1992, pp. 162–168.
6. E. H. Dooijes, *Analysis of Handwriting Movement*, PhD thesis, Univ. Amsterdam, Netherlands, 1983.
7. K. S. Fu, *Syntactic Pattern Recognition and Applications*, Prentice-Hall, Englewood Cliffs, NJ, 1982.
8. J. M. Hollerbach, "An oscillation theory of handwriting", *Biol. Cybern.* **39** (1981) 139–156.
9. A. Kundu and P. Bahl, "Recognition of handwritten script: a hidden Markov model based approach", *Proc. IEEE ICASSP*, 1988, pp. 928–931.
10. S.-H. Lee, K.-Y. Lee and Y. Lee, "A generalized character recognition using SEJONG-NET", *Proc. 2nd Pacific Rim Conf. AI*, Seoul, Korea, Sept. 1992, pp. 947–952.
11. S. Mori, C. Y. Suen and K. Yamamoto, "Historical review of OCR research and development", *Proc. IEEE* **80** (1992) 1029–1058.
12. R. Plamondon and F. J. Maarse, "An evaluation of motor models of handwriting", *IEEE Trans. Syst. Man Cybern.* **19**, 5 (1989) 1060–1072.
13. R. Plamondon, W. Guerfali and X. Li, "The generation of oriental characters: New perspectives for automatic handwriting processing", *Proc. 17th ICCPOL*, Hong Kong, April 1997, pp. 113–120.
14. A. B. Poritz, "Linear predictive hidden Markov models and the speech signal", *Proc. IEEE ICASSP*, May 1982, pp. 1291–1294.
15. S. Roucos and M. O. Dunham, "A stochastic segment model for phoneme-based continuous speech recognition", *Proc. IEEE ICASSP*, Dallas, Texas, April 1987, pp. 73–76.
16. M. J. Russell and R. K. Moore, "Explicit modeling of state occupancy in hidden Markov models for automatic speech recognition", *Proc. IEEE ICASSP*, Tampa, FL, Mar. 1985, pp. 5–8.
17. B.-K. Sin, *An HMM-based Statistical Framework for Modeling On-line Cursive Script*, PhD thesis, Korea Advanced Institute of Science and Technology, Feb. 1995.
18. B.-K. Sin and J. H. Kim, "Nonstationary hidden Markov model", *Signal Process.* **46**, 1 (1995) 31–46.
19. B.-K. Sin and J. H. Kim, "Ligature modeling for online cursive script recognition", *IEEE Trans. Patt. Anal. Mach. Intell.* **19**, 6 (1997) 623–633.
20. C. C. Tappert, "Cursive script recognition by elastic matching", *IBM J. Res. Dev.* **26**, 6 (1982) pp. 765–771.
21. C. C. Tappert, C. Y. Suen and T. Wakahara, "The state of the art in on-line handwriting recognition", *IEEE Trans. Patt. Anal. Mach. Intell.* **12**, 8 (1990) 787–808.
22. A. J. Viterbi, "Error bounds for convolution codes and an asymptotically optimum decoding algorithm", *IEEE Trans. Inf. Theory* **13** (1967) 260–269.

Bong-Kee Sin received B.S. degree in mineral and petroleum engineering from Seoul National University in 1985, and M.S. and Ph.D. degrees in computer science from Korea Advanced Institute of Science and Technology (KAIST) in 1987 and 1995 respectively. Since 1987 he has been a member and now a senior member of the research staff in Korea Telecom Research Center.

His current research interests include character recognition, stochastic and adaptive learning, theoretical and practical aspects of intelligent agents, and information retrieval.

Jin-Hyung Kim received the B.S. degree in engineering from Seoul National University, Korea, in 1971 and the M.S. and Ph.D. degrees in computer science from the University of California, Los Angeles, in 1979 and 1983, respectively. He was a research engineer at the Korea Institute of Science and Technology from 1973 to 1976, an engineering programmer at the County of Orange, California, USA, from 1976 to 1977, and a senior staff member at Hughes Artificial Intelligence Center, Calabasas, California, USA, from 1981 to 1985. He joined the faculty of KAIST in 1985. He was a visiting scientist at IBM Watson Research Center from 1990 to 1991. He is now on the editorial board of International Journal of Information Processing and Management, International Journal of Robotics and Autonomous Systems, and International Journal of Intelligent and Fuzzy Systems. He is currently holding the position of Director General at Korea R&D Information Center (KORDIC).

His research interests include pattern recognition, intelligent man-machine interface, agents and information retrieval, and AI for Education.

COMPARISON OF FEATURE PERFORMANCE AND ITS APPLICATION TO FEATURE COMBINATION IN OFF-LINE HANDWRITTEN KOREAN ALPHABET RECOGNITION*

KUKHWAN SEO, JONGYEOL KIM, JONGMIN YOON and KYUSIK CHUNG†

Department of Electronic Engineering, Soongsil University
1-1 Sangdo 5-Dong, DongjakGu Seoul, 156-743, Korea

This paper presents (1) a quantitative performance comparison of the features used in off-line handwritten Korean alphabet recognition, and (2) some experimental results based on the feature combination approach. We classified the features into three: geometrical/topological, statistical and global. For each class, we selected four or five features and performed recognition experiments with PE92 database using neural network classifiers. We compared their recognition performances and selected the top four among those thirteen features: Up Down Left Right Hole, Gradient, Structure, and Mesh. With the combination of some or all of the four features, we repeated recognition experiments. Experimental results show that (1) as a whole, geometrical/topological features outperform the other two feature classes in terms of the recognition rate, and (2) UDLRH and Gradient features in geometrical/topological feature class outperform the other features, (3) the feature combination approach can result in performance improvement.

Keywords: Optical character recognition, feature extraction, feature selection/combination.

1. INTRODUCTION

On-line/off-line handwriting recognition has been one of the most active research areas in the past several years. In on-line handwriting recognition there has been considerable progress in research so that some commercial products are available. However, in off-line handwriting recognition there is relatively little progress due to its additional difficulties. Further efforts should be made to solve the problems of off-line handwriting recognition with new approaches. So far for most off-line Hangul (Korean character) handwriting recognition, they have focused on the classification stage of the character recognition process so that little attention has been paid to other stages such as preprocessing, feature extraction or postprocessing.[6,7] One of the directions in breakthroughs on handwriting recognition is a systematic selection of distinctive features and the optimal combination of the recognition techniques.[9] It is very desirable to select a set of distinctive features so that they are insensitive to shape deformation as much as possible, and also they make a contribution to the improvement of the performance in terms of the recognition accuracy and speed as much as possible.

*This work was supported by NONDIRECTED RESEARCH FUND, Korea Research Foundation.
†Corresponding author. E-mail: {tatata,jykim,boramae,kchung} @q.soongsil.ac.kr

Advances in Oriental Document Analysis and Recognition Techniques (1998) 251–261

In order to select a subset of distinctive features, we need to compare the features to evaluate their power. A research paper[9] on this issue compares recognition techniques from the view of the features chosen. It classifies features into three: geometrical/topological, statistical and global. The relative merits of the features/recognition techniques were compared on the following criteria: (1) sensitivity to the deformation of the image, and (2) practical implementation of the techniques. However, only qualitative comparisons of features used were shown in the classifiers. In this paper, we present a quantitative comparison of the recognition performance of the features used in the recent off-line handwritten character recognition. This research aims at providing the basis for the feature combination in order to improve not only the recognition rate but also the efficiency of the recognition system. Based on the above classification scheme,[9] we classify those features used in the recent off-line handwritten character recognition into three: geometrical/topological feature, statistical feature and global (image transformation) feature. For each class, we selected four or five features which are more frequently used and easier to be implemented. With 13 features, we performed recognition experiments for Korean alphabets using neural network classifiers.

Korean characters called Hangul consist of 24 phonemes (alphabet). Fourteen of them are consonants and the rest are vowels. The phonemes are combined together to form a syllable (character). More than 11,000 syllables can be created, but 2350 of them are used for daily life. A Korean character is a structural combination of either two or three letter types: initial consonant, middle vowel and final consonant. Each type can appear only at a specific position in a character, and written in the order as initial, middle, and final letters. Note that a Korean alphabet corresponds to a phoneme level whereas an English alphabet corresponds to a syllable (character) level. Therefore, it is an issue which level recognition is more suitable for Hangul recognition: character-level recognition or alphabet-level recognition. In the former, the number of character classes is so large that the classifier design matters. In the latter, the number of alphabet classes is small so that the classifier design does not matter. However, the segmentation of a character into the alphabets matters. In this paper, we adopt the latter approach since it allows to exploit the structural properties of Hangul character.[4]

This paper is organized as follows. Section 2 gives a detailed description of the features. Section 3 explains the experiments and Sec. 4 describes the conclusion.

2. FEATURE DESCRIPTION[1–3,9]

Features used for character recognition can be classified into three: geometrical/topological, statistical and global.[9] Table 1 summarizes the characteristics and examples of the three feature classes. For each class, we compared several types of features based on the following criteria: (1) frequency of its use in the recent character recognizers, and (2) possibility of its practical implementation. Among them, we selected the top four or five features in each class.

Table 1. Feature classification.

Feature class	Extraction method	Example
Geometrical topological features	extract features which describe the geometry and topology of the drawing in an image	– polygonal approximation – convolution feature – stroke split – topological contour tracing
Statistical features	extract features from the statistical distribution of point in an image	– zoning – moments – n-tuples – characteristic loci – crossing and distance
Global features	extract features from the state of all points in an image or the state of a transformed image	– template matching and correlations – transformation and series expansion

2.1. Geometrical/Topological Features[1]

This feature describes the geometry and topology of the drawing. It may represent global and local properties of the character. The main advantage of such features is their high tolerance to distortion and style variations. They can also tolerate a certain degree of translation and rotation.[9]

2.1.1. Gradient feature

The gradient features are computed by convolving two Sobel operators on the binary image. These operators approximate the x and y derivatives in the image. The vector addition of the operators' outputs is used to compute the gradient of the image. Since the gradient is a vector with magnitude and direction, only the direction is used in the computation of the feature vector. The direction of the gradient can lie in the range from 0 to 359 degrees. This range is split into non-overlapping regions, each of 360/12 degrees. In each sampling region (4×4 grid), a histogram is taken of each gradient direction at each pixel which lies in the region. After the normalization of the histogram, these features are represented by $4 \times 4 \times 12 = 192$ real-valued components ranging from 0 to 1.

2.1.2. Structure feature

The structure features are obtained by extracting 12 special patterns from the gradient map, which is expressed by four groups as

(i) two kinds of horizontal line
(ii) two kinds of vertical line
(iii) two kinds of diagonal rising and
(iv) two kinds of diagonal falling and four kinds of corner.

These four groups are classified according to the gradient range of the 8-nearest neighboring pixels belonging to each pixel of the image. After accumulating 12 kinds of features included in each area of 4×4 grid, we normalize the accumulated result. These features are represented by $4 \times 4 \times 12 = 192$ real-valued components ranging from 0 to 1.

2.1.3. Coarse Pixel Density (CPD)

The input image is divided into 16 sampling regions (4×4 grid) and the number of black pixels in each grid is counted. After the normalization of the numbers, these features are represented by $4 \times 4 = 16$ real-valued components ranging from 0 to 1.

2.1.4. Large Stroke Feature (LSF)

The input image is divided into 16 sampling regions (4×4 grid) and the existence of large horizontal and vertical black strokes is checked. In each grid, run lengths of the horizontal and vertical strokes are computed. If the length is larger than half of the grid size, it is represented by '1'. Otherwise, it is represented by '0'. Thus, these features are represented by $4 \times 4 = 16$ binary-valued components.

2.1.5. Up Down Left Right Hole (UDLRH)

The UDLRH concavity features are computed as follows. Rays from each white pixel of the image is shot in four directions. Concavity is detected if a ray hits at a black pixel in that direction. In this way, upward, downward, left and right pointing concavity are detected along with holes. In each sample region (4×4 grid), results from each pixel are accumulated and normalized within the sample region. Thus, these features are represented by $4 \times 4 \times 5 = 80$ real-valued components ranging from 0 to 1.

2.2. Statistical Features

Features are extracted from the statistical distribution of points in an image. These features are less sensitive to distortion and style variation than global features. Compared to the other features, they provide a high speed and low complexity for implementation.[3]

2.2.1. Mesh features

The input image is divided into 64 sampling regions (8×8 grid) and the number of black pixels in each grid is counted. After the normalization of the numbers, these features are represented by $8 \times 8 = 16$ real-valued components ranging from 0 to 1.

2.2.2. Projection features

The input image is normalized into 32×32 and projected into X and Y axes, respectively. For each projection, the number of black pixels is counted. After the normalization of the numbers, these features are represented by $32 + 32 = 64$ real-valued components ranging from 0 to 1.

2.2.3. 8-direction zero crossing features

The input image is normalized into 32×32 and scanned into 8 directions from its mass center to its boundary. For each scan, the number of crossings to strokes is counted. After the normalization of the numbers, these features are represented by 8 real-valued components ranging from 0 to 1.

2.2.4. Zero-crossing features

The input image is normalized into 32×32 and scanned in the vertical and horizontal directions, respectively. During each scan, the number of changes from a white pixel to a black pixel is counted. After the normalization of the numbers, these features are represented by $32 + 32 = 64$ real-valued components ranging from 0 to 1.

2.3. Global Features

Features are extracted from every point which lies within a rectangle circumscribing the character. These global features can be extracted easily and are essentially unaffected by minor local changes or noise. Moreover, some are free from translation or rotation. But, they are dependent on the position alignment and are highly sensitive to distortion or style variation.[9] In our experiments, we first normalize the input image into 16×16 and then apply one of the following transformations to the image.

2.3.1. Fast Fourier Transformation (FFT)

After applying FFT to the input image, we obtain 16×16 transform coefficients. They are symmetric with respect to the origin and most large coefficients exist in the low frequency part. Thus, only coefficients in the second quadrant are used. These features are represented by 8×8 real-valued coefficients ranging from 0 to 1.

2.3.2. Walsh transformation

Unlike Fourier transformation, which is based on trigonometric terms, Walsh transformation consists of a series expansion of basic functions whose values are $+1$ or -1. Similarly as in FFT, only coefficients in the second quadrant are used. These features are represented by 8×8 real-valued coefficients ranging from 0 to 1.

2.3.3. HAAR transformation

HAAR transformation takes the differences of samples or the differences of local averages of the samples of the input vector. Thus, transform coefficients are the difference along the rows and columns of the local averages of the pixels in the image. Similarly as in FFT, only coefficients in the second quadrant are used. These features are represented by 8×8 real-valued coefficients ranging from 0 to 1.

2.3.4. Discrete Cosine Transformation (DCT)

As many transform coefficients in DCT are small, most of the energy of the data is packed in a few of them. Thus, DCT has excellent energy compaction. DCT is very close to the KL transform. Also, DCT is real and orthogonal. Similarly as in FFT, only coefficients in the second quadrant are used. These features are represented by 8×8 real-valued coefficients ranging from 0 to 1.

3. EXPERIMENTS AND RESULTS

3.1. Experiment Environment and Methods

Experiments are performed for the selected 13 features in IBM-PC 486DX2-66 and their performances are measured using a neural network simulator called NWORKS.[8] Given an input image, a bounding box is placed around it and a slant correction is applied. Then, depending on the feature type used, size normalization or skeletonization is applied. Then, the features are computed from the image. After the feature extraction, the feature vectors are presented as the inputs to a neural network classifier. The classifier is a multi-layered perceptron with one hidden layer trained with backpropagation algorithm. The reason why a MLP neural network classifier is chosen is because it is the most popular classifier for recent off-line character recognition. The training and test data for experiments are taken from PE92 database.[5] As PE92 contains handwritten Hangul syllables, some of them are manually segmented into initial consonant, middle vowel, and final consonant and then, are collected for our experiments. Table 2 shows the number of patterns used in our experiments where IC, HV and VV denote initial consonant, horizontal vowel, and vertical vowel, respectively.

Table 2. Number of patterns in the experiment.

Letter type		Train set	Test set
Korean alphabet	Initial Consonant (IC)	5377	4579
	Vertical Vowel (HV)	4041	1962
	Horizontal Vowel (VV)	2000	500

3.2. Experimental Results

Tables 3–5 show the classification results for Hangul initial consonants, Hangul vertical vowels, and Hangul horizontal vowels, respectively. The field of recognizer structure in the tables represent the number of input nodes $\times$ the number of hidden nodes $\times$ the number of output nodes in each experiment. The recognition rates in those tables indicate the correct recognition rates without considering rejections. For the comparison of feature performances, the same data set is used. Experimental results show that, as a whole, a high recognition rate is achieved in the order of geometrical/topological features, global features, and

Table 3. Classification result for initial consonants [unit:%].

	Feature type	Recognition rate		Recognizer
		Train set	Test set	Structure
Geometrical/ topological features	Gradient	98.29	90.70	$192 \times 96 \times 19$
	Structure	97.36	84.34	$192 \times 96 \times 19$
	CPD	81.81	74.36	$16 \times 16 \times 19$
	LSF	88.75	76.94	$32 \times 19 \times 19$
	UDLRH	98.81	94.46	$80 \times 40 \times 19$
Statistical features	Mesh	95.89	83.00	$64 \times 35 \times 19$
	Projection	88.67	73.71	$64 \times 35 \times 19$
	8-direction	52.72	47.41	$8 \times 19 \times 19$
	Zero-crossing	49.28	29.37	$64 \times 19 \times 19$
Global features	FFT	78.87	61.48	$64 \times 19 \times 19$
	DCT	89.19	69.77	$64 \times 32 \times 19$
	Walsh	90.40	68.09	$64 \times 32 \times 19$
	HAAR	91.41	80.50	$64 \times 19 \times 19$

Table 4. Classification result for vertical vowels [unit:%].

	Feature type	Recognition rate		Recognizer
		Train set	Test set	Structure
Geometrical/ topological features	Gradient	98.64	87.77	$192 \times 45 \times 9$
	Structure	96.76	84.96	$192 \times 45 \times 9$
	CPD	85.97	54.13	$16 \times 16 \times 9$
	LSF	89.41	74.31	$32 \times 19 \times 9$
	UDLRH	98.96	93.12	$80 \times 40 \times 9$
Statistical features	Mesh	98.66	87.36	$64 \times 40 \times 9$
	Projection	95.20	80.84	$64 \times 40 \times 9$
	8-direction	62.80	61.40	$8 \times 9 \times 9$
	Zero-crossing	72.14	54.89	$64 \times 20 \times 9$
Global features	FFT	71.22	61.47	$64 \times 9 \times 9$
	DCT	87.26	76.40	$64 \times 9 \times 9$
	Walsh	85.15	65.04	$64 \times 9 \times 9$
	HAAR	87.60	80.28	$64 \times 9 \times 9$

Table 5. Classification result for horizontal vowels [unit:%].

	Feature type	Recognition rate		Recognizer
		Train set	Test set	Structure
Geometrical/ topological features	Gradient	98.75	87.86	$192 \times 30 \times 5$
	Structure	96.30	80.54	$192 \times 30 \times 5$
	CPD	92.05	70.60	$16 \times 5 \times 5$
	LSF	95.75	79.82	$32 \times 12 \times 5$
	UDLRH	99.45	90.18	$80 \times 40 \times 5$
Statistical features	Mesh	99.75	82.86	$64 \times 5 \times 5$
	Projection	99.10	95.80	$64 \times 30 \times 5$
	8-direction	70.25	72.60	$8 \times 5 \times 5$
	Zero-crossing	75.80	64.80	$64 \times 20 \times 5$
Global features	FFT	78.35	78.40	$64 \times 5 \times 5$
	DCT	91.15	87.60	$64 \times 5 \times 5$
	Walsh	88.15	80.80	$64 \times 5 \times 5$
	HAAR	96.20	91.00	$64 \times 5 \times 5$

statistical features. The reason for this result seems as follows. Lines are the basic components to form a Hangul character. However, as the combinations of lines form a Hangul character, shape variations may occur accordingly. Also, similarities may exist between letters and their high style variations. These variations are easily handled by the geometrical/topological features. In the case of horizontal vowels, the three feature classes show a very similar performance. This seems to happen since the shapes of the vowels are relatively simple. Among the statistical features, mesh feature shows a relatively high performance for all types of letters. The projection feature shows high performance for vowels. This seems due to the feature being superior in representing the characteristics of vowels which mostly consist of horizontal and vertical line segments. Among global features, DCT and HAAR transform display a high performance. This seems due to this feature being superior in representing the direction components of Korean letters. Among geometrical/topological features, gradient and UDLRH features outperform the others for all types of letters. This seems due to the fact that they are superior in representing the characteristics of Hangul letters consisting of line segments. Table 6 shows the average execution time required to extract individual features. Among the three feature classes, global features take the longest time to be extracted whereas statistic features take the shortest time.

Table 6. Feature extraction times [unit:ms].

	Feature type	Feature extraction times
Geometrical/ topological features	Gradient	44.0
	Structure	86.0
	CPD	6.4
	LSF	11.0
	UDLRH	123.0
Statistical features	Mesh	13.0
	Projection	16.0
	8-direction	4.0
	Zero-crossing	13.0
Global features	FFT	45.0
	DCT	1475.0
	Walsh	778.0
	HAAR	843.0

3.3. Experimental Results on Feature Combination

Among the 13 features, we select four which show higher discrimination power: UDLRH, Gradient, Structure, and Mesh features. After some or all of their feature vectors are combined, they are presented to the neural network classifier. With the same data set, we repeat the experiment. Table 7 shows its classification results. Compared to the results in Tables 3–5, performances are improved as a whole.

Table 7. Classification result for feature combination [unit:%].

<table>
<tr><th colspan="4" rowspan="2">Feature combination</th><th rowspan="2">Letter Type</th><th colspan="2">Recognition rate</th><th rowspan="2">Recognizer Structure</th></tr>
<tr><th>Train set</th><th>Test set</th></tr>
<tr><td colspan="2" rowspan="3">Gradient</td><td colspan="2">Structure</td><td>IC</td><td>98.51</td><td>92.68</td><td>384 × 96 × 19</td></tr>
<tr><td colspan="2">UDLRH</td><td>IC</td><td>99.18</td><td>94.58</td><td>272 × 36 × 19</td></tr>
<tr><td colspan="2">Mesh</td><td>IC</td><td>98.83</td><td>93.89</td><td>256 × 45 × 19</td></tr>
<tr><td colspan="2" rowspan="2">UDLRH</td><td colspan="2">Mesh</td><td>IC</td><td>99.14</td><td>95.96</td><td>144 × 36 × 19</td></tr>
<tr><td colspan="2">Structure</td><td>IC</td><td>99.11</td><td>94.85</td><td>272 × 68 × 19</td></tr>
<tr><td rowspan="2">Gradient</td><td>UDLRH</td><td colspan="2">Mesh</td><td>IC</td><td>99.44</td><td>97.14</td><td>336 × 68 × 19</td></tr>
<tr><td>Structure</td><td colspan="2">UDLRH</td><td>IC</td><td>98.99</td><td>96.99</td><td>464 × 116 × 19</td></tr>
<tr><td>Gra</td><td>Str</td><td>UDLRH</td><td>Mesh</td><td>IC</td><td>99.29</td><td>97.49</td><td>528 × 132 × 19</td></tr>
</table>

Although this feature combination results in the increase of the complexity in its implementation, it can be viewed as an approach to improve performance.

4. CONCLUSION

In this paper we present experiments and have compared the recognition performance of the features used in the recent off-line handwritten Korean character recognition. We classified features into three: global feature(image transformation), statistical feature, and geometrical/topological feature. For each class, we selected four or five features based on the following criteria: (1) frequency of its use in the recent character recognizers, and (2) possibility of its practical implementation. With 13 features, we performed recognition experiments for Korean initial consonants, horizontal vowels, and vertical vowels, respectively. The classifier used in our experiments is a multi-layered perceptron with one hidden layer which is trained with backpropagation algorithm. The training and test data in the experiment are taken from PE92. Experimental results show that

(1) as a whole, geometrical/topological features outperform the other two feature classes in terms of recognition rate,
(2) UDLRH and gradient features outperform the others in geometrical/topological feature class,
(3) the feature combination approach can result in performance improvement.

The use of different Artificial Neural Network is expected to result in a slightly different performance for the features, but the global comparison among the three feature classes seems to remain the same. Not only the performance comparisons with different types of classifiers but also a detailed analysis of the feature combination will be needed in future research.

REFERENCES

1. J. T. Favata, G. Sirikantan and S. N. Srihari, "Handprinted character/digit recognition using a multiple feature/resolution philosophy", *IWFHR- IV*, 1994, pp. 57–66.
2. R. C. Gonzalez and R. E. Woods, *Digital Image Processing*, Addison Wesley Publishing Company, 1992.
3. A. K. Jain, *Fundamentals of Digital Image Processing*, Prentice-Hall International Edition, 1989.
4. S. . Jang, S. M. Kang, H. G. Kim, W. S. Rho and D. J. Kim, "A study on Hangul character recognition using GRNN", (Korean Ed.), *J. KITE* **31-B**, 1 (1994) 81–87.
5. D. H. Kim *et al.*, "Handwritten Korean character image database PE92," *Proc. 2nd Int. Conf. Document Analysis and Recognition*, 1993, pp. 470–473.
6. S. W. Lee, *Character Recognition — Theory and Practice* (Korean Ed.), Hongreung Science Publishing, Korea, 1993.
7. S. W. Lee, *The State of the Art in Off-Line Handwriting Recognition Research* (Korean Ed.), The Second Character Recognition Workshop, Sept. 1994, pp. 3–37.
8. *Neural Works Professional III and Neural Works Explorer*, Neural Ware Inc., 1989.

9. C. Y. Suen, M. Berthod and S. Mori, "Automatic recognition of handprinted characters — The state of the art", *Proc. IEEE* **68**, 4 (1980) 469–487.

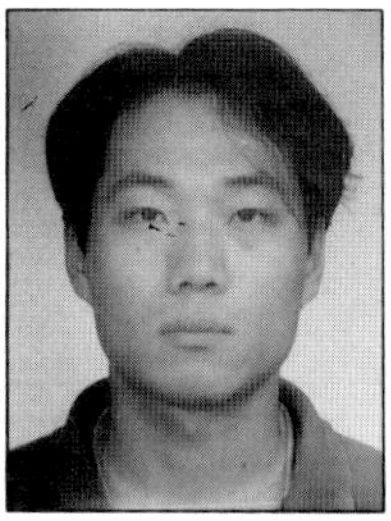

Kukhwan Seo received the B.S. and M.S. degrees in electronic engineering from Soongsil University, Korea, in 1996 and 1998, respectively. Since 1998, he is on the research staff of the Handysoft Com. in Seoul.

His research interests include artificial intelligence, image processing and pattern recognition.

Kyusik Chung received the B.S. degree in electronics engineering from Seoul National University, Korea in 1979, the M.S. degree in computer science from Korea Advanced Institute of Science and Technology, in 1981, and the M.S. and Ph.D. degrees in computer engineering from the University Southern California, Los Angeles, in 1986 and 1990, respectively. Since 1990, he has been on the faculty of the School of Electronic Engineering, Soongsil University in Korea, where he is currently an associate professor.

His research interests include artificial intelligence, pattern recognition and multimedia.

Jongmin Yoon received the B.S., M.S. and Ph.D. degrees in electronic engineering from Soongsil University, Korea, in 1991, 1993, and 1998, respectively. Since 1998, he is on the research staff of the Institute of Industrial Technology in Soongsil University.

His research interests include pattern recognition, neural network theory and application and character recognition.

Biography and photograph of Jongyeol Kim are unavailable.